THE DIARY OF ANTERA DUKE,
AN EIGHTEENTH-CENTURY AFRICAN SLAVE TRADER

The Diary of Antera Duke, an Eighteenth-Century African Slave Trader

STEPHEN D. BEHRENDT

A. J. H. LATHAM

DAVID NORTHRUP

With the assistance of the
International African Institute

OXFORD
UNIVERSITY PRESS

Oxford University Press, Inc., publishes works that further
Oxford University's objective of excellence
in research, scholarship, and education.

Oxford   New York
Auckland   Cape Town   Dar es Salaam   Hong Kong   Karachi
Kuala Lumpur   Madrid   Melbourne   Mexico City   Nairobi
New Delhi   Shanghai   Taipei   Toronto

With offices in
Argentina   Austria   Brazil   Chile   Czech Republic   France   Greece
Guatemala   Hungary   Italy   Japan   Poland   Portugal   Singapore
South Korea   Switzerland   Thailand   Turkey   Ukraine   Vietnam

Published by Oxford University Press, Inc.
198 Madison Avenue, New York, New York 10016
www.oup.com

First issued as an Oxford University Press paperback, 2012.

Oxford is a registered trademark of Oxford University Press.

Library of Congress Cataloging-in-Publication Data
Behrendt, Stephen D.
The diary of Antera Duke, an eighteenth-century African slave
trader / Stephen D. Behrendt, A. J. H. Latham, and David Northrup.
p.   cm.
Includes bibliographical references and index.
ISBN 978-0-19-537618-0 (hardcover); 978-0-19-992283-3 (paperback)
1. Duke, Antera—Diaries.   2. Slave traders—Nigeria—Old Calabar—Diaries.   3. Slave traders—
Nigeria—Old Calabar—Biography.   4. Slave trade—Nigeria—Old Calabar—History—18th
century.   5. Old Calabar (Nigeria)—History—18th century.   6. Old Calabar (Nigeria)—Biography.
I. Duke, Antera.   II. Latham, A. J. H.   III. Northrup, David A.   IV. Title.
DT515.9.O48B44 2009
306.3'62092—dc22 [B]   2009012872

Portions of the text are reproduced from *Efik Traders of Old Calabar*, edited by Daryll Forde (London: Oxford
University Press, 1956), with permission of the copyright holder, the International African Institute, School of
Oriental and African Studies, Thornhaugh Street, Russell Square, London WC1H OXG.

Printed in the United States of America
on acid-free paper

Preface

Extensive extracts of the three-year diary of Efik merchant Antera Duke (1785–1788) of Duke Town, Old Calabar (Calabar, Nigeria) survive today because of the efforts of William Valentine and Arthur W. Wilkie a hundred years ago. Valentine, a clerk in the Foreign Mission Office of the Free Church of Scotland, discovered and preserved the bound diary, which he found in a pile of rubbish. Wilkie, a missionary on furlough from Duke Town in 1907, transcribed most of the words to preserve the information and perhaps use it in a future study of Calabar life and customs. After the diary was misplaced in Edinburgh during the Second World War years, Wilkie prepared a typescript of his handwritten extracts and translated Antera Duke's words into a more readable "modern English" version. In November 1951 he brought his Antera Duke material to the attention of Professor Daryll Forde, director of the International African Institute, seeking advice as to the possibility of publishing the diary. Wilkie achieved his goal of seeing his work in print in 1956, two years before his death.

Efik Traders of Old Calabar, Containing the Diary of Antera Duke, an Efik Slave-Trading Chief of the Eighteenth Century was edited by Daryll Forde and published in 1956 by Oxford University Press for the International African Institute. The 166-page book included an introduction by Forde, essays by Donald C. Simmons and G. I. Jones on Efik ethnography and the political organization of Old Calabar, respectively, Antera Duke's diary extracts, a "translation" of the diary by Wilkie and Simmons, notes to the diary by Simmons, and an addendum by Jones on the Efik lineage system. Forde,

Simmons, and Jones discussed how best to present Antera Duke's material and decided that it was important to include both the original diary extracts—as transcribed by Wilkie—and the translation. In *The Diary of Antera Duke, an Eighteenth-Century African Slave Trader* we have followed their decision to publish the diary and "translation" but have offered an updated version rendered into standard English and have displayed the original diary and "translation" on facing pages with footnotes. Rather than including or updating the valuable contributions of Forde, Simmons, and Jones, we instead have written new chapters to help place the important diary in historic context.

Three coauthors collaborated on *The Diary of Antera Duke*, A. J. H. Latham taking the lead in chapter 1 and the appendices, Stephen D. Behrendt in chapters 2, 3, and 5, and David Northrup in chapter 4. The three, as editors, reworked Antera Duke's diary into standard English and reinterpreted several key passages. The three also edited 80 of the 100 notes from the 1956 version and added 165, many concerning ships and cargoes.

Victoria University of Wellington students Emily Boyd, Peter Carter, Karen Cheer, Nicholas J. Radburn, and Craig Watterson worked on the project as research assistants; in particular we thank Carter and Cheer for helping to create a database on African produce and Radburn for helping to analyze shipping accounts and to edit the diary and appendix A. We acknowledge research support from the Faculty of Humanities and Social Sciences, Victoria University of Wellington. We also thank Linda R. Gray for reading and suggesting changes to successive versions of the manuscript, Emma Cole and Robin Law for identifying errors or omissions, and Nona Parry for designing figure 2.1 and maps 1.1, 4.1, and 4.2, and for her contribution to the book cover. Librarians at the New College Library, University of Edinburgh, helped to locate Wilkie's typed transcription of the diary. A. J. H. Latham would like to acknowledge the help and encouragement over many years of the late Chief (Mrs.) Ekei Esien Oku (née Eyo), January 22, 1924–October 16, 2004, formerly Chief Librarian, Calabar. Finally, we thank Elizabeth Dunstan, Murray Last, and other members of the publications committee of the International African Institute, University of London, for encouraging the project a decade ago, and the institute for allowing us to republish Antera Duke's diary.

Contents

List of Maps, Figures, and Tables

THE DIARY OF ANTERA DUKE,
AN EIGHTEENTH-CENTURY AFRICAN SLAVE TRADER

Introduction

In about 1907, William Valentine, senior clerk to the Foreign Mission Committee of the Free Church of Scotland, discovered a curious manuscript in the "Church offices" at 121 George Street, Edinburgh.[1] In "an old press filled with all sorts of rubbish" Valentine found a "large folio bound volume; the paper of a blueish tint" that "had the appearance of a book originally intended for use as a Ship's Log-Book."[2] Opening the volume, Valentine saw that it was a diary written in Pidgin English without punctuation, with entries dated from January 18, 1785, to January 31, 1788. The clerk, who "had a Librarian's sense of the great value of ancient books and documents, and a real love of such valuable records," realized that the manuscript might have come from Calabar in Nigeria, where Scottish missionaries had been working since 1846. Consequently, Valentine loaned the book to thirty-one-year-old Arthur W. Wilkie, then a missionary at Duke Town, Calabar, during one of Wilkie's "early furloughs" in Edinburgh.[3] As Wilkie recalled, Valentine thought the book "might interest me."[4]

When Reverend Wilkie saw "antera Duke Ephrim" written on the first page, he realized that the diarist was from "Old Calabar," as it was referred to in precolonial times. Having studied Efik, the language of Calabar, an Ibibio dialect, he understood that "Antera" and "Ephrim" were anglicized versions of the Efik names Ntiero and Efiom,[5] and he also knew that Antera Duke was the traditional name for the male head of the Ntiero family in Duke Town. Indeed, Wilkie likely would have met an "Antera Duke" or "Duke Antera" during his mission. Glancing over the entries, Wilkie grasped that the diarist

worked as a merchant and slave trader and also commented on the "daily life
and the customs of the peoples in the Calabar area." Wilkie knew, as he wrote
later, that the diary was a unique document from "those far-off day[s] in Calabar."[6] He certainly had seen nothing like it before either in Duke Town or
in Edinburgh libraries.

Who was the man who kept this remarkable eighteenth-century diary?
Antera Duke—Ntiero Edem Efiom to use his full Efik name[7]—probably was
born in the 1730s. His anglicized trade name appears first in 1769 in documents concerning the Liverpool slaving ship Dobson. In May of that year a
merchant in Liverpool purchased six 4-pound and six 3-pound brass basins
with the words "Antera Duke" engraved on them.[8] Two months later at Old
Calabar, "Antera Duke King of Warr"[9] sold Captain John Potter two male
slaves for two basins and an assortment of textiles, iron bars, beads, powder
kegs, guns, and copper rods. Over a five-month period, July 1769–January
1770, Antera sold Potter fifty slaves—the second-highest total among Efik
businessmen. Clearly Potter dealt with a senior trader. Antera Duke last appears in the documentary record on January 18, 1805, when English explorer
Henry Nicholls called upon "another chief and trader, Antera Duke, whose
appearance and countenance did not at all please me, having a bold and dar-
ing countenance, with some appearance of malignity lurking about it: he
possesses apparently great activity of mind." Because Nicholls does not say
that Antera was aged in appearance, perhaps he was about seventy years old.[10]
We then learn that "Duke Antera" headed the family in October 1809, confirming that his father Antera Duke had died before that date.[11]

Antera Duke, like his father and grandfather, learned to write and speak
trade English to communicate with British sailors. English language learning
at Old Calabar started in the second half of the seventeenth century, as the
trading community, located forty-five miles north of the Atlantic–Cross
River confluence, began brokering shipments of slaves and ivory for overseas
markets. Trade names appear first in 1698, when James Barbot mentioned
Cross River dealers Duke Aphrom, King Robin, Captain Thomas, Mettinon,
King Ebrero, King John, King Oyo, William King Agbisherea, Robin King
Agbisherea, and Old King Robin. By 1720 greater numbers of leading Calabar notables and merchants had adopted trading names that combined an
English forename and an anglicized Efik family name, such as "Tom Cobham" or "Young Henshaw" or "Gentleman Honesty."[12] In the 1740s young
Antera Duke began picking up English words from visiting sailors, eventually learning an English commercial vocabulary. The Efik use of English abbreviations, such as "Jno" for John, demonstrates that language learning occurred via written correspondence as well. Like other Efik traders Antera

Duke would master the names of many European and Asian goods, measurements, Arabic numbers, adjectives, and verbs.[13]

The diary of Antera Duke is the most extensive surviving African text from precolonial Old Calabar. It contains 10,510 words and reveals that Antera Duke had a working vocabulary of 400 English words. Other Efik kept diaries or account books, but they have not surfaced and may no longer exist.[14] Antera's diary ends on January 31, 1788, probably when he reached the last folio in the bound ledger. If he continued his diary in a new book, a likely possibility, it too has been lost or remains in some family's possession. We assume that Antera also penned letters, notes, or cursory debt tallies in trade English, as there are seventeen such Efik-authored documents from the period 1767–1804. In two letters to Liverpool merchants in 1773, Grandy King George (Ephraim Robin John) wrote 1,608 words, and the next-longest surviving Efik document contains 333 words. Of these sixteen documents, only six still exist in manuscript.[15] The others, like Antera Duke's diary, were fortunately transcribed and published, thus preserving some of Old Calabar's history.

As a diary, Antera Duke's journal gives historians information otherwise not found in documents written by Africans in the precolonial era. These documents include earlier writings in Arabic by inland Muslim West Africans and writings in European languages from coastal Africans going back to the early sixteenth-century letters of King Afonso of Kongo. In addition, in the late eighteenth century there was considerable writing and publication by sub-Saharan Africans residing in Europe and North America.[16] Among these important historical sources, only Antera Duke, the sole extant diarist, chronicles the day-to-day social and cultural life of an African community. Another unique feature of diary writing appears with the initial phrase of Antera Duke's diary: "I be angry with my Dear awaw ofion" (I was angry with my dear [wife] Awaw Ofiong). The diarist reveals intimate thoughts that one finds only in an account written for oneself. Antera Duke's first dated entry, January 18, 1785, discusses a dispute between Efik traders Egbo Young Ofiong and Little Otto, one resolved by the Ekpe society of Old Calabar to which wealthy Efik men belonged. Here is local eyewitness history not found in the business correspondence between coastal African traders and ship captains, or in diplomatic discussions between African leaders and the Portuguese Crown, or in writings from Africans living in the Americas.

Antera Duke's diary, written in his own hand and for his own use, is a candid account of daily life in an African community during a period of great historical interest. Antera wrote his thoughts at a peak period of trade when Efik merchants, over a three-year period, sold Europeans 15,000 slaves,

500,000 yams, and 100 tons of ivory, palm oil, dyewood, and pepper. The 1780s ushered in a trade in palm oil, which would be the source of Efik foreign trade income for several generations after the abolition of the British slave trade in 1807–1808. Heightened competition from slaving merchants based in Bonny, located eighty-five miles to the southwest, prompted Cross River traders to diversify their export trades. Antera Duke writes in the aftermath of internecine battles between Duke Town merchants and rivals from nearby Old Town; the diary period marks the midpoint in the history of Duke Town's ascendance and in that of the family of Duke Ephraim, Antera's paternal uncle. Antera's voice is that of a major African businessman from an important commercial center in the eighteenth-century Atlantic world.

The History of the Diary and Its Loss during the Second World War

What is the history of the diary? After Antera Duke's death between January 1805 and October 1809, the book may have passed to his eldest son, Duke Antera, a name documented in 1813 and 1830.[17] Duke Antera died before 1842, the first year when his son Antera Duke appears in sources. Scottish missionaries arrived in 1846 and met this grandson of the diarist Antera Duke (ca. 1735–ca. 1809). Antera Duke signed five treaties with British officials from 1847 to 1857,[18] and may have given the diary to a missionary. Wilkie's wife recalled that no one working in the Free Church of Scotland in the early 1900s knew the history of the diary, and thus "it must have been there some time."[19] In the 1850s missionary Hugh Goldie began building his own private library in Duke Town, which perhaps included some Efik material written in trade English. Goldie or one of his assistants may have shipped Antera Duke's diary, perhaps before a Duke Town fire in early 1855 or the "great fire" there in April 1862.[20] In 1892 William Marwick began cataloging the Mission Library in Duke Town, formed from Goldie's collection. He found numerous books about the slave trade but did not mention Efik diaries or journals.[21] Many missionaries and their wives, such as Elizabeth Marwick, shipped home boxes containing "Calabar curiosities." Perhaps Antera Duke's diary was one such "curiosity" sent to Edinburgh in the 1850s or 1860s.[22]

Before returning to Duke Town to resume missionary work in 1908, Wilkie copied by hand extensive extracts from the diary, then returned the volume to clerk Valentine. He planned to use the information in a future study of Efik life in the Old Calabar region and perhaps even, some day after

his missionary service ended, to publish the diary. Wilkie also wanted to preserve a copy of Antera Duke's record before the original deteriorated further.
Already the script was difficult to decipher, Wilkie recalled, "for frequently
the paper is discoloured, and the ink has faded." Wilkie recommended to
Valentine "that the original Diary should be deposited in a secure place, suggesting one of the Scottish National Libraries, or in the Library of New College, Edinburgh." The volume, however, remained in the Free Church of
Scotland office building, perhaps in the Missionary Lending Library.[23]

Wilkie renewed his Old Calabar studies and interest in Antera Duke's
diary after the Second World War, having settled in Edinburgh upon retiring
from active service. His missionary work in Calabar and then on the Gold
Coast (1918–1931) and in South Africa (1931–1941) prevented any earlier
opportunities for such scholarly activity. He soon learned that the Antera
Duke diary disappeared during the early 1940s. As Wilkie wrote in 1951:

> During the late war many valuable books and documents were re-
> moved from the upper storey of the Church Offices to the basement
> in case of any bomb attacks.
>
> Shortly before his death, Mr. Valentine informed me that he was
> trying to re-create order in the books and documents that had been
> brought into great disorder in the upper story and in the basement of
> the Offices during the war. Unfortunately he had not been able to
> find any trace of the original Diary, but he had not given up hope of
> ultimately re-discovering it. I am assured by Foreign Mission officials
> in the [Foreign Mission Committee] offices that the search will be
> continued, but success is uncertain for it is just "possible" that a bomb
> may have destroyed it.[24]

Church officials did not find Antera Duke's diary; recent efforts to locate it also
have proved unsuccessful.[25] The city of Edinburgh was not targeted during
World War II, however, and thus someone possibly discarded the rare volume.[26]

The First Edition of Antera Duke's Diary

During 1951 Wilkie prepared his Antera Duke materials with the aim to
publish the important Efik diary. He sought advice from Church of Scotland
missionaries, acquaintances in the Foreign Mission Office, and others inter-
ested in Old Calabar history. Believing that Antera Duke's trade English
would prove difficult to read for those unfamiliar with the Efik idiom, Wilkie

made a "Translation (or interpretation) of the Diary." On June 26, 1951, he then completed a four-page introduction, which included an appendix on the "Number of slaves taken by the trading ships, with names of Captains." He gave a copy of his diary extracts and translation to the Foreign Mission Office, and a secretary there typed three copies. Only one of these three typed copies is extant: that which he donated to the library at New College, University of Edinburgh.[27]

When Daryll Forde, director of the International African Institute, University of London, received information about Antera Duke's diary from Wilkie, he agreed that it warranted publication.[28] Forde believed that the work needed to be published with background material on Efik history, notes to explain some of Antera Duke's passages, and a reexamination of Wilkie's translation (or interpretation). By mid-1954 Forde had contacted anthropology student Donald C. Simmons, who then revised and annotated Wilkie's translation and added a chapter based on his recent fieldwork in Creek Town and Duke Town. Forde also enlisted the expertise of anthropologist G. I. Jones, and in 1956 Oxford University Press published *Efik Traders of Old Calabar, edited by Daryll Forde, Containing the Diary of Antera Duke, an Efik Slave-Trading Chief of the Eighteenth Century together with an Ethnographic Sketch and Notes by D. Simmons and an Essay on the Political Organization of Old Calabar by G. I. Jones.*

The New Edition

Since the publication of *Efik Traders*, scholars have located new sources to document Old Calabar's precolonial history. When Simmons researched published material on Old Calabar, standard works were missionaries' and travelers' testimonies from the 1830s through 1860s.[29] The few sources that documented Old Calabar history during Antera Duke's lifetime included parliamentary evidence given by seven British mariners who traded at Old Calabar, 1740s through 1770s, and eight Calabar letters and memos, written from 1767 to 1783, published by Gomer Williams in 1897.[30] In the past fifty years the discovery of new documents has yielded information on the names of Old Calabar merchants in 1720, the goods imported by Efik businessmen, the personal linkages between Efik and British traders, the slave and produce trades, and Calabar in 1805. There are now twelve Liverpool and Bristol captains' letters written at Old Calabar during the period of Antera Duke's diary, and sailor Henry Schroeder's recollections of his slaving voyage to Old Calabar in 1786.[31] These materials, unknown or unavailable to Simmons, confirm some of Antera's diary dates and information.

Simmons and the contributors to *Efik Traders* published before databases on the slave trade enabled sources such as newspapers to be examined for information on Old Calabar's export trades. The creation of the consolidated slave trade database in 1999, now available online, allows researchers to search for voyages by names of vessels and/or captains, the standard identifiers in shipping lists or cargo advertisements.[32] Weekly gazettes such as the *Manchester Mercury* (founded in 1752), *Williamson's Liverpool Advertiser* (1756), and *Liverpool General Advertiser* (1765) list slaving ships and cargoes arriving from "Africa" and their American markets. By cross-referencing the ships with the slave trade database, one can determine the African location of trade for a majority of ships and their cargoes. The consolidated slave trade database has allowed today's researchers not only to identify all slaving ship captains mentioned by Antera Duke in his diary but also to determine whether these ships carried ivory, palm oil, or other agricultural commodities in addition to slaves.

Building upon older and more recent scholarship, the editors here have made a new translation of Antera Duke's diary and have written additional chapters on Old Calabar's history. From its first publication, the diary has been a focus for scholarship. The authors in the 1956 edition drew upon the diary to outline Efik customs and political history, and a 1960 anthology cited snippets of Antera Duke's diary as an example of precolonial Nigerian history and writing.[33] In the past fifty years the diary information has supported linguistic studies on Efik written "pidgin" or "broken English," work on the slave trade in the Bight of Biafra, and historical studies on Old Calabar–European credit relations and trading conflicts. The two senior members of the authorial team wrote pioneering monographs on the history of Old Calabar and its trading region; the junior member brings special expertise on the eighteenth-century slave and produce trades.[34] Our goal is to incorporate new primary source evidence with information contained in recent scholarly works to reemphasize the importance of Antera Duke's diary and to place it in the wider context of the history of Old Calabar and the Bight of Biafra.

Chapter 1 places information in Antera Duke's diary in the context of eighteenth-century Old Calabar political, social, and religious history. We chart how Duke Town eclipsed Old Town and Creek Town through military power, lineage strength, and commercial acumen. By the mid-1780s Duke Ephraim, Egbo Young Ofiong, and Antera Duke, all from Duke Town, became three of the strongest Efik—Duke Ephraim holding the position of *obong* (chairman of the town council and principal foreign spokesman) and Egbo Young the position of *eyamba* (principal legal authority and head of Ekpe society). We discuss how rivalries among Efik families intensified after the death of Obong Duke Ephraim on July 4, 1786; sacrifices of slaves weakened the power of some leading families, and so did witchcraft ordeals, which also reduced the number of merchants competing for shares of European trading goods. Preserving lineage strength required rising men to survive a competitive and volatile political system that rewarded wealth and sagacity. Ekpe, the society to which leading Efik men belonged, did not curb the interfamily tensions triggered by Duke Ephraim's death. Separate from these issues, Antera's diary is the only source that documents the deaths of other Efik notables, including King Calabar, the priest of the tutelary deity who retained ceremonial and religious importance.

In chapters 2 and 3 we detail the eighteenth-century Calabar slave and produce trades. Our discussion of Calabar's export slave trade, circa 1650–1838, focuses on Antera Duke's lifetime and in particular the 1760s–1780s period when Antera Duke emerged as a leading merchant who traded principally with Liverpool ship captains—including John Potter, whose *Dobson/Fox* accounts in 1769–1770 we analyze in detail. During these three decades the Old Calabar export slave trade reached its height and, as we outline in chapter 3, Efik merchants began shipping large quantities of palm oil—thus beginning their fifty-year dominance in oil exports. Though Efik traders brokered and European ship captains purchased slaves, produce, and provisions, we treat the slave and produce trades separately. In the 1780s the compatibility of the trades was clear: few Guineamen arrived at Old Calabar to load only human cargoes, and indeed slaving captains, among European traders, purchased the greatest quantities of ivory and agricultural commodities in space they otherwise would have reserved for human cargoes. In these chapters we contrast the economic histories of Old Calabar and Bonny, and we emphasize how personal relationships between British and Efik merchants formed the nexus of trade at Old Calabar.

To build a picture of Old Calabar's regional trading networks, chapter 4 draws upon information contained in Antera Duke's diary, other contemporary sources, and shipping records from the 1820s. Antera and other Efik worked as itinerant merchants, often walking or canoeing overnight on trading or diplomatic missions. Their commercial ties extended to Ibibio lands on the west bank of the Cross River, north up the Cross River to Umon, a three-day journey, east to the Cameroon grasslands located 250 miles beyond the riverine zones, 45 miles south toward Tom Shott's Point on the Atlantic coast, and southeast to "Little Cameroons," on the western slopes of Mount Cameroon. Within a 30,000-square-mile commercial hinterland, merchants such as Antera Duke bought and sold yams, slaves, ivory, palm oil, dyewood, pepper, fish, plantains, salt, alcohol, canoes, metal goods, textiles, and other manufactures. Although the diary presents evidence of conflict among African groups, between Europeans, and between Europeans and Efik, it nonetheless reveals that systematic trading patterns prevailed.

Chapter 5, comments on the diary text, discusses the accuracy and comprehensiveness of Wilkie's early twentieth-century transcription and problems with the diary's first "translation." We explain decisions taken in revising the English version and identify problematic diary passages that resisted translation. Antera Duke's trade English suggests that he learned his second language informally in Old Calabar by speaking and corresponding with British sailors. His first language was Efik, words from which have helped our interpretation of his trade English diary.

Part II reproduces the original diary of Antera Duke, as transcribed by Reverend Wilkie circa 1907, typed in 1951, and published in 1956. A new rendering of the diary into standard English appears on facing pages, and we have advanced the annotation completed by anthropologist Donald Simmons in 1954 by editing 80 and adding 165 footnotes, retaining only 20 notes as written by Simmons. The updated reference information, 265 footnotes, incorporates new primary and secondary source material on Old Calabar and specifies where our editorial decisions differ from those made by Wilkie and Simmons.

Reflecting upon reading and transcribing Antera Duke's words, Reverend Arthur Wilkie knew that he had helped to preserve a document of lasting historical value. Antera Duke, a leader and slaving merchant from Old Calabar, wrote the 1780s diary, giving readers an insight into life in Old Calabar and the organization of the slave trade. He left us with a glimpse into eighteenth-century Efik society. "Antera Duke must have been a very able man and highly respected in his day," the retired missionary remarked, and "It is right that there should be an historical record of the actual extent of this inhuman trade." "But one is grateful also to the Diarist," Wilkie concluded, "for giving to us such a 'living picture' of the daily life and the customs of the peoples in the Calabar area."[35]

PART I

CHAPTER ONE

The Diary and Old Calabar's History

The history of precolonial African Atlantic societies is told through tradition, archaeology, accounts of European visitors, and writings from Africans themselves. The mix of oral, physical, and written sources differs by location and time period. To study the Old Calabar of Antera Duke's lifetime (ca. 1735–ca. 1809), and the Efik who lived there, historians rely on almost as many African as European narrators, making the documentary record of the Cross River region most unusual. Antera Duke and other Efik merchants learned trade English—the British were the most frequent visitors to Old Calabar—and some of their correspondence survives, as do extensive extracts from Antera Duke's diary. Europeans did not maintain trading posts in the Bight of Biafra, so there are no archaeological sites or corpus of written material from fort administrators, like those that exist from other African coastal regions. Fortunately, in the period 1735–1809 there are eighteen letters from ship captains at Old Calabar, recollections of nine sailors, one account book written there, and one explorer's remarks. In the years after Antera Duke's death, the British wrote much more of the surviving material from Old Calabar. In the 1820s and 1830s adventurers renewed and publicized explorations of the Cross and Calabar rivers; missionaries arrived first in 1846, and ministers Hope Masterton Waddell, William Anderson, and Hugh Goldie subsequently wrote extensively about Calabar society.

Antera's journal contains details on Efik society not documented elsewhere. Before Reverend Wilkie preserved Antera's words, the only known

Efik writings from eighteenth-century Old Calabar were eight letters and memos written to Liverpool traders from 1767 to 1783. These documents, authored by Efik merchants other than Antera Duke, concern disputes over customs payments from British captains and requests for specific trading goods. Only two letters mentioned cursorily Old Calabar's uniquely African institution Ekpe (anglicized Egbo), a society to which wealthy Calabar merchants belonged.[1] Similarly, an Efik letter to a Liverpool captain in 1803 and seven Efik notes to British captains transcribed in 1827 discussed business transactions.[2] By contrast, Antera Duke mentions Ekpe throughout his diary, as in his first entry, January 18, 1785, when men in Ekpe, including Antera, adjudicated a dispute between Egbo Young Ofiong and Little Otto, and fined each man. That same day readers learn that sixty-four men in the society put in money presumably for twenty new initiates. Antera also mentions squabbles between family members, deaths of men and women, disputes between Efik and non-Efik, and political intrigues in Old Calabar.

In this chapter we discuss Antera Duke's kinsmen and the families in Old Calabar, an "enlarged village"[3] of small Efik settlements on the Calabar River. To set his diary in historic context, we draw upon Old Calabar information before and after Antera Duke's lifetime. The Efik emerged as middlemen in the late seventeenth century, and merchants and families competed for shares of overseas trade and anchorage fees, or "comey," which we detail in subsequent chapters. Trade increased competition between families; marriage alliances helped to diffuse tensions, as did the development of Ekpe, which features in one in four diary entries. Nonetheless, internecine warfare erupted from time to time and notably during the mid-1760s. To better understand family rivalries, we examine the political structure within Old Calabar and the positions of "King Calabar," the Ndem priest and religious leader; *eyamba* (president of Ekpe); *ebunko* (vice president of Ekpe); and *obong* ("king" or mayor). Obong Duke Ephraim's death, recorded by Antera Duke in his diary on July 4, 1786, triggered a political crisis that remained unresolved eighteen months later, when Antera closed the last folio of his book.

Tradition and Early Efik History

Building a historic context for biographical information in Antera Duke's diary requires one to first examine early Efik history. Efik society was built upon extended families; Antera Duke wrote the word "family" twenty-two times, often in discussion about how different kinsmen viewed issues concerning Ekpe society or conflicts with European traders. Similarly, in their correspondence Efik and British merchants often sent greetings to each other's families. Neither Antera nor other eighteenth-century Efik writers wrote about the early history of "Callabar," and no author used the word "history."[4] But the Efik of Antera Duke's lifetime certainly passed on their histories and traditions by word of mouth. Antera reveals such a recollected history in his diary. When men from two towns wanted to pay Ekpe fees in one day (rather than over several days), Antera wrote, "wee say never Been hear that for weer grandy grandy father."[5] Antera Duke had never heard about a town paying Ekpe in one day. Consulting elders confirmed that the practice was unknown, as far back as the time of Antera's great-grandfather.

Tradition traces Antera's lineage beyond his great-grandfather's generation to Efik settlement at Old Calabar. According to oral testimonies, transcribed by scholars and officials interviewing Efik elders in the 1950s and 1960s,[6] Ema and Efiom Ekpo were the two progenitors of the Efik families that settled "Old Calabar." These two men lived in Uruan, a village located west of the Cross River in Ibibioland. At some point in history Efiom Ekpo, Ema's son Eyo Emo, and Ema's three grandsons, Oku Atai, Ukpong Atai, and Adim Atai, migrated with their wives, children, slaves, and other retainers fifty miles southeast to Ikot Etunko. Known later as Creek Town, this settlement is located on a creek between the Cross and Calabar rivers. Ibibio claim that they gave this group of migrants the name "Efik," derived from the Ibibio verb *fik*, to oppress or suppress, and thus Efik means "the oppressors." They support this assertion by recalling that Efik warriors captured and enslaved nearby peoples whom they sacrificed, incorporated into Efik society, or sold to local dealers.[7] Antera Duke—in Efik, Ntiero Edem Efiom—is a descendant of founding father Efiom Ekpo.

After the five extended families settled at Creek Town, it is said that disagreements arose and several families relocated nearby. The Ukpong and Adim Atai groups settled fifteen miles south, on the east bank of the Calabar River, in what became known as Obutong and later, to the British, as "Old Town." After Efiom Ekpo died, tradition holds that his daughter Okoho bore twins, whom his second son Edem Efiom secretly took away to a small island in the Cross River. This action prevented the twins from being killed, as was custom. After reaching adulthood, the twins, Ofiong Okoho and Efiom Okoho, settled lands three miles south of Obutong at Atakpa, "New Town," known to Europeans by the turn of the nineteenth century as "Duke Town." Other Efik migrated fifteen miles north up the Calabar River and lived in a group of hamlets on both banks known as Adiabo, or "Guinea Company." At some point others settled to the west in three Efik villages on the Cross River known collectively as Mbiabo, or individually as Mbiabo

Edere (Akani Obio), Mbiabo Usin Ufot (Ikot Offiong), and Mbiabo Usuk (Ikonetu). These settlements are remembered as Old Ekrikok, Tom Ekrikok, and George Ekrikok, names given to and adopted by English captains, who would define those in Creek Town, Old Town, and Duke Town as from "Old Calabar" (see map 1.1).[8]

As descendants multiplied, distinct families emerged within founding kinship groups at Creek Town, Old Town, and Duke Town. Families cleared bush and built compounds; people lived in wattle-and-daub huts, and there were residences for freemen, wives, and slaves. Different clusters of buildings enclosed yards. These extended family units, living in their own geographically defined space, are "houses" (in Efik, *ufok*) or "wards," to use a twentieth-century convention.[9] Eventually two wards emerged from the Ema lineage in Creek Town—the Ambo and Cobham (*akabom*). In Duke Town, the Efiom Ekpo lineage split into the Henshaw (*nsa*), Ntiero (Antera Duke's ward), Duke, and Eyamba sections, and in the mid-nineteenth century the Archibong (*asibong*) ward developed in Duke Town. The Eyo ward also lived in Creek Town, tradition holding that founder Eyo Nsa (Eyo Willy Honesty) was an "outsider" or "stranger,"[10] who sided with the Efik to defeat rivals in the Cross River. Bravery earned Willy Honesty his advancement and the hand in marriage of an Ambo "princess," and the Eyo ward resided in Creek Town along with the Ambos and Cobhams, each family in separate compounds.[11]

Efik naming patterns help chart generations and ward development. In Efik a father's first name becomes the son's second name, for example, Nsa Efiom and Edem Efiom were sons of Efiom Ekpo. Consequently, second-, third-, and fourth-generation descendants of Efiom Ekpo by his daughter Okoho are Efiom Okoho, Ekpo Efiom, and Edem Ekpo. This naming sequence transferred to anglicized trading names, and thus Duke Antera is Antera Duke's son, probably his eldest son with one of his principal wives. Over time compound Efik and English trading names developed as families intermarried and lineages grew. Ntiero Edem Efiom (Antera Duke) would be the three names of an individual from a generation later than that of true agnates or ward founders.

By relying on traditions and legends, one can create an Efik genealogical tree that includes major branches descending from Ema and Efiom Ekpo. "Word-of-mouth" evidence gives some indication about the development of wards; legend holds, for example, that the Ambo and Cobham wards are senior branches of the Ema lineage, and they perhaps were the two remaining groups when others left Creek Town. Similarly, it is remembered that the Henshaw, Ntiero, Duke, and Eyamba families emerged as independent wards from the founding Efiom Ekpo group. But oral histories do not assign dates to events or tell us whether our diarist Antera Duke was the first Ntiero ward

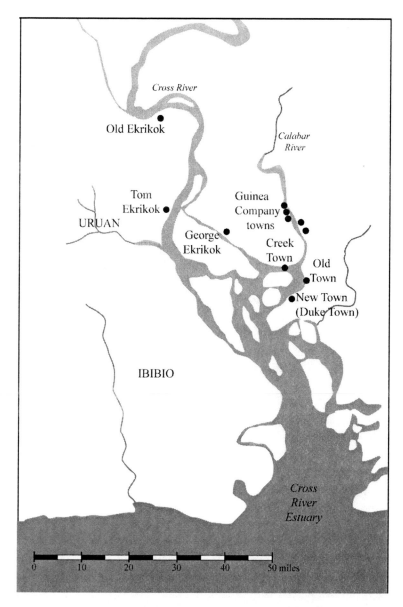

MAP 1.1. The Cross River Region, ca. 1785–1788

leader. To place the growth of Efik families and development of wards in historic time, one must turn to written sources. Those most important to charting early Efik history include three details: African names; ages or dates of death; and payments of port fees at Old Calabar that suggest an individual's status.

Written Sources and Early Efik History

Any document on early Efik history is precious, more so if authors dated their works and recorded biographical information on Cross River peoples. Before the publication of Antera Duke's diary in 1956, scholars knew the precise date of death for only one pre-1850 obong—Efiom Edem ("Great Duke Ephraim"), who died on October 14, 1834. Missionary Hope Waddell gleaned this information in 1846 when he was shown a "journal of transactions in English," written by "Mr. Young" (perhaps Egbo Young) from Duke Town: "Old Calabar, October 14, 1834.—Ephraim Duk diad in five o'clock this evening, and we put him for Groun next morning."[12] Antera Duke also recorded an obong's death, that of Ephraim Duke's father, Duke Ephraim (Edem Ekpo), on July 4, 1786: "[A]bout 4 clock morning Duk Ephrim Dead soon after come up to Look way putt to grown" ("About 4 o'clock in the morning Duke Ephraim died. Soon after we came up to look where to put him in the ground"). Before the discovery of the diary, it was known only that Edem Ekpo died a generation earlier than his son.[13]

Though we do not know the birth years or ages at death for Edem Ekpo and son Efiom Edem, explorer Henry Nicholls establishes that some Efik dignitaries lived long lives. Nicholls noted in January 1805 that Egbo Young Eyambo "is between sixty and seventy" and that King Calabar "is a very old man, at least eighty years of age." There is no additional information on Efik ages, other than from those later missionaries who observed the elder status of men from Old Calabar.[14] There are no tombstone inscriptions of Efik until the twentieth century. If one assumes a life expectancy of seventy years for those who survived infancy and follow Efik naming patterns, we can work backward from the death dates of the two Duke ward obongs to locate Efik migration from Uruan to Creek Town in the late sixteenth century.[15] Grandsons of Ema and Efiom Ekpo then would have settled Old Town and New Town in the first half of the seventeenth century (table 1.1).[16]

Two seventeenth-century reports record names of Cross River individuals and provide further information on the Duke family. In the first written account of Old Calabar, a tract published in 1668, sailor John Watts referred to King "E-fn-me." Here an Englishman tried to spell phonetically an unusual-sounding African name, most likely Efiom, and thus we assume he had seen or heard about an Efiom family dignitary, perhaps Efiom Okoho, obong and cofounder of Duke Town, a man who then might have been about sixty years of age.[17] Thirty years later Cross River merchants had adopted anglicized trading names; James Barbot, working on a London-based slaving vessel, traded with at least six Efik: Duke Aphrom,

TABLE 1.1. Efik settlement dates at Creek Town and the Duke ward lineage

Name	Years	Remarks
Efiom Ekpo	ca. 1540s–ca. 1610s	Cofounder of Creek Town
Okoho Efiom (daughter)	ca. 1590s–ca. 1660s	Mother of illegitimate twins
Efiom Okoho	ca. 1610s–ca. 1680s	Cofounder of Duke Town
Ekpo Efiom	ca. 1660s–ca. 1730s	Son of Efiom Okoho
Edem Ekpo[1]	ca. 1700s–July 4, 1786	Duke Ephraim in the diary
Efiom Edem[2]	ca. 1755–Oct. 14, 1834	"Great Duke Ephraim"

[1]Death date documented by Antera Duke in his diary.
[2]"Great Duke Ephraim." Death date documented in Mr. Young's journal and shown to missionary Hope Waddell in 1846.

King Oyo, King Robin, Old King Robin, King Ebrero, and King John.[18] Duke Aphrom, or "Duke Ephraim," was probably Ekpo Efiom, then about thirty years of age, too young to be a principal Calabar spokesman or "king" (see table 1.1). Legend and later written sources place King Oyo (Eyo Ema) in Creek Town and King Robin in Old Town. As "kings" they were town leaders and the men who brokered major disputes with ship captains. King John headed some of the Guinea Company villages;[19] King Ebrero perhaps spoke for a different Efik village and may have been an ancestor of the Ebros in Duke Town.[20]

We learn much more about early African families in the Cross River region from Scottish supercargo Alexander Horsburgh's accounts from 1720. Horsburgh's ledger, found in the 1990s in Edinburgh archives, is the most important source concerning early eighteenth-century Calabar history.[21] Whereas Barbot mentioned six Efik with whom he traded at Old Calabar in 1698, Horsburgh records twenty-six Cross River notables, including at least twenty Efik—and ten from the Ambo, Cobham, and Henshaw families, senior branches of the Ema and Efiom Ekpo lineages. Horsburgh writes names of men to whom he paid anchorage fees (comey), differentiates between traders and nontraders, and specifies comey per individual. His list of comey recipients includes all the important Efik, since the fees covered both trading duties and ransom for four sailors captured near the Cross River estuary. These payments, made in copper bars ("coppers"),[22] Calabar's currency unit, reveal the comparative position of Cross River elders, ward leaders, and merchants.

The tally of comey indicates that in 1720 there were between five and seven wards in Creek Town, Old Town, and Duke Town combined. Horsburgh paid the most monies to two kings—King Ambo (80 copper bars) and King John (72 coppers). King Ambo was the leader of Ambo ward in Creek Town; King John, referenced by Barbot in 1698, probably headed the Guinea

Company villages. Horsburgh made payments equal to or greater than 50 bars to Duke Ephraim (70 coppers), Tom Henshaw (65 coppers), Tom Cobham (50 coppers), and Grande Robin (50 coppers). Duke Ephraim (Duke Aphrom in 1698) headed the Duke ward in Duke Town. Tom Henshaw must have been the elder and leader of Henshaw ward, which tradition places in Duke Town. The Cobham ward, it is remembered, resided in Creek Town; Grande Robin, related to Old King Robin and King Robin with whom Barbot traded, was, we believe, the Robin (Obutong) ward leader in Old Town.[23] Horsburgh also paid 40 coppers' comey to Robin Honestie and 35 coppers to Robin John. In documenting these families for the first time, the supercargo may have established that the Honesty (Creek Town) and Robin John (Old Town) wards had developed by 1720. If so, there were then seven wards in the three Old Calabar villages.

The supercargo's accounts from 1720 also tell us that eight Efik families dominated Old Calabar about fifteen years before Antera Duke's birth. Horsburgh made total comey payments of 819 copper bars, including 649 copper bars to traders and 170 coppers to "men of no trade in Callabar." Among the Efik families we have identified, the distribution is as follows: King John's family (136 coppers); the Ambo family (129 coppers); Duke Ephraim and Young Ephraim (103 coppers); the Henshaws (87 coppers); the Robin family (72 coppers); the Cobham family (63 coppers); the Honestie family (44 coppers); and Robin John (35 coppers). Horsburgh paid 80 percent of his comey to these eight families. The Ambo recipients were King Ambo, Tom Ambo, King Ambo's wives (perhaps seven, since Horsburgh paid the group seven copper bars), Young Robin Ambo, and John Ambo. Barbot does not mention the Ambos in 1698, though in 1714 a London ship captain stated that one of the two kings he usually traded with was King Ambo.

For Europeans, King Ambo (either Esien Ekpe Oku or his brother Ekpenyong Ekpe Oku) was certainly a key Efik merchant and leader. He was Horsburgh's first comey recipient, and he received the greatest fee (80 coppers). In 1724 a Bristol slaving ship was named *King Amboe*—no other Calabar leader was so honored.[24] When he died in March 1729, a Bristol sailor wrote: "We are just now firing half Minute Guns for the Death of Amboe King of Calabar. Our Captain is gone ashore to the Funeral, with our Piper, Fidler and Drummer."[25] As we will discuss later in the chapter, King Ambo's prominence in the 1720s suggests that he was the president of either Ekpe (eyamba) and/or obong. His death in 1729, like that of other Efik leaders, may have triggered witchcraft accusations and power struggles within Calabar society.[26]

Horsburgh's ledger presents a snapshot of Efik society about five generations after settlement at Old Calabar. Significantly, only two compound trading names are documented by Horsburgh: Young Robin Ambo and Yellow Robin Cobham. Maximal lineages in the principal Efik villages consisted of true agnates in 1720, recent descendants of either Ema or Efiom Ekpo. This written evidence of compound names supports stories that the Ambo and Cobham wards developed first and perhaps were the only remaining groups when others left Creek Town. Further, initial migrant groups had not yet grown sufficiently large to split into more than five to seven wards or separate branches. Though oral tradition suggests that the Ntiero ward broke from the Efiom Ekpo lineage before the extended Duke family, Horsburgh does not give comey to Antera Duke's father, who may have been a teenager in 1720. Barbot, however, documents Duke Ephraim in 1698, and Horsburgh pays his son Young Ephraim the comparatively large fee of 33 copper bars. The Eyamba ward, important in Antera Duke's diary, also had not yet emerged by 1720.

The few extant written accounts before Antera Duke's lifetime supplement legends to chart the early history of Efik families at Old Calabar. About a century after Efik migrated from Creek Town, groups settled the Guinea Company villages to the north and Old Town and Duke Town to the south. Though one cannot date these migrations to specific years, it is reasonable to suggest that the Efik arrived at Creek Town in the late sixteenth century and families settled new villages in the first half of the seventeenth century. Following Efik tradition, European documents confirm the senior status of the Ambo, Duke, Henshaw, Robin, and Cobham families. King John from Guinea Company was an important trader in 1698 and 1720, but little is known about his lineage. Antera Duke's family, the Ntiero, is not mentioned in any early written accounts. His father, we assume, was a youth when Scottish supercargo Alexander Horsburgh arrived at Old Calabar in 1720. He and his son Antera would extend the Ntiero family's influence in the mid-eighteenth century and gain sufficient strength to break from the Duke lineage and form their own ward in Duke Town.[27]

Efik History and Families during Antera Duke's Lifetime

Antera Duke witnessed significant changes in the families of Old Calabar. He and his father developed the Ntiero ward; by the time of his diary, 1785–1788, Duke Town had subjugated Old Town, and Duke Ephraim, Egbo Young Ofiong, and Antera Duke were its three power brokers. Willy Honesty had emerged in the 1760s as the leading merchant and spokesman from Creek Town—the Honesties supplanting the Ambos and Cobhams. Henshaw

Town, under the leadership of Tom Henshaw, had by then become established one mile south of Duke Town's compounds; their family became less important, though, during the next two generations. Intra-Efik warfare and intrigues reduced the power of, most notably, the Robin and Robin John families from Old Town, and Antera Duke probably participated in a massacre of many of their traders and canoemen in 1767—a key historical event remembered in Efik history. Battles broke out again in 1768 and the 1770s between Duke Town and Old Town; a decade later, during Antera's travels up and down the Calabar and Cross rivers, he mentions only a dozen Old Town traders. By 1805, only 500 people lived in Old Town and 300 hundred in Henshaw Town; these figures compare to 2,000 and 1,500 residents in Duke Town and Creek Town, respectively.[28]

The few sources that document the history of Old Calabar from approximately the 1730s through 1765—Antera Duke's youth, teenage years, and early adulthood—suggest that rivalry between the Henshaw and Duke wards in Duke Town culminated in the founding of Henshaw Town. A Liverpool captain placed the establishment of one Efik village after 1748, a confusing date that may refer to either the resettling of Old Town or Duke Town or the foundation date for Henshaw Town.[29] In 1761 a Liverpool merchant was pleased to learn that Tom Henshaw had become "first man"—the head of Henshaws.[30] This man was probably the son of the Tom Henshaw who received comparatively large comey from Alexander Horsburgh in 1720. On his visit to Old Calabar in 1786 sailor Henry Schroeder learned some details about the history of the Henshaws. He believed that Henshaw Town "derived its name from its founder, Enshee Tom [Tom Henshaw], who was a man of martial enterprise, and independent spirit, and who, opposing the government of Duke Town with effect, a war was the consequence, which for some time banished trade from Old Calabar." He continued: "[T]he contending parties became reconciled, and the site of Enshee Town was granted, and guaranteed to Tom and his adherents, who view it with pride, as a memorial of their prowess."[31] Tom Henshaw acquired sufficient wealth to oppose the Duke family and founded Henshaw Town, one assumes, by the late 1750s or early 1760s.

We know much more about Calabar in the mid-1760s and early 1770s because the "massacre at Old Calabar" in 1767 generated testimonies from surviving Efik and Britons. In 1773 Ancona Robin Robin John and Little Ephraim Robin John, relatives of Old Town king Ephraim Robin John (Efiom Otu Ekon), arrived in Bristol, England, after five years of slavery in Barbados and Virginia. They had been kidnapped during the massacre in 1767 and reported their ordeal to religious figures in Bristol. After protesting their unjust enslavement before the Court of King's Bench in 1773—transcriptions of which remain—they gained their freedom and returned to Old

Calabar. In 1787 abolitionist Thomas Clarkson learned about the two "Calabar princes," and on a fact-finding journey through England he interrogated sailors who confirmed the main details about the massacre, twenty years earlier. Seven of these men appeared before parliamentary counsel in 1790 and 1791: John Ashley Hall, Ambrose Lace, Isaac Parker, James Morley, Henry Ellison, George Millar, and Richard Story. Lace, a retired captain, also kept some correspondence from Efik and Britons; these rare documents, now lost, appeared in print in the late 1800s and help to fill gaps in the tumultuous history of Old Calabar in the 1760s and 1770s.[32]

Contemporary written sources tell us that rivalries among Efik in the 1760s led to the outbreak of violence in summer 1767, pitting Duke Town and Creek Town against Old Town.[33] With the connivance of at least five British captains, in mid-August 1767 Duke Town warriors made a surprise attack upon a fleet of Old Town canoes.[34] Eyewitnesses believed that 300 to 400 men were killed, including Amboe Robin John, Archibong Robin John, John Robin John, Otto Robin John, and Tom Robin.[35] British sailors captured Little Ephraim Robin John and Ancona Robin Robin John; Duke Town leaders demanded their heads, but the youths were instead carried off to the Americas as slaves. Ephraim Robin John escaped to shore; other Old Town notables who survived the incident include Orrock Robin John, Young Archibong Robin John, and Otto Ephraim.[36] Duke Town's Imo Duke fought in the skirmish, as did, one assumes, "Antera Duke King Warr" and his kinsman Ebee.[37]

Sporadic intra-Efik warfare continued through 1768. Writing from Old Town in July 1768, Liverpool captain George Colley stated:

> Our purchase here at present is very small, owing to a hot and troublesome war amongst the natives, which the day I came here [ca. April 1, 1768] was hotly contested between the people of the [Duke] Town and those of the Old Town, wherein the latter (tho' the others were ten to on[e]) killed and wounded upwards of 300, and totally routed them. However, hope it will be quite subsided, as they seem to be pretty quiet at present. The battle was all in sight, not above a gun shot from the ship, and by that have received the thanks of the [Duke] Town people, for not firing at 'em, as it was [Duke] Ephraim's particular desire, not to interfere, but to let them fight it out themselves.[38]

According to Colley's testimony, Old Town warriors, though outnumbered ten to one, reversed some of their losses to Duke Town. The captain also identifies Duke Town's Duke Ephraim as the Robin John family's principal rival.

Analysis of a unique set of Liverpool-Calabar business papers illustrates how Efik warfare in 1767–1768 reduced the number of Old Town merchants.[39] During six months from July 1769 to January 1770, Captain John Potter transacted business with fifty-four African merchants from Old Calabar. He documents for the first time names of twenty-seven men, including nine Henshaws: Cobham Tom Henshaw, Ephraim Jemmy Henshaw, Jimmy Henshaw, Ephraim Robin Henshaw, Frank Jemmy Henshaw, Keneby Willy Henshaw, King Egbo Solomon Henshaw, Old Keneby William Henshaw, and Robin Henshaw (see appendix A). Potter traded with only one Old Town dealer, though: on August 30, 1769, he bartered for a "boy" from Little Otto Ephraim Robin John. His kinsman Ephraim Robin John does not appear in Potter's accounts. In all, the captain transacted two-thirds of his business from merchants from Creek Town and Duke Town, headed by Willy Honesty and Duke Ephraim. Grouped by families, the Honesties, Dukes, Nteiros, and King John's family purchased half of Potter's cargo of textiles, metal goods, beads, alcohol, and firearms. The Curcocks (Efik on the west bank of the Cross River), the Henshaws, the Cobhams, and the Ambos of Creek Town purchased most of Potter's other goods. The Old Town Robins and Robin Johns are noticeably absent from the accounts (table 1.2).[40] We discuss Captain Potter's accounts in more detail in chapter 2.

Further conflicts among Efik merchants and between Efik and Europeans occurred in 1773. In two letters written by Ephraim Robin John to Ambrose Lace,[41] we learn that three British slavers, the *Maria* (Captain Bishop) of Bristol, *Integrity* (Captain Jackson) of Liverpool, and Jackson's tender, fired on Old Town "without the least provecation and continued it for twenty-four hours." Ephraim fired back, leading Bishop and Jackson to hoist one of his sons to the yardarm of each vessel. Jackson then threatened to sail from Old Calabar with the Old Town youths, and that if Robin John tried to board Bishop's vessel Jackson would cut off his head and send it to Duke Ephraim. Responding to the challenge, Ephraim Robin John "put that out of his power [to cut my head off or carry away my pawns][42] "by stoping his [long]boats and sum of his people [crewmen]." The conflicts ended later that year, as Ephraim Robin John wrote that since "war be don Wee have all the Trade true [through] the Cuntry so that wee want nothing but ships to Incorige us and back us to cary it on." The captains who would arrive, he said, "shall be used with Nothing but Sivellety and fare trade."

In spite of his call for renewed British business, by 1780 Ephraim Robin John had been marginalized, and so had the market power of Old Town. Writing to Liverpool merchants on June 24, 1780, King Henshaw, Duke Ephraim, and Willy Honesty stated that "we was war again with one part our country [Old Town] now we make peace again one King [obong] for all Callabar and trad one places We Belive no war tell Longtime now." Though

TABLE 1.2. Old Calabar families selling slaves to the Liverpool ship *Dobson,*
July 1769–January 1770

A. Grouped by families			
Calabar family	Total	Slaves sold (1769–1770)	From the trust book (1768)
Honesty	135	108	27
Duke	85	69	16
Antera (Ntiero)	73	65	8
King John	59	52	7
Ecricock families	56	56	0
Henshaw	43	42	1
Ambo	28	26	2
Cobham	22	19	3
Ebro	18	16	2
Tom Egbo	14	14	0
Eyamba	4	4	0
Robin John	1	1	0
Unknown families	27	27	0
Totals	*565*	*499*	*66*

B. Grouped by location			
Calabar village(s)	Total	Slaves sold (1769–1770)	From the trust book (1768)
Creek Town	187	155	32
Duke Town	181	155	26
Guinea Company villages	67	60	7
Ekrikok (Itu) villages	56	56	0
Henshaw Town	43	42	1
Tom Shotts Point	3	3	0
Old Town	1	1	0
Traders from unknown villages	27	27	0
Totals	*565*	*499*	*66*

Source: Dobson Calabar account, Hasell MS, Dalemain House, Cumbria.

war between Old Town and Duke Town/Creek Town had ended, its impact
on the size of the Calabar merchant community was clear: "now We fewer,"
the letter reveals.[43] Old Town suffered major losses in 1767, as did Duke
Town in 1768, but ships would now anchor off one settlement and "trade at
one place": Duke Town. The Henshaw families' increased prominence at Old
Calabar is confirmed: King Henshaw was the letter's first signatory. Duke
Ephraim and Willy Honesty were the leaders and major slaving merchants from
Duke Town and Creek Town. All three wanted to assure British merchants

that they spoke for "Old Callabar Country"—not for "one man or one family." No Old Town leader signed this letter from 1780.

In addition to identifying important merchants, Antera Duke's diary helps historians gauge the relative size of Efik families in the mid-1780s. In all, Antera pens names of 101 men and 5 women from Old Calabar and several surrounding Cross River settlements; only his diary records most of these people, and no other premissionary source preserves as many names. Given that Antera lived in his family compound in Duke Town, he socializes frequently with his family members and with his neighbors in other Duke Town sections. Yet he travels most days to Creek Town, Old Town, or Henshaw Town, often to discuss issues concerning Ekpe or commerce. Antera also made one journey northwest to Itu and three southeast to Little Cameroon. Antera recorded information, including names of people with whom he conversed, from many of these short and long-distance travels (see appendix A).

The diary documents men mostly from four families from Duke Town and three from Creek Town. The Ntiero, Duke, Archibong, and Eyamba wards of Duke Town feature in two-thirds of the diary entries, often in the context of Antera's travels with Esien and his brother Egbo Young Antera, referred to in several passages as "wee 3." Antera mentions Duke Ephraim thirty times up to and including his death on July 4, 1786; then his name appears in eleven later entries concerning obsequies. Egbo Young Ofiong and Coffee Duke are clearly important figures, named in twenty and twelve diary entries, respectively. Coffee Duke, a man documented first in 1769, was likely a cousin of Duke Ephraim and became embroiled in witchcraft accusations, as we discuss later. From the Creek Town Ambo, Cobham, and Eyo families, Antera has most contact with Sam Ambo and Willy Honesty, ward leaders, merchants, and senior Ekpe members. The Cobhams appear infrequently; though lesser merchants, they still retained ritual importance through their maintenance of the Ndem priesthood.

Though Old Town and Henshaw Town are located only a few miles north and south of Duke Town, respectively (see map 1.2), Antera had little day-to-day contact with the Robin, Robin John, and Henshaw families. Our diarist mentions eleven Old Town men on twenty-seven different days. He had the most interaction with Willy Tom Robin, whom he meets on nine occasions, including Christmas dinners in 1786 and 1787. Antera documents George Old Town (October 31, 1787) and Old Robin John (January 9, 1788); neither of these men is Ephraim Robin John, who styled himself "Grandy King George." Young Tom Robin, who died on July 29, 1785, was the only Robin he mentioned by name. The Henshaws were reduced by the mid-1780s, as Antera refers to only six family members. Cobham Tom Henshaw, Ephraim Jimmy Henshaw, Frank Jemmy Henshaw, Keneby Willy Henshaw, King Egbo Solomon Henshaw, Old Keneby William Henshaw, and Tom Henshaw, names documented from 1761 to 1770, do not appear in Antera Duke's diary. The Henshaws, one suspects, declined in importance after the death of Tom Henshaw—perhaps the "King Henshaw" of 1780.[44]

By 1805, toward the end of Antera Duke's life, Duke Town and Creek Town had eclipsed Old Town, "formerly the principal town of Calabar," as explorer Henry Nicholls learned that year. The 1767 massacre and later military defeats certainly reduced Old Town's wealth and power. Indeed, Nicholls arrived when Old Town had been "at war" with the "Calabar natives"—soldiers from Creek Town and Duke Town—since 1798. In Duke Town Nicholls witnessed a "visit from king John of Guinea Company, who came [fifteen miles downstream] to return the chiefs of Calabar thanks for getting him away from Old Town out of the power of Willy Tom." Willy Tom Robin, prominent in Antera's diary, was still leader of Old Town; Nicholls called his village "Willy Town" and estimated its size as "perhaps five hundred people," though he did not visit the settlement. Nicholls met three "chiefs" and traders in Duke Town—Egbo Young Ofiong, Duke Ephraim, and Antera Duke—and another in Creek Town, Eyo Honesty. He walked to Henshaw Town and "called upon the principal traders, Jemmy Henshaw and Gentleman Honesty." Later he met Momo Dick at King John Ambo's Town, a small village northeast of Duke Town). Of the group of seven, Duke Ephraim was "by far the greatest trader."[45]

Traditional Religion, "King Calabar," and the Arrival of Ekpe at Old Calabar

Antera Duke's diary helps scholars understand the Cobham family's importance in Efik religion and provides the first written evidence about the Ekpe society.[46] Given Antera's often-cryptic remarks, one must read the diary along with firsthand observations from nineteenth-century explorers and missionaries. Travelers Henry Nicholls (1805) and James Holman (1828) yield the most information about Ekpe before the arrival of the United Presbyterian Church Mission in 1846. The Reverends Hope Masterton Waddell and William Anderson resided at Duke Town for twelve and thirty-three years, respectively, and, as missionaries, they paid particular attention to local religious practices. One hundred years later, in the 1950s and 1960s, Efik recalled their traditions to anthropologists and historians, as well as to a commission that heard disputes about the obong-ship at Calabar. Their recollections add to our understanding of precolonial Calabar religion.

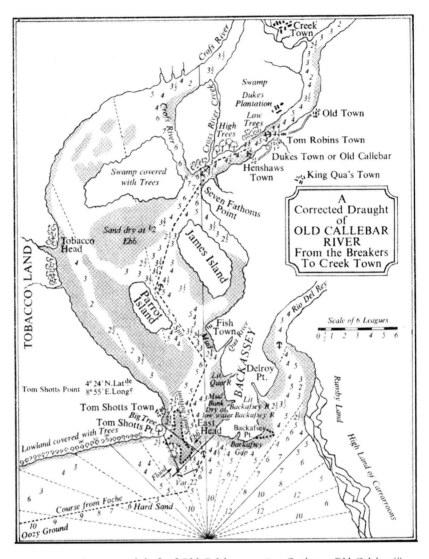

MAP 1.2. A corrected draft of Old Calabar, ca. 1820 (Latham, *Old Calabar*, ii)

  It is remembered that Ndem Efik was the tutelary deity at Old Calabar
and was revered by all Efik since the origins of the tribe and early years at
Creek Town.[47] This serpentlike water god supposedly lived in the river near
Parrot Island, and men sacrificed albino or light-colored girls to Ndem Efik
by throwing them in the water. Legend holds that it was a good omen if the
girl disappeared under the waves instantly, as the *Ndem* had accepted the
offering; if she floated, however, it was a bad omen, as the *Ndem* had rejected
the offering. The guardian of the cult of Ndem Efik was the head of religion,

known as Oku Ndem Efik. Elders say that Oku Ndem has always come from the Cobham family, direct descendants of Eyo Ema, the eldest son of Ema, the senior Efik founding father.[48] The role of the Oku Ndem has continued, and as late as 1966 one could see the shed of the serpent (Efe Asabo) in downtown Duke Town, then an inconspicuous building made from traditional materials with a thatched roof.

The first missionaries who lived at Duke Town in the mid-1800s confirm traditional stories about the cult of Ndem Efik and identify his anglicized title "King Calabar." As Waddell wrote in 1846: "There is another person who, by a misuse of the title, is called 'King Calabar.' He is the remains of the greatest man in the country, being the nearest approach to a *Pontifex Maximus* that their native superstition admits of. He had charge of the *Ndem Efik*, or Great Calabar juju. To him the chiefs of the land made lowly reverence, while he made obeisance to none, and before him and his idol the covenants of tribes and families were sealed by oath." Waddell also learned that "[o]n certain occasions a human being was sacrificed to some river or sea god to hasten the arrival of ships,"[49] but he did not identify Ndem Efik as one of these water spirits to whom human offerings were made. These details entered the missionary record from William Anderson, who reported that in waters off Parrot Island Efik sacrificed albino girls to Ndem Efik. As Anderson stated on March 28, 1856: "It is with deep sorrow that I am constrained to record that the greater portion of Duke Town gentlemen went this afternoon to the neighbourhood of Parrot Island, and there sacrificed a poor albino girl. Some say such sacrifice is made to Ndem Efik, to make him bring plenty ships to the country, while others say the rite is intended to keep away sickness from the town. . . . Have not heard of any sacrifice of the kind being made since 1851." Two days later Anderson recorded the death of Edem Oku, "who took an active part in the murderous ceremonial of the 28th." Anderson's "Edem Oku" is clearly an anglicization of Oku Ndem, the guardian of Ndem Efik. Sacrificing albino girls appears to have occurred about every five years. In addition to the instances in 1851 and 1856, Anderson learned that in June 1862 Duke Town gentleman "took a poor Albino girl slave down the river to the neighbourhood of Parrot Island, and there murdered her to Ndem Efik."[50]

The Presbyterian missionaries at Old Calabar contrasted Efik reverence to Ndem Efik and Oku Ndem, King Calabar, with the poverty of his office. Animals and humans were sacrificed to the water spirit to ward off fire or to honor the installation of a new "high priest of the Ndem." In 1853 Reverend Anderson, given a leopard cub, learned that Efik tradition entitled King Calabar to this animal, and when the priest "heard that he had been deprived of a portion of his perquisites, he became quite outrageous." He threatened to "bring the curse of Ndem Efik on Duke Town, unless the little leopard were carried to him." A group of Efik begged the missionaries to present the cub to King Calabar. A decade later, after the installation of a new Oku Ndem, Anderson noted how King (Obong) Archibong "and all the gentry spent several hours this morning adorning Ndem Efik's house."[51] Other than some animals and reptiles, King Calabar received few financial entitlements. In 1847 Waddell observed that the "office has fallen into disrepute, and the emoluments are so trifling that only a decayed gentleman can be found to accept the honour. A poor, little, old man, who often got his dinner as an alms at the mission-house, was the dignitary at the time of which we write."[52]

Similarly, during diarist Antera Duke's time the Oku Ndem had little conspicuous wealth but retained crucial ceremonial and religious importance. On August 23, 1785, Antera writes, "[A]ll wee go with King on bord Captin fairweather for comey." This "king" who accompanied Antera and others on board Captain Fairweather's ship, we suggest, is "King Calabar." This is the only time Antera records the "king" boarding a ship, and, since Fairweather was the senior and most important captain, the priest's visit may have had particular significance.[53] In one of the more puzzling diary entries, on September (October) 8, 1785, Antera wrote, "[S]o I have give King up Tabow Besides Chap so I killd goat and Deash him & peoples about 30 copper besides mimbo and Brandy[.]" Admittedly King "up Tabow" is obscure, but if the "king" is King Calabar, the Oku Ndem, then "up Tabow" may be an anglicization of the Efik verb *täb-ä* or *töbö*, to stand or lie low or inferior in height to some other thing.[54] Thus Antera bent low or prostrated himself in obeisance to the Ndem priest and his shrine, sacrificed a goat, and dashed (gave) the priest and his attendants thirty copper rods (the value of a goat), palm wine, and brandy.

Antera gives clues that the Cobham family provided the Oku Ndem, as maintained by Efik tradition. On May 18, 1786, he writes that a Cobham "father" had died recently, and his family cut off seven men's heads in the funeral ceremony. A deceased Cobham elder, perhaps Tom John Cobham, had been the previous Oku Ndem, since there are later discussions among Efik elders in the Cobham ward of Creek Town about who will be the next King Calabar. On March 24, 1787, Willy Honesty calls all the Efik gentlemen to Egbo Cobham's cabin "for know who wee will give King of Old Calabar" ("to decide who we will make King of Old Calabar"). This is the only diary passage referring to Egbo Cobham. Three weeks later, on April 13, Antera and others dined at Egbo Young Ofiong's house, still needing to "settle about King of Callabar." Witchcraft accusations into the death of Tom John Cobham may have delayed the settlement: on December 11, 1787, Tom John Cobham's wife or wives undertook the poison bean ritual. By January 31,

1788, when the diary ends, it is not clear whether a new Ndem priest had been chosen.

Discussions about the vacant office of Oku Ndem Efik in 1787 reveal that during the period of Antera's diary Ekpe stood side by side with Ndem as the principal religious cults in Old Calabar. Egbo Young Ofiong and Willy Honesty hosted meetings about choosing the Ndem priest, because these two men were key Ekpe leaders. As recorded in the diary, on February 16, 1787, retainers from these two men dressed Grand Ekpe (Idem Nyamkpe), a costumed figure, in the palaver house. In 1805 Nicholls refers to Egbo Young "Eyambo" and Eyo Honesty "King of Ebongo," and later testimonies identify these titles as the president (eyamba) and vice president (ebunko) of Ekpe society.[55] At some point, probably in the nineteenth century, Ekpe officials excluded the Ndem priest from trading with Europeans, which reduced the market power of the Cobham ward.[56] When explorer Nicholls visited the "king" (King Calabar) in Creek Town in 1805, he thought he was a "nobody," his rank "being a mere nominal title, the traders possessing all the power."[57] What was Ekpe, and when did the Ekpe secrets arrive at Old Calabar?

Ekpe was an invisible forest spirit, which had to be propitiated for the well-being of Calabar. Similar beliefs in forest spirits exist in other communities in southeastern Nigeria and western Cameroon, and in many the spirit manifested itself as a leopard and traveled from the bush to interact with humans. Ekpe means "leopard" in Ibibio and Efik, and in Ejagham, the Ibibio dialect in southwestern Cameroon, Ngbe means "leopard." Since humans captured the spirit, it tries devious ways to escape, and indeed it was revered as a trickster.[58] Leopard societies developed to worship the forest spirit and unite villagers around a supernatural entity. These Ngbe and Ekpe societies created elaborate masquerades in which villagers performed rituals and plays associated with the spirit's proclivities.[59] Because amazed Europeans wrote about these ceremonial spectacles, locating descriptions of costumes or masks establishes dates when the societies functioned.

In a little-known work, English sailor Silas Told, at Old Calabar in mid-1729, gives historians the earliest reference to the Ekpe figure. After arriving in the Cross River, Told went on shore, "heard an uncommon shrieking of women," and saw

> *Egbo*, a native, in a fine silk grass meshed net, so curiously made to fit him, that nothing but his hands and feet appeared; the end ended with a fringe, not unlike ruffles. This man is looked upon as both God and devil, and all stand in the most profound awe of him, from the highest to the lowest.

I stood still to see the sequel of his caprice, and observed that in his hand he had a green bough, wherewith he was whipping the women's posteriors, as they went naked, and chasing them out of one house into another; and as they were exceedingly terrified, and considered it a heavy curse when Egbo struck them, therefore they fled from him as we would flee from hell flames.[60]

Told observed a basic raffia-suited Ekpe masquerade, which accords with the more elaborate costume observed a hundred years later by British traveler James Holman. At Old Calabar in 1828, Holman stated that Egbo "wears a complete disguise, consisting of a black network close to the skin from heat to foot, a hat with a long feather, horns projecting from his forehead, a large whip in his right hand, with a bell fastened to the lower part of his back and several smaller ones round his ankles."[61] The Ekpe messenger (Idem Ikwo), as later evidence confirms, whipped nonmembers—women, youths, and poorer freemen and slaves.

That Silas Told arrived at Old Calabar within a generation of the establishment of Ekpe is supported by the fact that neither James Barbot (1698) nor Alexander Horsburgh (1720) mentioned King Egbo or King Bunko.[62] In particular, if Ekpe society had developed by 1720, one might have expected to see an Ekpe officer listed as one of Horsburgh's comey recipients. It must be noted, however, that the supercargo paid the largest comey (80 coppers) to King Ambo, and "King" could refer to Ekpe leadership. As British sailor John Ashley Hall, recalling his visit in 1775, believed: "At Calabar they had Three Kings, one of which had the Civil Government, the other was at the head of the Religion, and the third at the Head of the Law."[63] Oral histories support the proposition that King Ambo was "the head of the Law" (eyamba) in 1720. At some early time Esien Ekpe Oku of Ambo ward purchased the Ekpe secrets, established the cult in Creek Town, and became its first eyamba.[64] "King" also could refer to the head of "civil government," the obong. But Efik do not remember the obong-ship residing in the Ambo family. If this oral history is accurate in time placement, Horsburgh paid the largest comey to the eyamba, and King Ambo established Ekpe no later than 1720. If Efik legends are inaccurate in regard to timing and King Ambo was obong in 1720, then he purchased the secrets between 1720 and 1729.

The Organization and Function of Ekpe Society

Before the publication of Antera Duke's diary and Henry Nicholls's letters, traveler Holman (1828) and missionary Waddell (1846) penned the earliest firsthand observations about Ekpe's organizational structure. Holman established that there were five steps or grades of Ekpe, headed by the rank of "Yampai" (the fifth "step"), which in 1828 cost an entry fee of 850 "white copper rods." To attain that position one needed to have purchased admission into the previous four ranks of "Abungo," "Aboko," "Makaira," and "Bakimboko." In contrast, Waddell learns in 1846–1847 that Ekpe includes "ten branches of various degrees of honour and power, some low enough for boys and slaves to buy as a sort of initiation, others so high that only freemen of old family and high rank can procure them." Wealth, family position, and freed status—not age—were criteria to purchase different Ekpe grades. A young man such as Young Eny Cobham, for example, "a great gentleman's eldest son" who "bought all Egbo," would have completed his payment for all degrees up to and including "Yampy Egbo." To acknowledge his "Yampy" (Nyamkpe) membership, he received "three marks of yellow powder on his forehead and arms."[65]

The different numbers of Ekpe grades recorded by Holman and Waddell suggest that between the 1820s and 1840s the society's membership expanded because Efik merchants increased earnings and the numbers of slaves they owned. The Old Calabar export palm oil trade doubled during these three decades as British demand increased and French and Portuguese slave trades ended.[66] Antera Duke's sons and grandsons would have reinvested palm oil profits in domestic and agricultural slaves, swelling the bonded population. Ekpe leaders advanced the number of steps from five to ten to ease social tensions caused by rising traders and restless farm slaves. With greater numbers of low rungs, more slaves initiated into the society; greater numbers of high rungs differentiated those from established lineage and wealth from the new rich. Nyamkpe, which remained the top grade, became reserved for wealthy freemen from old families who controlled Ekpe offices and the positions of obong and King Calabar.

Ekpe expansion from five to ten steps within a generation contrasts with the incremental change to the society's structure during the two decades before and two decades after the abolition of British slaving. Antera Duke remarked on October 17, 1787, that he and others shared out 115 coppers "for all 4 Callabar Egbo," and then two weeks later that Jimmy Henshaw paid dues "for 4 Callabar Laws" to head an Ekpe grade.[67] Though Nyamkpe members received the payments, which totaled 192 copper rods and four goats,[68] they comprised, symbolically, one set of dues for each of the four grades. In 1805 explorer Nicholls heard that Old Calabar had four "laws," and that the laws were headed by the "king of Ebongo," "king of Congo," "king of Egbo," and "king of Yampia." He understood that one needed to purchase each law, and before "buying yampia," for example, "they must first purchase Egbo, which costs them eight boxes of copper rods, with brandy and chop, which is likewise divided among their chiefs."[69] Officials perhaps created a fifth Ekpe rung, Holman's entry-level "Bakimboko," because there was a rise in palm oil exports and incomes in the decade after European wars ended in 1815.

Though there remained four Ekpe "laws" circa 1785–1807, new initiates entered the first step and others undoubtedly had accrued sufficient monies to attain higher levels. In eight diary entries Antera gives cursory evidence about members "putting in money" for new initiates. For example, on January 18, 1785, all the Ekpe men joined together to "putt moony for 20 men." His broken English makes it unclear whether people "putt in moony" (denominated in copper rods) for twenty new Ekpe members or put in money to the value of twenty men slaves. In his last reference to initiation fees, on February 16, 1787, Antera writes, "[W]e Did bought Egbo 344 men be Callabar new Egbo." If our diarist remarks that new initiates paid entry fees to the value of 344 men slaves, those fees would total 60,000 to 70,000 copper rods—entry fees from 60 to 70 new Ekpe initiates. We doubt that society membership increased by a fifth on just one day.[70] Thus Antera's cryptic remark may refer to 344 total Ekpe members, or perhaps that 344 men moved up a step. Waddell thought that in 1847 Ekpe included 1,000 members in ten branches, so perhaps 344 Ekpe members in four branches in 1787 is realistic.[71]

Many Ekpe members at Old Calabar in February 1787 would have been initiated into the rites of the lowest grade. Some newcomers worked as Ekpe "runners," young men who helped to enforce the society's laws for the greater Efik community. We believe that Antera refers to these "leg men" when he mentions "wowo Egbo men" canoeing to meet Ibibio fishermen and "wawa Egbo" cutting firewood. He had difficulty rendering the concept "Ekpe runner" into English and, as in two other diary entries, reverts to Efik to convey his meaning.[72] Efik words most similar to "wowo"/"wawa" are the verbs *wärä* and *wara*. Missionary Goldie defined *wärä* as "To come forth; to come out; to proceed from; to issue" or "To come up, grow up." He defines *wara* as "To make haste, to be speedy, quick."[73] Each definition suggests movement or speed. Egbo runners, wearing terrifying masks, ran between family compounds, subjugating slaves and women. Runners also accompany the Ekpe figure to the houses of those offenders who break Ekpe law. In 1828 Holman observed Ekpe followed by "half a dozen subordinate personages fantastically dressed, each carrying either a sword or stick."[74]

Ekpe functioned as a governing council to resolve intra-Efik disputes as well as disagreements between Efik and non-Efik, including European traders.[75] Nyamkpe made binding legal decisions, and the second grade, called Okpoho during Reverend Waddell's mission, implemented them. The society could seize people's property for nonpayment, in the manner of a bailiff. For Europeans, the ability of Ekpe to force Efik merchants to pay debts gave them increased confidence to advance credit, and indeed lowered the cost of credit. Ship captains, though, feared having Ekpe "blown" on them, as they could not transact business until parties settled the dispute. The society's punishments also included execution, home detention, or fines.[76] In an extraordinary incident, in 1774 Liverpool captains Edmund Doyle and Thomas Fidler were seized, imprisoned, and "poisoned" by men from Duke Town.[77] Were they detained for violating Ekpe rules? Poisoned by accident?[78] Financial penalties could be crippling, as Creek Town merchant Eyo Willy Honesty learned in the 1810s. According to Waddell, who heard the story in 1847, jealous enemies in Nyamkpe trumped up a charge against Willy Honesty, and he was "condemned to pay an enormous fine which nearly ruined him. They ate him up, or, as they expressed it, 'chopped him all to nothing.'"[79]

Because of the power wielded by Ekpe, ambitious men coveted the offices of eyamba and ebunko. Evidence from Antera's diary in 1787 suggests that Egbo Young Ofiong was eyamba, and that there were then three vice presidents of Ekpe: King Ambo, Willy Honesty, and Young Duke Ephraim, perhaps thirty years of age. Egbo Young Ofiong had become eyamba by 1805, and Efik tradition recalls that his predecessor was Ekpenyong Ekpe Oku, of Ambo family, senior half brother of the founder of Ekpe society.[80] Yet Egbo Young Ofiong was a major figure in Ekpe at the time of the diary. When on October 31, 1787, Jimmy Henshaw paid dues to be "King Egbo," obong, here referring to the head of one of the Ekpe grades,[81] Egbo Young Ofiong received twenty-five rods and a goat, the biggest share of all. Surely he must have been eyamba? Three men each received twenty rods and a goat, Willy Honesty, Young Duke Ephraim, and King Ambo. Willy Honesty was the leading man in Creek Town, vice president of the society by 1805, and a renowned Efik warrior. Young Duke Ephraim, though perhaps a decade younger than his fellow officers, was already an important Efik notable.[82]

Ekpe, then, in these days was an exclusively male society that enacted and enforced laws for the greater Efik community, helped reduce tensions between individuals and families, and stabilized the business environment for both local and overseas traders. A wealthy merchant, Antera Duke was a member of Nyamkpe, the highest of four Ekpe grades functioning during the last twenty years of his life. Though Antera did not hold a specific Ekpe office and was not included in the list of Jimmy Henshaw's payments in October 1787, to be able to list the payments he must have been a crucial member close to all important decisions. These Efik in Nyamkpe dined together frequently, occasionally with ship captains, to foster good relationships. Ekpe could not control all intra-Efik jealousies, though, as battles between Old Town and Duke Town prove. Given that the power of Ekpe also could be invoked to marginalize rivals, tensions would have risen following the deaths of obongs as elders forged alliances to support candidates from specific families.

The Death of Duke Ephraim and
His Funeral Obsequies

The big event in Antera Duke's diary is the death of Duke Ephraim (Edem Ekpo) at about 4:00 A.M. on July 4, 1786. Duke Ephraim was the leader of civil government, holding the title obong—defined by European traders as the principal ruler, foreign minister, or "king."[83] The diary provides the earliest death date of an obong, a crucial fixed point in time needed to anchor a series of obongs in Calabar history. Antera records human and animal sacrifices in honor of Duke Ephraim, nervousness about probable intra-Efik conflict, and Duke Ephraim's funeral obsequies that occurred in November 1786. British sailor Henry Schroeder, at Duke Town from late July to mid-December 1786, later wrote extensively about his months at Old Calabar and provides more information about Duke Ephraim's interment ceremonies.

Antera confirms the importance of the obong and that Duke Ephraim held the position until he died in July 1786. We know from Efik traditions that the obong-ship passed from the Henshaw to the Duke ward,[84] but there is little written evidence about the Duke family before the mid-nineteenth century. Waddell's potted history of Old Calabar, for example, did not mention Great Duke Ephraim's father Edem Ekpo (ca. 1710–1786).[85] The Duke Ephraim of Antera's diary handled disputes between Efik and their African neighbors and between traders and ship captains. When in March 1785 a British captain threatened to sail to Cameroon unless his anchorage fees were reduced, Duke held a meeting with Willy Honesty and other Efik to discuss the situation. Later that year British sailors fought some Efut people near the Cross River estuary. Antera Duke and others "go to meet for Duk to know Duk think for Doe" (went to meet Duke Ephraim to know what he was thinking to do about it). In January 1786 Duke and Efut leader King Tom Salt sacrificed a goat after resolving a disagreement. Six months later Duke Ephraim helped distribute copper rods, a fine paid by Tom Salt, and sent a payment of forty rods to Ibibio people.[86]

Duke Ephraim's death, like those of four other Efik notables documented by Antera Duke, prompted ritual human sacrifices at the burial and during later ceremonies. The Duke had been sick since July 2, 1786, died on July 4, 1786, and was buried by high-ranking Ekpe members in secret at 5:00 A.M.

the following day, along with nine adult men and women, possibly free relatives and wives.[87] Antera and others may have buried Duke Ephraim in his family compound or in the bush.[88] The previous year, on June 29, 1785, Antera records that young Tom Robin died after having been sick for seven days, and three weeks later, on July 19, 1785, an undisclosed number of heads are cut off in his funeral ceremonies. On May 18, 1786, John Cobham's family "mak play" for their father and cut off the heads of seven men. On June 7, 1787, Robin Tom King John and Otto Tom King John cut a woman's head off for Duke Ephraim, and seven men for Antera's own father—again, rituals occurring months after the burials.[89] Such burial and funeral sacrifices continued at Old Calabar until 1850, when pressure from British missionaries, diplomats, and slaves—usually the victims—supposedly ended the rituals.

In the interim between Duke Ephraim's burial and funeral obsequies, the Ntiero allied with other families in anticipation of possible internecine violence caused by the obong's death. Four days after Ephraim died, Antera Duke's family traveled to Creek Town to "chop Doctor" with Cobham gentlemen at George Cobham's yard. The next day they "chop Docter with henshaw family" at Long Dick Ephraim's "cabin" (small house) in Duke Town. A week later, on July 18, all Calabar elders, including those in Antera Duke's family, "Drink Docter" with King Aqua, the leader of Qua peoples to the east, nominal owners of Calabar River land. The following day Ntiero elders "Drink Docter" privately with King Aqua, and at night they "Drink Docter" with Willy Tom Robin of Old Town. The terms "chop Docter" and "drink Docter" in this context refer to oath-swearing rituals between families, equivalent to swearing on a holy text. Parties swore on *mbiam* (oath) not to use mysterious force to cause harm. *Mbiam*, said to possess supernatural power to detect falsehoods, was usually in water, though the potent liquid might be mixed with sacrificial food. Oath takers would drink or "chop" (eat) "doctor" (a ritual) from a small amount of *mbiam* placed in a gourd.[90]

Efik leaders planned funeral ceremonies for Duke Ephraim to begin November 4, exactly four months after the obong's death. British sailor Henry Schroeder witnessed preparations for what he termed the "grand pageant." At some time in October, "Couriers were immediately dispatched to Cameroons, New Calabar, and other places, to apprise the chiefs, when the sacred rites would be performed; and three weeks were allowed them to furnish their quota of slaves, goats, and fowls; for each chief had to provide a certain number, in proportion to the rank he held." [91] Sixty years later Presbyterian missionaries also learned about the four-month interval between burial and obsequies. In both 1786 and 1847, funeral planners presumably waited for the rainy season to end, but the significance of four months is not known.[92]

Loud crying from men and women in Duke Town on November 4 marked the commencement of the ten-day funeral ceremonies for Duke Ephraim.[93] After hearing the wails, Antera sent all his "people" away to the woods in two canoes, so they would not become victims during the ensuing mass sacrifices. According to Schroeder, African visitors in "a very large fleet of canoes" began arriving on the afternoon of November 5, and, as they steered up the Cross and Calabar rivers, they "were so formidable in appearance, as to create alarm in the minds of the English captains, whose ships were anchored opposite [Duke Town]." Soon the "beach was lined with spectators, to welcome their approaching friends; the profoundest silence prevailed, well suited to the occasion of the visit." Schroeder does not name these visitors, and our diarist mentions only a dignitary from "TaEon town." Schroeder's captain, Jenkin Evans, and other British commanders learned that "the sacrifice would commence at about two o'clock in the morning [of November 6], [and] they proposed leaving the ships at that hour, in order, if possible, to witness the inhuman ceremony from its commencement."

On November 6, 1786, all the elders met in Duke Town's palaver house, perhaps at 2:00 A.M., and at 5:00 A.M. executioners began to cut off slaves' heads for Duke Ephraim. Antera tells us that fifty slaves died that day—the "grand sacrifice," as Schroeder remembered. Meanwhile, drumming and dancing continued, as it had throughout the day in every yard in Duke Town. There also was a feast of fifteen calabashes of food and twenty-nine cases of brandy, and "fires were kept burning during the whole night."[94] Schroeder heard, presumably from his captain, Jenkin Evans, that during the funeral ceremony a "grand procession was formed, consisting of chiefs, inferior traders, and visitors. The chiefs, according to rank, took precedency, and walked two and two, followed by the others, among whom numbers appeared, wearing white aprons, apparently goats' skins and carrying muskets, some in their hands, others on their shoulders." They walked to the grave site of Duke Ephraim, forming a circle around it.[95]

The next day Efik and their foreign guests witnessed a "sacrifice of a more simple nature": Duke Ephraim's possessions "sacrificed" near the Duke Town beach. Schroeder reports how

the whole moveable property belonging to [Duke Ephraim] was deposited near the newly-erected tents; even his canoe, which was chained to a large tree; kettles, pans, and every kitchen utensil; all his wearing apparel, forming a most valuable wardrobe, chiefly of English and French fabric. The small cattle, goats, and fowls, which the other chiefs provided for the occasion, were now killed, and their blood sprinkled, or rather thrown, over the whole of the wearing apparel, drapery, &c.; when every thing of European manufacture was hung up in the two tents; the utensils, and other articles from the same quarter of the globe, were also placed therein; while the natural products, or the works of African ingenuity and industry, were laid on the ground, arranged with great regularity. All were rendered useless; the canoe, as well as the vessels used for the culinary and domestic purposes, were broken, but not materially altered in form. With this destruction terminated the sacrifice; and the remainder of the day was spent according to the inclination of the assembled multitudes.

Workers raised mud walls "to surround the sacred deposit" of broken property, and sentinels guarded the ground day and night.[96] Antera Duke and the gentlemen dined that night at Esien Duke's house. On the morning of November 8 the foreign visitors canoed from Duke Town. The gentlemen later dined at Egbo Young Ofiong's house. That day executioners beheaded four slaves, including one woman sacrificed to honor Antera Duke's father.

Following the departure of guests paying their respects to the deceased obong, the final obsequies concerned Duke Ephraim's fellow Nyamkpe members, kinsmen, and surviving wives. On November 11, Efik notables, including Antera Duke, walked to Duke Town's palaver house, dressed in "Long Cloth & Egbo cloth & Hatt and Jacket and Everry fine thing."[97] Afterward, masked Ekpe messengers ran through the town to announce the end of the ceremonies. Even then the obsequies had not concluded. On the twelfth retainers took the costumed Grand Ekpe figure (Idem Nyamkpe) to women in Duke Town and ordered more feasting and dances. On the morning of the thirteenth runners ordered all the Duke house women to pay ten copper rods to Ekpe. At 8:00 P.M. all members of Ekpe met in Duke Town's palaver shed and ordered Duke Ephraim's wives to walk from his compound to the palaver shed to weep and wail—"cry Egbo." The Duke's chief wife would have led the ceremonial procession, followed by other widows, relatives, freeborn and slaves.[98]

Witchcraft Accusations and Old Calabar Politics

In the Old Calabar of Antera Duke's time and even among some Efik of Calabar today, witchcraft might have explained the sickness (July 2–4) and death (July 4) of Duke Ephraim.[99] Antera's diary provides the earliest evidence about witchcraft fears at Old Calabar, and on October 22, 1787, he wrote that Duke Ephraim's sister had accused Coffee Duke of using witchcraft to kill her brother.[100] Those accused of practicing witchcraft were forced to "chop nut"—to consume the poisonous *esere* bean (*Physostigma venenosum*), ground into a potion, to try to prove their innocence. Since most died from the ordeal, the poison ritual made witchcraft accusations a powerful tool against relatives and enemies. In Efik society, accusations generally target male blood relations, wives, or in-laws. Unrelated persons were not usually accused, so there were, for example, no witchcraft attacks on Europeans. Coffee Duke, we suggest, was Duke Ephraim's cousin (see figure 1.1) and one of the candidates to succeed Duke as obong.[101] Though the obong-ship remained unfilled by the time Antera's diary ends, Coffee Duke was defeated eventually, as we know that Egbo Young Ofiong emerged triumphant at some time between 1788 and 1805. Ofiong is remembered by the Efik as the first man to be both eyamba and obong, an achievement replicated in the 1820s by Duke Ephraim's son, the "Young Duke" of the diary.[102]

Coffee Duke and Egbo Young Ofiong were two of the leading half dozen Efik gentlemen during Antera's diary years and viable contenders to succeed Duke Ephraim as obong. The two appear first in the historical record in Captain John Potter's Calabar accounts, 1769–1770. Coffee Duke sold twenty-eight slaves to Liverpool captain John Potter—the captain's sixth most important supplier. "Egboyoung" brokered the sale of two slaves for "King Warr"—Antera Duke.[103] Both men, we suggest, were born about the year 1740.[104] By 1785 Egbo Young had a two-story wooden house imported from Liverpool ("Liverpool Hall"), a privilege allowed only to important men, and indeed he had attained the presidency of Ekpe.[105] When he fell sick on August 29, 1785, Antera wrote that they had a "Bad Sunday." On Christmas Day in 1785 Egbo Young shared Christmas dinner with British ship captains, Coffee Duke, Antera Duke, and other Efik dignitaries.[106] After Duke Ephraim died, Esien Duke, Egbo Young, and Coffee Duke walked to Antera's house to examine debts itemized in Duke's comey book. On March 24, 1787, the Duke Town gentlemen met at Coffee's cabin to settle their disputes and sacrificed two goats. Their actions did not prevent Duke Ephraim's sister, five months later, from charging Coffee with witchcraft.

Busy events on October 22, 1787, concerning Coffee's alleged witchcraft prompted one of Antera Duke's longest diary entries. Antera and three colleagues, including, probably, Egbo Young Ofiong, had heard about Duke Ephraim's sister's accusation, and the four men swore on *mbiam* that they would not associate with Coffee Duke. Coffee Duke had by then fled to Captain Fairweather's ship for safety, but Ekpe officials ordered Coffee to King Ambo's palaver house, where it was decided that Coffee must drink the witchcraft ordeal with Duke Ephraim's sister. When challenged to take the ordeal, Coffee Duke refused. After a discussion, Willy Honesty sent two Ekpe drums

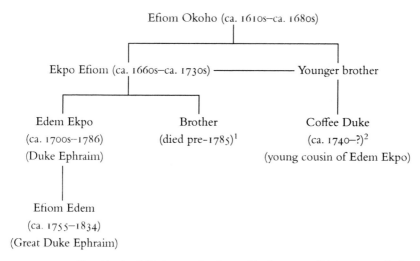

Efiom Okoho (ca. 1610s–ca. 1680s)

Ekpo Efiom (ca. 1660s–ca. 1730s) ———————— Younger brother

Edem Ekpo   Brother   Coffee Duke
(ca. 1700s–1786)   (died pre-1785)[1]   (ca. 1740–?)[2]
(Duke Ephraim)   (young cousin of Edem Ekpo)

Efiom Edem
(ca. 1755–1834)
(Great Duke Ephraim)

FIGURE 1.1. Hypothesized Duke ward relationship between Edem Ekpo (Duke Ephraim) and Coffee Duke. [1] Before Antera Duke's diary begins, and hence death not recorded by the diarist. [2] In 1769–1770 Coffee Duke was a significant merchant, selling twenty-eight slaves to a Liverpool ship. We assume, then, he was about thirty years of age, and thus about forty-five to fifty years of age at the time of older cousin Duke Ephraim's death.

with men to escort Coffee to his house and confine him there. Antera Duke and his allies ("wee 4") agreed that they would not settle their differences with Coffee Duke unless he "Drink Docter."

We learn nothing more about Coffee Duke's predicament until two of Antera's last diary entries from January 1788 and brief notes from Bristol sailors in 1790 and 1792. On January 8 one of Willy Honesty's men heard that Coffee Duke had threatened to set fire to all his houses in Duke Town. So Antera carried two Ekpe drums to warn everyone not to sleep in Coffee's houses. On the seventeenth there was indeed a big fire in town in Potter Antera's yard. Antera Duke and all the town's people tried to put it out; Old Town's Willy Tom Robin assisted, as did Liverpool captain John Tatem's mate and six African boat boys. The fire burned four houses; whether the conflagration resulted from Coffee's threat is not clear, but it looks suspicious. In 1790 a Bristol captain moored off Duke Town and paid "Duke [Ephraim] and Egboe Youn and Antera for Anchorage." Two years later, a mate noted how they landed goods "under the care of Duke Ephraim, Egbo Young, and Antera Duke, and taken their receipts." Duke Town's Coffee Duke is not mentioned in either letter.[107] Though Antera's diary ends before Coffee Duke was forced to consume the poisonous draft, if he ever did, the fact that

Egbo Young Ofiong later emerges as obong implies that Coffee was defeated, perhaps killed as early as February 1788.

Interestingly, rivalry between Duke Ephraim's family and that of Coffee Duke appears to have continued for two generations. When Duke Ephraim's son (Efiom Edem or Great Duke Ephraim) died on October 14, 1834, accusations of witchcraft were lodged, and two days later sixteen Efik were forced to undergo the poison ordeal in the Duke's yard.[108] Missionary Waddell transcribed the entry from Mr. (Egbo?) Young's diary:

> '16 October 1834.—This morning all country and Calabar come, and we go for Mr. Young, and stop little, not long, after that we go for Duk Palaver house, with all country, and our people, about the Duk Ephraim sick, and we go in for his yard, so all our people chop nut. The name of them:—
>
> Erim Cooffee Duk chop, dead. His son chop, no dead. Orrock Cooffee and two his son, dead. Cooffee Copper, dead. Egbo Eshan, dead. Egbo Young Egbo, dead. Bashey Archiebong Egbo Duk, dead. Erim Egbo Duk Ephraim, Otto, dead. Young Old Archiebong, dead. Erim Odoor, mother, dead. Otto Ecarnum, dead. One Otto slave, dead, for street. Egbo Eshen, mother, dead *to-night*.

The first six Efik forced to take the potion were members of the Coffee family, and five died: Erim Coffee Duke; Orrock Coffee and two of his sons; and Coffee Copper. The Duke ward had a long-standing rivalry with the Coffee family, and ward members seized the opportunity immediately after Great Duke Ephraim's death to try to eliminate three men and their eldest sons.[109]

Moving back to the eighteenth century, with the support from Efik elders such as Antera Duke, Willy Honesty, Sam Ambo, and Willy Tom Robin, Egbo Young Ofiong succeeded Duke Ephraim as obong. Efik tradition places Egbo Young Ofiong's obong-ship between the offices of Duke Ephraim (ca. 1700s–1786) and his son Great Duke Ephraim (ca. 1755–1834). He appears to be obong in 1805, as early in that year explorer Nicholls calls Egbo Young the "principal chief" who "is obliged to entertain all strangers, and if required, give them his protection"—classic duties of the obong, which included foreign diplomacy. Duke (later Great Duke) Ephraim, then about fifty years of age and "by far the greatest trader," was one of several other "chiefs" identified. Nicholls did not meet Coffee Duke, who apparently died after Antera Duke's diary ended on January 31, 1788.[110] Egbo Young Ofiong was then already eyamba and he must have seen Coffee Duke, a rival of similar age, as someone who would contest the obong-ship.

Forty years after the elder Duke Ephraim's death, a garbled story from a British ship surgeon provides an intriguing postscript to the political turmoil that engulfed Coffee Duke. While at Cameroon in 1826, surgeon Robert Jackson learned about a bitter feud between two half brothers, following the death of King Bell. Jackson recounted how in 1792 an "elder Brother, the heir-apparent" to the king

> had become by the commission of several cruel murders, & many other atrocities extremely obnoxious to the Natives, & the decease of their father taking place at this period, the whole place became a scene of anarchy and confusion, the inhabitants neglecting their accustomed avocations, to engage in the state broils, & thereby putting a stop to the trade of the river. Fifteen Slave Ships then lay moored in the harbour, & Capt. Fairweather of one of them, being an experienced man, was delegated by the others, to reason with the population, & restore them in some degree to their former tranquility. After many vain efforts the leading Chiefs at length agreed to refer the matter in dispute, to the arbitration of the Slave Commanders & it was decided by a Majority of one, that the present King should become sole Monarch & absolute as his father before him.

The British captains, headed by Captain Patrick Fairweather, enforced the one-vote majority decision with "powder & Ball," and the heir apparent, in revenge and despair, "set fire to the Town, and immediately afterwards, blew out his brains with a blunderbuss."[111]

That this story circulated more than a generation after the feud shows the interest it held for people, but it is unclear whether the struggle occurred at Cameroon or Old Calabar. In 1792 Captain Patrick Fairweather traded at Old Calabar, and on October 19 he assumed command of a recently arrived Liverpool ship to enable him to remain in the river through June 1793.[112] Further, in contrast to Old Calabar, the slave trade then at Cameroon was insufficiently large to support "Fifteen Slave Ships." Could Jackson's phrase "the decease of their father taking place at this period" refer thus to the death of Duke Ephraim in 1786? Were the older brother and "heir apparent" a misunderstanding of the relationship between Coffee Duke and Egbo Young Ofiong? Before the conflict related here, in October 1790 a Bristol captain at Old Calabar predicted trouble: "I cannot say what Quantity of slaves I can Purchase more yett, here is great talks of a war."[113] If a war indeed erupted, one suspects that its root cause was the contested battle for the obong-ship after the death of Duke Ephraim in 1786.

Conclusion

Antera Duke's 10,510-word diary, January 1785–January 1788, is one of the key sources that document Old Calabar's precolonial history. The diary, the most extensive Efik-authored writing, anchors local political, legal, and religious traditions in time. Antera confirms that deaths of Efik dignitaries, as nineteenth-century missionary sources indicate, triggered human sacrifices and witchcraft accusations—giving historians the earliest evidence of such practices at Old Calabar. Frequent references to Ekpe reveal that the society's obligations occupied many hours of Antera's time each week. Antera, a member of the highest Ekpe grade, Nyamkpe, gained monies from men paying dues to enter any four of the grades then functioning. Families competed to advance in Ekpe, those in Nyamkpe holding positions of obong, eyamba, or ebunko. Comparing Efik names in the diary with those from captains' accounts from 1720 and 1769 indicates that Duke Town's Ntiero, Eyamba, Coffee, and Duke families emerged in the mid-eighteenth century to challenge men from senior branches of the Ema and Efiom Ekpo lineages.

Antera Duke came of age during heightened competition among the principal families living in Creek Town, Old Town, and Duke Town. Ekpe could help to minimize tensions between Efik traders. Battles between the Dukes and Henshaws resulted in the founding of Henshaw Town in the mid-eighteenth century; rivalries between merchants exploded in a massacre of Old Town canoemen and traders in 1767 and continued intermittently until Antera's death, sometime between 1805 and 1809. Internecine warfare strengthened Duke Town and Creek Town merchants, as they gained large shares of the comey payments and business held earlier by their Old Town rivals. Duke Ephraim (Edem Ekpo) and Egbo Young (Ekpenyong) Ofiong are two of the power brokers in Antera's diary. Obong Duke Ephraim's death on July 4, 1786, presented opportunities for rising men to fill the political vacuum. For Egbo Young to emerge triumphant as obong, he would need to gain the support of Antera Duke, Young Duke Ephraim, and leading Ekpe members, including senior men from the Cobham family that held the Ndem priesthood. Egbo Young and his allies used the power of Ekpe and traditional witchcraft accusations to thwart the challenge of Coffee Duke, a younger kinsman of Duke Ephraim (Edem Ekpo) seen as a threat to the Duke family.

Antera Duke and his contemporaries discussed in this chapter were merchants who competed for shares of local and long-distance trade. They profited from their middlemen position in towns near the confluence of the Cross and Calabar rivers, selling slaves and animal and agricultural commodities in return for boxes of textiles, metals, firearms, and beads, and barrels of alcohol, gunpowder, and salt. The growth of overseas trade in the late seventeenth and early eighteenth centuries heightened frictions between Efik towns and between their businessmen and Europeans. King Ambo, a leading merchant in the 1710s and 1720s, purchased the Ekpe secrets, perhaps to diffuse tensions and maintain his family's market power. The Creek Town Ambos were leading slave traders, but by midcentury they had lost some shares of the overseas slave trade to merchants from Duke Town, such as Antera Duke. Antera's diary is an important source written by an African slave trader, and his information helps scholars understand the operation of an eighteenth-century African town, Old Calabar, and the organization of the slave trade there, the topic of chapter 2.

CHAPTER TWO

The Slave Trade at Old Calabar

In the seventeenth and eighteenth centuries, African demand for Atlantic goods transformed fishing communities along the Calabar River into the entrepôt "Old Calabar," trading European, Asian, and African commodities. Some of the small-scale traders who shipped fish, salt, and yams up and down the Cross River and tributaries would become wealthier middlemen merchants. They were principally Efik, who maintained fleets of canoes and retinues of slave porters and canoemen. For African businessmen residing in the Cross River region, the export slave trade remained the chief source of overseas trading revenue until palm oil earnings rose in the 1820s and fewer and fewer French, Portuguese, and Cuban slavers frequented the estuary. Parliament abolished the British slave trade in 1807, and British diplomatic pressure on European and African polities, culminating in Efik-British anti–slave trade treaties signed in 1841 and 1842, ended Calabar's export trade in human cargoes.[1] British missionaries who arrived later then worked with Efik leaders to abolish domestic slavery—the slave workforce that supported the economy at large, including transport, agriculture, and the export palm oil and ivory trades.

Antera Duke lived during a period in Old Calabar history marked by expansion in the export slave trade and the growing power of Duke Town. He was born in the generation after Efik merchants had begun dominating trade in the Cross River. He died shortly before or after Parliament abolished the British slave trade, an event that severed ties temporarily with ship captains and merchants from Liverpool—Efik merchants' principal business partners. The time period of Antera's diary, January 1785–January 1788, saw the height of Old Calabar's export slave trade. Diary entries provide a firsthand African account to help scholars understand the history and organization of the late eighteenth-century slave trade at Old Calabar. In writing about interactions with Europeans, Antera Duke mentioned the officers with whom Duke Town merchants traded; foreign buyers not documented by Antera transacted business with other Efik communities as well as with non-Efik competitors. As we will discuss, Liverpool and Duke Town merchants emerge in the diary as key transatlantic partners, with senior captains and Efik elders dominating the cross-cultural trading relationship.

This chapter examines the slave trade at Old Calabar to explain Antera Duke's diary entries and place "his book," *ejus Liber*,[2] in historic context. We first present an overview of Calabar's slave trade, and we then detail the rise of Efik middlemen. Third, in analyzing Efik market power, we discuss the key quarter century (1750–1775) when Old Calabar doubled its share of the transatlantic slave trade and Antera Duke began working as a merchant. To illustrate how Britons and Efik transacted trade, we spotlight one Liverpool slaving venture to Old Calabar: the paired voyages of *Dobson* and *Fox* in 1769–1770, whose senior captain purchased 499 slaves over six months from individual Efik traders. This venture, documented by the ships' outfit at Liverpool and the barter transactions at Old Calabar, discloses the range of goods sold for slaves (and for ivory and provisions, a discussion we reserve for chapter 3) but also what types of goods were given as presents, paid as comey (anchorage fees), or credited on "trust" for future deliveries. By using *Voyages*, the online, consolidated slave trade database,[3] we then will identify all captains later mentioned by Antera Duke in his diary. Finally, slave-trading information from Antera's diary jottings allows us to map how Efik merchants networked with different groups of European traders, networks that hinged upon personal relationships that formed the nexus of cross-cultural trade.

An Overview of Old Calabar's Overseas
Slave Trade, Circa 1650–1838

African merchants based in the Cross River region sold slaves to European ship captains from the mid-seventeenth century, when Caribbean cash-crop plantations began developing, to the late 1830s and the final British-led diplomatic and naval push to abolish the transatlantic slave trade.[4] Though Portuguese captains were the first to visit the Rio da Cruz (Cross River), which they named as early as 1502,[5] they did not trade significantly at Old Calabar until 1707–1715. British captains dominated each decade of the Old Calabar slave trade until Parliament banned the trade in 1807–1808. Captains sailing from London, Bristol, or Liverpool purchased three-quarters of all enslaved Africans sold at Old Calabar, and from 1662 to 1807 at least one British captain traded with Efik merchants each year. After British aboli-tion, Portuguese slavers reentered the Calabar trade, and in 1815 French captains returned, many hoping to profit from the expanding Cuban slave market. By 1838, when British cruisers captured two Portuguese-flagged slavers from Old Calabar—perhaps the final two slaving ships—palm oil revenues had exceeded those of slaving for a generation. Exporting approximately 275,000 slaves from 1650 to 1838, Old Calabar ranked fifth in total slave exports behind Luanda and Benguela (in Angola), Bonny (Nigeria), and Ouidah (Benin).[6]

Dating the early slave trade from Creek Town and nearby villages is as difficult as establishing the timing of Efik migration to the confluence of the Cross and Calabar rivers. Seventeenth-century narratives and shipping sources often refer to "Calabar" or "Calabari" slaves. For example, in 1615–1616 the Jesuit father Manuel Alvares mentioned the Portuguese slave trade at "Calabar," and in 1616 some "Calabar" slaves worked on the Bahia sugar plantation "Santana." In 1620 another Portuguese document references a "Rey de Calabar"—king of Calabar.[7] In 1622 and 1625 the Portuguese slavers *Nossa Senhora del Rosario* and *Candelaria* arrived in the Spanish Americas with slaves from "Calabar."[8] But because none of these early sources specify "Old Calabar," the African peoples are "Calabari" slaves, those Ijo peoples shipped from Elem Kalabari, the port "New Calabar" situated northwest of Rio Real, the estuary of the New Calabar and Bonny rivers.

We can date an export slave trade from Old Calabar in the 1640s and 1650s with more confidence. From 1638 to 1645 eight Dutch West India Company ships traded at "Calbary," and the English organized sixteen voyages to Calabar in 1645–1647, responding to the demand for slaves in Barbados. In a Dutch map from about 1650–1654, "Calbray" is placed between the Rio Real and Rio del Rey, in Old Calabar's approximate location, and Jansson's *Nigritarum Regnum*, from 1658–1664, charts, from west to east, "R. Real de Calabari," "Calabari" (New Calabar), "Bani" (Bonny), "Oud Calbari" (Old Calabar), and the "Rio del Rey."[9] In 1658 the Prerogative Court of Canterbury proved the will, written in September 1657, of James Bentham "late of the Shipp Edward of London Cooke then riding at Anchor in old Callabar river."[10] This first written source documenting a slaving ship in the "Old Calabar River" might not refer to the Calabar River, which at Seven Fathoms Point branches northeast from the Cross River, thirty-five miles from the estuary. Instead it may refer to the stretch of the Lower Cross from the bar upriver, twenty miles, to Parrot Island (see map 1.2).[11] Similarly, those other early "Calabar" ships may have plied waters closer to the Atlantic coast. In 1642–1646 nine Dutch captains traded for slaves in the swampy Rio del Rey estuary, and six more did so in 1653–1658, suggesting that the Dutch, at least, did not venture far from the coastline.[12]

In contrast, our first written narrative about "Old Calabar" relates that when the London ship *Peach-tree* anchored in the Cross River in 1668, the captain sailed to or beyond Parrot Island. Sailor John Watts describes how the *Peach-tree* moored off the Gold Coast, "where they staid not long," and then sailed to Old Calabar, entering "a river called the *Cross* river into *Paratt* island." About a year earlier, some English sailors had kidnapped "a native" on shore; in retaliation, Watts was seized, enslaved, and marched inland. Several weeks later he was presented to king "E-fn-me"—perhaps Efiom Okoho and perhaps in Creek Town or Duke Town (see chapter 1). An English captain redeemed Watts for "forty-five copper and, iron bars, each copper bar being about the bigness of a youth's little finger, the iron bars a little bigger." Old Calabar's economy was therefore monetized in 1668, and here we read for the first time about the copper rods and iron bars that were units of account (they also were goods included in barters).[13] Watts does not mention where the *Peach-tree* moored, though there was a later anchorage off northeast Parrot Island. His English rescuers had sailed "into the road"—that is, into a roadstead, or anchorage—but unfortunately the ship's location was not specified.

The creation of the London-based Company of Royal Adventurers (1660) and its successor the Royal African Company (1672) encouraged British commercial endeavors in the Lower Cross River. Surviving company papers document that at least sixty-eight English slavers traded at "Old Calabar" from 1662 to the outbreak of King William's War in 1689, their competition limited to five Dutchmen, who appeared in 1677, 1681, 1684, and 1686.[14] The majority of slaves, about 15,000, shipped from Old Calabar on board British company vessels were disembarked at Barbados, Jamaica, Nevis, and Antigua. In contrast to British endeavors in Upper Guinea and the Gold Coast, the three to four captains who arrived at Old Calabar annually planned to purchase mostly slaves, though they did load some quantities of ivory and redwood to offset mortality risks, as we discuss in chapter 3. The British captains purchased, on average, 250 enslaved Africans over a six-month trading period in the Cross River region. We assume not only that some of these captains steered up into the Calabar River but also that daily contact between British mariners and African traders stimulated English language acquisition among some Efik and their neighbors.

In the second half of the seventeenth century, Cross River merchants, including the Efik based at Creek Town, Old Town, and Duke Town, sold perhaps 25,000 Africans into the transatlantic slave trade. They traded mostly with captains who worked for London-based companies, men who arrived on sailing vessels. Cross River peoples did not allow company trading agents—factors—to reside on shore, and there were no European houses, forts, or fixed factories anywhere in the Cross River region until 1846.[15] By 1700 the European demand for slaves began to outstrip supply: in that year a London slaving merchant told his captain "there is soe many Ships gone to Old Callebarr that you cann have no trade there."[16] Tensions between Europeans and Africans presumably increased if captains faced lengthy sojourns in the river or a ship needed to depart, owed slaves. In 1702 Efik merchant Grande Robin, probably from Old Town, was killed on board the London slaving ship *Hunter*.[17] This incident, the first documented murder of either an African or a European trader at Old Calabar, further depressed London's share of the trade, already narrowed after Parliament removed the London-based Royal African Company's monopoly in 1698. London ships still frequented the Cross River, but by 1717 Thames merchants would lose their business at Old Calabar to Bristol traders.

Bristol merchants dominated the slave trade at Old Calabar, 1717–1737, controlling 80 percent of the British market and 70 percent of the total European slave trade there. During these twenty years, at least 108 British captains purchased slaves at Old Calabar. Of this sample, Bristol's share of 87 ventures dwarfs those of London (13) or Liverpool (3). The Bristol traders moved into an African market slowly relinquished by the Royal African Company in the 1690s as more and more company ships sailed to Upper Guinea, the Gold Coast, and Whydah (Ouidah). After the War of Spanish Succession (1702–1713) ended and insurance costs dropped, Bristol merchants expanded their slave trade to the Cross River region. When the Glasgow-based *Hannover* arrived at Old Calabar in May 1720, for example, six Bristol ships recently had departed with 1,000 enslaved Africans, and a seventh still rode at anchor. The *Hannover*'s supercargo, Alexander Horsburgh, noted that "our iron," a commodity essential in all assortments of trading goods, "they do not like, being the barrs are not quite so long as the Bristoll man's."[18]

During the 1750s, Liverpool merchants began overtaking Bristol's dominant position at Old Calabar.[19] Merchant William Whaley accepted William Davenport (1725–1797) as an apprentice in 1741[20] and owned shares of four Liverpool-Calabar ships, 1748–1752. William Earle (1721–1788) commanded one of these, the *Chesterfield*, on voyages in 1750 and 1751, and Davenport invested as a junior partner. Earle returned to Liverpool in 1753 to settle as

a merchant, transferring command of the ship to Patrick Black, a ship's surgeon, who then slaved at Old Calabar on four voyages, 1753–1757. In the
1750s Liverpool vessels embarked an estimated 15,000 slaves, more than dou-
bling Bristol's total (6,450). The only other Europeans in the Cross River
then were skippers from Nantes: six French-flagged ships embarked 1,200
slaves at Old Calabar. In the 1750s Cross River merchants doubled slave exports from 1,250 to 2,500 per year, perhaps drawing upon new supplies brokered via the rising Aro commercial empire a hundred miles northwest of
Old Calabar.

Slave exports from Old Calabar increased again during the peacetime
years 1764–1775 and 1783–1792. Peak periods of the overseas slave trade, exceeding 5,000 slave exports, occurred twice: in 1785, the first year of Antera
Duke's diary, and in 1791, two years before the Wars of the French Revolution (figure 2.1). Increased European demand began to pressure hinterland
slave supplies, as it did throughout the latter half of 1785. Captain Peter Potter arrived at Old Calabar in June 1785 to find four other Liverpool ships and
one from Bristol. In late July he wrote, "[W]e have been six trading ships ever
sence and very little trade for any." On August 17, trade "is still very slack,"
and on November 3, "Trade is yet but slack and we are no less till Six
Trading Ships to devide it." By mid-December "Trade begins to be a little

Calabar Slave Exports 1650–1838

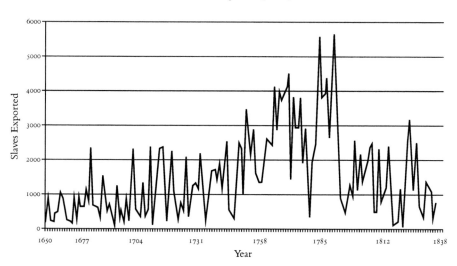

FIGURE 2.1. Cycles of the export slave trade from Old Calabar, 1650–1838. *Sample:* 900
voyages embarking an estimated 254,900 slaves, 1650–1838. *Source:* www.slavevoyages.org.

brisker," and Potter was optimistic that he could depart the river in late January or by the middle of February.[21] Similarly, in late 1787 demand exceeded the capacity of the Efik slaving networks. When Bristol captain Richard Rogers arrived in October, he "found no less than eight purchasing Ships many had been in the River sixteen months & Slaves at this instant are very scarce." Later that month he had "but eleven Slaves on board many in the River have not purchas'd half that Number in the time."[22]

Old Calabar's export slave trade dropped after the peak in 1791 and then declined after French (1794) and British (1807–1808) abolition. It dropped further after the Napoleonic Wars, even though Portuguese and French slavers returned to the region. In the period 1815–1838 at least sixty French-, Portuguese-, and Spanish-registered Guineamen attempted to purchase enslaved Africans at Old Calabar. Antislave patrols captured half of these vessels; the rest avoided seizure to disembark 6,500 to 7,500 slaves in the West Indies or Brazil. In 1838 British cruisers captured two Portuguese-flagged vessels, the *Felicidade* and *Prova*, which had embarked 784 slaves at Old Calabar, and escorted them to Sierra Leone. In 1841 and 1842 British representatives negotiated slave trade abolition treaties with leaders from Creek Town and Duke Town. One final European slaving ship, the French slaver *Luis d'Albuquerque*, arrived at Old Calabar in 1843. Little is known about this venture, the last to Old Calabar, as the French Admiralty proceedings did not state a clear outcome. If Captain Emile Bellet purchased slaves, he probably would have done so in the Lower Cross River or Rio del Rey.

The Rise of Efik Middlemen in the Cross River Region

The British dominated trade in the Cross River region before the Efik achieved similar market power. The Efik settled near the Cross/Calabar rivers at the turn of the seventeenth century but did not broker slave shipments to Europeans until the mid-1600s. They slowly increased their dominance in the region, becoming powerful middlemen by 1720. During Antera Duke's diary years, Efik market power extended south to the Cross River estuary; they faced little competition from their closest neighbors, such as the Qua, located just east of Old Calabar, and southern groups, such as the Effiat, sold few if any slaves to Europeans. Antera notes that those slaving captains refusing to pay prices demanded by Efik merchants had to proceed to the Cameroon River.[23] In 1821, Duke Town warriors extended Efik power to the Atlantic estuary, crushing Effiat peoples at Tom Shott's Town, at the western entrance of the Cross River, to gain control of the salt and palm oil trades and supposedly to root out pirates. Duke Ephraim and his warriors also forbade European ship captains to trade in the Rio del Rey, a minor location of trade since the mid-1600s.[24]

Effiat, Ibibio, Efik, Qua, and/or Efut peoples probably encountered the first European mariners who arrived in the Cross River in the mid-seventeenth century. Written sources provide no clues as to the ethnicities of Cross River peoples until 1698, when agent James Barbot, working on a London-based slaving vessel, traded with Captain Thomas, Mettinon, William King Agbisherea, Robin King Agbisherea, King John, King Ebrero, King Oyo, Duke Aphrom, King Robin, and Old King Robin.[25] Following other historians, we assume that Captain Thomas resided in Salt Town (later Tom Shott's Town), settled by Effiat people; merchants William King Agbisherea and Robin King Agbisherea worked from "Egbosherry," that is, Ibibio, towns on the west bank of the Cross River; and Duke Aphrom, King Oyo (Eyo), and the Robins were leading Efik traders from Duke Town, Creek Town, and Old Town, villages along the Calabar River, "Old Calabar" proper, as we discussed in chapter 1. Mettinon, a name not documented, cannot be placed in a settlement. King Ebrero may be an ancestor of the Ebros of Duke Town; scholars have linked King John to Creek Town, Guinea Company, or Ibibio villages.[26]

Though not mentioned by Barbot, Qua merchants also challenged Efik attempts to dominate the Old Calabar slave trade. The Qua were original owners of the lands east of the Calabar River, an ownership acknowledged by the Efik. King Aqua headed Qua Town, located on the Great Qua River, three miles northeast of Duke Town. On his voyage to Old Calabar in 1704 London-based captain William Snelgrave remarked that King Aqua boarded his slaving vessel, and on his voyage to Calabar in 1713 he stated that "Acqua" was a major chief at Calabar.[27] On the London slaving ship *Florida*, which arrived in the Cross River in 1714, Captain Samuel Paine purchased "about 20 Slaves in going up ye River, before we came to an Anchor." Once moored in the Calabar River, "there were but 2 Kings, that we usually traded with, one of them was call'd King Ambo, & ye other Aquaw." Because the *Florida* departed Old Calabar with 360 slaves, Kings Ambo (Efik) and Aqua (Qua) were substantial traders.[28] Though Creek Town, Old Town, and Duke Town had become important Efik commercial centers by the early eighteenth century, Effiat, Ibibio, and Qua merchants also earned incomes from international trade.

By 1720, Efik merchants had gained the dominant position in the Cross River's Atlantic trade. In that year supercargo Alexander Horsburgh of the Glasgow-based slaver *Hannover* arrived and penned a detailed account of comey—anchorage fees—paid in copper bars to African merchants and "men of no trade in Callabar."[29] Among the twenty-two men Horsburgh denoted as traders, Efik received 93 percent of comey payments. He paid the largest fees to King Ambo (80 copper bars), King John (72 coppers), Duke Ephraim (70 coppers), Tom Henshaw (65 coppers), Grande Robin (50 coppers), and Tom Cobham (50 coppers). These payments reflect the comparative position of these men as elders within Efik society, as well as their relative shares of trade with Horsburgh. The "men of no trade" included King Aqua and Grande Robin Aqua, to whom Horsburgh paid comey of 35 and 20 copper bars, respectively. Significantly, King Aqua, a major trader with Captain Paine in 1714, received anchorage fees only because Qua were nominal owners of the land.[30]

Horsburgh also paid ransom to the Efik for four of the *Hannover*'s sailors held hostage at Tom Shott's Point, in Effiat country. Upon arriving in the Cross River estuary, four sailors "went ashoar armed out of the boat," at Tom Shott's Point, "perhaps with a Design to take the whole Continent of Africa." Seized immediately (with one sailor being killed), the supercargo paid a ransom, in assortments of trading goods, worth 808 coppers or £60 12s (the price of twelve adult male slaves). He paid most of this ransom to Effiat peoples, but Efik received at least 85 of 170 coppers' ransom paid to others in the Cross River region. As Horsburgh wrote: "I was obliged to Comie them in order to get the white men again, otherwise I would not have given any of them so much as one Copper barr." This incident demonstrates not only comparative European weakness along the African coast but also that, by 1720, Efik influence extended forty-five miles south to the Cross River estuary.

Though Efik commercial power increased during the eighteenth century, it could never completely prohibit other small-scale merchants from selling slaves to Europeans. Mariner James Morley, at Old Calabar in the 1760s, purchased slaves in Qua country, east of Duke Town. He recalled "an instance of one [slave who] was offered to the ship I belonged to; I saw that Slave at work in the plantation myself, when out at Aquaw getting slaves." Slaving ships often purchased a few slaves at the Cross River estuary. Isaac Parker, after departing Old Calabar in mid-1767, purchased some people "with the goods we had left" near the estuary's sandbar. Merchants based along the banks of the Rio del Rey sold slaves, occasionally in sufficient numbers to fill a small slaving ship. John Ashley Hall sailed on two voyages from London to the Rio del Rey in the 1770s. His captain slaved at Del Rey on the first voyage, but after arriving there on the second voyage, "finding trade very dull, we went from thence to the river Old Calabar, where we slaved."[31]

Outfitting Ships for Old Calabar:
Efik Demand for Commodities

To profit from the slave trade at Old Calabar, European merchants needed to offer commodities sought by Cross River merchants. Antera Duke's diary does not give much detail about the types of goods he selected, mentioning only five commercial items: basins; bottles of brandy; Guinea stuff (a type of cloth); India goods ("Inder"); and romals, a type of Indian cloth. Fortunately, the records of the two largest British merchants, William Davenport and James Rogers, trading in this period at Old Calabar have survived. Their accounts contain information on the outfit of twenty-seven ships, 1761–1792.[32] There are also scattered references to the commodities Europeans traded at Calabar in the late 1600s and in 1714, as well as lists of goods in Efik merchants' letters from the 1760s and 1770s. We thus can evaluate how "consumption patterns" in the Cross River region changed over time.[33]

In the later 1600s and early 1700s, as Old Calabar merchants gained market power relative to other ports, they purchased from ship captains broader assortments of high-quality consumer products. We detect shifting consumption patterns from three accounts. On the *Blackamore*, an early English ship at Old Calabar in 1662, Captain John Major's cargo valued £867 and included mostly copper rods (£601) and iron bars (£84). European and Indian textiles constituted a small percentage of the *Blackamore*'s outfit and were still only 3 percent (by value) on a London-Calabar ship in 1698.[34] When Captain Samuel Paine arrived at Old Calabar in 1714, however, a sailor on board commented, "The chief Commodities that are brought to truck with them are Strip'd Cottons of the East Indies, bars of Iron & Copper, small arms, Hats, Knives, Beads, Pewter ware as Diskes, Plates, Tankards, Basons &c."[35] These Indian cottons, now listed first, were probably handcrafted pieces of white cloth printed with blue stripes, such as the nicanees popular throughout the era of the transatlantic slave trade.[36]

During the second half of the eighteenth century, Old Calabar businessmen imported more consumables—particularly cottons, which now made up 40 percent of the value of any bundle of goods received for slaves. Responding to African demand, European merchants also increased shipments of household goods, beads, gunpowder, firearms, and liquor (usually French brandy). As calculated by David Richardson, on twenty-seven ventures to Old Calabar, 1761–1792, outfitted to purchase 9,000 to 10,000 enslaved Africans, merchants Davenport and Rogers loaded goods valued at £133,479, two-fifths of which were East India (24.3%) and Manchester (17.2%) textiles. The additional major trading items included hardware (15.2%), bar iron

(7.3%), firearms (6.7%), gunpowder (6.5%), liquor (6.4%), and beads (3.7%). Lesser goods, by value, included leather, writing paper and implements, and salt. From 1700 to 1800 slave prices more than doubled from 75 to 180 copper rods per slave, or from £6–£8 to £15–£18, reflecting how the terms of trade shifted as Efik merchants gained dominance.[37]

Merchants tried to outfit cargoes to meet the changing demands of Old Calabar merchants, and they followed recommendations from their ship captains. In particular, they relied on information about new fashions for textiles. "The Trade is much alter'd, my Chintz is not the least in demand which was the Commanding article last Voyage," Captain Richard Rogers wrote from Old Calabar in 1787.[38] Liverpool merchant Davenport sent his captains to shop for textiles in Manchester and London. Travels to London totaled £10 to £13 per person—costs that included carriage transport and lodging near the East India Company warehouses. In 1768 and 1770, Davenport's partner Patrick Black, a retired captain, and that year's captain of the *Dalrymple* traveled to London; Black presumably instructed his protégés how to select India textiles most suited for Old Calabar. One such protégé was Patrick Fairweather, who subsequently purchased India goods in London in 1772, 1773, 1775, and 1777 and, by 1777, was the senior captain at Old Calabar.[39]

European merchants also knew what types of cargoes were in demand at Old Calabar because Efik traders, needing to broker goods regionally, placed specific orders. In July 1783, for example, Duke Town merchant Egbo Young (Ekpenyong) Ofiong informed his Liverpool partners that their Captain Burrows had arrived with "very fine Cargo only we wante[d] more iron bar[s] and Romalls and [gun]powde[r] and ordinance and phota[e]s as them be Finest thing for our trade." On the captain's return voyage he also should bring "very Little Salt and muggs" and "Round White & Round green & round yellow bead[s]."[40] Efik also requested specified personal items, such as dressing gowns, silver canes, writing paper, books, ink cakes, wafers, and a range of other trade goods and household items. "Please to have my name put on Everything that you send for me," Ephraim Robin John reminded Liverpool merchant Ambrose Lace.[41]

The most detailed "shopping list," from Robin John to Lace circa 1773, importantly distinguishes between goods "for trade," for "coomey," or for personal use ("for me" or "for my Salf"). Trade goods include hats, hand mirrors, pewter and brass drinking containers and basins, flintlock muskets, butter, and sugar. Among the shorter list of goods for comey are drinking horns, cushtaes, caps, canes, and nails. Robin John's biggest request is for household and personal goods. He asks for a large mirror, one table, six chairs, two armchairs "for my Salf to sat in," two small writing desks, and a stool. He also requests twelve pewter plates, four dishes, twelve knives, twelve forks, two large table spoons, a trowel, one pair of balances, and one case of razors for shaving. To support his slave trades, Robin John wanted new canvas to make sails for his canoes, large leg manillas with locks, and large iron manillas for his "Room of irons" (prison). Textiles are clearly important. He specified a hundred yards of chintz "for me," and then a hundred yards of nicanees, photaes, romals, cushtaes, and bafts, presumably for trade and comey.[42] If these India goods "be Right good," he wrote, Lace's ship will "no stand long" in the river. Ephraim Robin John's personalized items included business clothes: a gold-mounted long cane, and two coats with gold lace, one red and one blue, "to fit a Large man." When Efik socialized with ship captains, they "dressed as white men," as Antera Duke phrased it.[43]

The Davenport accounts confirm that Liverpool slaving ships loaded various personal gifts for Efik traders. On Davenport and Company's ship *Dobson*, Captain John Potter transported twelve brass basins engraved "Antera Duke." In 1771 Creek Town merchant Willy Honesty received two coils of cordage addressed to him, and the next year the *Dalrymple* loaded thirty basins inscribed "WH."[44] The Liverpool ship *Hector*'s trading cargo in 1771 included eighteen copper leg manillas engraved with 488 letters. Given that on each manilla were approximately twenty-seven letters, the words probably included an African and a Liverpool merchant's name as well as a date.[45] Other British merchants also paid workmen to engrave names on firearms, bells, and canes.[46] Captains transported wood, iron, bricks, and other building supplies across the North Atlantic to construct houses for principal traders, and they shipped a range of furniture.[47] In 1805 traveler Henry Nicholls lodged in one of Duke Ephraim's guesthouses furnished with twenty-seven large mirrors, three sofas, twelve chairs, two writing desks, a marble sideboard, two wine racks, six tables, six paintings, twenty large engravings, "an immense quantity of glasses, china and earthen ware," and seven clocks. A "pretty jumble of furniture it is," remarked Nicholls.[48]

Efik-British Transactions, 1769–1770: The Liverpool Slaving Ships *Dobson* and *Fox*

To analyze Efik-British transactions in detail, we consider the voyages of the Liverpool slaving vessels *Dobson* and *Fox* in 1769–1770, owned by William Davenport and partners. There are complete copies of the *Dobson* and *Fox*'s outfit in Liverpool, accounts itemizing the quantity and price of all trading goods loaded on board the two craft. From Old Calabar there survive the *Dobson* captain's transactions from July 16, 1769, to January 12, 1770, handwritten in a ruled ledger (114 folios), for slaves, ivory, and provisions.[49] For his slave purchases, Captain John Potter records the days, specific goods sold, number of slaves and their prices, and the names of the Efik businessmen with whom he traded. We therefore can determine the market share of individual African slaving merchants, including Antera Duke, and analyze their specific transactions. Potter's ivory and provisions purchases, also dated, itemize quantities bartered and prices but do not record individual Efik dealers. We discuss his ivory trade in more detail in chapter 3. Captain Potter purchased commodities for both the *Dobson* and *Fox*, and by comparing trading goods purchased by Efik in this unique Calabar-based document with the corresponding Liverpool invoices, one can analyze which assortments Davenport and Company earmarked for trade, comey, or gifts.

In early 1769 William Davenport, working as ship's husband, began assembling trading goods for the *Dobson's* return voyage to Old Calabar. The ship had arrived in Liverpool in October 1768 from Calabar, Antigua, and St. Kitts, under the command of Francis Lowndes. Lowndes probably reached Old Calabar in late July or early August 1767 and thus would have witnessed the massacre of Old Town canoemen and traders (see chapter 1). He had left, on credit, trading goods worth £400, the value of fifty-five slaves. From January to May 1769 porters loaded goods on board the *Dobson* and *Fox* that totaled £5,642. Captain John Potter traveled to London to purchase the India textiles, and Potter, in command of the *Dobson*, cleared customs for Africa on May 14, 1769. After Potter steered into the Cross River estuary, an African mariner piloted the ship from Parrot Island twenty-five miles upriver to the anchorage off Duke Town's beach. Potter first would need to pay comey, divided later among leading Efik merchants, and then give presents to Antera Duke and other traders. He began his trade on July 16, purchasing nine small pieces of ivory. Two days later he initiated his slave trade, buying one man and one girl from Willy Honesty for 200 coppers and one woman from Dick Ebrew for 93 coppers. Potter, as senior captain, would purchase all slaves, ivory, and provisions for the *Dobson* and his tender, the *Fox*, which would arrive sometime in August.

On board the *Dobson* were hundreds of containers of textiles, hardware, bar iron, beads, firearms, gunpowder, liquor, and miscellaneous items, such as salt, horns, food, and one crimson ensign. In the £5,642 outlay, East Indian and Manchester textiles constituted 36 percent of all goods (by value), followed by hardware (15%), bar iron (14%), weaponry (firearms and gunpowder, 10%), beads (7%), and alcohol (5%). The accounts record garments as single items, such as the two blue coats priced £5 each or the 1,872 three-shilling caps. Fabric was measured in yards and loaded in 10- to 18-yard rolls or in pieces. Fifteen different types of cloth measured 11,579 yards and to-

taled £701 2s, more than half of which were Indian chintz, chelloe, and
photaes (6,520 yards valued £418 10s). There were pieces of checks and red-
striped Turkey bar cloth, each piece sufficiently large to wrap a person's body.
Hardware included 15,625 copper rods—essential items in all assortments
sold at Old Calabar—metal basins, manillas, lead bars, knives, pipes, bells, and
a variety of glassware and bottles. Potter carried 4,028 iron bars, each costing
Davenport 3s 10d, different-colored round and cylindrical pipe beads, a range
of musketry, gunpowder, brandy, rum, wine, beer, and some bushels of salt.

In preparation for trade, Potter assembled his goods in groups to follow
the customary barter "rounds" with Efik merchants. Such a method of trade
may have been common along the African Atlantic coast. In an anonymous
account written by a Liverpool surgeon, circa 1775, the doctor notes, probably referring to the Windward Coast: "The trade in this district is made in
rounds; so many are given upon a slave, the price here as every where else
fluctuates, we have known from eight to twenty [rounds] sometimes more.
1 round consists of a piece of cloth, a musquet, & a keg of powder."[50] A series of 2 to 10 rounds resulted in one transaction or "trade" between Captain
Potter and an Efik merchant. In all, Potter completed 2,011 rounds to effect
316 transactions (average 6.4 rounds). Each round usually paired two types of
trading goods, and, invariably, the first round included iron bars and gunpowder kegs. In round one with each Efik merchant, there were only twelve
transactions that did not include iron bars, and only seven did not include
gunpowder. In all 316 transactions, round two included some type of cloth.
In general, textiles were offered in the middle rounds, along with various
metal manufactures. Captain Potter's final round included disproportionate
amounts of beads and copper rods compared with the amounts in earlier
rounds. Since the notional currency at Old Calabar was copper rods ("coppers"), the final payment in these rods "rounded" fractional prices. In Potter's
first transaction for his employers, he purchased a man and a girl from Willy
Honesty after ten rounds of trading, adding fourteen copper rods at the
barter's end to reach the price of 200 coppers (table 2.1).

Captain Potter's sales ledger demonstrates that protracted slave trading
occurred at Old Calabar. He purchased, over a 178-day period, 499 slaves in
316 separate transactions on 131 days. On those days he purchased slaves, he
bartered for, on average, 4 individuals. His greatest purchases took place on
September 20, when Willy Honesty sold Potter 12 women and 11 men in
four separate barters totaling twenty-seven rounds. Barters, though several
could happen daily, generally involved 1 or 2 slaves. In 207 transactions Efik
merchants sold the captain 1 slave, and in 69 transactions they sold 2 slaves
to him. Antera Duke, for example, sold slaves in lots of 1 (seventeen times),

TABLE 2.1. Willy Honesty's first transaction with Captain John Potter, July 18, 1769, selling two slaves for 200 coppers in ten barter rounds

July 18		Coppers	Total	No.	M	W	B	G
Willy Honesty					1			1
10 iron bars	3 gunpowder kegs	64						
2 pieces nicanees	1 romal	32						
1 cushtae	10 photaes	20						
1 brawl	1 Guinea stuff	9						
1 Silesian cloth	1 trade gun	14						
2 flagons	2 basins	14						
2 bunches purple pipe beads	2 bunches dove beads	16						
1 bunch round red beads	4 manillas	9						
12 knives	6 yards chelloe	8						
14 copper rods		14	200	2				

Sample: Willy Honesty's first transaction with Captain Potter, July 18, 1769. In total, Willy Honesty completed 170 barter rounds in 25 transactions for slaves with Potter between July 18 and January 10, 1770.

Note: We standardized names of trading goods and wrote them out, when abbreviated. Nicanee, romal, cushtae, photae, and chelloe are Indian textiles; Guinea stuff refers to a type of cotton cloth made for the African market. M, W, B, G, as recorded on the manuscript ledger, abbreviate men, women, boys, girls.

Source: Dobson Calabar account, Hasell MS, Dalemain House, Cumbria.

2 (four times), 3 (five times), 4 (once), and 6 slaves (once, on September 6, 1769). On fifty-three days Potter purchased 1 slave from one Efik trader. Potter traded every day of the European calendar week, the two busiest, Monday and Friday (110 barters for 177 slaves), "bookending" the smaller weekend trades (71 barters for 109 slaves). Efik traders sold slaves on 131 of the 178 days, slaves or ivory on 146 days, and then slaves, ivory, or provisions on 154 days. There were thus 25 days on which no transactions occurred with Captain Potter—some were "Calabar Sundays"[51]—but there were only three instances when trading stopped for a 2-day period.

This one Calabar sales ledger indicates that a coterie of Efik traders from Creek Town and Duke Town wielded considerable market power. The six traders Willy Honesty, Antera Duke, Gentleman Honesty, Duke Ephraim, Tom King John, and Coffee Duke sold, in total, 256 (51.3%) of 499 slaves. By price, they sold 256 slaves valued 30,901 coppers, 52.7 percent of the total (of 58,620 coppers).[52] In January 1770 these top six merchants also delivered 44 of the 55 slaves purchased on trust in 1768. Liverpool captains thus did not advance goods on credit to Efik merchants indiscriminately—they trusted valuable cargoes mostly to major merchants who could call in debts. In total, fifty-four Efik merchants sold slaves to Captain Potter, half the traders selling fewer than 5 slaves each. Four merchants delivered slaves "on Acc^t First Trade," including Young Antera (one of Antera Duke's sons), who gifted Captain Potter a woman and boy—no barters or prices were recorded. Egboyoung Tom Ecricock, as a penalty "For Theft," delivered one adult male slave.[53] The fact that Creek Town and Duke Town businessmen brokered 368 of 565 slaves situates the *Dobson's* voyage, as we noted in chapter 1, after the reduction of Old Town in 1767 (table 2.2).

To spotlight Antera Duke's trade with Captain Potter, over a twenty-three week period in 1769–1770 he sold 50 slaves (22 men, 18 women, 5 boys, and 5 girls). In the 181 rounds of trading (in twenty-eight transactions), he received goods worth 6,649 coppers and sold men for approximately 135 coppers, boys for 127, women for 105, and girls for 97 coppers.[54] Antera Duke's sales returned 782 copper and brass rods, thirteen different types of textiles, including 500 yards of cloth, 221 iron bars, 99 bunches of beads (totaling about 15,000 beads), 88 kegs of gunpowder, 68 leg and arm manillas, 62 gallons of brandy, 36 muskets, 25 basins, 11 flagons (usually pewter), and 12 knives. The goods valued at Calabar at 6,649 coppers cost Davenport and partners £294 16s in Liverpool, and hence slave prices averaged £5 18s. By value, 48.4 percent of Antera's imports comprised Indian and Manchester cotton textiles, including luxury chintz and photaes (table 2.3).

The distribution and quality of goods purchased by Antera Duke, Willy Honesty, or other leading Efik slaving merchants varied little from those bought by minor dealers. All Calabar businessmen, even those eleven who sold one slave, received bundles of goods in at least four categories: all barters included textiles and gunpowder; ten of the eleven smallest traders received, in addition, hardware and bar iron; and most received beads in their assortments. Only firearms and liquor were absent from most of these minor traders' transactions. Those who sold two or more slaves always received the range of European and Indian manufactures and semifinished goods. Comparing the transactions of the six Efik traders selling at least twenty-five slaves with those selling fewer reveals modest differences only in firearm and alcohol purchases (table 2.4). That almost all Efik merchants received the same types of products is not surprising, given that each transaction required, on average, six trading rounds. In each round an Efik trader negotiated with Captain Potter over the prices of goods in two categories, closely examining the size, weight, color, or other quality of, for example, various textiles or hardware.

Significantly, trading goods amounting to one-third of the total value

TABLE 2.2. Efik merchants who delivered at least five slaves to Liverpool captain John Potter at Old Calabar, July 1769–January 1770

Old Calabar merchant	Slaves sold (1769–1770)	On account first trade	From the trust book (1768)	Total
Willy Honesty	69	0	22	91
Antera Duke	50	0	6	56
Gentleman Honesty	39	0	5	44
Duke Ephraim	38	0	5	43
Tom King John	32	0	1	33
Coffee Duke	28	0	5	33
Keneby Willy Ecricock	21	0	0	21
Messimbo Tom King John	17	0	0	17
Young Tom Ecricock's brother	16	0	0	16
Dick Ebro	14	0	2	16
King Egbo Solomon Henshaw	14	0	0	14
Tom Egbo	14	0	0	14
George Cobham	11	0	1	12
Captain John Ambo	10	2	0	12
Ebee	11	0	0	11
Captain Dick John Ambo	9	0	0	9
King John	3	6	0	9
Angoy	8	0	0	8
Rice Cobham	7	0	1	8
Gentry Tom Ecricock	7	0	0	7
Jemmy Henshaw	6	0	0	6
Doctor Guinea Company	5	0	0	5
John Willy	5	0	0	5
King Ambo	5	0	0	5
Tom Henshaw	5	0	0	5
Robin Henshaw	4	0	1	5
Young Antera	3	2	0	5
Young Duke	3	0	2	5
Subtotals	454	10	**51**	515
26 other traders	*45*	*1*	*4*	*50*
Totals	**499**	**11**	**55**	**565**

Notes: Table ranks 28 of 54 traders who sold/gifted at least five slaves. In addition, Egboyoung Tom Ecricock delivered 1 adult male slave as a penalty "For Theft." Hence Calabar traders delivered 566 slaves, July 18, 1769–January 10, 1770.

Source: Dobson Calabar account, Hasell MS, Dalemain House, Cumbria.

loaded on the *Dobson* and *Fox* in Liverpool in spring 1769 were not sold for slaves, ivory, or provisions. Of the *Dobson/Fox* original outlay for Old Calabar, £5,612,[55] Captain Potter purchased 499 slaves valued £2,929, 613 pieces of ivory valued £362 8s, and provisions (mostly yams) valued £406. The remaining goods not sold, valued £1,957 2s, include products that do not

TABLE 2.3. Quantity, type, and British value of goods received by Antera Duke from his sale of 50 slaves to Captain John Potter, July 31, 1769–January 10, 1770

	Value		Value
1. Textiles*		4. Beads	
400 yards cushtaes	£26 6s	66 bunches pipe beads	£26 8s
540 yards romals	£25 4s	33 bunches round beads	£3 6s
373 yards photaes	£23 16s		**£29 14s (10.1%)**
164 yards chintz	£20 8s		
340 yards nicanees	£16 14s	5. Arms	
38 pieces Guinea Stuff	£7 14s	23 trade guns	£7 14s
32 pieces brawls	£7	5 Danish musquets	£3
116 yards chelloe	£5 4s	5 bayonet musquets	£2 12s
52 yards bafts	£3 4s	3 musquetoons	£1 10s
8 Silesias	£2 8s		**£14 16s (5.0%)**
38 yards patches	£1 16s		
20 yards French striped	£1 4s		
14 yards calico	£1 4s	6. Gunpowder	
10 yards Turkey red striped	12s		
6 caps	2s	88 kegs gunpowder	£15 10s
	£142 16s		**£15 10s (5.3%)**
	(48.4%)		
2. Bar iron		7. Liquor	
221 iron bars	£41 8s	62 gallons brandy	£5 14s
	£41 8s		**£5 14s (1.9%)**
	(14.0%)		
3. Hardware			
782 copper and brass rods	£36 16s		
68 manillas	£3 6s	Totals	
25 basins	£2 16s	Trading goods valued	
11 flagons	£1 18s	**£294 16s** for the sale	
12 knives	£0 2s	of 22 men, 18 women,	
	£44 18s	5 boys and 5 girls	
	(15.2%)	(average **£5 18s**)	

★Two-thirds Manchester goods, one-third India cottons.

Sources: Trading Invoices and Accounts, *Dobson* and *Fox*, 1766, 1771, Davenport Papers, MMM; *Dobson* Calabar account, Hasell MS, Dalemain House, Cumbria.

appear in Potter's barters. Take, for example, the crimson ensign, probably measuring six feet by six feet, purchased along with 360 yards of bunting. Valued £9 12s (and stuffed in a 2 1/2-shilling sail bag), this large flag and accompanying pennants, made by Liverpool sailmakers Joshua Rose and James White,[56] was the most expensive single item purchased by Davenport

TABLE 2.4. British sterling value of goods received by Efik traders for the sale of 499 slaves, July 18, 1769–January 12, 1770, Liverpool ships *Dobson* and *Fox* (by category of goods and share of trade)

	Efik transactions for 499 slaves[1] (58,620 coppers)		Efik traders[2] selling 25+ slaves[3] (30,901 coppers)		Efik traders[4] selling 1–24 slaves[5] (27,719 coppers)	
Textiles	£1,391.6	47.5%	£715.7	46.9%	£675.9	48.2%
Hardware	459.0	15.7	237.6	15.6	221.4	15.8
Bar iron	428.8	14.6	226.9	14.9	201.9	14.4
Beads	286.9	9.8	151.8	9.9	135.1	9.6
Arms	161.4	5.5	94.5	6.2	66.9	4.8
Gunpowder	139.2	4.8	78.7	5.2	60.5	4.3
Liquor	61.0	2.1	22.1	1.4	38.9	2.7
Salt	0.6	0.0	0.1	0.0	0.5	0.0
Horns	0.5	0.0	0.1	0.0	0.4	0.0
Totals	£2,929.0	100.0%	£1,527.5	(52.2%)	£1,401.5	(47.8%)

[1] 217 men, 124 women, 79 boys, 79 girls.

[2] Willy Honesty, Antera Duke, Gentleman Honesty, Duke Ephraim, Tom King John, and Coffee Duke (the top six traders) sold 256 of 499 slaves.

[3] 115 men (44.9%), 70 women (27.3%), 28 boys (10.9%), 43 girls (16.8%).

[4] 43 (of 49) other Efik traders sold 243 slaves.

[5] 102 men (42.0%), 54 women (22.2%), 51 boys (21.0%), 36 girls (14.8%).

Sources: Trading Invoices and Accounts, *Dobson* and *Fox*, 1766, 1771, Davenport Papers, MMM; *Dobson* Calabar account, Hasell MS, Dalemain House, Cumbria.

and associates. It was not sold in any of Captain Potter's 2,011 trading rounds. Clearly this ensign/bunting was a gift for one of the leading Efik, to be flown, we assume, from a ceremonial or war canoe.[57] Similarly, goods engraved with Efik merchants' full names or initials, like the basins engraved "Antera Duke" in 1767 or "WH" (Willy Honesty) in 1772, were probably gifts. Other items, probably not inscribed, were paid as comey, dashed formally, or simply given as personal gifts. Thus Davenport purchased six dressing gowns, each valued 16s 9d, but Potter sold only four of these expensive garments.

The items that do not appear in any of Captain Potter's Calabar barters—whether for slaves, ivory, or provisions—include consumables, drinking containers, and castor hats. Foodstuffs such as rice (14,816 pounds), split beans (4,634 pounds), and stockfish (3,380 pounds) were slaves' provisions. Potter supplemented these eatables by purchasing, at Old Calabar, 82,935 yams, 740 jars of palm oil, 10 goats, 2 cows, 143 coppers' worth of plantains, and unspecified quantities of fish, fowl, pepper, greens, and limes. In addition to food, the following items do not appear in any barters: 348 "true glasses" (val-

ued £157 10s); 168 beaver or felt imitation "castor hats" (£50 8s)[58]; 315 gallons of rum (£41 18s); 720 bottles of beer (£17 6s); 890 pounds of tobacco
(£14 16s); 47 gallons of port wine (£14 2s); 31 "bastard glasses" (£8 4s); 50
oblong-shaped, two-quart wine bottles called gardevines (£4 2s); 160 yellow
bottles (£3 3s); and 792 various-sized mugs, decanters, and jars (£9 14s).
Sailors on the *Dobson* or *Fox* may have imbibed some of the liquor, but most
gallons likely were paid as comey or dashed. Breakable glassware would be
included in all of these exchanges. Tobacco could have been given to the Efik
or smoked on board ship. Castor hats, at 6s each, apparently were given to
many Efik, as were shoes, stockings, trousers, shirts, duffel jackets, coats,
frocks, and taffeta (table 2.5).

Captain Potter carried many durable garments and textiles, metal goods,
beads, and brandy bottles that he needed both to "break trade" and later to
purchase slaves, ivory, or provisions. There were numerous goods "partially
traded," and the percentages varied significantly. The captain sold, for example, 90 percent of his romals but only 20 percent of his nicanee rolls. He
traded 74 of 660 one-shilling hats (11% of them) and 1,023 of 1,872 four-
pence caps (55%). He sold 76 percent of his trade guns but 58 percent of
his musquetoons. He exchanged 77 percent of his pipe beads but 50 percent
of his round beads and only 7 percent of his beads packed in chests. One
might suppose that the captain, unable to sell unwanted goods, carried them
back to Liverpool. But no "returned goods" appear as credits in the *Dobson/
Fox* accounts from mid-1770, when Davenport tallied the venture's profits
and losses.[59] We thus believe that Captain Potter included these and other
bundles as either formal comey or dash payments, or that he trusted some
of the trading goods on credit for the next year's voyage. There was also
an unknown quantity of damaged items that he must have discarded at Old
Calabar.

What goods Captain Potter reserved for comey, dashes, or credit depended upon their ceremonial function, durability, and standardization. In
October 1787 Bristol captain Richard Rogers specified goods paid in comey
at Old Calabar: "500 Iron Bars for one article, 32 Boxes Rods [4,000 copper
rods], 15 Puncheons Rum & Brandy & Cloth in proportion."[60] We thus assume that in 1769 many of Captain Potter's 1,149 iron bars, 4,326 copper
rods, 1,867 bottles of brandy, 315 gallons or rum, and yards of cloth—goods
not traded—were paid as comey. Captains dashed brandy, rum, and other "re-
freshments" to break trade; and evidence from the mid-1800s includes as
dashed items firearms, luxury cloth, knives, nightcaps, mugs, plates, and tobacco pipes.[61] Given that drinking ceremonies occurred before and after individual barters, perhaps Potter reserved most of his brandy and rum for
dashes. Trusted goods would include large numbers of iron bars and copper

TABLE 2.5. Goods loaded on the Liverpool slaving vessels *Dobson* and *Fox* but not traded for 499 slaves, 613 pieces of ivory, or provisions, Old Calabar, 1769–1770 (by sterling value)

Goods not traded (units)	Value (£)	Not traded (%)	Probable usage (in order)
Iron bars (1,149)	215.4	28.5	Comey, dash, credit
Copper rods (4,326)	203.3	27.7	Comey, dash, credit
Brandy bottles (1,867)	171.1	71.9	Dash, comey
True glasses (348)	157.5	100.0	Dash
Rice lbs. (14,816)	92.6	100.0	Provisions
Pipe bead bunches (192)	76.8	23.1	Credit
Sham stores (156)	58.5	97.5	Dash
Round bead bunches (572)	57.2	50.4	Credit
Byrampauts (69)	55.2	98.6	Dash, comey
Chelloe yards (1,135)	51.1	39.2	Credit
Castor hats (168)	50.4	100.0	Dash, comey
Cushtae yards (752)	47.6	58.8	Credit
Photae yards (672)	42.1	37.7	Credit
Rum gallons (315)	41.9	100.0	Dash
Stockfish lbs. (3,380)	40.7	100.0	Provisions
Gunpowder kegs (218)	38.4	18.2	Comey, credit
Musquetoons (70)	36.0	42.2	Credit, comey
Nicanee yards (560)	35.5	80.0	Credit
Romals (60)	33.6	10.7	Credit, comey
Brawls (144)	31.6	32.1	Credit, comey
Hats (586)	29.3	88.8	Dash, comey
Patches (49)	26.2	80.3	Credit
Trade guns (73)	24.3	24.3	Credit, comey
Split beans lbs. (4,634)	20.7	100.0	Provisions
Chintz yards (198)	19.0	10.8	Credit
Beer bottles (720)	17.3	100.0	Dash
Tobacco lbs. (890)	14.8	100.0	Dash, provisions
Caps (849)	14.6	45.4	Dash, comey
Port wine gallons (47)	14.1	100.0	Dash, comey
Guinea stuff (58)	11.8	12.9	Credit, comey
Bayt musquets (21)	11.0	52.5	Credit, comey
French stripe yards (191)	10.5	54.6	Credit
Bead chests (26)	10.4	92.9	Credit
Totals	£1,760.5		

Sample: Table includes quantities and value of 33 goods not sold (minimum £10). The total value of all goods not traded, £1,957 2s, equals 34.9% of the £5,612 outfit.

Sources: Trading Invoices and Accounts, *Dobson* and *Fox*, 1766, 1771, Davenport Papers, MMM; *Dobson* Calabar account, Hasell MS, Dalemain House, Cumbria.

rods and other, standardized items, such as textile rolls or pieces that could be marketed later in the hinterland. Merchants instructed captains to avoid bringing cottons, firearms, or other perishable goods back to England.[62]

Assuming Captain Potter set aside trading goods worth £400 to advance to Efik merchants on credit for future deliveries of slaves and ivory, as did the *Dobson*'s captain in 1768, provisions loaded in Liverpool cost £200, then comey, dashes, and damaged/discarded goods at Old Calabar would have totaled £1,380, one-quarter of the *Dobson/Fox* outlay. Writing in 1822 when retired, a British captain active in the 1790s, John Adams, believed that ships paid £250 anchorage fees at Calabar, half going to Duke Ephraim.[63] But these figures apply to the palm oil trade circa 1820.[64] His comey estimates are far too low for Old Calabar's late eighteenth-century slave trade. In 1785 Liverpool captain Peter Potter's comey totaled 25,000 to 27,000 coppers, the value of 140 to 150 slaves. Similarly, in 1787 Bristol captain Rogers complained that his comey payments "had taken near 150 Slaves goods." On each of these two ventures, comey amounted to at least £1,800 per ship.[65] In 1769 Captain John Potter's comey may have been half that inflated figure,[66] but for individual Efik in either period, goods received as comey or dashes thus amounted to considerable earnings. Comey, divided in "proportion" to merchants' market shares, as Captain Rogers noted, increased the wealth of Willy Honesty, Antera Duke, and other elite traders. In 1773 Otto Ephraim Robin John, a minor trader from Old Town and perhaps in his twenties, specified that his comey amounted to 1,600 coppers. Willy Honesty's comey must have far exceeded that amount, and in each of Willy Honesty's 170 rounds of trading with Captain Potter, he would have received goods "in dash," augmenting his already considerable profits.

A detailed analysis of the *Dobson/Fox* accounts, then, reveals how Efik merchants transacted business with one European ship captain. They demanded a wide array of European and Indian goods, and there were established trading protocols. Captains paid substantial amounts of comey as a privilege to anchor and trade, dashed individual merchants, such as Antera Duke, and an average of five days per week conducted protracted barter rounds for small numbers of slaves. Six Efik merchants sold the majority of slaves to Captain Potter, and these creditworthy businessmen also delivered the greatest number commissioned from the *Dobson*'s previous voyage. Willy Honesty, Antera Duke, and other major merchants purchased the same assortments of goods as did other Efik traders—but in much greater quantities, and comey was paid in proportion to their trading shares. "[You] Know very well we Cant Do without Some Coomy," wrote King Henshaw, Duke Ephraim, and Willy Honesty in 1780.[67] Taking the 1769–1770 *Dobson/Fox* accounts as a benchmark, if Antera sold, on average, 50 slaves per Guineaman and sold to five captains per year, over a forty-year trading career he would have brokered 10,000 slaves. In return, he would have purchased consumer goods that he or his agents would have marketed throughout the Cross River region. Antera Duke also would have received various gifts—clothing, flags, or personalized basins—that demonstrate the importance of the individual trade relationships between an Efik trader and a European merchant.

"Ship and Tender Voyages" at Old Calabar and the Importance of Senior Captains

The *Dobson/Fox* venture in 1769–1770, outfitted by William Davenport and partners, was one of the first "ship and tender voyages" at Old Calabar, a paired enterprise that became routine by the period of Antera Duke's diary. Davenport sent Captain John Potter with a crew of thirty to Old Calabar in May 1769 to transact all business for Potter's *Dobson* and the *Fox*, commanded by William Brodie, a smaller vessel that would arrive about six weeks later. Potter first would supply the *Fox*, sending Captain Brodie on his Middle Passage with letters to carry back to Liverpool to inform his employers about any new commodities demanded by Efik merchants. Potter then would complete purchases for the *Dobson*. This strategy eventuated, as the *Fox* departed Old Calabar in early November with 180 slaves, and arrived in Dominica on December 16, 1769. Meanwhile, Potter continued trading with Efik merchants and did not depart Old Calabar until mid-January 1770, arriving at Barbados on March 19 and then at Liverpool on June 22. Davenport had learned in February 1770, when the *Fox* returned to Liverpool, about new commodities in demand at Old Calabar and began to order goods for the next *Dobson/Fox* venture. He thus "turned around" the *Dobson* with its £7,000 "double cargo" in just two months, Captain Potter again departing (on August 28) six weeks ahead of the *Fox* with Captain John Beard (October 9).

The first "ship and tender voyages" we have identified occurred in 1766 in response, we suggest, to increased transaction costs at Old Calabar. In 1766 William Davenport outfitted the *Dalrymple* and *Little Britain*, the larger *Dalrymple*, under the command of senior captain Alexander Allason, to depart eight weeks ahead of the smaller *Little Britain*. That same year William and John Crosbie and associates sent the 150-ton *Hector*, under the helm of experienced trader John Washington, two months ahead of the 30-ton *Polly*, commanded by novice John Power. In both paired voyages, the senior captain at Old Calabar loaded the small craft before his own, enabling the "tender" to depart the river first.[68] Prior to these ventures, all European merchants who organized slaving voyages to Old Calabar either sent out one ship, or, if they outfitted two vessels, both would trade separately, each departing the Cross River once the captain had completed his business.[69] The innovative "ship and tender" system allowed merchants to obtain information about market conditions at Old Calabar more quickly, and it certainly enabled "tenders" to load more slaves per day. It may have developed in response to the increasing delays slaving captains encountered. In 1763 six ships at Old Calabar embarked, on average, six slaves per day, loading rates that dropped to one to two slaves per day in 1765–1766 because of supply constraints.[70]

In a European maritime context, the *Fox* and other tenders would function as auxiliary sloops and schooners to larger ships, such as the *Dobson. Falconer's Naval Dictionary* defined a tender as a "small vessel employed to attend a larger one, to supply her with stores, to carry intelligence, &c."[71] In an Efik context, though, "tender" described the hierarchical relationship between two captains who commanded vessels owned by the same firm. For example, on February 14, 1785, Antera writes, "Captin Brown Tender go way with 430 slaves." A small vessel cannot have stowed 430 Africans, and, indeed, the fourteen "tenders" in Antera Duke's diary averaged 179 tons—including the largest ship trading then in the Calabar River, the 428-ton ship *Three Brothers*. Mariners at Old Calabar adopted this Efik usage for "tender." A Bristol captain, referring to the *Three Brothers*, wrote, "The last Tender that sail'd lay in the River 9 Months [and] came after 500 Slaves."[72] Tenders—junior captains—were not necessarily young men. In 1785 Antera Duke traded with forty-one-year old John Langdon, the senior Bristol captain who traded on behalf of his thirty-three-year old tender, Matthew Morley.[73] Other "captains," as opposed to "tenders," might be younger than Morley: status, authority, and personal ties with Calabar traders, not strictly age, were key considerations to Antera Duke and other Efik.

The importance of senior ship captains to the Efik is apparent when one glances at the entries in Antera Duke's diary: he pens the names of "captains" and not the surnames of "tenders" or the names of the vessels they commanded.[74] In the diary entry dated January 21, 1785, for example, Antera remarks, "I go Captin Savage to tak goods for slav." Then, a week later, "wee two go Bord Captin Smal with 3 slave so his tak two and wee com back." At Old Calabar in 1828, British adventurer James Holman termed this Calabar practice as identifying "the ship in the captain." And, according to Holman, when trading disputes arose, Efik merchants did not know the names of the ships concerned.[75] Though Holman may have overstated Efik ignorance about ship names,[76] Antera Duke's three-year diary refers to only one craft: on October 9, 1786, he writes: "his be Captin Johnston ship will Tender of Captin Aspinall" ("It was Captain Johnston's ship *Will*, the tender of Captain Aspinall"). By contrast at Bonny, kings who transacted business with Europeans identified each captain by his ship. "Name but a Vessel," one British surgeon wrote in 1826, and King Pepple "will instantly recollect her Commander, how long she lay in Bonny, how many times she traded there, [and] what number of Slaves she carried."[77]

Contrasting emphases on senior captains at Old Calabar and ship names at Bonny reflects the different market structures at the two Bight of Biafra ports. Prior to 1808, at Old Calabar almost every day of the week an experienced, well-known captain such as John Potter traded for small lots of slaves or other commodities. Such senior captains might remain in ships moored in the Calabar River or on shore for up to twenty months. Their mates did not transact any business, though they learned the intricacies of barter-round trading.[78] At Bonny, captains, too, managed the trade, though by the latter 1700s they might receive 5 to 10 slaves per day to inspect on board ship alongside their officers. Bonny's "wholesale market for slaves," as Captain Adams termed it, attracted large European slaving ships that generally loaded 375 to 400 enslaved Africans within two to four months. Experienced, senior captains, those who had worked their way up from brigs to three-masted ships, traded at Bonny, and ships that arrived first at Bonny received cargoes before latecomers.[79] Lacking distinctions between captains, there were no "ship and tender voyages" at Bonny. During the years of Antera Duke's diary, fourteen "tenders" averaged 100 days at Old Calabar; thirteen "captains" averaged 364 days there—a career's African coastal stay to a Bonny captain (table 2.6).

Differing credit mechanisms enable us to plumb the relative depths of individual business relationships between senior British ship captains and African merchants at Old Calabar and Bonny. Captain Adams believed that captains advanced credit "even more extensively" at Old Calabar than Bonny,[80] and the fact that Captains Lowndes (1768) and Potter (1770) of the *Dobson* each credited trading goods valued at least £400 until their return on a subsequent voyage six to twelve months in the future supports Adams's statement. Hugh Crow, a veteran Liverpool captain at Bonny, 1798–1807, mentioned selling "some goods on credit to the extent of £600 or £800," but these were short-term advances, redeemed before he departed the river and in the same trading cycle. On his 1798 voyage to Bonny and Jamaica, Crow sold to Kingston merchants £1,200 "worth of return goods, which I had saved from my outward cargo."[81] At Old Calabar, captains rarely kept

TABLE 2.6. Captains and their tenders at Old Calabar during the period of Antera Duke's diary

Captain (voyage)[#]	Vessel (tons)	Principal owner	Port	English departure	Days at Old Calabar[†]
John Burrows (3)	*Lion* (250)	Wicksted	Li	7/28/1784	315
John Ford (1)★	*Edwards* (180)	Wicksted	Li	10/20/1784	34
John Langdon (5)	*Constantine* (200)	Coulson	Br	8/3/1784	214
Matthew Morley (1)★	*Juba* (110)	Coulson	Br	12/6/1784	24
Peter Comberbach (2)	*Gascoyne* (294)	Gregson	Li	3/12/1785	265
Edward Aspinall (1)★	*William* (160)	Gregson	Li	5/26/1785	67
Thomas Cooper (2)★	*Quixote* (158)	Heywood	Li	4/29/1785	332
James McGauley (1)	*Highfield* (230)	Heywood	Li	7/21/1785	136
Patrick Fairweather (10)	*Tarleton* (342)	Tarleton	Li	6/23/1785	180
Barton Overton (2)★	*Fanny* (100)	Tarleton	Li	8/21/1785	41
Patrick Fairweather (11)	*Tarleton* (342)	Tarleton	Li	8/26/1786	281
Robert Harrison (1)★	*Mary* (164)	Tarleton	Li	8/26/1786	18
Thomas Smith (1)★	*Banastre* (93)	Tarleton	Li	3/31/1787	65
William Brighouse (7)	*Preston* (100)	Earle	Li	2/15/1786	476
Jenkin Evans (1)★	*Hudibras* (200)	Earle	Li	5/26/1786	136
John Cooper (6)	*Liverpool Hero* (211)	Heywood	Li	2/19/1786	414
Bryan Smith (1)★	*Hannah* (192)	Heywood	Li	8/4/1786	67
John Ford (3)	*Ellis* (280)	Bent	Li	4/19/1786	576
John Holliwell (1)★	*Renown* (196)	Bent	Li	8/12/1786	213
Edward Aspinall (2)[d]	*William* (200)	Gregson	Li	5/8/1786	324
Thomas Johnston (1)★	*Will* (128)	Gregson	Li	8/4/1786	104
John Tatem (3)	*Langdale* (209)	Lake	Li	6/1/1786	602
John Keatin (1)★	*Three Brothers* (428)	Lake	Li	9/20/1786	288
Peter Comberbach (3)	*Gascoyne* (294)	Gregson	Li	2/22/1787	364
Thomas Johnston (2)★	*Will* (128)	Gregson	Li	8/15/1787	93
Peter Potter (3)	*Iris* (268)	Galley	Li	3/20/1787	395
John Spencer (1)★	*Ned* (193)	Galley	Li	6/4/1787	117
Summary	Thirteen captains:	364 days at Old Calabar			
	Fourteen "tenders":	100 days at Old Calabar			

Br, Bristol; Li, Liverpool.

[#]Voyage as captain in the slave trade to Old Calabar.

[†]Some voyage times based on an estimated outward passage of 68 days and a Middle Passage of 72 days.

★Referred to in the diary as "tenders."

[d]Died at Old Calabar.

Sources: www.slavevoyages.org; Antera Duke's diary (see part II).

untraded goods in such quantities, instead depositing the goods with Efik traders on trust for deliveries up to a year later. Further, for spot credit at Old Calabar, but not at Bonny, captains received human pawns, who legally could be enslaved if Efik did not repay debts promptly. Leaving pawns, sometimes traders' kinsmen or wives, with senior captains highlights the importance of one-to-one business relations at Old Calabar.[82]

During Antera Duke's diary period, Liverpool captain Patrick Fairweather was the senior European trader at Old Calabar and key European liaison. Among the shipmasters named in the diary, January 1785–January 1788, Antera Duke mentions Fairweather most frequently—twenty-seven times.[83] On September 26, 1785, Antera canoed to shore to tell Fairweather in person that he had sighted the captain's tender downriver. After Duke Ephraim died in July 1786, sailor Henry Schroeder, on board the *Hudibras* in the Calabar River, recollected that they "were informed that, as soon as Captain Fairweather arrived, preparations would be made to commence with [the funeral obsequies]. He was expected with impatience, and hailed with rapturous congratulations, on his landing."[84] Fairweather departed Old Calabar in late December 1787 after residing three months at Duke Town, in an Efik trader's guesthouse, and eleven months in harbor.[85] Merseyside men such as Fairweather, who lived one-half of his adult life at Old Calabar, worked as de facto British representatives in an African region in which Europeans maintained no onshore settlements. Whereas Duke Ephraim as obong spoke for Efik interests, Fairweather as senior ship captain represented British concerns.

Captain Patrick Fairweather (ca. 1735–1799)[86] arrived first at Old Calabar in 1755,[87] at a time when Liverpool traders eclipsed Bristol merchants' forty-year dominance with Efik merchants. Surviving Guinea voyages during his twenties, by 1765 Fairweather advanced to the position of chief mate on the *Dalrymple*, Captain Alexander Allason.[88] He gained command of the ship when Allason died in 1768, a year that marked the rapid decline of Bristol's Calabar trade vis-à-vis Liverpool. Between 1770 and 1775 Fairweather steered the *Dalrymple* on five voyages to Old Calabar, and by the *Dalrymple*'s final voyage to Old Calabar in 1777, he had achieved the mantle of senior ship captain. By then he had trained future Liverpool-Calabar captains John Cooper, William Brighouse, William Begg, John Reynolds, Robert Harrison, and John Keatin.[89] During the 1778–1782 war years Fairweather commanded two of the six slavers that reached the Cross River region. He retired from sea after seven further voyages to Old Calabar from 1783 to 1792, the decadal height of the Liverpool-Calabar slave trade.[90]

Networks of Trade among Efik and
European Merchants

Captain Patrick Fairweather's prominence in the diary highlights the growing dominance of Liverpool and Duke Town traders in the late eighteenth-
century Old Calabar slave trade, and the key roles played by senior ship captains and Efik merchant-elders. New sources on the transatlantic slave trade,
unavailable to the first editors of Antera Duke's diary, allow us to identify
each sailing master at Old Calabar, 1785–1788, as well as his ship and its
tonnage, home port, and the partnership that outfitted the venture.[91] To dis-
cover the names of tenders, we looked for paired Calabar vessels organized
by the same firm, keeping in mind that senior commanders departed Europe
several months before their tenders, or junior captains. Further, with access to a comprehensive listing of all Guineamen, we identified captains
who frequented the Cross and Calabar rivers but were not mentioned by
Antera Duke—masters who traded principally with Creek Town or Old
Town merchants.

In his diary entries from January 1785 to January 1788, Antera Duke references forty-two slaving voyages.[92] He mentions one Bristol and one Liverpool captain who slaved previously at Old Calabar, in 1784, and two Liverpool
brigs that anchored in the Cross River estuary en route to Cameroon. Embarking slaves were thirty-two Liverpool, five Bristol, and one La Rochelle
Guineaman. Antera notes surnames of twenty European captains, the most
prominent being Patrick Fairweather from Liverpool, linked to three voyages (table 2.7). By comparing Antera's list with the slavers compiled in *Voyages*, the online slave trade database, we find that the diarist identifies thirty-
eight of the forty-nine European vessels at Calabar in the three-year period.[93]
Ten of the eleven captains not mentioned by Antera sailed from France (table
2.8). Further, the thirty-eight Calabar slaving voyages in the diary loaded 81
percent of all captives, and Liverpool merchants controlled 72 percent of the
Old Calabar slave trade (table 2.9).

French captains did not purchase many slaves from Duke Town dealers.
Antera does not identify any French captain by surname, referring only to
a "funchmen" that sailed upriver to Old Town or Creek Town and then
downstream, en route to the Americas, four months later. This slaver, the
Aurore from La Rochelle, probably traded with Creek Town leader Willy
Honesty, who held its "comey" (customs) book, and the French captain also
paid customs to merchants at Henshaw Town.[94] Another possible French-
flagged craft in the Calabar River in August 1785-July 1786 was the Liverpool

TABLE 2-7. European captains and slaving vessels referred to in Antera Duke's diary

Diary reference (original text)	Diary date*	Captain	Vessel (tons)	Port†	Principal owner(s)#
I go Captain Savage for tak goods for slav	1/21/1785	John Savage	Liverpool Hero (211)	Li	Thomas & William Earle
wee two go Bord Captin Smal	1/28/1785	John Smale	Perseverance (300)	Li	Thomas & William Earle
we have go Captain Brown	1/29/1785	John Burrows	Lion (250)	Li	Wicksted, Mason & Bourne
Captin Loosdan Tender	2/5/1785	Matthew Morley	Juba (110)	Br	Thomas Coulson
Captin Brown Tender go way	2/14/1785	John Ford	Edwards (180)	Li	Wicksted, Mason & Bourne
I go Bord Captin Loosdam for break book	2/23/1785	John Langdon	Constantine (200)	Br	Thomas Coulson
to till Duk about news ship com	3/6/1785	Robert Bibby[1]	Will (128)	Li	John Gregson
what owe about Captin Morgan [1784]	5/10/1785	William Morgan[2]	Pearl (350)	Br	William Tapscott
his be the Captin Combosboch	5/26/1785	Peter Comberbach	Gascoyne (294)	Li	John Gregson
wee com about Captin Osatam	6/25/1785	John Tatem	Fair American (180)	Li	Thomas Lake
wee see Captin Opoter arrived	6/25/1785	Peter Potter	Essex (150)	Li	William Davenport
give Captin fairwether [1784]	7/17/1785	Patrick Fairweather[2]	Tarleton (342)	Li	Tarleton & Backhouse
Captin of Combesboch tender	7/24/1785	Edward Aspinall	William (160)	Li	John Gregson
go on bord Captin Collins	8/7/1785	Thomas Collins	Martha (90)	Br	John Collard
his be Captin Hughes com up	8/19/1785	Joseph Hughes	President (263)	Li	Gill Slater
wee go with King on bord Captin fairwether	8/23/1785	Patrick Fairweather	Tarleton (342)	Li	Tarleton & Backhouse
Captin William	10/26/1785	Joseph Williams	Little Pearl (72)	Br	William Tapscott
wee get on bord his be Captin Overton	10/26/1785	Barton Overton	Fanny (100)	Li	Tarleton & Backhouse
Tom Cooper Tender go way	1/22/1786	James McGauley[3]	Quixote (158)	Li	Benjamin Heywood
Tom Cooper go way	5/21/1786	Thomas Cooper[3]	Highfield (230)	Li	Benjamin Heywood
com up Captin ford	6/10/1786	John Ford	Ellis (280)	Li	Ellis & Robert Bent
one funchmen ship	6/10/1786	Moël de Kerfraval	Aurore (800)	LR	Dumoutier & de Jarnac
Captin Savage arrived	7/5/1786	John Savage	Rodney (200)	Li	Parke, Heywood, Earle
one mat beLong to Brighouse Tender	9/4/1786	William Brighouse	Preston (100)	Li	Thomas & William Earle
and one John Cooper whitman	9/4/1786	John Cooper	Liverpool Hero (211)	Li	Parke, Heywood, Earle

his be John Cooper Tender	10/5/1786	Bryan Smith	*Hannah* (192)	Li	Benjamin Heywood
Captin Johnston ship will Tender	10/9/1786	Thomas Johnston	*Will* (128)	Li	John Gregson
Tender of Captin Aspinall	10/9/1786	Edward Aspinall	*William* (200)	Li	John Gregson
brow for Captin Fairwether	10/26/1786	Patrick Fairweather	*Tarleton* (342)	Li	Tarleton & Backhouse
Captin Fairwether Tender go way	12/9/1786	Robert Harrison	*Mary* (164)	Li	Tarleton & Backhouse
Captin Brikhouse Tender	12/19/1786	Jenkin Evans	*Hudibras* (200)	Li	Thomas & William Earle
Captin ford send his Tender way	5/21/1787	John Burrows	*Renown* (196)	Li	Hodgson & Bent
wee Done coomy on bord Potter	5/21/1787	Peter Potter	*Iris* (268)	Li	Galley & Pickop
Little ship belong to [Captin] Hughot	6/11/1787	Joseph Hughes	*President* (254)	Li	Gill Slater
Captin fairweather Tender go way	8/25/1787	Thomas Smith	*Banastre* (93)	Li	Tarleton & Backhouse
wee have Tatam Tender go way	9/16/1787	John Keatin	*Three Brothers* (428)	Li	Thomas Lake
Little snow Brsh ship was in Comrown	9/20/1787	John Foulkes[1]	*Searle* (137)	Li	John Tomlinson
wee for com on bord Rogers	10/9/1787	Richard Rogers	*Pearl* (375)	Br	James Rogers
Potter go way with Tender go way	12/22/1787	John Spencer	*Ned* (193)	Li	Galley & Pickop
wee have Captin … John Tatam	12/25/1787	John Tatam	*Langdale* (209)	Li	Thomas Lake
wee have Captin … Combesboch	12/25/1787	Peter Comberbach	*Gascoyne* (294)	Li	John Gregson
wee have Combesboch Tender go way	1/23/1788	Thomas Johnston	*Will* (128)	Li	John Gregson

*First reference date in original text (references with same names are subsequent voyages).

[1]Br, Bristol; Li, Liverpool; LR, La Rochelle.

[#]For British voyages, preferred principal owners.

[1]Vessel slaved at Cameroon.

[2]Antera Duke refers to voyages the previous year (1784).

[3]Thomas Cooper arrived at Calabar June 26, 1785, on the *Quixote* and transferred command to James McGauley; McGauley arrived in September on the *Highfield* and transferred command to Thomas Cooper.

Sources: Cols. 1–2: see part II, original text of the diary of Antera Duke; cols. 3–6: www.slavevoyages.org.

TABLE 2.8. Documented European slaving voyages at Old Calabar, January 1785–January 1788, not recorded in Antera Duke's diary

Vessel (tons)	Captain	Principal owner(s)	Port*	Approximate trading dates at Old Calabar
Amour (400)	Pierre Duchesne	Langevin & Langevin	Na	August–October 1785
Uni (350)	Joseph-Marie Le Roux	Ducoundray-Bourgault	Na	September–October 1785
Asia (100)	Michael Loughman	John, Christopher Shaw	Li	August 1785–July 1786
Cérès (443)†	Julien Guichet	J. Mosneron-Dupin	Na	July 1786
Uni (350)	Joseph-Marie Le Roux	Ducoundray-Bourgault	Na	September–December 1786
Légère (410)†	Jean Deloge	J. Mosneron-Dupin	Na	October 1786
Elizabeth (78)	Vanier	Premord & Sons	Ho	August–September 1787
Cérès (443)	Julien Guichet	J. Mosneron-Dupin	Na	July–September 1787
Amour (380)†	Mathurin Ringeard	Langevin & Langevin	Na	August 1787
Folie (205)	H. Fr. Chalumeau	Langevin & Langevin	Na	August 1787–January 1788
Négresse (260)†	Magouet	Antoine Baudoin	Na	September 1787

*Ho, Honfleur; Li, Liverpool; Na, Nantes.
†Slaved also at Bonny; perhaps no slaves were embarked at Old Calabar.

Source: www.slavevoyages.org.

merchants John and Christopher Shaw's *Asia*, captained by Michael Loughman. The Shaws are one of the few British slaving firms that maintained links with French Guinea concerns, reflagging at least two Liverpool-based vessels in France in 1785 and 1790.[95] Perhaps Captain Loughman traded off Old Town or Creek Town with other French Guineamen, since he is not mentioned in Antera Duke's diary.

The assumption that French merchants lacked long-standing commercial ties with Duke Town holds true as well with Bristol and London. The smaller merchant community of Bristol, including such traders as Thomas Jones, a Calabar captain in 1760 and 1763, developed their closest commercial relationships with Old Town. Jones's links with Old Town are best illustrated by a bell preserved by the Bristol Society of Merchant Venturers, inscribed "The Gift of Thomas Jones of Bristol to Gr[a]ndy Robin John of Ol[d] Town Ol[d] Callabar 1770."[96] In 1761, 1763, and 1771, James Morley crewed on three Bristol voyages to Old Calabar. When he testified to Parliamentary counsel in 1790, two of the three Efik traders he mentioned were Archibong Robin John and Orrock Robin John—both from Old Town.[97] In 1776, Liverpool captain William Brighouse, off Duke Town, noted that "at old town there is one Bristol Snow & [one] Expected, 2 Lond[on]ers & 1 French Snow."[98] Brighouse references the Bristol snow *Cato*, owned by Thomas Jones, then at anchor at Old Town; the snow *Africa* (expected, but shipwrecked on the

TABLE 2.9. The European slave trade at Old Calabar, January 1785–January 1788

Port	(A) Old Calabar slave voyages mentioned in Antera Duke's diary		(B) Old Calabar slave voyages not mentioned in Antera Duke's diary		(C) Total slave voyages at Old Calabar	
	Voyages	Estimated slave exports	Voyages	Estimated slave exports	Voyages	Estimated slave exports
Liverpool	32	12,683 (87.4%)	1	213 (7.2%)	33	12,896 (72.0%)
Bristol	5	1,436 (9.9)	0	0	5	1,436 (8.0)
Nantes	0	0	9	3,084 (89.9)	9	3,084 (17.2)
La Rochelle	1	400 (2.7)	0	0	1	400 (2.2)
Honfleur	0	0	1	85 (2.9)	1	85 (0.5)
Totals★	38	14,519 (81.1%)	11	3,382 (18.9%)	49	17,901

★Antera Duke's diary reports 8,165 slave exports on 24 British vessels. Slave exports for 8 other voyages come from various sources, cited in www.slavevoyages.org. Slave export estimates for 14 voyages are based on slave import data and estimated slave mortality loss on the Middle Passage of 23%.

outward passage); the *Venus* and *Neptune*, the only two Londoners in the Calabar River; and one of the five Nantes slavers then trading at Old Calabar.[99] The *Neptune*, according to one of its mates, "lay abreast of the Old Town."[100] Significantly, Brighouse does not mention any Liverpool captains at Old Town, even though by 1776 Merseyside outfitted three in four Guineamen at Calabar.

Liverpool's rise at Old Calabar occurred in the 1750s and 1760s when merchants such as William Earle and William Davenport created networks with Duke Town merchants. In the two decades after the massacre of 1767, Merseyside businessmen almost doubled their market share—mostly at the expense of Bristol traders. Between 1768 and 1777, fifty-one Liverpool slavers competed against only eight vessels from Bristol, seven from Nantes, and two from London.[101] Bristol's Calabar trade dropped by half in 1768, suggesting that the massacre of Old Town merchants in 1767 crippled trading networks created between the Efik village and southwest English port. Old Town's and Bristol's share of the trade in the 1770s and 1780s thus declined together, and only Liverpool merchants successfully made the transition from trading with a number of Efik merchants to purchasing slaves largely through the rules of trade established by Creek Town merchants and rising Duke Town traders.

To the Efik, Captain Fairweather's relation to an extended Liverpool partnership was that of a junior, non-kin member absorbed into a multigenerational family of businessmen. Fairweather worked for William Davenport, and Davenport's partners included William Earle, Patrick Black, James Berry, and Ambrose Lace—all former slaving captains to Old Calabar, and all men well known to the Efik. In 1773 Ephraim Robin John, for example, asked Lace to give his complements "to the gentlemen owners of the brig Swift Mr Devenport Marchant Black and Captn Black and as also Mr Erll." Lace had by then entered into Calabar slaving partnerships with Edward Chaffers, and in 1773 Otto Ephraim Robin John, who lived in Liverpool for two years, asked Lace to "Remember me to your Wife and Mr. Chiffies [Chaffers]." Similarly, British merchants maintained their connections to Efik families. In 1761 merchant (and former captain) William Earle asked Duke Town's Duke Abashy (Abasi) to send greetings to several Efik merchants and their families.[102] Personal connections between Efik and European merchants were also long-standing and passed between generations. For example, thirty-three-year-old second mate (later captain) Hamnet Forsyth, writing from Old Calabar in 1792, told of his "great friendship" with the "principal traders" at Old Calabar who knew his father and brother. His father Robert Forsyth had last traded at Old Calabar in 1771—twenty years earlier.[103]

Conclusion

The history of the slave trade at Old Calabar during Antera Duke's lifetime is the history of the rise of Duke Town and Liverpool merchants. Businessmen from both settlements emerged in the 1750s, challenging their Efik and British rivals from Creek Town, Old Town, and Bristol, respectively.[104] Antera Duke and Patrick Fairweather probably met first in 1755, when both men were about twenty years of age. Unlike many others, they survived to prosper from the slave trade, accumulate market power, and become key cross-cultural brokers. They helped to engineer the rise of Duke Ephraim in the 1760s and 1770s and to secure the position of his son after the father's death in July 1786. The decision by ship captains in 1792 to strengthen Egbo Young Ofiong's and Duke Ephraim's positions in Efik society allowed Duke Town merchants to dominate trade and drive up comey and slave prices. British firms without access to Liverpool senior captains' market power could not compete profitably in a trade controlled by a tight transatlantic partnership. Bristol merchant James Rogers's captains realized their weak position upon arriving in the Calabar River in the late 1780s. When they entered Duke Ephraim's house, they walked into a building constructed in Liverpool in 1785 and transported to Duke Town by Patrick Fairweather. When they met the fifty-year-old Liverpool captain, they quickly advised their employer, James Rogers, that Fairweather was the man to consult about the slave trade at Old Calabar.[105]

Our analysis of the Old Calabar slave trade has highlighted the importance of individuals, free or enslaved, African merchants or European mariners. Efik families competed to increase kin and non-kin members and to purchase and store international goods in demand throughout the Cross River region. To Efik traders, ships' officers they met descended from those charter captains or merchants—"common ancestors"—who traded first with Calabar families. Similarly, European partnerships functioned as extended families, and the hierarchical relationship between merchant, captain, and mate mirrored age-sets in Calabar society and the paramount role of Efik elders. Both groups, European and African, retained individuals to collateralize debts: captains held free African men and women as "pawns" in lieu of trading goods advanced; Efik merchants occasionally seized sailors as commercial hostages to redress grievances. Intricate and long-standing personal relationships between African and European families, forged through commerce and language communication, distinguish Calabar from other communities in Atlantic Africa.

Duke Ephraim and other Duke Town merchants continued to strengthen their position after Fairweather retired from the sea in 1793. By 1804 they had squeezed some Henshaw merchants out of the slave trade,[106] and by 1805 Duke Ephraim had become "by far the biggest trader."[107] The Duke's power grew throughout the 1810s and 1820s, so much so that his warriors extended their power to the Atlantic estuary—crushing Tom Shott's Point in 1821—to gain control of the salt and palm oil trades. After Willy Honesty died, probably in the 1810s, Duke Ephraim, already obong, also became eyamba, or president of Ekpe. As Latham remarks, "Consequently his dominance was unchallenged, and he set about consolidating and extending his vast power." By 1828, in his late sixties or early seventies, Duke Ephraim became "the most influential man in Efik history." He was "*Obong, Eyamba*, sole comey recipient, and virtual monopolist of the external trade." It was "Great Duke Ephraim" who managed Calabar's transition from the slave to palm oil trades after the abolition of the British slave trade.[108] The Calabar export produce trade first developed in the seventeenth and eighteenth centuries, and it is to this topic that we now turn.

CHAPTER THREE

The Produce Trade at Old
Calabar

On "June 24the 1780," King Henshaw, Duke Ephraim, and Willy
Honesty—senior Efik businessmen from Henshaw Town, Duke Town,
and Creek Town—wrote a letter to Liverpool "Gentlemen," encouraging
them to send vessels to Old Calabar to trade for slaves and ivory. In the past
two years only Captain William Begg, a surgeon and mariner trained by
Patrick Fairweather, had arrived in the Calabar River: "we no been See 24
moonth no more Captain Beggs Come for tooth [tusks]." Atlantic privateering during the American Revolutionary War made it difficult to send ships
to Africa and the Americas, but Henshaw, Ephraim, and Honesty wanted to
assure Liverpool merchants that they would profit from the security of trade
in Old Calabar, as had Captain Begg, then purchasing ivory.
The Efik merchants emphasized that they "all go for Country"—that they
journeyed to hinterland suppliers—thus enabling British ships that arrived
to load quickly. Knowing that captains would need distant markets to sell
slaves, they wrote, "[W]e think as soon as your have way for Sell Slaves that
your will send Ship for Slaves and tooth Tooth together that will be better for
us[.]"[1]

Efik merchants brokered slaves and "tooth tooth," or elephants' teeth
(ivory tusks),[2] profiting from selling human cargoes and ivory "together."
The export trade in ivory and other produce figured more importantly than
the June 1780 letter indicated, however. A Liverpool newspaper documents
that Captain Begg purchased as many as 1,280 ivory tusks, 25,000 gallons of
"exceeding fine palm oil," and 1 ton of redwood.[3] Similarly, Antera Duke's

diary gives little indication that Cross River middlemen sold large quantities of animal and agricultural commodities. He mentions ivory only twice, without counting tusks: on January 23, 1786, he wrote that traders Egbo Young Antera and Apandam arrived at Duke Town from Umon with slaves and "Toother" (tusks); two weeks later Antera wrote that "Combesboch," Liverpool captain Peter Comberbach, departed with "639 slave & Toother."[4] In fact, Comberbach loaded 2.5 tons of ivory and also purchased 5,880 gallons of palm oil and 13 tons of pepper.[5]

In the period 1752–1808 many Lancashire gazettes record Liverpool ships' cargoes. These years coincide with Antera Duke's adulthood and growing prominence as a Cross River merchant. Liverpool imports allow us to examine Old Calabar's produce trade in a comparative Bight of Biafran context, since Liverpool captains dominated business at Bonny, New Calabar, Old Calabar, and Cameroon.[6] In the fifty years before British abolition in 1807–1808, Cross River merchants monopolized the modest, but growing, African palm oil trade and sold 20 percent of the ivory entering England, the latter mostly from the Cameroon backcountry. While Cross River traders brokered slaves, ivory, redwood, palm oil, pepper, and yams, Bonny and New Calabar merchants specialized in the export slave and yam trades. By developing ancillary trades in these commodities, Efik merchants hoped to attract more European slave traders to Old Calabar and compete more effectively with Bonny, forty miles to the west of the Cross River estuary. The strategy was not particularly successful in increasing Old Calabar's share of the slave trade from the Bight of Biafra, but when Britain moved to end the slave trade after 1807, the Efik would be much quicker than their neighbors in capitalizing on these alternative exports.

The Produce Trades from Old Calabar and the Bight of Biafra, 1650–1750

Old Calabar began exporting ivory along with slaves in the mid-1600s. Both trades grew slowly from the 1650s to 1690s, as more and more Efik merchants began working at Creek Town near the Calabar River. Palm oil was produced for local consumption but not as an export commodity. In the early 1700s redwood appears in the cargoes of British ships returning from Old Calabar, and quantities were sufficiently large in 1720 to support the first documented "redwood ship" at Old Calabar. English ivory imports increased in the 1720s, a decade when greater numbers of Bristol and Liverpool ships frequented Old Calabar and Bonny, abandoning New Calabar. By the time of Antera Duke's birth, probably in the mid-1730s, Dutch ivory ships had begun trading in Cameroon, Cape Lopez, and Gabon, and Mayumba had become important as a redwood center.

Limited evidence survives on Old Calabar's early produce trade with Europeans. A word list from approximately 1642 to 1655, written by an anonymous Dutch trader, lists seventy-one terms from Cameroon–Rio del Rey–Old Calabar, including African (mainly Duala) words for ivory, yam, palm oil, palm kernel, and palm wine.[7] In 1662 Captain John Major of the London slaving ship *Blackamore* purchased 217 slaves and 81 ivory tusks at Old Calabar.[8] Captain Major probably also bought yams and palm oil for the coast and Middle Passage. The *Blackamore* loaded unspecified amounts of ivory on its subsequent voyage to Old Calabar in 1664. In January 1665 the Company of Royal Adventurers of England Trading to Africa advertised 42.5 tons of ivory that had arrived in London on four ships, including the *Blackamore*. The majority of the 4,449 tusks came from New Calabar.[9]

By the turn of the eighteenth century, Old Calabar's ivory exports rivaled New Calabar's. A 1672 report about the Royal African Company mentioned that "many ships are sent to trade at New and Old Calabar for slaves and teeth, which are there to be had in great plenty."[10] Referring to evidence from 1698 and perhaps earlier, James Barbot believed that African merchants in "villages and hamlets" banking the Cross and Calabar rivers shipped most of the ivory that arrived in England.[11] In 1699 customs officials recorded forty-five tons of ivory imported into England, a little more than half of which arrived via the Americas on slaving vessels.[12] If Barbot is correct, Old Calabar dealers sold about twenty-five tons of ivory to captains trading on five to ten ships.[13] In 1703–1704 Jean Grazilier believed that New Calabar merchants each year shipped thirty to forty tons of "elephants teeth, all very fine and large, most by Dutch ships."[14] Though Grazilier exaggerated his totals, New Calabar's ivory trade remained comparatively large in the late 1600s.[15]

In the first two decades of the eighteenth century, redwood appears with ivory as a commodity sold by Cross River merchants.[16] The first documented Bristol ships were the slavers *Stonedge Gally* in 1707 and *Leopard Gally* in 1709, which returned to Bristol from Old Calabar and Virginia with 1/2 ton each of the dyewood.[17] In 1714 Captain Samuel Paine, on board a London slaver at Old Calabar, noted, "Here they have no gold, but great abundance of Elephants teeth, & of all Sizes from those of 5 or 6 Pound weight to 100# [pounds] & more; they have a sort of Red wood, which is a very valuable Dye."[18] Busy trades in redwood and ivory continued at Calabar in 1719–1720. The slavers *Berkley, Callabar Merchant, Cornwall, Rebecca,* and *Tiverton* arrived in Bristol from Old Calabar and the Americas with at least fifteen tons of redwood and two tons of ivory.[19] The *Leah* of London, a nonslaver commanded by Theophilous Boucher, sailed from Old Calabar in June 1720 "bound directly for London with Red wood."[20]

As Cross and Calabar River businessmen began dealing slaves, ivory, and redwood, they attracted European merchants who earlier would have sent ships to New Calabar. New Calabar's export trades fell precipitously after 1700, losing regional business to Old Calabar and then, in the mid-1720s, to Bonny.[21] There are only 15 documented European voyages that slaved at New Calabar from 1700 to 1750, compared with 186 that traded at Old Calabar and 142 ventures at Bonny.[22] As the port's slave trade declined, so too did its ivory trade. Dutch ivory merchants shifted business from New Calabar to Agathon (on the Benin River) and Ouidah in the Bight of Benin, and then in the 1730s they began sending ships to Cameroon, Cape Lopez, and Gabon.[23] New Calabar did not recover its business with European ship captains until the 1750s, but by then nearby Bonny sold 80 percent of the slaves from the eastern Niger Delta.[24]

Evidence suggests that in the first half of the eighteenth century Old Calabar merchants sold more redwood than Bonny and equal amounts of ivory. Bristol merchants dominated trade in the Bight of Biafra,[25] but unfortunately the African locations of trade are recorded for only two in five Bristol ships.[26] In spite of these source limitations, we know that redwood and/or ivory arrived on twenty-three of ninety Bristol vessels that traded at Old Calabar (1707–1742) and twelve of seventy-two that traded at Bonny (1725–1735). From this sample, Old Calabar produce shipments totaled 81 tons of redwood and 13 tons of ivory; Bristol slaving ships to Bonny loaded 20 tons of redwood and 12 tons of ivory.[27] Bristol captains generally loaded 125 to 250 tusks at either Old Calabar or Bonny.[28]

The size of Bristol's redwood trade warrants special attention, as the city's dockworkers in one peak year (1725) unloaded redwood in amounts that almost equaled London's redwood imports on Royal African Company vessels from 1674 to 1713.[29] In the sixteenth and seventeenth centuries Bristol textile manufacturers produced dyed woolen cloth and were famous for "Bristol Reds." In the late seventeenth century the industry shifted up the Severn River, centering upon the Cotswolds northeast of Bristol.[30] Strong local demand for dyestuffs prompted Bristol captains to trade for camwood (also producing red dye) south of Sierra Leone, and to buy redwood in the Cross River region and "Angolan" coastline between Cape Lopez and the Congo River. Cutters harvested Cross River redwood from two kinds of trees, *Baphia nitida* and *Pterocarpus tinctorius*,[31] a wood distinct from *Pterocarpus soyauxii*, generally called "barwood," that grew in Gabon.[32] Bristol captains probably purchased the greatest quantities near Mayumba, the major redwood port in Lower Guinea, through which Gabon traders shipped redwood from the Setta Cama region.[33]

In contrast to the woolen textile industry, Bristol and southwest England played a minor role in the country's ivory crafts. The most common ivory products before 1700 were London-made combs.[34] Later, more and more ivory was worked into cutlery handles, piano keys, furniture inlays, billiard balls, and numerous other luxury items.[35] Brokers sold ivory in pieces or in lots to dealers who then shipped parcels to manufacturers in England and Scotland. Some ivory remained in Bristol, lathed by the few ivory turners in the city.[36] The closest major ivory market was Birmingham, a manufacturing center for buttons, snuffboxes, chests, cases, and other decorative objects. An advertisement for "J. Taylor, Gold and Silversmith, Jeweller, Tortoiseshell and Ivory Box and Toy Manufacturer" included an elephant and a ship on the sides of the engraving. John Taylor (d. 1775) founded the firm in Birmingham in the early eighteenth century, and undoubtedly some of the ivory shipped to Bristol found its way to his shops.[37]

Whereas African merchants warehoused and brokered dyewoods and ivory for export markets, palm oil was consumed locally and on ships. Early visitors to Guinea mentioned supplies of oil and palm nuts, and slaving captains purchased small amounts of oil as food (to supplement beans and yams) for slaves confined on the coast and Middle Passage.[38] Palm oil imports remained minute until the mid-1760s, on average, only a couple of hundred gallons a year arriving in English customshouses. All early traders mention palm oil loaded in "jars," rather than in the larger puncheons used in the 1780s.[39] The oil palm grows between 12° north latitude and 12° south latitude, and it is likely that most of these early shipments arrived in London from Sierra Leone, the Gold Coast, or the Bight of Benin. Since the greatest concentration of oil palm trees is in southeastern Nigeria, Old Calabar merchants sold some of the small quantities of palm oil.[40]

Incomplete information makes it difficult to gauge the scale and comparative importance of Old Calabar's produce trades in the first half of the eighteenth century. The British dominated trade in the Bight of Biafra, but it is not possible to identify the majority of ships calling at either Old Calabar or Bonny. Although English customs ledgers aggregated imports from "Africa" or from broadly defined regions such as "British West Africa" (1699–1714) or "West Africa" (1700–1714),[41] we know that merchants from Old Calabar brokered ivory as early as 1662 and redwood as early as 1707. Among Lower Guinea ports, redwood imports from Old Calabar ranked behind shipments from Mayumba. Regarding ivory, it is not a coincidence that

English imports more than doubled in the two decades after 1718, a period
when first Bristol and then Liverpool slaving merchants outfitted more and
more ships to Old Calabar and Bonny.

Old Calabar and the Bight of Biafra's
Produce Trades, 1750–1807

Extensive source material allows a confident comparison of the Bight of
Biafra's produce trades in the latter 1700s. On March 3, 1752, Joseph Harrop
published the first issue of his weekly *Manchester Mercury*, which reported
ships' cargoes that arrived in Liverpool, twenty-two miles west of Manchester. *Williamson's Liverpool Advertiser* began in 1756, followed by the rival *Liverpool General Advertiser* in 1765.[42] In addition, there are extant copies of the
Liverpool Trade List from August 1798 to January 1800.[43] Combined, these papers advertised cargoes arriving in Liverpool for most weeks between 1752
and the abolition of the British slave trade in 1807–1808.[44] After the 1770s,
British colonial shipping lists from the Americas, such as those from Jamaica,
more frequently record African produce, adding to and confirming cargoes
advertised in Lancashire gazettes.[45] A trove of business documents survive
from British merchant William Davenport (trading at Old Calabar, 1751–
1786) and some others from James Rogers (trading there 1787–1792). The
Davenport papers include voyage accounts, which total quantities of ivory,
dyewood, and palm oil purchased, and both sets include some captains' letters from Old Calabar that discuss trades in these commodities.

   In the second half of the eighteenth century, Cross River middlemen,
losing business to slaving merchants based at Bonny, developed larger ivory
trades and began to respond to a small rise in the European demand for palm
oil. In the 1750s and 1760s Efik traders at Old Calabar increased trades with
Cameroon grasslands ivory dealers, and in the 1760s and 1770s they began
pursuing more oil barters with the Mbiabo Efik, situated on the west bank
of the Cross River. Business pressures heightened during the American Revolutionary War, as the threat of privateers in the Caribbean led British slaving merchants to dramatically reduce the number of Guineamen they outfitted for Old Calabar. Threatened with a loss of income, more and more Efik
who specialized in the export slave trade turned to alternative investments.
By the period of Antera Duke's diary almost all British ships' captains purchased slaves and ivory, some supplementing cargoes with palm oil, pepper,
and redwood. Old Calabar became one of the most economically diversified
ports in Lower Guinea, later helping Efik merchants to minimize the economic impact of the abolition of the British slave trade in 1807–1808.

In considering the various export trades from the Bight of Biafra in the eighteenth century, one must emphasize the importance of ivory, transported to Europe mostly on slaving vessels via the Americas.[46] Ivory was the third most valuable commodity exported from Africa (after gold and slaves) and was priced eight times the sterling value of palm oil per hundredweight (112 pounds).[47] Tusks could bear the cost of transatlantic freight and, depending on the mortality risks of enslaved Africans, might prove a better speculation than purchasing human cargoes. Captains took into account mortality risks when deciding how to pack in each square foot of between-deck space. As early as 1725 a Bristol firm reminded its captain to judge the comparative risks between purchasing slaves or ivory, as "in that Commodity there's no Mortality to be fear'd."[48] The value of ivory was such that British slaving merchants often instructed captains to transship tusks to homeward-bound vessels if they faced delays selling their slaves in the Americas. They paid captains commissions of 2 to 3 percent on ivory, insured it separately, and, during wartime, sought heavily armed ships to transport the luxury good to England.[49]

Old Calabar's Ivory Trade

In the second half of the eighteenth century, Old Calabar's ivory exports doubled to 7 to 11 tons per year. Limited evidence from the 1750s indicates that six slaving ship captains returned to Liverpool, 1753–1758, with 553 ivory tusks (an average of 92 per ship), and a French privateer captured one Liverpool-Calabar slaver with 2 tons of ivory.[50] After the Seven Years' War, a better documented period, we estimate that 152 British slaving ships, mostly from Liverpool and Bristol, loaded 146 tons of ivory at Old Calabar, 1763–1775, exports increasing on the Liverpool slaving ships to 179 tusks per vessel. Record ivory cargoes left Old Calabar during the depressed American Revolutionary war years, when few craft entered the Cross River region and ivory stocks were plentiful. Four vessels returned to Liverpool in 1781–1783 with 10,000 pieces of ivory—about 64 tons. One of these was the slaving ship *Liverpool Hero* co-owned by Liverpool merchant William Davenport, which transported 2,586 tusks, one of the highest loads for a slaving ship. From 1783 to 1808 Liverpool ships returning from Old Calabar delivered 217 tons of ivory, 7.5 tons per year. During this final period these British slaving captains loaded, on average, 204 pieces of ivory.

William Davenport was the most important buyer of Old Calabar ivory for a generation and the largest ivory dealer in England outside London. From 1754 to 1786 his ships returned to Liverpool with at least twenty-six

ivory cargoes—twenty-three on slaving vessels via the Americas—from Old
Calabar, totaling 11,800 tusks and 75 tons. Accounts document the weight of
ivory on twenty-one of his slaving ventures, 1765–1777. On these his captains delivered 5,793 tusks or pieces of ivory (276 per ship), weighing 83,463
pounds (37 tons); the average weight of the tusks was 14.4 pounds. In his Liverpool warehouses Davenport divided ivory into lots, pieces averaging from
2 to 114 pounds per lot. His captains purchased many small "teeth"—juve-
nile elephant tusks ("scrivilloes"), a few hippopotamus tusks ("seamorse" or
"seahorse" teeth), or broken shards.[51] On the *Swift*, which arrived in Barbados from Old Calabar in 1777, for example, Davenport's colonial agent took
the ivory pieces "out of the store" and found 176 "teeth" weighing 7,750
pounds (average 44 pounds) and "six hundred scrivilloes" weighing 3,783
pounds (average 6.3 pounds).[52]

For two of Davenport's vessels, the *Dobson* and *Fox*, there survive detailed
accounts of ivory purchases at Old Calabar in 1769–1770. As we discussed in
chapter 2, Captain John Potter of the *Dobson* purchased slaves, ivory, and provisions for both vessels, first loading and sending his "tender" to the Americas. Potter began his ivory trade on July 16, 1769, when he purchased six
scrivilloes weighing thirty-two pounds for an assortment of goods valued
thirty-five coppers. Over the next six months he purchased ivory in 179 separate transactions totaling 410 barter rounds. All told, Potter traded goods valued 8,429 coppers for fifty-eight tusks and 555 scrivilloes. The ivory accounts
do not record the names of the Calabar sellers until final transactions settle
debts. Potter paid "Sundry loose Coppers" for ivory to balance the accounts
of Gentleman Honesty, Antera Duke, and Dick Ephraim Duke. Then, on
January 9, 1770, he received a single fifty-pound tusk, valued at seventy coppers, to settle Duke Ephraim's account. Since these four men are Efik, we assume Potter purchased all ivory from Efik merchants, as he did when he
bought slaves.

Captain Potter purchased the ivory offered for sale on most days during
his six-month trade at Old Calabar. Though Davenport's orders to Potter do
not survive, others instruct Calabar-bound captains to first purchase small
scrivilloes, and then, "what goods remain lay out for Teeth of any size"
(1751),[53] or to "be looking out for Ivory, and purchase all that you can of the
very best" (1762), or to purchase ivory "from the beginning of your trade"
(1762).[54] In Potter's July 1769–January 1770 ivory transactions he bought
whatever ivory Efik merchants brokered. He did not purchase piles of scrivilloes, for example, in the first few months of trade or more and more large
tusks in December and January. He was offered more ivory in November
than other months. Since Efik sold mostly small pieces, valued, on average,
14 coppers, they usually completed sales in one to two rounds of trading.

Only four transactions required five barter rounds, the most protracted concerning Potter's purchase on December 2 of the largest tusk, one weighing 84 pounds, for 129 coppers. Potter and Efik traders valued this tusk more than most of the African captives they bought and sold. That same day, for example, Tom King John sold Potter one girl for 115 coppers.[55]

Efik merchants selling ivory demanded different bundles of goods than in their rounds of slave trading. By value, Antera Duke and others purchased 40 to 50 percent textiles whether they sold ivory or slaves. The five major types of Manchester-imitation and Indian cloth—romal, cushtae, photae, chintz, and nicanee—appear in most slave and ivory transactions. But whereas romal tops the list of textile purchases in all commodity transactions, other cloth ranked differently. Cushtaes, the second most important cloth in slave transactions, ranked seventh in ivory sales. By contrast, the second-ranking "ivory cloth"—chelloe—placed eighth in slave sales. The greatest difference was in a manufactured English textile: Efik merchants purchased 562 caps in their ivory barters, but only 62 in all 2,011 rounds of slave trading with Captain Potter. They demanded slightly more hardware in their ivory negotiations, in particular, manillas, knives, tankards, and lead bars. Davenport loaded, for example, fifty tankards, and Potter sold thirty-nine for ivory but only seven in all his slave rounds (the remaining four tankards he probably paid as comey). As in their slave barters, Efik merchants demanded copper rods in almost all ivory trades—in 172 of 179 transactions with Potter. Disproportionate amounts of brandy appear in the ivory sales ledger; disproportionate bunches of beads appear in Potter's slave purchases (tables 3.1 and 3.2).

Whereas Captain Potter's trade at Old Calabar in 1769–1770 concerned mostly transactions for slaves (80 percent of his trade, by value), during the American Revolutionary War William Davenport fitted out his brig *William* for Old Calabar with cargoes to trade principally for ivory and other African produce. In 1778 Atlantic privateering risks in the Caribbean, "positively forbade"[56] merchants such as Davenport from outfitting slaving vessels. Davenport thus sent the *William* on three "produce voyages" in 1780 and 1781 to return direct to Liverpool. Measuring "about Fifty Tons"—probably fifty feet in length by sixteen feet in breadth[57]—the *William* was one of the earliest nonslaving vessels to anchor off Duke Town. Davenport stated the importance of ivory's potential profitability in 1780, on a voyage that would trade at Old Calabar and then the Windward Coast. As he wrote to his captain, William Begg, "Ivory will produce clear to the Owners per ton [£]330," palm oil £74, malagueta pepper £60, rice £15, beeswax £130, and camwood £30 per ton, commodities listed according to their south (Calabar) to north (Sherbro Island) markets.[58]

On the *William*'s late 1781 voyage from Liverpool to Old Calabar,

TABLE 3.1. British sterling value of goods received by Efik traders for the sale of slaves, ivory, and provisions, July 16, 1769–January 12, 1770, Liverpool ships *Dobson* and *Fox* (by category of trade goods)

	Transactions for 499 slaves[1] (58,620 coppers)		Transactions for 613 pieces of ivory[2] (8,429 coppers)		Transactions for provisions[3] (10,574 coppers)	
Textiles	£1,391.6	47.5%	£155.8	43.0%	£156.3	38.5%
Hardware	459.0	15.7	85.2	23.5	135.4	33.4
Bar iron	428.8	14.6	41.3	11.4	69.8	17.2
Beads	286.9	9.8	16.3	4.5	9.1	2.2
Arms	161.4	5.5	16.6	4.6	3.2	0.8
Gunpowder	139.2	4.8	22.7	6.3	10.9	2.7
Liquor	61.0	2.1	21.6	6.0	9.7	2.4
Salt	0.6	0.0	1.2	0.3	11.6	2.9
Horns	0.5	0.0	1.7	0.5	0.0	0.0
Totals	£2,929	(79.2%)	£362 8s	(9.8%)	£406	(11.0%)
	£5 17s/slave		£0.59 (11.8s)/piece			

[1]217 men, 124 women, 79 boys, 79 girls. Trading goods are specified for transactions concerning these 499 individuals. Captain Potter also received 67 slaves for unspecified goods credited the previous year.

[2]58 teeth and 555 scrivilloes (total weight 6,312 lbs.).

[3]82,935 yams, 740 jars of palm oil, 10 goats, 2 cows, 143 coppers' worth of plantains, and unspecified fish, fowl, pepper, greens, limes, and mats.

Sources: Dobson and *Fox* accounts, William Davenport Papers, MMM; *Dobson* Calabar Account, Hasell MS, Dalemain House, Cumbria.

Davenport gave Captain Peter Comberbach, Begg's successor, detailed trading instructions. His letter to Comberbach reads:

> you have herewith Invoice of a very choice Cargoe shipped on the Brig *William* amounting to the sum of £1393 10s 8d Sterling and 37,768 Coppers very suitable for the River Old Callabar, where you are to barter the same for Elephants' Teeth and as much palm Oyle as your vessal can store. . . . On your arrival in the River you are to send your Boat on shore for Pawns, and having recd them from whom you know are good you may then go on shore to the Dukes, and agree with them to trade on the same footing that Capⁿ Begg did Last voyage, Viz. 1000 Coppers to be divided amongst them as the thing proper, the Particulars of which you have in [Begg's] trust & trade Book; the prices for Scarveloes one Copper [per] pound, from 18 to 25 pounds 1[1/2] and teeth from 25 pounds and upwards 2 Copper per pound but you are to be guided by any other Ships that may be in the River, and as your cargo is better than any other Vessal that are

TABLE 3.2. Quantity, type, and British sterling value of goods received by Efik merchants from the sale of 613 ivory tusks, July 16, 1769–January 10, 1770, Liverpool slaving ships *Dobson* and *Fox*

	Value		Value
1. Textiles[1]		4. Beads	
780 yards roman	£36 8s	87 bunches round beads	£8 14s
449 yards chelloe	£22 10s	18 bunches pipe beads	£7 4s
20 handkerchiefs	£22	1 bead chest	8s
595 caps	£10 4s		**£16 6s (4.5%)**
50 pieces Guinea stuff	£10 4s		
190 yards nicanee	£10 2s	5. Arms	
128 yards cushtae	£8 8s	36 trade guns	£12
119 yards French stripe	£6 12s	Shot	£3 4s
42 yards chintz	£5 8s	Flints	18s
93 yards Turkey bar	£5 2s	1 bayonet musquet	10s
81 yards photae	£5 2s		**£16 12s (4.6%)**
50 yards baft	£3 2s		
13 brawls	£2 18s		
45 hats	£2 6s	6. Gunpowder	
5 blue jackets	£1 16s	129 kegs gunpowder	£22 14s
2 dressing gowns	£1 14s		**£22 14s (6.3%)**
19 yards calico	£1 14s		
6 India mats	6s		
4 yards French patch	4s		
	£155 16s		
	(43.0%)		
2. Bar iron		7. Liquor	
220 Iron bars	£41 6s	236 gallons brandy	£21 12s
	£41 6s		**£21 12s (6.0%)**
	(11.4%)		
3. Hardware		8. Horns and salt	
1,154 copper rods	£54 4s	55 horns	£1 14s
320 manillas	£14 10s	132 coppers' salt	£1 4s
33 pewter flagons	£5 12s		**£2 18s (0.8%)**
522 knives	£4		
39 tankards	£3	Totals	
82 lead bars	£2 4s	Trading goods valued **£362 8s**	
15 basins	£1 14s	for the sale of 58 tusks and	
	£85 4s	555 scrivilloes (average **11.8s/piece**)	
	(23.5%)		

[1]Two-thirds Manchester goods, one-third India cottons.

Sources: Trading Invoices and Accounts, *Dobson* and *Fox*, 1766, 1771, Davenport Papers, MMM; *Dobson* Calabar account, Hasell MS, Dalemain House, Cumbria.

gone out, you are desired to give as much as them Let the price be
what it will, but be well assured that they give more than you do before you rise the prices; you must endeavour by all means to get the
traders to go into the Country for you and particular to the Country of Orrop, w[h]ere you may send 6 or 8000 Coppers divided
amoungst the different Traders minding to procure the best pawns
that are to be had, by which means you will insure your Debts.[59]

Davenport had calculated the Old Calabar value of his goods in coppers, and
he confirms that Efik traders—the "Dukes," certainly Duke Ephraim, and including either Esien Duke, Coffee Duke, and/or Antera Duke—would
credit captains with pawns, human collateral, as receipts for trading goods to
be bartered for ivory. He also identifies the "Country of Orrop" as an ivory
supply center. We discuss this Efik trading network—east toward Ododop—
in chapter 4, but here we briefly will mention Old Calabar's links with the
Cameroon grasslands.

Ivory Supplies in the Bight of Biafra

No contemporary of Antera Duke identified Old Calabar's large ivory trade.
Captain John Adams, reflecting upon his experience in the 1790s, wrote that
ivory is purchased "more abundantly in some places than in others." He
noted that there were large stocks, not surprisingly, along the Ivory Coast,
but few tusks sold from villages along the western Gold Coast. From "Accra
to Bonny the trade is again extensive," wrote Adams, "particularly at Popo
and Benin." Passing over the Cross River region, Adams then remarked, "Camaroons is celebrated for its ivory, which is of a very superior quality, being less
porous, and more free from flaws than that which is obtained at the former
places. A very considerable quantity is procured on the coast of Angola, particularly at Ambrize, Loango, and Majumba." Mayumba, in particular, had
ivory "of a superior quality."[60] Even slaving surgeon Elliot Arthy, writing in
1804 after he returned to England from Old Calabar, considered ivory "a
general product of Africa," as it "appears by its abundance at most parts of the
western coast." He spotlighted only Old Calabar's monopoly of the palm oil
market.[61]

Since writers placed significant ivory sources in the Cameroon region
rather than at Old Calabar, Antera Duke and his associates traded either with
the Duala or with their ivory suppliers. We know that the greater Cameroon
region, a new ivory frontier in the Atlantic world, still had large stocks beyond Antera Duke's lifetime. Captain Crow's memoirs, edited in the 1820s,

referred to "immense herds" of elephants at Cameroon.[62] British naval officer Edward Bold, in his 1822 African pilot, located a supply center 200 miles
southeast from Cameroon, in "an immense tract of desert with a contiguous
morass, where the elephants came in droves to quench their thirst."[63] In 1847
missionary Hope Waddell, based in Duke Town, learned that "[i]vory does
not come our way, but goes all to Camaroons, the next port south."[64] Here
he refers to how Efik and Duala competed to buy ivory from dealers toward
the Cameroon grasslands. Given that, previously, Antera Duke and other Efik
did not canoe to or beyond the Wouri estuary, intermediaries must have
boated and walked several hundred miles east to trade with grasslands brokers.

In the second half of the eighteenth century the Cross River demarcated
ivory zones in the Bight of Biafra. Our large sample of Liverpool ivory imports, 1750–1808, reveals that shipments from Old Calabar, Cameroon, and
Gabon were eight times larger than those from Bonny and New Calabar.
Though the Efik brokered the greatest volume of ivory, individual slaving
ship captains purchased, on average, thirty to forty more tusks per consign-
ment from Duala dealers at Cameroon. New Calabar, an ivory center in the
1600s, shipped fewer ivory pieces per ship than did Bonny. In total, 350 tons
of Biafran ivory arrived in Liverpool (table 3.3), one-half of Merseyside's aggregate ivory imports. If Bristol and London captains loaded similar numbers
of tusks per ship, we estimate that English imports from the Bight totaled
1,000 tons, 20 percent of the ivory trade.[65]

While Old Calabar merchants increased their ivory trades after 1750, those
from Bonny and New Calabar began to specialize in slaving. Bonny had
matched Old Calabar's slave exports by the 1730s and then exceeded them in
all but one year from 1748 to 1775. During these decades merchants at Bonny
exported twice as many slaves as did Efik traders. At the outbreak of the
American Revolutionary War in 1775 they tripled Old Calabar's annual total
of 2,000 slave exports. We have not identified any ship at Bonny or New Calabar, during Antera Duke's lifetime, whose captain loaded animal or agricultural products without also embarking large numbers of enslaved Africans. In
the late 1780s former slaving surgeon Alexander Falconbridge commented
that Bonny has "little Trade but Slaves, and some Ivory." To sustain their large-
scale slave trades, Bonny's merchants imported a "great Quantity of Yams"
from Andoni to the east and "Creek" (Okrika) to the north.[66] In the three
years before the abolition of the British slave trade, 75,000 enslaved Africans
arrived in the British West Indies, and forty to fifty tons of ivory entered English customshouses. Whereas merchants at Bonny supplied 20 percent of
the late British slave trade, African merchants in the Cross River region supplied 20 percent of all British ivory imports. Bonny and nearby New Calabar began developing as specialist slaving ports during the 1750s through

TABLE 3.3. Ivory exported on British ships from the Bight of Biafra, 1750–1808

Trading location	Estimated ivory exports (tons)	Sample voyages[1]	Ships loading ivory	Estimated ivory tusks and pieces	Average shipment (tusks)
Old Calabar	196.7	194	181	33,895	220.1
Cameroon	68.2	62	58	11,755	250.1
Bonny	64.9	378	323	11,185	36.3
Gabon	15.3	21	18	2,641	155.4
New Calabar	5.5	62	48	953	22.2
Totals	350.6	717	628	60,429	84.3

[1]Voyages with identified African places of trade and whose cargoes are recorded in British Colonial Office shipping lists and/or Lancashire newspapers. The sample of 717 voyages includes 89 British slaving ships in the Bight of Biafra that did not load ivory.

1770s as Old Calabar businessmen began diversifying exports—not only in ivory but also in palm oil, redwood, and pepper.

Palm Oil, Redwood, and Pepper

No African merchants in the Bight of Biafra challenged Old Calabar palm oil brokers during the initial years of the transatlantic palm oil trade. In the decade before the American Revolution, Cross River merchants and those in the Niger Delta began to increase palm oil production for overseas export.[67] From 1764 some palm oil arrived in English customshouses every year, and 25,400 gallons[68] entered ports from 1764 to 1775—an average of 2,120 gallons per year.[69] The prewar oil trade peaked in 1775, when captains unloaded 7,380 gallons.[70] The first significant palm oil shipment to England arrived in 1772, when the slaver *Sportsman*, named after an English racehorse, entered Liverpool from Old Calabar and Grenada with forty casks of oil (3,360 gallons)—a speculative gamble that probably paid off. Of the fifty-seven ships returning to Liverpool with palm oil that year, thirty-nine loaded at Old Calabar, eleven at Bonny, four on the Sierra Leone/Windward Coast, two at Porto Novo (Benin), and one at New Calabar. By volume, in 1772–1775 Liverpool and Old Calabar controlled 80 to 90 percent of the Anglo-African palm oil trade.

Old Calabar maintained its 80 to 90 percent share of the palm oil trade, extending its exports from 14,000 gallons per year in 1783 to 56,000 gallons in 1792 and then to 80,000 to 100,000 gallons by abolition. Totals rose rapidly after the last British slaving vessel departed Old Calabar in mid-1808: in

1815 Liverpool warehouses received 473,000 gallons of palm oil,[71] mostly from the Cross River region. Between 1783 and 1808, from a sample of 115 Liverpool ships trading at Old Calabar, 97 carried oil back to England, with average loads of 5,640 gallons. By contrast, 68 of a sample of 234 Liverpool slaving vessels at Bonny loaded palm oil, in average consignments of 617 gallons. Old Calabar (86.6 percent market share) was by far the most important oil center in Africa, followed distantly by Bonny (6.6 percent), and the Bight of Biafra supplied 97 percent of all palm oil entering England in 1783–1808.[72]

In the period between the Seven Years' War and the outbreak of the American Revolutionary War, 1764–1775, redwood remained a minor commodity shipped from the Bight of Biafra posts compared with major dye exports from Gabon and northern Angola. Gazettes record only two unspecified "wood" shipments (in 1764 and 1765) from Bonny and Old Calabar, compared with substantial redwood imports farther south. Between November 1775 and March 1777, for example, five nonslaving ships arrived in Liverpool from "Angola": the *Liverpool*, with 400 tons of redwood; the *Jamaica* (with 420 tons); the *Fisher* (250 tons); the *Greenwood* (400 tons); and the *Sparling* (260 tons). Redwood's low value to bulk ratio required captains to load hundreds of tons to trade profitably. Merchant William Davenport did not instruct his Calabar-bound captains to trade for dyewoods; on one of his Cameroon slave and ivory ventures, though, he encouraged his captain to test Gabon's plentiful and moderately priced barwood market.[73] Bristol's redwood trade, prominent earlier in the century, declined to only 38 tons imported from 1771 to 1778, most probably arriving in 1775 on the slavers *Jason* and *King George* from Angola and Jamaica.[74]

After a lag in redwood shipments from Old Calabar through the 1790s, loads increased during the final seven years of the British slave trade. From 1801 to 1808, sources record African produce cargoes for thirty-four Liverpool ships that traded at Old Calabar. Thirty-two of these carried, in total, 1,500 tons of the dyewood. Three nonslavers transported 450 tons in the space that slaving ship captains reserved for African captives. Renewed British demand for redwood prompted Efik merchant Jemmy Henshaw to specialize in the business. As he wrote to Liverpool captain James Phillips in July 1803, "now I be trade for red-wood, and every stock you may want I sell."[75] Demand from British dyers pushed up the price of redwood, encouraging more Cross River merchants to broker billets of *Baphia nitida* and *Pterocarpus tinctorius*. Certainly there were still plentiful supplies of the wood —Captain John Adams remarked, recalling his trading experience in the 1790s, "Barwood grows, in great abundance, in the country surrounding

Old Calabar." By 1847, though, missionary Hope Waddell commented:"Red-wood was formerly largely exported [from Old Calabar], but cannot now be easily obtained."[76]

While redwood had featured early in Old Calabar's trade, Cross River merchants began regularly selling pepper for European markets, not just for shipboard consumption, after the American Revolution.[77] The shipping sources we have examined first place a pepper cargo from Old Calabar in 1767, when the *Nelly and Nancy* arrived in Liverpool in April with two bar-rels (392 pounds) of "Guinea pepper."[78] Additional pepper cargoes departed Calabar in 1774 and 1779, and then from 1783 to 1808 fifty-three Liverpool slaving ships at Old Calabar loaded 250 tons of the cultivars. As at Bonny, the pepper bought from Old Calabar would have been spicy cayenne (red) pep-per (*Capsicum annuum*), not the similar malagueta pepper (*Capsicum frutescens*) that thrived along the Windward Coast.[79] As newspaper adverts confirm, Cross River dealers sold "pepper" (29 instances), "Guinea pepper" (16), "long pepper" (8), and "long Guinea pepper" (2). The advertisements do not iden-tify these grains as malagueta pepper, "grains of paradise," or "Guinea grain," as they do for cargoes from Upper Guinea. In 1780 William Davenport in-formed Captain Begg that he sold his "long pepper," pods about two to four inches in length.[80]

Old Calabar's Produce Trade during the Period of Antera Duke's Diary

The growing diversification and size of Old Calabar's eighteenth-century produce trade helps us place Antera Duke's diary years in historic context. Antera started his diary—or, more properly, opened a new bound folio[81]—on January 18, 1785, just as Cross River merchants began to recoup incomes from seven years of recession during the American War of Independence. Since the few British captains who arrived at Old Calabar during the war demanded large quantities of ivory and palm oil, Antera and other Efik traders would have worked to increase supplies by strengthening networks with a range of ivory dealers and Ekrikok palm oil brokers.[82] Ibibio house-holds also would have had to increase their production of palm oil to meet the rising demand. Because there is no tradition in this area of planting oil palms, the increase most likely came from harvesting the fruits of wild trees that had not previously been exploited for domestic consumption. To supply the sharply expanded palm oil trade after British abolition in 1807–1808, Ibibio households must have greatly increased their labors to harvest fruits even more distant from homestead, extract the oil, and carry the heavy oil to waterside depots. Such efforts only can be explained by these communities' demand for the trade goods received in return.

During the period of Antera Duke's diary, almost all ship captains who purchased slaves at Old Calabar also loaded ivory, most bought palm oil and pepper, and some also loaded tons of redwood. Though Antera does not record produce cargoes,[83] thirty-one of the thirty-two Liverpool captains he mentioned, 1785–1788, embarked 50 tons of ivory—an estimated 7,832 pieces (245 per ship). Of the thirty-one ships taking ivory, twenty-five carried at least 100 tusks, and ten captains purchased at least 300. Twenty-one captains loaded, in total, 69,000 gallons of palm oil, seventeen transported 58 tons of pepper, and nine masters stored 97 tons of redwood. Six Liverpool slaving commanders purchased all four commodities: ivory, palm oil, pepper, and redwood. Only the slaver *Hannah* departed Old Calabar without African produce—other than the yams, firewood, and water for the Middle Passage that all ships loaded (table 3.4). In addition, we know that Captain Rogers of the Bristol slaving ship *Pearl*, referenced by Antera Duke in October 1787, purchased about 1.5 tons of ivory, twenty-eight to thirty puncheons (2,352–2,520 gallons) of palm oil, and 5 to 7 tons of redwood.[84]

To Antera Duke and other Efik merchants, the importance of diversifying exports heightened when overseas demand shrank for slaves, as during the American Revolutionary War. In the June 1780 letter cited at the beginning of this chapter, three Efik merchants, writing on behalf of the "Old Callabar Country Country [Countries]," stated that only Captain Begg had arrived in the past twenty-four months. They knew that once war in the Caribbean ended, captains would "have way for Sell Slaves." After his 1780 voyage in the *William*, Captain William Begg returned to Old Calabar, in 1781, via the Windward Coast, and docked at Liverpool with 2,300 ivory tusks (weighing twelve tons), 4,130 gallons of palm oil, one ton of redwood, and eight slaves to be reexported to the West Indies. In 1781 three Liverpool ships chanced wartime risks by clearing for Old Calabar; in 1782 one Liverpool and two Bristol slavers sailed to Old Calabar. Prewar trading levels did not resume until October 1783–March 1784, when six to eight European ships (all British) rode at anchor in the Calabar River. Such a sudden drop in slaving ships at Old Calabar, as occurred in 1778–1782, would next confront Efik merchants in 1808.

The Efik needed to offer a greater range of commodities to overseas buyers because, in contrast to Bonny's merchants, they were able neither to expand their annual slave exports beyond 5,000 people nor to sell healthier individuals. In the key 1750s–1780s period, not only did slaving ships' loading

TABLE 3.4. Liverpool ship captains' purchases at Old Calabar, 1785–1788 (during the period of Antera Duke's diary)

Slaving vessel[1]	Enslaved Africans[2]	Ivory (lbs.)[3]	Palm oil (gallons)	Pepper (lbs.)	Redwood (lbs.)
Liverpool Hero	513	[3,168]	1,596	2,400	0
Perseverance	[327]	[2,592]	2,770	11,592	8,960
Lion	[409]	[6,149]	16	0	0
Edwards	430	[4,291]	3,190	9,856	0
Gascoyne	639	5,600	5,877	28,336	0
Fair American	395	[4,018]	0	0	0
Essex	284	1,000	0	0	0
William	325	[4,219]	0	0	0
President	484	[5,746]	0	600	0
Tarleton	440	[1,512]	4,915	9,800	17,920
Fanny	250	[792]	0	0	0
Quixote	383	7,840	43	1,200	0
Highfield	381	[6,048]	0	0	672
Ellis	[429]	[8,453]	2,477	0	0
Rodney	[494]	[5,587]	924	0	0
Preston	320	1,257	420	1,960	0
Liverpool Hero and William [4]	560 328	[4,306]	3,654	4,312	0
Hannah	420	0	0	0	0
Will	300	2,240	1,259	6,160	0
Tarleton	377	[648]	9,600	11,760	112,000
Mary	280	[806]	0	1,176	22,400
Hudibras	420	[4,637]	2,436	17,640	4,480
Renown	330	[7,517]	3,897	2,800	13,440
Iris	[549]	[1,397]	5,964	0	0
President	[390]	[1,627]	3,024	4,312	17,920
Banastre	210	[1,368]	0	0	0
Three Brothers	330	2,665	4,198	0	0
Ned	350	6,720	4,198	0	20,160
Langdale	[405]	1,800	0	0	0
Gascoyne	[651]	[5,026]	6,804	13,552	0
Will	280	[2,779]	2,267	2,464	0
Totals	12,683	111,808 (49.9 tons)	69,529 (286.8 tons)	129,920 (58.0 tons)	217,952 (97.3 tons)
Ships loading	32/32	31/32	21/32	17/32	9/32

Column 1 organized by the first instance Antera Duke references the ship's captain (see table 2.3).

[1] Table includes 32 Liverpool slaving ships at Old Calabar, recorded by Antera Duke.

[2] Antera Duke records numbers of enslaved Africans embarked on some vessels; brackets record estimated numbers, based on American import data and Middle Passage mortality loss estimates of 23%.

[3] Ivory totals in brackets are recorded as "elephants' teeth" and converted to a weight measurement based on 14.4 lbs./ivory piece.

[4] After disembarking slaves, the William shipwrecked at or near Dominica, and the captain transshipped his produce on the Liverpool Hero. The Manchester Mercury grouped together the two ships' ivory, pepper, palm oil (Manchester Mercury, Dec. 18, 1787).

rates increase at Bonny, but merchants' opinions also improved as to the
"quality" of enslaved Africans shipped from there. In a letter from approximately 1762, a Liverpool merchant remarked how a captain "sold Last Voyage at Barbadoes with Messrs Wood & Simmons the best Bonny or Bite car-
goe of Negroes Imported for many Years by the Factors own Account."[85] In
June 1784, West Indian agents told merchant William Davenport that slaves
would be in demand in St. Vincent from September to December, "and
should any Vessels arrive here about that time from the Windward Coast,
Gold Coast, or Bonny they cannot fail of coming to a good Market."[86] The
new West Indian preference for slaves from Bonny provides a proxy for measuring health, and indeed the proportion of slaves who died on the Middle
Passage from Bonny declined from 25 to 40 percent before 1760 to about 15
percent.[87] Outbreaks of epidemic mortality skew data from the later Bonny
slaving ships, which, in general, lost 10 to 12 percent of their human cargo
during the two- to four-month journey to the Americas, levels similar to
those from nearby New Calabar.

Changing opinions as to the health of human cargoes from Bonny contrast with continued high mortality of "Calabar slaves." When in 1762 one
Liverpool merchant had identified the "best Bonny cargo... imported for
many years," another Merseyside firm reminded their captain that Old Calabar was "Remarkable for great Mortality in Slaves."[88] In the period 1750–
1807, 20 to 25 percent of slaves died on the Middle Passage from Old Calabar, and that figure varied little year by year.[89] Old Calabar also had the worst
rainy season health conditions in any African Atlantic market, almost a third
of all enslaved Africans embarked from June to December later dying on the
Middle Passage.[90] James Jones, the largest Bristol slaving merchant in the
1780s and 1790s, fitted out half of his ships for Bonny or New Calabar. "As
to Old Callabar and the Camaroons," he stated in 1788, "I have always declined sending to those two Rivers, as they are Sickly, and the Slaves inferior
to any other, very Weakly and liable to great Mortality."[91] In his diary, Antera Duke records slave exports for twenty-seven British vessels. There are
corresponding slave import totals for twenty-five of these ships. Of 9,072
Africans embarked at Old Calabar, at least 2,077 individuals died on the
Middle Passage, a mortality loss of 23 percent.

Conclusion

To Efik merchants like Antera Duke, unable to sell as many healthy slaves
as those African merchants at Bonny or New Calabar, it was vital to import
animal and agricultural commodities to offer European captains options.

Fostering long-distance links with ivory suppliers was a strategic decision made by Efik during Antera Duke's lifetime, likely in the mid-1700s when Cameroon's ivory and slave trades expanded. By the last quarter of the eighteenth century, Old Calabar brokers sold ivory, palm oil, pepper, and redwood in quantities sufficiently large to enable captains to load craft with cargoes other than enslaved Africans. Whereas small brigs like the *William* traded for palm oil in 1780 and 1781, in 1803 Liverpool merchants outfitted for Old Calabar the three-masted produce ships *John and Henry* (264 tons) and *Mary Ann* (276 tons), which returned to Liverpool with combined cargoes of 27,200 gallons of palm oil and 350 tons of redwood. Located just forty miles west of the Cross River estuary, the market at Bonny could not support a produce-only export trade.

By the time of Antera Duke's diary, merchants knew that the Cross River separated the Bight of Biafra into two commercial zones: to the west, Bonny and New Calabar (slaves and yams); to the east, Old Calabar and Cameroon (slaves, ivory, palm oil, redwood, pepper, and yams). Importantly, understanding the history of Old Calabar's ivory trade helps to solve a conundrum in Atlantic history: given the great Middle Passage mortality risk and associated American planters' "dislike" of slaves shipped from Old Calabar, why would British merchants outfit vessels to the Cross River region? Planters expressed their dislike of "Calabar slaves" by offering lower prices for Africans from this outlet in the Bight of Biafra. Nonetheless, the sustained demand for enslaved laborers gave merchant William Davenport of Liverpool confidence that his captains could sell any cargo of slaves from Old Calabar.[92] Significantly, Davenport's captains had the option to also purchase ivory and agricultural commodities. Without these opportunities to diversify commodities one wonders whether Davenport would have risked ventures to the Cross River, known for high slave mortality. Thus a captain like John Potter of the *Dobson/Fox* venture in 1769–1770 purchased ivory as well as slaves on most days of his six-month trade at Old Calabar.

Sales of agricultural and animal produce provided significant income to Efik traders during Antera Duke's lifetime. As is well known, Old Calabar became the preeminent palm oil export center from the late eighteenth century through to the 1830s. In chapter 3 we have located its nascent oil trade in the 1760s and 1770s, demonstrating that shipments steadily increased before British slave trade abolition in 1807–1808. Graduated increases suggest that each year Ibibio farmers west of the Cross River harvested the fruits of more and more wild oil palm trees, the largest stimulus occurring during the American Revolutionary War when African merchants realized that their reliance on European slaving merchants—many of whom refused to trade in 1778–1782, reduced regional wealth. Similarly, pepper shipments from

Calabar increased after the ending of the American war. Old Calabar's red-wood and ivory trades, though, date from the seventeenth century and first contact with European captains. The ability of Efik traders to maintain stocks of dyewood and ivory suggest that, when local supplies dwindled, they sought suppliers from afar. By the period of Antera Duke's diary, most captains purchased slaves and produce, and 10 to 15 percent of Efik incomes from overseas trade came from sales of ivory, redwood, pepper, and palm oil.

By diversifying prior to 1807–1808, Efik merchants withstood better than their rivals in the eastern Niger Delta the shock of the abolition of the British slave trade. Historians have debated whether African communities, linked to the Atlantic world via the slave trade, faced a "crisis of adaptation" after the abolition of overseas slave exports. Regarding the Bight of Biafra, other than palm oil, there is little discussion of ivory, dyewood, or spice trades bridging the period of abolition.[93] British abolition would have led to a much greater drop in export revenues from Bonny than Old Calabar; efforts to maintain overseas slave trades, correspondingly, must have been greater at Bonny. All African merchants in the Bight would have lost significant earnings in the generation after 1807–1808. At Old Calabar, comey paid to the fifty Efik slaving merchants during Antera Duke's diary years—the peak period of the export slave trade—totaled £1,800 to £2,000. During Old Calabar's palm oil years, comey increased from £250 in the early 1820s to perhaps only £500 to £625 by the 1850s.[94] Comey and other trade earnings, though, would have been much less if Efik merchants had not begun to seek out new commodity suppliers in the Cross River region.

CHAPTER FOUR

Old Calabar's Trading Networks

Efik merchants like Antera Duke were middlemen acting between European ship captains calling at Old Calabar and African traders farther inland. Although they drew upon a network of land and water routes across the Cross River basin and adjacent regions, Old Calabar traders rarely ventured beyond a ring of markets that lay within forty or fifty miles of their hometown, and they never sailed their canoes in the open Atlantic. Many other African communities supplied the slaves, foodstuffs, and other commodities that Old Calabar exported overseas, and the return flow of trading goods from overseas also passed through a vast commercial network covering some 30,000 square miles. By the mid-1780s the trading links that Efik merchants operated enabled Antera Duke, Duke Ephraim, Egbo Young Ofiong, and others to broker annually as many as 5,000 export slaves, 500,000 yams, twenty-five tons of ivory and redwood, and 2,000 barrels of palm oil.

The network of markets, traders, and economic interests that tied Old Calabar to the expanding Atlantic economy had much in common with trading networks elsewhere in West Africa, but there was a notable difference from some of them. Unlike the powerful new kingdoms of Asante and Dahomey that dominated the trade of the Gold Coast and Slave Coast in the eighteenth century, Old Calabar was no more than a city-state, and a very decentralized one at that, as were the neighboring coastal trading communities of the Niger Delta, Bonny and New Calabar, and the Duala villages at the Cameroon River estuary. Efik merchants' inland partners also remained largely free of centralized political forces, even as the trading networks integrated the region economically and linked into the larger Atlantic economy. Small-scale kinship-based political organization continued to be the norm among the inland Igbo- and Efik-speaking communities[1] and other smaller groups.

Political decentralization helped keep Old Calabar free of the large-scale warfare in other parts of Africa that provided so many captives to the Atlantic slave trade. Antera Duke's diary mentions only one instance of his people and other Efik obtaining slaves through raids (entry for January 30, 1785).[2] But an English visitor in 1766, Isaac Parker, testified that he accompanied Efik merchant Dick Ebro (Ebrow, Ebrero) on two marauding expeditions twenty to thirty miles "up river," launching nighttime raids on local villages. The first Efik raid captured forty-five men, women, and children; on the second, "higher up the river... we were gone eight or nine days plundering of other villages; we got much the same as we did the first."[3] Because so many diary entries document the peaceful purchase of slaves at regular markets, it is hard to know whether the situation in the 1780s represented a recent maturing of the trade or if the earlier accounts of Efik raids represented exceptional captive taking to settle particular disputes. During the diary years there were certainly frequent disputes and skirmishes with neighbors, usually over trade or seizing market women, but Antera does not link these conflicts to his slave trades.[4]

In this chapter we examine evidence from Antera Duke's diary and European visitors to analyze Old Calabar's trading expeditions in the Cross River region. We identify and highlight three main commercial networks. The first, to the Middle Cross River, led to the densely populated Igbo and Ibibio communities west of the river. A second pathway linked Old Calabar to the Upper Cross River and Cameroon grasslands, via both water and overland routes. Old Calabar's third trading connection radiated to the lands east of the Lower Cross River to the western slopes of Mount Cameroon (table 4.1, map 4.1). All three routes required Efik to supply local and foreign-produced goods demanded by many African trading partners residing in independent villages. Because our diarist records no information on slaves' homelands or ethnicities, though, to understand the origin of "country slaves," the term used by coastal slave traders, we turn to evidence from nineteenth-century explorers' accounts, missionary records, and "Calabar slaves" themselves—those individuals captured by British antislaving patrols in the 1820s and interviewed by British officials in Sierra Leone.

TABLE 4.1. Hinterland peoples and places mentioned in Antera Duke's diary (grouped by trade region)

Trade region	Diary name	Modern name	Diary references
Middle Cross River	Egbo Sherry	Ibibio	Nov? 4, 11, 1785; Jan. 29, June 10, Oct. 14, 1786; Dec. 9, 1786; Oct. 25, 1787
Middle Cross River	Curock (River)	Ekrikok (Mbiabo Efik)	Oct. 14, 15 & 19, 1786
	[Tom] Curock	Ikot Offiong	Apr. 21, Nov.? 3, 5, 1785
	old Curock Landing; old Curock Town; Curock town	Itu	Nov.? 5, 7, 10, 1785
Middle Cross River	Enyong; Enyang; the Enyong Creek; Enyong town	Enyong	Aug.? 7, Oct,? 8, Nov.? 7, 1785; Apr. 20, 1786
Upper Cross River	Boostam	Umon	Feb. 14, July? 21, Nov.? 7, 10, 1785; Jan. 22–23, Dec. 23, 1786; Feb. 17, Dec. 4, 1787
Upper Cross River	Orroup	Ododop	Apr. 21, July? 2, 29, Dec. 23, 1785; Dec. 11, 1787; Jan. 3, 9, 1788
Lower Cross River	Commrown; Comrown	Cameroons (Efut)	Mar. 7, Nov.? 3, 1785; Feb. 11, 1786; Sept. 20, 1787
Lower Cross River	aqua Bakassey, aqua Bakasy; aqua Bakassey Crik	Akwa Bakasi; Akwa Bakasi Creek	Jan. 1, Feb. 8, May, 1, 4, 1786; Jan. 31, Nov. 1, 1787

Middle Cross River Trading Network: Ikot Offiong, Itu, and Enyong Creek

In the early evening of November 3, 1785, toward the end of the rainy season when rivers and creeks were high, Antera Duke loaded goods into Egbo Young Antera's trading canoe, and at midnight their expedition set out for "Curock." By early morning the paddlers had descended the Calabar River to its confluence with the Cross River, a place the English had named Seven Fathoms Point. A rainstorm that afternoon may have slowed their progress up the Cross River, as they did not reach their destination until the morning of November 5, when the traders and crew had their first real meal in a day and a half. That day Antera Duke called on Tom Curock, and after coming ashore at Old Curock landing, he walked up to the house of the local

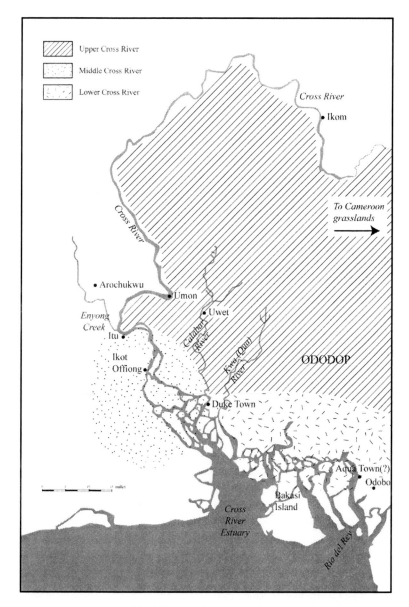

MAP 4.1. Old Calabar trading networks, ca. 1785–1788

chief, Andam Curcock, to whom according to custom he presented four brass rods and a case of brandy. Antera Duke's diary records little information about the trading at Curcock during the six days the Old Calabar traders were there in November 1785, other than the purchase of one slave from Andam. At 3:00 P.M. on November 10, the expedition set off for home.

Traveling all night, the Efik party arrived back at the Duke Town landing at about 9:00 A.M. on November 11.

Where were these "Curcock" locations? Scottish missionary Hope Waddell's journal and map from the 1840s make it possible to identify Tom Curcock's town as Ikot Offiong and Old Curcock as Itu, both settlements of the Mbiabo Efik on the west bank of the Cross River.[5] Ikot Offiong lies about thirty miles up the Cross River from Seven Fathoms Point, and Itu is another ten miles upstream. These locations dovetail with Antera Duke's entry: he arrived at Tom Curcock's about dawn and reached Old Curcock by early afternoon; Itu has a canoe beach from which one must walk uphill to the town. Antera's "Curcock" is his version of Ekrikok, and these Efik-speaking peoples shipped almost all the palm oil from "Old Calabar" during Antera Duke's lifetime and through the 1820s, as we saw in chapter 3. In November 1785 Antera and his party traveled to these Ekrikok villages, though, to purchase small numbers of slaves, not palm oil, which was not then in season.[6]

From Itu, Antera Duke and other Old Calabar Efik journeyed northwest up the Enyong Creek between lands that would have been dense with secondary forest and palm tree vegetation. The Enyong joins the Cross River at Itu (see map 4.1), and during his November 1785 visit Antera Duke canoed up the Enyong Creek to visit kinsman Potter Antera's mother. Not finding her there, he went to Enyong Town, and soon after he arrived, he received the gift of four copper rods and two yards of romal (Indian cloth) from Potter's father's family. Potter Antera earlier (August 7, 1785) traveled from Duke Town to Enyong to trade for slaves. Then, in October 1785, Antera sent Robert Enyong from Duke Town to trade at Enyong on his behalf. In spite of his relationship with Robert Enyong, conflict between Antera and the "Enyong people" could break out, as on the morning of April 20, 1786, near the Duke Town beach, when armed men seized one of Antera's canoes, two canoe boys, one of his sons, and a group of perhaps thirty threatened Antera with small muskets (they "Look for shoot me"). At 9:00 P.M. the Enyong "Let me hav canow & all my men Back," and the conflict was resolved.

During his November 1785 visit to Itu and Enyong Town, Antera does not mention the Aro, known to the Efik as "Inokun," though they traded with Mbiabo Efik and Enyong.[7] Fifteen miles—a two-day canoe journey up the Enyong Creek—from Itu is the town of Arochukwu, whose traders, the Aro, had established far-flung settlements and trading partners across much of Middle Cross region. Within much of the hinterland between the Niger and the Cross River the Aro had built up an exceptionally large trading sphere, but, in keeping with the decentralized forms of organization typical of the region, it was a loose federation of Aro commercial colonies. Different Aro clans constructed spheres of operations and forged alliances with prominent local patrons who provided protection and profited from the alliance. They also used the prestige of their religious oracle to boost their standing and invulnerability. At times the Aro deployed force or the threat of force to expand and defend their operations. Armed conflict and trade wars sometimes broke out among the Aro, but annual conclaves at Arochukwu helped moderate intra-Aro conflicts and expand the frontiers of pan-Aro dominance.[8]

Old Calabar was not the main outlet for the Aro, who had substantial connections through intermediaries with the frontier markets at the edge of the Niger Delta and with lower Niger River commercial networks. Those networks supplied more than twice as many slaves to Bonny as to Old Calabar. Although there is no way to date the development of the various components of the Aro trading connections with precision, the network of markets and large fairs they dominated was in place from the middle of the eighteenth century, if not earlier, because slave exports from Bonny doubled in the 1740s and doubled again in the 1760s.[9] By 1780 Efik merchants, well aware that rival merchants from Bonny had built up hinterland slave-supply lines, wrote a letter to Liverpool merchants to remind them that they "have Slaves Same a[s] Bonny or other place[s]."[10]

Antera Duke gives few details about the vast populations of Ibibio- and Igbo-speaking people west of the Cross River. When he references the Ibibio, "Egbosherry," to use Efik trade English, Antera usually discusses only their fishermen and canoes in the Cross River. In November 1785 en route to Itu, Antera encountered an early-rising Egbosherry fisherman with whom he swapped a drink of brandy for some freshly caught fish. During an Ekpe palaver arranged by Duke Ephraim, runners took forty copper rods to send to the Ibibio district; Ekpe operated west of the Cross River, but it is striking that Antera does not discuss the Aro traders of Arochukwu, the crucial intermediaries handling trade that flowed across the lands of the Igbo and Ibibio. Since a seasoned trader like Antera Duke could not have been ignorant of the vast inland trading networks of the Aro, his diary likely records what he personally experienced. The fact that Antera had no direct contact with the Aro underscores the system of distinct trading spheres within which the Efik operated. In the 1780s Efik merchants journeyed no farther northwest through Ibibio country than Enyong Town, perhaps Asang, located on the west bank of the Enyong Creek, halfway between Itu and Arochukwu.

From the vantage point of Old Calabar's overseas traders, during Antera Duke's lifetime the Middle Cross River trading network was principally a slave-trading network, supplying small lots of slaves to Efik middlemen who then brokered captives to European ship captains. During his visit to Ikot Offiong, Itu, and Enyong Town, Antera only hints at the great volume of trade (detailed in chapters 2 and 3), and at the complex relations of these frontier towns with their own inland trading areas. By the period of Antera's diary the Mbiabo Efik had begun to expand palm oil production and export, which they were able to do while continuing to sell slaves. They traded oil directly with ship captains, only small quantities purchased and stored by Efik at Old Calabar. After the abolition of the British slave trade (1807–1808) and Antera's death (ca. 1809), the Middle Cross palm oil trades expanded dramatically, sustaining incomes to Mbiabo Efik and Enyong merchants who supplied palm oil exports for a generation, until farmers opened new sources in the Niger River region and east of Old Calabar.

Upper Cross River Trading Network: Umon, Ododop, and the Cameroon Grasslands

While at Itu on November 7, 1785, Antera Duke had a discussion with Apandam and Egbo Young Antera about Boostam, and then three days later their "Boostam canow com Down with 5 slave and yams.""Boostam" can be identified with the Umon town that was situated on an island in the Upper Cross River, fifteen miles upstream from Itu. Other sources of the same era rendered the name as "Bosum," "Boson," or "Boatswain" (pronounced BOH-s'n). Umon commanded trade moving, up, down, and across the river, and besides trade with the Efik, Umon merchants had trading connections with the Aro to the west and with various groups farther upstream. Its key position enabled the island-town to prosper. In 1805 Efik trader Otto Ephraim Robin John, educated at Liverpool, reported "Eerick Boatswain" was "the richest and most powerful king in the neighbourhood of Calabar."[11] The Upper Cross River trading network extended thirty miles east to Ododop, and then an additional ten miles east to the edge of the Cameroon grasslands. Traders journeyed to these slave, yam, and ivory markets by canoeing up and portering between the Cross, Calabar, Qua (Kwa), and Ifiong rivers.

Umon was an entrepôt for yams, slaves, ivory, and perhaps canoes and was the farthest point up the Cross River that Efik merchants traveled during Antera Duke's lifetime and through the nineteenth century.[12] We learn that Antera's yam canoe returned from Boostam on February 14, 1785, and later that day he sold Captain Savage 1,000 yams, 10 yams for a copper rod. In January 1786 Egbo Young and Apandam returned from Umon with slaves and ivory. When on November 10, 1785, Antera and his party departed Itu for Duke Town, they traveled with three small canoes purchased within the week. These small canoes probably came from Mbiabo riverain communities; they might have been purchased at Umon, though that market sold large trading canoes manufactured upriver at Akunakuna.[13] The diary does not record that Antera went to Umon, and he does not name any Umon/Boostam traders—referring, on February 17, 1787, only to a "Boostam man." This diary entry concerns Efik merchant Long Dick Ephraim's Ekpe palaver with the unnamed Boostam individual, verifying that Ekpe had extended as far north as Umon.[14]

Perhaps to bypass Umon's dominance of access to the Upper Cross River, the Efik and their allies developed overland trade routes that ran northeast from Old Calabar through thinly populated, mountainous country to the headwaters of the Cross, and then toward the densely peopled Cameroon grasslands. In Antera Duke's day, ambitious merchants were staking out waterfront property to the east and northeast of Old Calabar as the larger trading networks in the region began to "open up" the Upper Cross River around Ikom to trade with the Atlantic coast. Aro traders from Arochukwu were also moving into the riverain area from the west, as were Agwa'aguna traders from the east. One Old Calabar route went up the Calabar River to Uwet and overland to a market near Ikom. A number of identifiable individual captives from the "Atam" (Nde Ekoi) cluster were brought overland or down the river to Old Calabar and other ports in the 1820s and 1830s.[15]

The longest of the overland trade routes ran east from Old Calabar around the southern end of the Kwa mountains, then north through the sparsely populated foothills of the Cameroon mountains, and on to the populous Cameroon grasslands. The diary mentions the first stop on this route, Ododop (Duke's "Orroup"), more often than any other place as a source of small numbers of slaves. In 1785, for example, four entries concern "Orroup." In April of that year Esien Duke returned to Duke Town with seven slaves from Orroup. Three months later Awa Ofiong, one of Antera's wives, returned with a dead slave from Orroup.[16] In July Hogan Abashey Antera and Archibong Duke's son departed for Orroup, Archibong's boy returning with slaves in late December. Slaves from Ododop likely carried ivory tusks, as the Cameroon grasslands supplied much of the ivory warehoused at Old Calabar. As one Liverpool firm wrote to its ship captain in 1781: "you must endeavour by all means to get the [Duke Town] traders to go to the Country for you and particular to the Country of Orrop." The captain was instructed to exchange most of his trading goods for ivory, though, not slaves.[17]

It is not known whether the trade via Ododop extended to the Cameroon grasslands in Antera Duke's time, but it did by the 1820s. As a result of raids by Fulani and other marauders mounted on horseback, large numbers of individuals from the grasslands were captured in the 1820s and 1830s and sold through Old Calabar. Several of these grasslands people were liberated by the British and resettled in Sierra Leone. They included Awazi (known as Harry Johnson in Sierra Leone) of Ndob, taken prisoner in about 1828, and Kamsi (alias John Thomas) of Bali, captured four years later. People learned to flee for their lives at the approach of the raiders, but other unscrupulous individuals enslaved many of these refugees, either keeping them for their own use or selling them to slave dealers. This happened twice to Mbape (alias James John) of Ngoala, who was a young man of eighteen years in the mid-1820s:

> When the Tipala came to his country and burnt all the towns so that people had to flee for safety in every direction. He himself fled to Mbara, where he was seized and made a slave. When the Tipala burnt the Mbara towns likewise, his master fled with him to Param, where he was again seized, and at once carried toward the sea, a journey of one month's constant walking before they arrived at Kalabar [Old Calabar], where he remained for three years [before being sold into the overseas slave trade].

A not dissimilar fate befell many others who fled the invading horsemen. Two Baba (Ndob) men fled in different directions from a Bamum invasion; one was eventually sold from Old Calabar, the other from the Cameroon estuary. They were reunited in Sierra Leone with thirty others of their people.[18]

In the 1850s, missionaries learned that Ododop was known as "a principal slave route in former times" and was still "much esteemed" for domestic slaves. The Reverend Hugh Goldie named the principal stopping places on the route as far as "Eyefen," eight and a half days from Old Calabar, which he said was the most distant point Efik traders visited. The Eyefen or Eafen can be identified with the Obang Ekoi south of the town of Mamfe. Three days beyond Eyefen, the route reached the Anyang, a branch of the Bantoid cluster of peoples north of Mamfe. The Anyang, in turn, had connections with what Goldie knew as Mbudukom or Mbudikom, the Efik name for the Cameroon grasslands around modern Bamenda.[19] A four-year-old grasslands girl, whose parents had been captured in a Fulani raid, was "dashed" to the British consul in 1858 by an Old Calabar chief. She had been brought from the grasslands to the Anyang, to the Ododop ("Orroup"), and finally to Old Calabar, evidently along the same route described by Goldie.[20]

Whereas the Aro supplied slaves southwest to the Niger Delta and southeast to the Middle Cross trading network, hinterland merchants in Ododop and the Cameroon grasslands supplied slaves to Old Calabar and the Cameroon estuary. In July 1792 Bristol captain Hamnet Forsyth, anchored off Duke Town, mentioned these competing supply lines, telling his employer he "could not procure more Male Slaves being so scarce, oweing to marching them through the Country for the Camaroons where they Receive a greater price for them."[21] Duala merchants on the banks of the Cameroon estuary were established ivory traders, and in the 1760s and 1770s they began selling increasing numbers of slaves to European ship captains. They encroached upon Efik merchants' grasslands supply networks, and, as Captain Forsyth remarked, growing Duala market power may have altered the sex ratio of enslaved Africans marched overland to Old Calabar.

Lower Cross River Trading Network: Akwa Bakasi and "Little Cameroon"

Antera Duke sent emissaries to Umon and Ododop but made personal journeys to key settlements in the Efik-dominated Lower Cross River trading network. In February 1786, during the dry season, he undertook a multiday trip to "aqua Bakassey" and "Commrown," two regions in the Ekpe zone. At early morning on the eighth, Antera was in "aqua Bakassey Crik," and that afternoon he found Archibong Duke. The two canoed to "new Town" and back. Three days later, at "Coqua Town," Archibong Duke asked Antera "to walk up for Commrown with him so I Did." During this trip the two Efik, accompanied by canoemen and porters, passed "3 Little Commrown town" and arrived at "Big town." There follows a three-week gap in Antera's diary (possibly omissions by diary transcriber Arthur Wilkie), a gap in the diary similar to those following two other trips Antera made to "aqua Bakassey": in May 1786 (a two-week gap) and November 1787 (a monthlong gap).

Efik traded frequently with merchants from Akwa Bakasi who resided in villages on the Bakasi River and western shore of Bakasi peninsula, fifteen to thirty miles downriver from Old Calabar. During his February 1786 trip, Antera Duke stayed at New Town and Coqua (Aqua)[22] Town, settlements not to be confused with Old Calabar's New (Duke) Town or Qua (or Big Qua) Town, eight miles east of Calabar, on the Qua River. Archibong Duke and Antera put the Grand Ekpe (Idem Nyamkpe) costume in the New Town palaver house, and an Ekpe event was staged. Three months later, on May 1, Antera again visited New Town in Akwa Bakasi and then canoed to an Old Town in Bakasi, firing one cannon in the creek. At Old Town he found Coffee Duke, and he called on the local Ekpe lodge, dashing the Ekpe men a case of brandy and some rods. On the fourth, Antera departed the Akwa Bakasi beach at 10:00 A.M. and arrived at Jock Bakassey's town nine hours later. He carried Grand Ekpe to the local palaver house, using the power of Ekpe to collect a debt he was owed by Bakasi merchants. Bakasi also supplied Efik with canoes that were essential to Old Calabar's trade. While at the Duke Town beach on November 1, 1787, Antera Duke went "on bord Everry ship to Let the[m] know I will go to aqua Bakassey to Buy Canow."

Ephraim Aqua Bakassey was the most important of several Bakasi or nearby merchants who traded with Antera Duke and ship captains. He features six times in the diary, including an instance when Antera delivered slaves to a captain to redeem Ephraim Aqua's pawns. Ephraim Aqua traveled up to Duke Town, trips that usually concerned Ekpe matters.[23] When on October 31, 1787, Jimmy Henshaw paid dues to head an Ekpe grade, Ephraim Aqua received five copper rods from the distribution; he was the only Bakasi recipient. Antera references a Bakasi trader again in an Ekpe context, when on September 4, 1785, Jock Bakassey paddled to Duke Town beach carrying the Grand Ekpe costume. Antera also mentions traders Commrown Backsider Bakassey (June 14, 1785; July 2, 1785), Abashey Commrown Backsider (July 27, 1785), and Backsider Drek Comroun (January 27, 1788).[24] Commrown Backsider Bakassey was a Bakasi merchant who, we suggest, resided in a "Backsider town"[25] in "Cameroon" on the backside (to the east) of Akwa Bakasi, as did the other two "Backsider" merchants.

In Antera Duke's day, "Cameroon" designated the coastal area east from the Cross River to Rio del Rey and on to the Cameroon estuary (or Cameroon River).[26] Cameroon(s) came into English from *camarãoes* (shrimp), the name that early Portuguese explorers gave to the shrimp- and crayfish-rich creeks that flowed to the coast east of the Lower Cross River. Efut peoples inhabited oases in mangrove swamps and numerous creeks fed by Rio Del Rey, the border between modern-day Nigeria and Cameroon, demarcated in the 1880s. The Efut, once Bantu-speaking immigrants from farther east, had been incorporated into the Efik houses and had adopted the Efik language. Missionary Hugh Goldie noted that the Efut country was called "Little Cameroons," and that Old Calabar people bought slaves, canoes, and palm oil there.[27]

From the northern limits of Bakasi lands, Efik launched overland journeys east and southeast to Little Cameroon. On February 11, 1786, after Antera Duke and Archibong Duke passed the three Cameroon villages and arrived at "Big town," their hosts killed a goat and gifted an iron rod and two copper rods. Antera then engaged in a long discussion about Archibong's trade goods. Their trip east to Big town, we suggest, follows the same route taken on two dry-season journeys in 1877 and 1878 by the Efik who led the Reverend Alexander Ross to Efut country (Little Cameroons). That party's first stop, King Archibong II's Farm (to the north of the Akwa Bakasi Creek), suggests the family continuity of the Archibong Duke whom Antera met on the Akwa Bakasi Creek on February 8, 1786. After a long canoe trip and a forty-minute walk, the Ross party reached the large, walled Efut town of Odobo, which impressed the visitors with its grid of lamp-lighted streets. Ross reported that the district was a dependency of Duke Town and had many Calabar traders in residence.[28] These circumstances suggest that the "Big town" Antera walked to in 1786 may well have been Odobo, a town fifty miles east from the entrance to the Great Qua River, which in turn lies twenty miles downriver from Duke Town (see appendix B, map 4.2).

In the nineteenth century the eastern limit of Efik commercial operations ran from Mbudikom in the Cameroon grasslands south to Lundu, on the western slopes of Mount Cameroon. Missionary S. W. Koelle interviewed two Bafia men from the grasslands who, as teenagers in about 1831, had been captured by the Bamum in war. One was sold from the Cameroon estuary and the other from Old Calabar.[29] The Efik of Old Calabar purchased slaves from Lundu, perhaps via the Efut settlements Antera Duke visited in Bakasi. As one late nineteenth-century observer interpreted it: "The Calabars were rich in goods and wanted people; the Barundus [Lundu] had nothing but brothers and sisters, children and poor hungry slaves—and they wanted to become rich." Perhaps such motives were responsible for the kidnapping and sale from Old Calabar of a Lundu named Bira (alias George Bailey) about 1828.[30]

The accounts in Antera Duke's diary suggest he confined himself to the 30,000-square-mile commercial zone bounded by Umon on the Upper Cross River (northwest of Old Calabar), Akwa Bakasi near the Cross River estuary (southwest), Odobo in Little Cameroon (southeast), and Ododop, on the fringe of the Cameroon grasslands (northeast). As Antera Duke's November 1785 diary entries suggest, Old Calabar traders traveled in small groups to the towns and markets on the frontiers. At these locations the Old Calabar Efik were welcomed by their African trading partners, who, in turn, had contacts with merchants still farther away. Each trading community had its own sphere of operations and jealously guarded entry by outsiders. The diary gives no conclusive evidence that individual Efik specialized in regional markets. Thus Antera Duke traded at Itu and Akwa Bakasi, and Andam Nothing journeyed to the "Curcock River" and to Ododop.[31] Since our diarist references Ododop ("Orroup") more than any other regional market, one can assume that in the 1780s the Cameroon grasslands had become an important supply center to Old Calabar. While we know the grasslands supplied large quantities of ivory, our diarist does not give sufficient evidence to determine its ranking as a slaving region. To help rank the slave trades from Old Calabar's three principal trading networks, we must turn to later sources that identify slave ethnicities.

Ethnicities of Enslaved Africans
Sold from Old Calabar

Explorer Henry Nicholls provides the most detailed account of Old Calabar's regional supply centers written during Antera Duke's lifetime. "Most of the slaves Calabar people get," Nicholls learned in 1805, "are Eericock [Duke's "Curcock"], Tabac, Eericock Boatswain [Duke's "Boostam"], and Ebeo

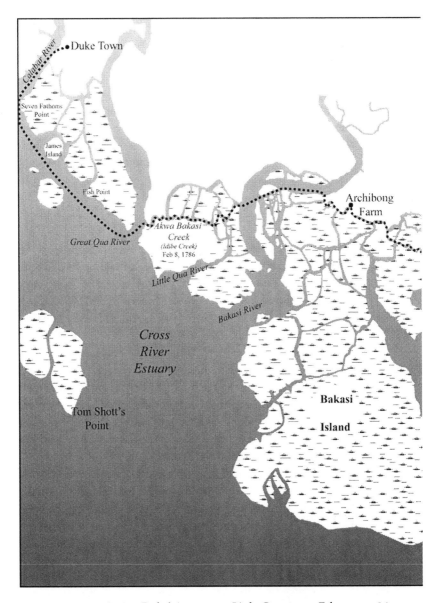

MAP 4.2. Antera Duke's journey to Little Cameroon, February 1786

[Igbo]; sometimes some Brassy slaves, and Cameroon slaves."[32] Four of these six places drew on the populations west of the Cross River. Nicholls's "Tabac" can be identified with the Adua, a branch of the Ibibio living north and south of the Oron Creek, which flows into the Lower Cross River. Generally considered a single people in the twentieth century, the Adua and

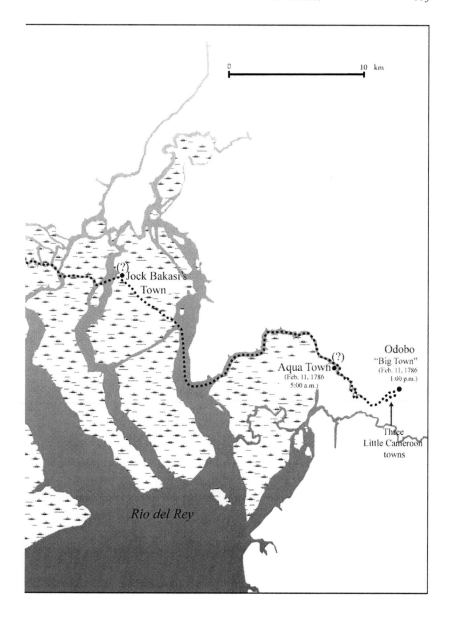

Oron were in a position to exploit their position along the Cross River and its western tributaries for trading purposes.[33] The identities of Nicholls's "Cameroon" and "Brassy" are less clear. Cameroon was either the Efut (Little Cameroon) area discussed earlier or the more distant Duala trading community on the Cameroon estuary. Brassy could refer to the distant trading community of Nembe Brass in the eastern Niger Delta but more likely refers to the Efut area. "Brass" or "Brassy" was a general term outsiders used to designate people from Efut, and oral sources support the existence of some slave trade from there.[34] Aside from the "Eboe," the names Nicholls lists are not ethnic or linguistic but simply the trading places where Efik merchants bought slaves. Though this is helpful in identifying Old Calabar's commercial partners, his list is of little use in identifying the many different ethnic identities of the slaves involved in these transactions. Nor does it reveal the relative proportion of slaves from different ethnic groups.

Additional evidence of the ethnic mix of peoples shipped through Old Calabar comes from the records of slave ships intercepted by British patrols in the 1820s. For a brief period British officials in Sierra Leone registered each liberated African by name and "country." These registers include ethnic identities from three, or perhaps four, Portuguese ships that traded at Old Calabar. The *Constantia, Conceição,* and *Defensora da Patria,* taken at Old Calabar in 1821–1822, all carried very high proportions of Igbo and "Calabar" (Efik-speaking), but the share of Igbo ranged from 15 percent to 60 percent of the total, and the proportion of Efik speakers ranged from 20 to 85 percent. The countries of the small number of others included one Hausa, two "Accoo" (Yoruba), and four Attam/Ahtop (Middle Cross River) (table 4.2).

The fourth Portuguese vessel, the *Esperença Felis,* though captured at Lagos in 1822, carried a mix of slaves that suggests an Old Calabar origin: 66 percent were recorded as Igbo, 27 percent "Moko," that is, Upper Cross River and Cameroon grasslands Africans, but only three were said to be Calabar, plus one Attam, one Yoruba, and one unidentifiable "Cumbally." The British captors rejected the Portuguese officers' claim that they had purchased the slaves at Molembo, a port south of the equator, where slaving was still legal, and had been blown off course to Lagos. Such alibis were often used by Portuguese who actually meant to trade in ports north of the equator, and, for their testimony to be true, there would have to have been a coastal trade (unknown from other sources) to Molembo from Old Calabar. In support of their charge that the vessel was illegally trading for slaves north of the equator, the British captors cited testimony from three "intelligent" Hausa speakers on board that they and all the other slaves had been loaded at Lagos the same day as the ship was seized. These witnesses and half the other slaves were lost when the British vessel carrying them sank on the way to Sierra Leone. This testimony also seems doubtful, because there is no record of a trade in slaves from the upper Cross River and Igbo country to Lagos. Given the composition of the slave cargo, it seems more likely that the slaves had been loaded at Old Calabar.[35]

Of the total 373 survivors from these four captured vessels from Old Cala-

TABLE 4.2. Origins of slaves on selected voyages from Old Calabar, 1821–1822

Ships	Date and place of capture		"Country" of origin of slaves			
	Date	Place	Igbo	"Calabar"	"Moko"	Other
Constantia	Apr. 9, 1821	Old Calabar	92	59		3
Conceição	Aug. 2, 1821	Old Calabar	8	46		
Defensora da Patria	April 1822	Old Calabar	60	16		5
Esperença Felis	April 7, 1822	Lagos	56	3	23	3
Totals			216	124	23	11

Sources: Great Britain, Public Record Office, Foreign Office, FO84/9, Woods to Bandinel, July 5, 1821, and FO84/15, Woods to Bandinel, Jan. 5, 1823, concerning the brigantine *Constantia* taken Apr. 9, 1821, the schooner *Conceição* taken Aug. 2, 1821, the sloop *Defensora da patria* taken in late April 1822, and the polucca *Esperença Felis*, taken on Apr. 7, 1822, at Lagos

bar, Igbo ("Heeboo") outnumbered Efik-speaking ("Calabar") by nearly two to one, a proportion that seems about right. However, it is improbable that only 9 percent of the slaves exported came from all the other places that served Old Calabar in the early 1820s and during Antera Duke's time. Indeed, the disturbances caused by the raids of the Fulani far to the north during the previous decade ought to have expanded the ethnic pool. Interviews by missionary Koelle of recaptives in Sierra Leone identified eleven individuals from this era who listed Old Calabar as the port from which they were sold, mostly from the grasslands of western Cameroon, and one was from north of the Benue River.[36]

A more critical look at the Sierra Leone lists reveals why the number of Calabar and Igbo identities was inflated. Recording the many languages and dialects of the recaptives was a daunting task that Sierra Leone officials soon abandoned altogether. The identities they recorded during the 1820s were not necessarily those individual Africans would have volunteered, but looser categories that were common among the growing liberated African population in Sierra Leone. The registrars must have assigned these identities on the basis of the languages understood by the Africans being liberated. Thus it is likely that individuals of other origins would have been assigned a "Heeboo" or "Calabar" identity if they had learned one of these trading languages before their capture or during the often lengthy period between their capture and their sale overseas.[37] Such language-based assignments of identity also would help explain the otherwise unlikely presence of Yoruba and Hausa speakers in the lists of those shipped from Old Calabar. Though an accurate count of places of origin is impossible, the slaves shipped from Old Calabar in this period may have been about 60 percent Igbo-speaking, 15 percent Efik-speaking, and 25 percent speakers of other languages. During Antera

Duke's later life and through the 1820s, then, the Middle Cross River was the largest source of slaves for export, followed by the Upper and Lower Cross trading networks, a ranking that is consistent with estimated population densities in the Cross River region.[38]

While nineteenth-century evidence thus expands knowledge of the possible origins of those who were enslaved beyond the scanty details in the diary, it stops short of providing an accurate list of particular ethnic groups and how their proportions changed over time. Still, it is clear that individuals were drawn from many different communities. Liverpool sailor Henry Schroeder, who traded off Duke Town in 1786, recalled that people from "fourteen different tribes or nations" were found among the first 150 slaves taken aboard their ship, but he does not name these peoples.[39] The evidence learned by explorer Henry Nicholls in 1805 and the few surviving individual accounts from the 1820s suggest how much detail is missing and how much, even before the captives began their ocean voyages, this diversity had begun to be simplified. Slaves were named for the market towns from which they came in the vicinity of Old Calabar, and by the time they reached the Americas they were often rebranded with the name of the port from which they had sailed.

Conclusion

Evidence from Antera Duke's diary and from other precolonial accounts indicates that Old Calabar merchants had connections to a range of African trading systems. For Old Calabar traders such diversity was advantageous, providing alternate sources of supply and encouraging competition among their brokers, even though, as with their European partners, much of the trade passed through a limited number of hands. In such a decentralized system disputes might shut down one or more branches of the trading system. In Antera Duke's day, trade on the Cross River frontier ports appears to have been mostly orderly and peaceful, but trade disputes of long or short duration were a feature of these competitive systems, as the various autonomous partners maneuvered to maintain or expand their positions. In the 1760s and 1770s there had been raids by Old Calabar traders against local villages along the Cross River, and in the 1840s and 1850s Itu acquired a reputation for using violence to defend its trading positions and to collect tolls from Efik traders en route to Umon. In 1848 Creek Town sent a fleet of sixty war canoes to intimidate the Umon chiefs into granting better trading terms.[40]

Violence and the threat of violence were part of the system, but the many separate partners working in the trading system held together because of the powerful mutual interest in its material rewards and the frequent personal visits and fellowship that the diary records. More difficult disagreements were resolved through the Ekpe society, to which, from the mid-eighteenth century, all Old Calabar merchants and their partners belonged. Ekpe provided cohesion in a highly fragmented region. Its hierarchy of membership grades, open to all who could afford the heavy fees, provided a meeting place where issues of kinship and ethnicity were minimized. In a trading system in which credit and debt were common among merchants, Ekpe also became a valuable mechanism for collecting debts. Though a private voluntary association, not a government, Ekpe had many coercive powers, enforced by its members and the religious powers it claimed. As is detailed in the diary, Ekpe chapters heard testimony, conducted ordeals to determine the truth, and imposed penalties to back up its decisions. The penalties included distraint, boycotts, fines, detention, and execution.[41] As chapter 1 detailed, the society also served to commemorate the deaths of its leading members.

Despite the limits of political authority, the decentralized trading system in the Cross River region functioned efficiently. Because of its many nodes of power, the trading network was capable of considerable flexibility. As in any free-market capitalist economy, individuals rose and fell, connections grew or shrank, and the entire system enlarged as the Atlantic connections expanded. Challenged in the early nineteenth century when Britain moved to shut down the transatlantic slave trade, the system weathered the crisis readily by continuing to sell slaves to the traders of other nations and rapidly increasing the export of palm oil, which became more valuable than slaves had ever been.

CHAPTER FIVE

The Diary of Antera Duke:
Comments on the Text

This chapter introduces the diary of Antera Duke, as transcribed by the Reverend Arthur W. Wilkie, and a new "standard English" version of the diary, which builds upon the efforts of Wilkie and anthropologist Donald C. Simmons. Some background to the 1956 and updated editions is warranted here. Wilkie's transcription is a partial record, thus bringing into question the representativeness of his selected passages. Antera's trade English and the intricacies of Calabar society challenged interpretation fifty years ago and still do so today. His vocabulary and sentence structures, we contend, suggest that he learned English informally in the Cross River region by hearing spoken words and seeing them written in captains' accounts and letters. By keeping in mind Antera's mainly aural language learning, we were able to reinterpret the meanings of some of his words. We close these introductory comments by discussing formatting changes that distinguish this new edition, and by pointing out several passages that proved problematic.

Reverend Arthur Wilkie's Transcription

In approximately 1907, upon opening Antera's 120-year-old diary, Wilkie noticed that discoloration had lightened many words, a discovery that influenced his decision to copy out Antera's text. Without access to the original folio, presumed lost in Edinburgh during the Second World War, it is not possible to double-check the accuracy of the transcription.[1] Wilkie, though, took care in copying passages. As he recollected in 1951: "I made those extracts from the original volume (now lost), + tried to retain the exact spelling of the original. I may have made an occasional 'slip'—for I cannot claim verbal inspiration—or veracity!; but I checked + rechecked with the original every word in my extracts before making my final 'Script,' so I do not think that there can be any 'serious discrepancies.'"[2] Wilkie avoided adding punctuation marks and inserted question marks next to words that were particularly faded or when he did not understand their sentence or Efik context. For example, in the first year's entries he queried words such as "Brown" (January 29, 1785) and "Brivon" (July 19, 1785)—presumably hard to read—and faded or unintelligible Efik-English words such as "Etutim" (January 18, 1785), "Cosoin" (June 1, 1785), and "Tabow" (September 8, 1785). In all, Wilkie questioned the spelling or meaning of 56 of 10,510 words that he preserved in the three-year diary.

Though Wilkie transcribed each entry to his best ability, he reformatted Antera's diary dates and removed trading day appellations. He used a British-style "day.month.year" format (as in 18.1.1785) to render all diary dates consistent, though Antera Duke undoubtedly spelled out dates. On the front page of the diary, for example, Antera writes "December 24 the 1787" and "January 27 the 1788," and later he recalls a meeting on "October 17th the 1787." Other Efik writers understood the English-language months of the year as well. Liverpool merchant-captain Ambrose Lace received letters from Calabar merchants dated "January 13, 1773," "July 19th 1773," "December 24th 1775," "August 23the 1776," and "March 20th 1783."[3] Egbo Young Ofiong dated a letter to Liverpool merchant William Earle "July 23, 1783," in which he mentioned the arrival of Captain Burrow on "4 Day may" and a possible return date to Liverpool as "15 or twenty Day March."[4] Unfortunately, Wilkie did not copy "days of week" terms, which headed each entry. These were, as he remembered: "Andrew Honesty Sunday, Market Day, King John Sunday, King Honesty Sunday, Sam Ebrow Sunday, Aqua Market, King War Sunday, Little King Sunday, Andrew Honesty Sunday, etc."[5] The eight different terms reflect the eight-day Calabar week. Without punctuation an original diary entry, then, might have read "Andrew Honesty Sunday January 18 the 1785."

Reformatting dates may have led to errors in date transcription or in ordering the diary's entries. Wilkie commented in 1951 how the secretary who typed his handwritten notation "got the paging rather confused," but that he "succeeded in re-arranging all in order." By "paging" perhaps Wilkie meant "dating," because if one follows the typed transcription, Antera muddled dates by heading two diary entries—thirteen entries apart—24 June 1785. Antera then follows his June 24 entry with one on June 25, but then the transcription continues 1, 2, 8, 9, 15, 17, 18, 19, 20, 21, 22, 23, 24 June (repeated), and Antera closes the month with entries on 27 and 29 June. Wilkie did not comment on these dating problems, nor did Simmons in 1954 when he decided that the 24–25 June entries, which appeared first, referred actually to 24–25 May. A Liverpool ship captain's letter, however, confirms one of Antera's diary dates: Antera recorded on June 25, 1785, that Captain Potter had arrived, and Potter wrote to his Liverpool employer that he arrived at Old Calabar "the 25th June after a Passage of 72 days."[6] Potter also confirms the arrival date of the Liverpool slaver *Fanny*, which arrived October 26, 1785 (though transcribed by Wilkie as September 26).[7] Thus we assume that the June–November 1785 transcribed diary dates are incorrect by one month; nonetheless, when one reads the entries, it is clear that the events proceed chronologically.[8]

We believe that a second major dating error in the first diary edition concerns events in August–October 1787. In Antera's entry transcribed and dated by Wilkie as August 31, 1787, we read that John Tom Cobham's wife hanged herself about the palaver on "October 17th the 1787"—seven weeks later. The entry then continues with Jimmy Henshaw's payments, in copper rods, to various Ekpe members to allow Henshaw to become "King Ekpe"—the head of one of the Ekpe grades. But in the entry dated October 17 there is information previous to that appearing in the "August 31" entry about sharing copper rods to make Jimmy Henshaw "King Ekpe." Given this chronological confusion, we think that Antera headed his October 31, 1787, diary entry "8er 31 the 1787," following the format that ship captains occasionally used to abbreviate October ("8er"). "Oct" is a homophone for the Gaelic *ocht* and Dutch/German *acht*—"eight." Moving the entry from "August 31, 1787" in the 1956 edition to "October 31, 1787" in this revised edition thus fits the chronology of the diary information about the women palaver and Jimmy Henshaw's payments.

It is reasonable to suppose that Wilkie's transcription contains most of Antera's words from the 187 entries, January 18, 1785 through January 31, 1788. Wilkie stated that his extracts "cover practically the whole of the original Diary" and that he transcribed "every entry of any real value . . . omitting only such entries as were merely repetitive, or very pedestrian." Ellipses begin 91 transcribed entries—here the missionary, in most cases, left out Antera's formulaic time-location-weather phrases, such as "at 5 am in aqua Landing with fine morning." He adds ellipses only in the middle of 11 entries and closes 3 with them—so here we lost, perhaps, what Wilkie considered "very pedestrian" information. Wilkie also recalled that the diary contained daily entries, a "day by day record of events in Duke Town, Calabar."[9] If literally true, then the folio must have contained about 1,100 entries over the three-year period.

It is probable, however, that Antera Duke maintained a frequent diary, and that Wilkie recalled how Antera labeled entries by the day.[10] Consider the writing instruments and paper Liverpool merchants shipped to their Calabar partners. In 1776 the *Hector*'s outward cargo to Old Calabar included the following:[11]

Three [books] 4 Q^{res} ½ Bound Journals Letter'd	15s
Three 3 ditto	12
1 ream course fools Cap	9
1 Box of Wafers	1
6 Papers Ink Powder	3
100 Common Quills	1

A quire consisted of twenty-four equally sized sheets of paper, probably linen,[12] and the two largest books shipped to Calabar were the four-quire book that contained ninety-size folios (192 verso and recto) or the three-quire book with seventy-two folios (144 sides). Wilkie commented that the "large folio bound volume" looked like a ship's logbook, and thus we suggest that Antera Duke's diary contained a maximum of 192 pages. Even in the largest books, Antera would have had difficulty writing paragraph-length daily entries for three years—unless he wrote very small characters.[13] Moreover, Antera may have wished to conserve his supplies of powdered ink or quills, and thus avoided writing each day. Ending his book January 31, 1788, certainly implies that he had reached the last page and continued his diary in a subsequent volume.

If one follows Wilkie's 1951 correspondence literally, then he may not have transcribed the information Antera recorded about European slaving voyages. Writing to Daryll Forde of the International African Institute, Wilkie stated how Antera recorded the country of origin for each sailing vessel, and that the captains "told the Chiefs the number of slaves they could take; and the Diarist records the bargaining before the price per slave was finally determined."[14] Antera mentions a vessel's nationality or its home port, however, in only four transcribed entries: on March 23, 1785, he saw a "small Bristall ship" coming up the river; on June 10, 1786, and September 4, 1786, he noticed slavers from France ("funchmen"); and then on September 26, 1787, he boarded a "Brsh [British] ship." In general, the transcription tells us that Antera identified ships by captains' surnames, as in "Captin Aspinall ship go way with 328 slaves."[15] Though slave exports appear, no transcribed extracts specify numbers of enslaved Africans captains planned to load, numbers totaling 500 slaves on the largest vessels. In spite of Wilkie's statement to Forde, few transcribed sentences discuss bargaining for slaves, ivory, or yams in detail; only two entries mention prices for yams in copper rods.[16] Recalling

Antera's diary after forty-four years, perhaps Wilkie remembered incorrectly some details the Efik writer included.[17]

The transcribed diary also lacks sufficient information on the extensive export commodity trades of Old Calabar. According to Wilkie's copy, Antera refers twice to elephants' "teeth" (ivory tusks), and two entries mention bulk cargoes of agricultural produce (two and four "towns," or tons, of unspecified goods). From the diary alone we would conclude that most captains departed Calabar only with enslaved Africans, as when Fairweather departed for the Americas on December 29, 1787, "with 377 slaves." But other sources indicate that almost all British slaving captains with whom Antera traded loaded agricultural goods, as we discussed in chapter 3. Fairweather, for example, arrived in Dominica with slaves and 45 ivory tusks, 100 puncheons of palm oil, 50 tons of redwood, and 60 barrels of pepper.[18] As transcribed by Wilkie, Antera does not mention any produce transactions in diary entries between March and December 1787, when Fairweather's ship moored off Duke Town, perhaps indicating that he did not sell these commodities. Alternatively, Wilkie may have purposively omitted words regarding these products of "legitimate trade" to focus attention on Calabar slaving.

Just as Reverend Wilkie might have excluded words indicating a "legitimate" produce trade, he may have included all passages discussing "ungodly" episodes. In his later correspondence Wilkie recalled that Antera "frequently" stated how "'so and so' were made to 'drink doctor.'"[19] For example, when suspected of witchcraft in cases of unexplained deaths, Efik upper-class men and women were forced to drink poison to prove their innocence. Twelve diary extracts refer to various Efik "drinking doctor." Wilkie also transcribed the information on human sacrifice. After the deaths of Young Tom Robin (June 29, 1785), John Cobham (April–May 1786), and Duke Ephraim (July 4, 1786), Antera detailed the numbers of slaves who were decapitated to honor the deceased leader. When they buried Duke Ephraim, "9 men & women go [went] with him," and then, on November 6, 1786, during the major obsequies, at "5 clock morning we begain cutt slave head of 50 head of by the one Day" ("at 5 o'clock in the morning we began to cut slaves' heads off, 50 heads off in that one day"). To missionary Wilkie, perhaps few such "un-Christian" incidents warranted excision if he wanted to demonstrate the progress of "civilization" at Old Calabar.[20]

Without access to Antera Duke's original folio, scholars should use care when quantifying information contained in Reverend Wilkie's selection of extracts. Wilkie transcribed the large majority of words, but he may have omitted certain details on Calabar produce trades or the substantial English business in the Cross River region. His status as a Christian missionary might guarantee that he copied all instances of "ungodly" poison rituals, slave trading, and human sacrifice. Regardless of possible biases, the transcription is the only remaining record of Antera Duke's diary; Wilkie claimed to have copied all informative entries, and most words not transcribed probably are Antera's formulaic time-place-weather phrases that began each diary entry and perhaps some details on the export produce trades.

Publishing Wilkie's Transcription and "Translation"

In 1951, believing that Antera Duke's broken English would prove difficult to read to those unfamiliar with the Efik idiom, Wilkie made, to use his words, a "Translation (or interpretation) of the Diary." When Daryll Forde agreed to publish Wilkie's material, he thought that the translation warranted reexamination. Wilkie concurred. As he stated in a letter to Forde in November 1951:

> I would like to say that in preparing the "extracts," my primary purpose was restricted to present it in a form that would make it available for a wider circle, interested in the "way of life" in olden times in the Calabar area. My so-called "interpretations" were merely intended to make intelligible to the "ordinary reader" the meaning of many of the phrases used—+ not a "scientific" document. I believed, however, that others with far more scientific "anthropological" training than I myself had might find it useful.

Forde also believed that the diary, "while being useful for its vividness, is not sufficiently explanatory, and could only be published with a commentary by someone who had specialized on Efik material." By mid-1954 Forde had contacted anthropology student Donald C. Simmons to proofread and edit Wilkie's translation and annotate the diary. Simmons, an Efik specialist like Wilkie,[21] had returned recently from his fieldwork in southeast Nigeria, having spent eleven months in Creek Town and three in Duke Town studying Efik language, folklore, and customs. He agreed to proofread Wilkie's work and suggested to Forde that he could offer footnotes to elucidate many of Antera's meanings and to identify Efik and European traders.

Comparison between the Wilkie and Simmons translations indicates that the anthropologist edited words in each of Wilkie's modern English renditions. As Simmons remarked: "I have spent some time on the diary especially attempting to translate it so it makes sense." Simmons's revised translation included more of Antera's words than the missionary's effort. To streamline the prose, Simmons removed most of Wilkie's parenthetical remarks, some of which reemerged in endnotes. Wilkie also had underlined references to slave trading, questioned confusing terms, and spotlighted local idioms with quotation marks—notations Simmons removed. The anthropologist corrected obvious mistakes in the translation (changing the diary entry of July 18, 1787, "cutt a cow for his good" to "cutt cow for his god"), and retained Antera Duke's terms, changed by Wilkie in the translation, that remain common in Old Calabar, such as the verb "to dash," the noun "comey," and Antera's anglicized Efik names Ephraim (instead of Efiom) and Coffee (instead of Kofi).[22] Simmons also changed Egbo to Ekpe, when Antera referred to the Ekpe society.

Simmons's annotation—ninety-eight endnotes—focused on placing Antera Duke's diary in the context of Efik social history and customs, areas in which he was knowledgeable. He based most references on his early 1950s fieldwork in Creek Town and Duke Town, information he acquired by conversations with Efik elders. His published references include nineteenth-century traveler and missionary accounts, such as those by adventurer James Holman and missionary Hope Masterton Waddell. Readers gained information on towns and peoples in the greater Cross River region with whom the first- and second-generation descendants of Antera Duke traded. Simmons explained the Efik names for anglicized words, discussed local customs, and gave insights into Ekpe, the society to which elder Efik notables belonged. The names of European ship officers warranted comment, but Simmons, given the sources at hand, identified only three of the captains mentioned by Antera Duke. The annotation most lacks information about the export slave and produce trades at Old Calabar and those foreigners who visited the river between January 1785 and January 1788.

The efforts of Wilkie and Simmons produced a readable "modern English" version of Antera Duke's diary with informative endnotes. To create a more straightforward narration, they added punctuation to split word streams into sentences, conjugated Antera's verbs, and inflected Antera's pronouns. Simmons's annotations placed numerous passages in the context of eighteenth- and nineteenth-century Efik life and identified some details from the European slave trade. Yet the 1956 translation did not render consistently Antera's verb tenses, sentence orderings, or usages of subordinating conjunctions. Additionally, they translated "Cosoin" in a non-Efik context, and the terms "Tabow," "Bar Room men," and "wowo"/"wawa" remained unexplained. Finally, Simmons's diary notes lacked full information on slaving ships, captains, and cargoes—details now available via ships' muster rolls and newspaper advertisements.

Revising the Diary Translation and Annotations

During the past half century, scholars have learned more about the transatlantic slave trade and Efik history, allowing a re-annotation of Antera Duke's diary to better place its information in historic context. British ships' muster rolls, examined first by abolitionist Thomas Clarkson in 1788 and reexamined in the 1980s, yield information on the British captains and crew members working at Old Calabar. Data on individual voyages slaving at Old Calabar, as we mentioned in the introduction to this book, are compiled in the consolidated online slave trade database. An extensive narrative from one mariner working at Old Calabar during the time of Antera Duke's diary has been identified: William Butterworth (pseudonym for Henry Schroeder) published information about slave trading at Old Calabar, July–December 1786, in his work *Three Years' Adventure of a Minor* (1822). Some material in his book, such as his recollection of hostilities between British captains and a French commander, corroborates Antera Duke's diary information, as do twelve letters written by British captains at Old Calabar between 1785 and 1788.

In addition to a new "translation" rendered into standard English and newly annotated, as an aid to readers the two versions of the diary appear on facing pages with footnotes.[23] We replicate Wilkie's original transcription of Antera Duke's text, including the exact number of ellipses Wilkie (or his secretary-typist Miss Bell) added, as well as the spaces between words that appear in the original transcription. We do not know whether Antera added spaces between words to indicate sentence or thought breaks—or whether Wilkie or Bell added these. By retaining the spaces we have chosen to replicate exactly Wilkie's 1951 typed transcription, which is the document closest to Antera's late eighteenth-century text. Our new "translation" has changed 10 to 15 percent of the words from the 1956 Wilkie-Simmons translation, in many cases placing verbs in the past tense. There are now 265 notes, placed beneath the text. Simmons's notes are indicated in this edition by [S]. New footnotes appearing in this revised edition conclude with [E]. If we edited Simmons's notes, by rewriting them and/or by adding new information, the reader will see the marker [S, E].

Linguistic analysis of Antera Duke's diary provided guidelines for revising the "modern English" version written by Wilkie and Simmons. Though Antera Duke's diary entries lack punctuation, his passages follow a consistent structure: he wrote in his diary after the day's activities and probably recalls events in chronological order. The diarist begins sentences with temporal markers and conjunctions. Antera employs the subordinating conjunction "so" either as an adverbial clause to indicate a sequential relationship or to indicate a causal relationship.[24] We kept in mind how Antera might have heard words, or the types of words he would have seen written by captains, merchants, or other Efik. The trade English employed by other Efik—particularly in the two lengthy letters (totaling 1,608 words) written by Ephraim Robin John of Old Town—informed the way we rendered Antera's diary into standard English. When Antera writes "Bliv" ("bee-leave" or believe), we see his aural language learning. Few of his written English words contained the silent "e" ending; words ending in "y" (such as "they," written as "the") proved tricky, as did "th" words in English, such as "there" (usually written as "here"). There is a clear correspondence between vowel sounds and the letters he writes, as when Antera pens "at" when he hears the number "eight."[25]

The best example of how Antera learned English—by hearing a sailor or reading business correspondence—is his use of "occasion." Twice Antera writes the term: as "Cosoin" in one passage and then as "cason" eighteen months later—in both instances translated by Simmons as "cousin." Antera writes we "have Ebrow Optter Cosoin to go Look them 7 men" and then "wee have us cason go up to guin Company." Wilkie questioned "Cosoin" and "cason," perhaps knowing that "cousin" is not an Efik kinship term. Reading letters written by contemporary ship captains would have aided Wilkie's translation. For example, in July 1785, one month after arriving at Old Calabar, Liverpool captain Peter Potter informed merchant William Davenport that he "lost about five tun of Salt ocationed by a lake."[26] Ten years earlier, in the Cameroon River, Potter informed Davenport how a ship arrived at Cameroon "in great distress Ocationed through [the captain] and all his people being Sick." And later he wrote, "Capt Dwyre as before mentioned arrived here in great disstres ocationed through death & sickness." Antera's adoption of the difficult-to-spell "occasion" thus explicates his diary passages: "Ebrow Potter had occasion to go look for those seven men"; and "we had occasion to go up to Guiney Company."

One of Antera Duke's most problematic passages is his phrase "I have give King up Tabow" (October? 8, 1785), which could be interpreted at least four ways. Wilkie noted his confusion over the remark, penning (?) after "Tabow"—a question mark that may also indicate that the script had faded. Efik writer Ukorebi Asuquo believes that King Up Tabow was King Etta Agbo from Qua territories east of Calabar. Or, Antera may be referring to a "king" of the "Tabac" people, a people referenced by Cross River explorer Henry Nicholls in 1805. Perhaps Nicholls referred to those groups living in Ekritobako towns, twenty miles southwest of Duke Town.[27] In a third interpretation, if "King" refers to King Calabar, the priest of the tutelary deity, Ndem

Efik, perhaps Tabow could abbreviate tobacco (as in tab^{ow}), and hence Antera gave the leaf to the priest. We suggest, however, that Antera's phrase might best be interpreted as Antera walking up to bow before King Calabar and the shrine.[28] Here we follow missionary Hugh Goldie's dictionary of the Efik language, which defines the verb *täb-ä* or *töbö*: "To be low; to stand or lie low, or inferior in height to some other thing; To be short in stature, but thick in body; to be squab or squat; To be or become low, inconsiderable in wealth or rank."[29] Though Antera does not intersperse many Efik words into his trade English diary, the link between the Efik verb *täb-ä* or *töbö* and the English "to bow" would explain his choice of "Tabow" to recall his actions that day.

We explain terms such as "Bar Room men," undeciphered by Wilkie and Simmons, by cross-referencing Antera's vocabulary with that used by Ephraim Robin John in two lengthy letters written in 1773. The most straightforward translation of "bar room" is "prison," and hence men confined in the room with bars are "prisoners." Indeed, in Efik prison is *ufok uquat* (iron-bar house). Alternatively, "Bar Room" could refer to the Mbarakom people of the Cameroon grasslands. The interpretation of "bar room" as prison gains weight from the fact that Ephraim Robin John used a similar term—"Room of irons"—in his letter to a Liverpool merchant, Ambrose Lace. Robin John requested that Lace send him some large leg manillas with hinges, screws, and locks and two large iron ones to serve "in the Room of irons."[30]

Readers should note that our standard-English rendition is the best attempt of three historians to elucidate fully the Efik writer's sentences; other scholars may decide upon alternate interpretations.

PART II

Antera Duke, His Diary

Extracts from the Original Text of the
Diary of Antera Duke, 1785–1788

antera Duke Ephrim

December 24 the 1787. I be angiry with my Dear awaw ofion   I Did
settle with him in January 27 the 1788

January 18 the 1785

About 6 am in Aqua Landing with fine morning so I walk with Egbo
men to go for Etutim so his Deash   1 Rods   & 1 small cas Bottle Brandy
soon after we hav all Egbo men go to Egbo Bush Bush   for mak bob about
Egbo Young & Little Otto   plaver so Egbo Young pay 1 goat & 4 Rods &
Little Otto pay 4 Rods so all Egbo men com Down for Duk plaver and be
join putt moony for 20 men all be 64 men put moony 45 for Duk family 19
for another family

---

1. The name Antera, "Ntiero" in Efik, is peculiar to the Ntiero family of Duke Town. Duke either is an anglicization of the Efik names "Orok" or "Eduk," or it derives from English captain Abraham Duke, who traded at Old Calabar in 1663. Ephrim (Ephraim, or ca. 1700 Aphrom) is anglicized from the Efik "Efiom" (Hair, Jones, and Law, *Barbot on Guinea*, 2:705n27). For a detailed explanation of Antera Duke's name, title, and genealogy—and attribution of the name "Ntiero Edem Efiom"— see Asuquo, "Diary," 36–38. We will use the name Antera Duke in these notes to the diary. [S, E]

2. Awa Ofiong, Antera Duke's principal wife. See also notes 142, 214 below. [E]

3. The Reverend Arthur W. Wilkie, the diary transcriber, changed Antera's date format, which likely would have read "January 18 the 1785." Regarding Wilkie's transcription, see chapter 5. [E]

4. Antera Duke's time references suggest that he owned a timepiece. [E]

5. Aqua is the diarist's transcription of the Efik adjective *akwa*, "big," rather than a reference to the neighboring village, Big Qua Town, whose inhabitants are culturally related to the Ejagham Ekoi and are called *abakpa* by the Efik. The "big landing" was presumably situated somewhere along the present marina at Duke Town. [S]

6. Men who belonged to a cult known as Ekpe, associated with a society with secret rituals, which, by the 1840s, had ten grades or "steps" of membership, each of which had to be purchased successively. Ekpe society made and enforced laws for the greater Efik community and functioned also as a social club. Having the power to collect debts and control credit, Ekpe functioned to reduce transaction costs for European and Efik merchants (Latham, *Old Calabar*, 28, 35–40; Lovejoy and Richardson, "Trust," 347–339). The Efik word *ekpe*, "leopard," is substituted for the diarist's word "egbo" even though "egbo" is sanctioned by continual English usage since the nineteenth century. Egbo, more properly *ekpo*, since Efik lacks the voiced labial velar *gb*, might be confused with the Ibibio masked society known as *ekpo*, "ghost," which did not exist among the Efik. [S, E]

7. Wilkie's transcription inserted "(?)" after "Etutim," indicating uncertainty about Antera's meaning or difficulty reading this particular word from the faded manuscript. Wilkie's transcription is the only surviving record of the important Antera Duke diary. [E]

8. The word "dash" is used extensively in West Africa to denote any gift or present. Van Dantzig and Jones offer three etymologies for dash (Marees, *Description*, 47n): the Portuguese *donação* (gift); the Akan *medasse* (thank you); and the Chinese *datjin* (a gold weight). [S, E]

Extracts from the Diary of Antera Duke, 1785–1788, Rendered into Standard English

[on front page of diary]: Antera Duke Ephraim [Ntiero Edem Efiom][1]

December 24, 1787. I was angry with my Dear wife Awa Ofiong.[2] I settled with her on January 27, 1788.

January 18, 1785[3]

About 6 a.m.[4] at Aqua Landing [Big Beach],[5] a fine morning. I walked with the Ekpe men[6] to go to Etutim's house.[7] He "dashed" [gave][8] us 1 copper rod[9] and 1 small case of bottle brandy. Soon afterwards all the Ekpe men went to the Ekpe bush[10] to "make bob about" [discuss][11] the Egbo Young [Ofiong][12] and Little Otto[13] palaver.[14] Egbo Young paid 1 goat and 4 rods and Little Otto paid 4 rods.[15] All the Ekpe men came down to Duke Ephraim's[16] palaver house and joined together to put in money for 20 men. In all 64 men put in money, 45 from Duke's family, 19 from another family.[17]

9. The Efik had a currency of copper or brass rods and wire. According to "William Butterworth" (Henry Schroeder), a crewman on the Liverpool slaver *Hudibras* in 1786 (see notes 95, 174, 176, 198), copper rods were "about eighteen inches long and one inch in circumference, valued at about one shilling each" (Butterworth, *Three Years Adventures*, 83). See also Latham, "Currency," 599–605. [S, E]

10. A plot of land belonging to the Ekpe society. [S, E]

11. A "bob" signifies a discussion (as in "bobbing heads together"). The term "bob" seems to be an abbreviation of the slang word "bobbery." There is a trade "bob" and a war "bob," as well as a hate "bob" and a respect "bob." [S, E]

12. Antera Duke refers to two Egbo Youngs—Egbo Young Ofiong and his brother Egbo Young Antera. See appendix A and note 96. In January 1805 explorer Henry Nicholls met Egbo Young Ofiong, sixty to seventy years of age (Hallett, *Records*, 199). Egbo Young is an anglicization of Ekpenyong, the name of a god or spirit, as well as a personal name. Persons so named are believed to be self-willed and unruly, since the actions of the Ekpenyong spirit-god are unpredictable. [S, E]

13. Otto is an anglicization of the Efik name "Otu." [S]

14. The word "palaver" derives from the Portuguese *palavra*, "word," and signifies any discussion, debate, dispute, or conference. The word is associated so intimately with the West African coast that Francis Grosse in his *Classical Dictionary* (1785) erroneously imputed to it an African origin. [S, E]

15. The judges evidently decided against Egbo Young Ofiong, since he contributed a goat as well as court costs. Both plaintiff and defendant pay equal fees to have a case adjudicated. The loser gives a goat (an "Egbo goat"—Hallett, *Records*, 203) to provide a feast for everyone and thus signifies that he accepts the judgment, bears no ill will to his opponent or the judges, and will comply with the decision. [S, E]

16. Duke Ephraim (Edem Ekpo) of Duke House (d. 1786), Antera Duke's uncle and obong (Old Calabar civil authority, or, to Europeans, "king"). [S, E]

17. This passage probably refers to 64 men putting in money for either 20 Ekpe initiates or 20 men slaves or money equal to the value of 20 men slaves. [S, E]

January 21 the 1785

at 5 am in aqua Landing with fine morning so I go Captin Savage for tak goods for slav

January 25 the 1785

about 4 am in Eyo Willy Honesty house so wee walk up to see Willy Honesty in yard so his killd 1 Big goat for wee soon after we walk up to see wee town & Did tak one great guns to putt for canow for two Egbo Young men Bring hom in aqua Landing so wee join to Henshaw Town and com Back and at 3 clock noon wee Everry Body go com to Deash Eyo Willy Honesty Daught .... 1496 Rods besides cloth & powder & Iron   so wee play all day befor night

January 28 the 1785

about 6 am in aqua Landing with fine morning so I hav work for my small yard   after 2 clock noon wee two go Bord Captin Smal with 3 slave so his tak two and wee com back

18. Captain John Savage of the Liverpool slaving ship *Liverpool Hero* (211 tons), which arrived at Old Calabar in September or October 1784. Efik traders identified "the ship in the captain," as British adventurer James Holman stated (Holman, *Travels*, 365–366). Antera Duke refers to sailing vessels by the name of their captains in all cases except one: the ship *Will* (see notes 179, 202). Information on slaving vessels and captains referred to by Antera Duke may be found in www.slave voyages.org. Unless indicated otherwise, all slaving voyage information (dates of sail, slave import totals) comes from this online slave trade archive. [E]

19. Captains purchased slaves by "trust-trade"—advancing trading goods for slaves to be delivered at a later date. See Simmons, "Ethnographic Sketch," 4–5; Latham, *Old Calabar*, 27–28. One Liverpool trader at Calabar in 1769 kept a "Trust Book" (Hair, "Antera Duke," 361). [S, E]

20. Eyo Willy Honesty is Efik leader Eyo Nsa of Creek Town, who died in 1820, according to the editors of Crow, *Memoirs*, 280. He is reputed to have decapitated the chiefs of Old Town, Enyong, and Itu through various stratagems. According to a British sailor, George Millar, Honesty decapitated an important Old Town merchant during a war in 1767 between Duke Town and Old Town, when the Duke Town warriors, with the connivance of British captains, attacked the Old Town warriors during a shipboard peace parley. Millar testified that Willy Honesty asked one British master, "Captain, if you will give me that man to cutty head, I will give you the best man in my canoe and you shall be slaved the first ship" (Lambert, *Commons Sessional Papers*, 73:392). [S, E]

21. The compound of an Efik merchant consisted of rectangular buildings and courtyards surrounded by a high wall of wattle and daub, the sloping roofs composed of rectangular thatch mats attached to a framework of poles. Slaves and loyal retainers inhabited the outermost courtyard to protect the dignitary in case of attack. The merchant's house was situated on one of the inner courtyards; his wives used other courtyards. See Bassey, "Architecture," 125–129. [S, E]

22. Efik hospitality requires the provision of food for visitors, as recorded incidents throughout the diary illustrate. A host who does not offer food and drink insults his guest. [S]

23. After visiting Willy Honesty in Creek Town, Antera Duke visited some of his people living there. He then walked up a hill to observe Duke Town across the river and then boated downstream to Aqua Landing (Duke Town's big beach). An alternative possibility: Willy Honesty may have maintained a home at Duke Town. [S, E]

January 21, 1785

At 5 a.m. at Aqua Landing, a fine morning. I went to Captain Savage[18] to take goods [to be exchanged] for slaves.[19]

January 25, 1785

About 4 a.m. we were in Eyo Willy Honesty's[20] house and we walked up to see Willy Honesty in his yard.[21] He killed 1 big goat for us.[22] Soon after that we walked up to see our town[23] and took one great gun [cannon][24] to put in a canoe[25] for two of Egbo Young [Ofiong's] men to bring home to Aqua Landing. We went together to Henshaw Town[26] and came back, and at 3 o'clock in the afternoon we and everybody went to "dash" Eyo Willy Honesty's daughter . . . 1496 rods besides cloth, gunpowder, and iron.[27] We "played"[28] all day before night[fall].

January 28, 1785

About 6 a.m. at Aqua Landing, a fine morning. I worked in my small yard. After 2 o'clock in the afternoon we two went on board Captain Smale's[29] ship with 3 slaves. He took two slaves and we came back.

24. The Efik fortified the beach with small cannon to be fired for military purposes, at funeral obsequies, or to salute the arrival of European sailing vessels. They also armed their canoes with these cannon. [S, E]

25. According to mariner Richard Story, who was in Old Calabar in 1766, Efik traders transported slaves "[c]hiefly in large canoes—what they call war canoes—carrying upwards of fifty men, with a three or four pounder in the bow." Similarly, Liverpool sailor Isaac Parker stated that Old Calabar war canoes "were fitted with ammunition, cutlasses, pistols, powder and ball, and two guns, which were three-pounders, fixed upon a block of wood; one in the canoe's stern, and one in the bow" (Lambert, *Commons Sessional Papers*, 82:8, 73:126). "Pounders" refer to the weight, in pounds, of the projectile. The length, diameter, and weight of the cannon are directly proportional to the size of the ball. The length of a three-pounder, for example, was about four feet (Falconer, *Naval Dictionary*, 58–65). Efik purchased various-sized canoes. On November 1, 1787, Antera Duke traveled to Akwa Bakasi to buy canoes. Umon (see note 37) was another source of canoes, manufactured farther upriver at Akunakuna. [E]

26. Henshaw Town, or Nsidung, is one mile south of Duke Town. Nicholls estimated its population at 300, when he visited in February 1805 (Hallett, *Records*, 206). [S, E]

27. Willy Honesty's daughter celebrated the wearing of her first cloth, which required her family, relatives, and friends to mark her newly acquired status by giving her gifts (see Simmons, "Ethnographic Sketch," 15). Or, she had just emerged from seclusion (see also notes 143, 254, 260). [S, E]

28. The Efik verb root *bre*, "play," signifies all types of singing, music, or dancing, whether performed by an individual or a group. As a noun ("play"), its specific meaning depends on context and can translate as "function," "ceremony," "celebration," "masquerade," or "festivity." [S, E]

29. Captain John Smale of the Liverpool slaving ship *Perseverance* (300 tons), which arrived at Old Calabar in July or August 1784. The *Perseverance* sailed from Old Calabar within the month (a departure not noted in the diary transcription) and later arrived in Liverpool with 33 puncheons palm oil, 5 butts and 1 puncheon Guinea pepper, 180 "elephants teeth" (ivory tusks), 4 tons "Guinea red wood," and West India produce (*Liverpool General Advertiser*, Aug. 18, 1785). [S, E]

January 29 the 1785

about 6 am with fine morning so I have work for my small yard all morning and at 2 clock noon we have go Captin Brown for tak good for slav and Com Back

January 30 the 1785

about 6 am at Aqua Landing with fog morning so I goin to work for my Little Yard   sam time wee & Tom Aqua and John Aqua be join Catch men

February 2 the 1785

about 6 am in Aqua Landing with great fog morning so I going to work in Little yard   after that Duke & all wee go to King Egbo for share Egbo moony for 40 men after that wee com way

February 5 the 1785

about 6 am in aqua Landing with Little fog morning so I go Down for Landing after . . clock noon wee 3 go to Egbo Young house Liverpool Hall for share 3 keg powder   soon wee hear news ship com up so wee Run for Landing for gett 5 great guns Redy for firs sam time wee see Little canow Com & till wee his be Captin Loosdan Tender

30. Wilkie's transcription inserted "(?)" after "Brown." Captain "Brown" (the "n" may be a loop extension of "w") refers to Liverpool captain John Burrows's (sounded out "B-row") ship *Lion*, which arrived at Old Calabar in late 1784, as the same merchants owned the *Lion* and *Edwards* ("Captin Brown Tender," see note 40). See also notes 58, 112. [E]

31. Nicholls, at Old Calabar January–February 1805, noted that at Duke Town fogs begin in February and "are sometimes so thick that you cannot see a man ten yards before you; these continue more or less till the rainy season commences again [in late May]" (Hallett, *Records*, 207). [E]

32. This is the *only* diary reference to the Efik capturing slaves, reflecting the fact that in the 1780s Efik merchants purchased most of their slaves from neighboring towns with which they had established trade relations. See also notes 91, 134, 201. [S, E]

33. King Ekpe, head of one of the grades of the Leopard (Ekpe) society. [E]

January 29, 1785

About 6 a.m., a fine morning. I worked in my small yard all morning, and at 2 o'clock in the afternoon we went to Captain Burrows's[30] ship to take goods for slaves and came back.

January 30, 1785

About 6 a.m. at Aqua Landing, a foggy morning.[31] I went to work in my little yard. At the same time we and Tom Aqua and John Aqua joined together to catch men.[32]

February 2, 1785

About 6 a.m. at Aqua Landing, a very foggy morning. I went to work in my little yard. After that Duke Ephraim and all of us went to King Ekpe[33] to share Ekpe money for 40 men.[34] After that we came away.

February 5, 1785

About 6 a.m. at Aqua Landing, a little morning fog. I went down to the landing. After . . . o'clock in the afternoon we 3 went to Egbo Young [Ofiong's] house Liverpool Hall[35] to share 3 kegs of gunpowder. Soon we heard news that a ship was coming up the river so we ran to the landing to get 5 great guns ready to fire. At the same time we saw a little canoe coming and he told us that he was Captain Langdon's tender.[36]

34. All members of the Ekpe society receive a share of the initiation fees received from new members. See also diary entry Jan. 18, 1785. [S, E]

35. Important Efik merchants such as Egbo Young Ofiong possessed two-story wooden houses imported from England in pieces and reassembled (see Simmons, "Ethnographic Sketch," 8). "Liverpool Hall" reflects the dominant position of Liverpool slavers in Old Calabar. [S, E]

36. Captain John Langdon of the Bristol slaving ship *Constantine* (200 tons), which arrived at Old Calabar in October 1784. Langdon's "tender" was Captain Matthew Morley of the ship *Juba* (110 tons). Efik traders used the term "tender" to describe the age-status relationship between two captains who commanded vessels owned by the same firm: Morley was junior to Langdon, and Bristol merchant Thomas Coulson owned both the *Constantine* and the *Juba*. In 1774 Langdon, captain of the Bristol slaver *Cato*, transported Little Ephraim Robin John and Ancona Robin Robin John, younger brothers of an Old Town leader, from the Cape Verde Islands to Old Calabar (Sparks, "Two Princes," 581). [E]

February 14 the 1785

about 5 am in aqua Landing with great fog morning so I hav see my Boostam yams canow com hom with yams so I have pay Captin Savage 1000 yams for 100 Coppers and at 12 clock night Captin Brown Tender go way with 430 slaves

February 15 the 1785

about 6 am in aqua Landing with Little fog morning so wee go on Bord Captin Loosdam Tender and com back after 10 clock noon wee hear Loosdam Tender go way with 230 slaves

February 23 the 1785

. . I go Bord Captin Loosdam for break book for 3 slave so I break for one at Captin Savage   so I tak goods for slav at Captin Brown and com back.

37.   Boostam is Bosun or Umon, a town on the Cross River above Itu, where Efik traders pur-chased slaves, canoes, ivory, yams, and other provisions. Most regional yam supplies came from Afikpo, Abakaliki, and Obubra, 100 to 150 miles farther upriver (Latham, *Old Calabar*, 5, 7). Uwet, north of Duke Town on the Calabar River, was one important local yam market (Northrup, *Trade without Rulers*, 181). [S, E]

38.   Ibo merchants sold "new yams" (see the entry Aug. 11, 1785) after the annual harvest. Sup-plies dwindled by March. The diary reports prices of ten yams per copper rod in this entry and the entry from Dec. 22, 1785. A Liverpool ship's account book in 1769–1770 also records a price of ten yams per copper at Old Calabar, as does explorer Nicholls in 1805 (Hair, "Antera Duke," 361–362; Hallett, *Records*, 207). Captains provisioned Guinea ships with one-half to two yams per slave per day, depending on the sizes of the tuber and the African individual. The species *Dioscorea alata* (the "greater yam") grows up to two feet long and nine inches thick. For the four major yam species that grow in West Africa, see Johnston, *Staple*, 112–116. [E]

39.   Antera Duke's diary indicates that there was no precise time when Guineamen departed Old Calabar, as movements depended on tides: two slavers sailed in the morning, two in the after-noon, three in the afternoon, two in the evening, two at midnight, and one sometime after midnight. Captains anchored off Seven Fathoms Point, six to seven miles downstream (see note 80), to prepare for the Middle Passage and await favorable water levels and winds. After captains navigated over sand-

February 14, 1785

About 5 a.m. at Aqua Landing, a very foggy morning. I saw my Boostam [Umon][37] yam canoe coming home with yams. Then I paid Captain Savage 1,000 yams[38] for 100 copper rods, and at 12 o'clock at night[39] Captain Burrow's tender[40] went away with 430 slaves.[41]

February 15, 1785

About 6 a.m. at Aqua Landing, a little morning fog. We went on board Captain Langdon's tender and came back. At 10 o'clock in the afternoon we heard that Langdon's tender has gone away with 230 slaves.[42]

February 23, 1785

. . . I went on board Captain Langdon's ship to "break book" [make an agreement][43] for 3 slaves. I "broke trade" for one slave with Captain Savage. Then I took goods for slaves from Captain Burrows and came back.

bars in the Cross River estuary, they likely followed the practice at Bonny of waiting until morning to take advantage of land winds (Lambert, *Commons Sessional Papers*, 73:385). It is doubtful that vessels departed Calabar secretly at night to prevent slaves, as surgeon Thomas Trotter stated on his Gold Coast voyage, from showing "signs of discontent at leaving the coast" (Lambert, *Commons Sessional Papers*, 73:86). Incoming tides helped carry ships upriver to Old Calabar. In 1786, the *Hudibras* and *Langdale* (see notes 198, 209) "taking advantage of the first flood-tide . . . got under way, arrived at Calabar the next morning" (Butterworth, *Three Years Adventures*, 26–27). [E]

40. Captain John Ford of the Liverpool ship *Edwards* (180 tons). Regarding the difficulty of identifying Captain Brown (Burrows), see notes 30, 58, 112. [E]

41. The *Edwards* arrived in Grenada April 12, 1785, with 350 slaves, 23 of whom died before sale. The ship arrived in Liverpool August 16, 1785, with 298 ivory tusks, 38 puncheons palm oil, 8 puncheons pepper, and West India produce (*Liverpool General Advertiser*, Aug. 25, 1785). The Naval Office list did not record this African produce (CO106/4, f.18, NA). European merchants identified Old Calabar as "Remarkable for great Mortality in Slaves" (Williams, *Liverpool Privateers*, 486). [E]

42. The *Juba*, Captain Matthew Morley, arrived in St. Vincent May 19, 1785, with 180 slaves and cleared in ballast. [E]

43. "Break book" signifies the establishment of a trading agreement and derives from the European trader opening his account book to enter the transaction. [S]

March 6 the 1785

about 6 am in aqua Landing with fine morning so wee have all Egbo men & Egbo Young go to Henshaw Town for get Egbo moony   after 2 clock noon see Duke send his wife for call wee   say Captin Loosdam send his mat to till Duk about news ship com   so I & Esien go Bord Captin Loosdam to know so wee see news ship mat on bord   so wee did ask him way ship be   so his say in pointstand   so wee com ashor and 7 clock night wee have all Egbo men com back   the say Henshaw Town putt moony for 19 men Cobham Town for 5 men one for Guin Company Egbo.

March 7 the 1785

about 6 am in aqua Landing with fine morning so I go down for Landing after 10 clock wee go chop for Egbo Young house Liverpool Hall and after 12 clock Day wee see news ship mat com & com to till his will not com heer Did go to Commrown so Duke say berry well may go way plase.

44. One of the mates on the Bristol ship *Constantine* (see note 36). [E]

45. This new ship, that sailed farther southeast to Cameroon (see diary entries Mar. 7, 1785, and Mar. 12, 1785), was most likely the Liverpool ship *Will*, Captain Robert Bibby. [S, E]

46. Esien, a close associate of Antera and his brother Egbo Young. Diary entries mentioning Crim, Eshin, Esien, Esim, Esin and Ewien refer to this man. See appendix A. Variant spellings illustrate Antera Duke's difficulty rendering the sound of the name in letters. Indeed, Esin is the Duke Town pronunciation of a name pronounced *Esien* in Creek Town, and is one of the few examples of variant pronunciation in Efik. [S, E]

47. One of the mates on the Liverpool ship *Will* (see notes 45, 51). [E]

48. Ships arriving in the Cross River estuary anchored off Parrot Island, twenty miles downstream from Old Calabar. As Nicholls reported in 1805, Parrot Island "takes its name from the vast flights of those birds which are daily hovering over it. The whole island, which is about nine or ten miles in circumference, is one complete bed of mud, overgrown with large mangroves, with their shoots hanging down from every branch. . . . We waited at Parrot Island two days for a pilot to take

March 6, 1785

About 6 a.m. at Aqua Landing, a fine morning. All the Ekpe men and Egbo Young [Ofiong] went to Henshaw Town to get Ekpe money. After two o'clock in the afternoon Duke Ephraim sent his wife to call us. She said that Captain Langdon had sent his mate[44] to tell Duke about a new ship[45] coming. So I and Esien[46] went on board Captain Langdon's ship to find out. We saw the new ship's mate[47] on board. We asked him where the ship was. He said at Parrot Island.[48] Then we came ashore, and at 7 o'clock at night all the Ekpe men came back. They said that Henshaw Town had put in money for 19 men, Cobham Town[49] for 5 men, and one for the Guinea Company[50] Ekpe.

March 7, 1785

About 6 a.m. at Aqua Landing, a fine morning. I went down to the landing. After 10 o'clock in the morning we "go chop" [had a meal] at Egbo Young [Ofiong's] house "Liverpool Hall," and after 12 o'clock noon the new ship's mate came to tell us that he will not come here but go to Cameroon. So Duke Ephraim said, "Very well, go away please."[51]

us over the shallow part of the river, which extends about three miles up the river: between Parrot Island and Duke Town, the channel is very shallow, and only three fathom water" (Hallett, *Records*, 198). [S, E]

49. Cobham Town, a section of Creek Town during Antera Duke's time, migrated in part to Duke Town in the middle of the nineteenth century. Cobham is an anglicization of the Efik name, *Akabom*. [S, E]

50. Guinea Company is the English name for a group of Efik villages, referred to collectively as Adiabo, situated on the banks of the Calabar River, twenty to thirty miles north of Duke Town (Waddell, *Twenty-nine Years*, 361). Most maps locate Adiabo on the west bank. The name "Guinea Company" suggests that at one time, probably in the mid-seventeenth century, Europeans set up a trading post there. No records of such a Guinea Company trading post have been found, however. [S, E]

51. The captain of the British ship (probably the *Will*), anchored off Parrot Island, tried to force Duke Ephraim to lower his anchorage fee (see note 86), but his "commercial brinkmanship" did not succeed, and he departed to Cameroon. [S, E]

March 12 the 1785

about 6 a m in aqua Landing with great rain morning so I go down for
see Duke I & Ewien in his plaver house soon wee have Willy Honesty to
meet for Duk with all genllmen for new ship Captin plaver so wee writ
to his for com ashor so his say will not com ashor   & wee 3 go on bord his
for ask him and his answer be & say he will not stay for us River soon that
wee com ashor and till all genllmen so the say verry well may go way his
plase to go.

March 23 the 1785

at 5 am in aqua Landing with fine morning so I goin to see Duke in his
yard so wee carry all wee yams & Rod for Egbo yams for guin Company to
share soon after see the Duke get his life from powder about one his yellow
wife pip so all wee go to deash him copper for that sam time wee see that
small Bristall ship com up again.

April 11 the 1785

at 5 am in aqua landing with fine morning so I go Down for Landing so
I see nothing all day Butt 7 clock night I see two my poepls Com I was send
to find Ephrim Aqua Bakasy & say canow over it for water and Loos Everry
thing & canow all Loos.

---

52. Hutchinson, writing in the 1850s, has left the best description of a palaver house: "The
palaver-house consists of two walls running parallel for about forty yards, terminated by a transverse
wall, about as many feet in length, and thatched with a stout bamboo roof. The end by which it is
entered is opened from side to side, a space of nearly eighteen inches intervenes between the tops of
the walls running lengthways and the roof; and there is an ascent from the road by half-a-dozen steps
to the floor, which is hard and smooth. In the centre of the entrance is a huge hollow brass pillar
reaching up to the roof; further in are two more of equally imposing diameter, whilst between them
are a large bell and a piece of wood. The latter is drum-like in shape, with a slit longitudinally in it,
and fixed to the pillar. This is the Egbo drum which is beaten to alarm the inhabitants in case of a
fire, to give notice of the attack of an enemy, or to signify the fact of a leopard having been captured,
each occurrence being indicated by a peculiarity of beating the drum, which is known as soon as the
sound is heard. In the farthest corner of the house is a private sanctuary into which none but the
privileged are admitted on occasions of Egbo meetings" (Hutchinson, *Impressions*, 119–120). [S, E]

53. Efik merchants wrote brief notes in broken English to captains, enquiring about commercial transactions. For example (Williams, *Liverpool Privateers*, 553), on December 30, 1777, "Egoboyoung Coffiong" (Egbo Young Ofiong) wrote "Friend William Brighouse" the following note: "I have
sent you one woman and girl by Shebol. I will come toomorrow to see you. Suppose you Some

March 12, 1785

About 6 a.m. in Aqua Landing, a very rainy morning. I went down with Esien to see Duke Ephraim in his palaver house.[52] Soon after Willy Honesty met us at Duke's house with all the gentlemen to discuss the dispute with the new ship's captain. We wrote[53] to ask him to come ashore, but he said he would not come ashore. Then we 3 went on board his ship to ask him and his answer was that he would not stay in our river. Soon after that we came ashore and told all the gentlemen. Then they said: "Very well, he may go away, please go."

March 23, 1785

At 5 a.m. at Aqua Landing, a fine morning. I went to see Duke Ephraim in his yard. We carried all our yams and rods for Ekpe yams for the Guinea Company people to share. Soon after the Duke got his life [saved] from powder because of his yellow wife Pip.[54] All of us went to "dash" him coppers for that. At the same time we saw that the small Bristol ship[55] was coming up river again.

April 11, 1785

At 5 a.m. at Aqua Landing, a fine morning. I went down to the landing. I saw nothing all day, but at 7 o'clock at night I saw two of my people come that I had sent to find Ephraim Aqua Bakassey, and they said that the canoe overturned in water and everything was lost, including the canoe.[56]

Coffee to spar. Please send me a Little." For Liverpool captain Brighouse, see note 174. For further examples of correspondence between Efik and Liverpool captains/merchants, see Lovejoy and Richardson, "Letters," 99–111. [E]

54. The Duke's wife either gave him a powder (medicine) or may have saved his life by preventing an explosion of gunpowder. Waddell (*Twenty-nine Years*, 289) records an explosion in the Duke Town market in 1846, which killed several and injured many more. "Yellow" refers to the wife's coloring. [S, E]

55. Probably the Bristol snow *Wasp*, which traded for slaves and provisions at New Calabar and Old Calabar. Sailing vessels rigged as snows stepped usual mainmasts and foremasts but also a small mast, carrying a trysail, abaft. Snows generally measured 100 to 150 tons. See also note 235. [E]

56. Canoes frequently capsize on the Cross and Calabar rivers. Efik believe that a supernatural female power called Udominyang, also known as Mami Wata (possibly derived from "mermaid water"), seizes goods that fall into the river. Canoes that carry any type of ceremonial play or a corpse always have the new leaves of the palm-oil tree hanging from the bow to prevent supernatural powers capsizing them. Regarding present-day Mami Wata devotion in Nigeria, see Bastian, "Married." [S, E]

April 12 the 1785

at 6 am in aqua Landing with fine morning so I walk up to market way and com down for see Duke soon after wee hear Duke was brow Egbo for one his son nam Egbo Abashey so that son no mind that Egbo so wee did go to Egbo Bush for call Egbo com and killd one his mother goat.

April 21 the 1785

at 5 am in Aqua Landing with fine morning so at 12 clock Day wee 3 go Bord Buowon so wee beg his to Trust slave to carry for pay   so he will not after that wee com back and wee have Eshen Duke com hom from Orroup with 7 slave so I have my fishman com hom with slave and Robin send me 1 girl & my first Boy com from Curcock with slave and 12 clock night wee go to Savage

April 22 the 1785

at 5 am in Coffee Duke canow so wee get Longsider Captin Savage   so we be join settle Everrything what we owe him so he Deash Crim 1 Big great guns and Deash wee so com way and Liv to the portsand.

April 30 the 1785

about 6 am in aqua Landing with small Rain morning so I have all Captin com ashor   so I Little sick   so I not drink no mimbo all Day   befor night I hear Coffee Duke killd goat for Egbo Young & Crim the play.

57. The editors of Crow's *Memoirs*, 282–283, note that " 'to blow Egbo' upon anyone who is a European . . . in cases of disagreement between the chiefs and the captains . . . causes a suspension of intercourse until the parties come to an understanding." This also applies between Efik, as the instance reveals. Since the youth flouted the authority of the Ekpe society, the members seized one of his nanny goats as punishment. Had the boy not been the son of the chief, the punishment would undoubtedly have been greater. [S, E]

58. Antera's last entry regarding Captain Burrows ("Brown" or "Buowon"), who would have departed Old Calabar in August 1785 with perhaps 350 to 400 slaves. Burrows died (Oct. 22, 1786) on his subsequent voyage to Calabar, shortly before arriving there (BT98/47,349, NA). See also notes 30, 40, 112. [E]

59. Orroup refers to the Ododop people who inhabit southern Cameroon. The Okoyong, who live north of the Efik, evidently migrated from the Ododop. According to Goldie, *Dictionary*, 353, Ododop "is reached by the way of the Qua River, and in going to it from Calabar, two days are spent

April 12, 1785

At 6 a.m. at Aqua Landing, a fine morning. I walked up to the market path and came down to see Duke Ephraim. Soon after we heard that Duke "blew Ekpe"[57] on one of his sons named Egbo Abashey, but that son did not obey Ekpe. Then we went to the Ekpe Bush to call Ekpe to come and we killed one of his nanny goats.

April 21, 1785

At 5 a.m. at Aqua Landing, a fine morning. At 12 o'clock noon we 3 went on board Burrows's[58] ship. We begged him to "trust" for slaves but he would not. After that we came back. Esien Duke came home from Orroup [Ododop][59] with 7 slaves. My fisherman came home with a slave, and Robin sent me 1 girl. And my first boy [head slave] came from Curcock [Ikot Offiong][60] with a slave. And at 12 o'clock at night we went [downriver] to Savage's ship.

April 22, 1785

At 5 a.m. in Coffee Duke's canoe. We got alongside Captain Savage's ship. We got together to settle everything we owed him. He "dashed" Crim [Esien][61] 1 big great gun and "dashed" us. We came away and left for Parrot Island.

April 30, 1785

About 6 a.m. at Aqua Landing, a little morning rain. I invited all the captains to come ashore. I was a little sick so I did not drink any mimbo [palm wine][62] all day. Before night I heard that Coffee Duke had killed a goat for Egbo Young [Antera] and Esien. They played.

---

travelling on the river, and one on land, when the village Ekonganaku is reached." Ekonganaku was the southernmost of several Ododop towns and villages Goldie listed. See also chapter 4. [S, E]

60. Curcock is the Efik town Ikot Offiong, also known as Tom Ekrikok's town, located twenty miles northwest of Duke Town. "Curcock" derives from "Ekrikok." [S, E]

61. Wilkie's transcription inserted "(Esien?)" after "he Deash Crim." See note 46. [E]

62. Mimbo is the sap obtained from tapping palm trees. Men tapped the raffia palm, whose palm wine they called *mmin efik* (Efik wine). Some believed that "should a woman tap the wine from the palm wine tree, the sap would dry up" (Noah, "Economic," 140). Waddell stated that mimbo is "a milky-looking liquor . . . of agreeable taste and unintoxicating nature," but then noted: "I may mention that by standing a day and fermenting, and especially by the infusion of certain leaves, it acquires a somewhat intoxicating quality which some prefer" (Waddell, *Twenty-nine Years*, 248, 281–282). [S, E]

May 9 the 1785

at 5 am in aqua Landing with fine morning so I goin Down for Landing
after that I see Duke mak Doctor for his god Bason   soon after wee have
great Rain Day.

May 10 the 1785

. . . . . . so I be goin work for my Cobin after that I see Sam Ambo carry
Egbo Drum to Dick Ephrim about Ephrim Watt send to Dick Ephrim for
pay what owe about Captin Morgan was stop them

May 26 the 1785

at 5 am in aqua Landing with fine morning so I go Down for Landing
after I com up to work for my Cobin soon after I see Esin Duke Bring new
Captin with him to my Cobin   his be the Captin Combosboch   so his say
ship in the porrots sand   so wee 3 Did Drishst whit men and go Down for
his Boat & one Big canow to Bring up.

---

63. "Make doctor" denotes any type of sacrifice, oath-swearing, or form of "medicine." It is a
literal translation of the Efik *nam ibok*. Here it is some form of libation or sacrifice to Duke Ephraim's
household god, usually represented by a small earthenware bowl with a certain plant growing by it.
[S, E]

64. The words "god basin" are a direct translation of *usan abasi*, "basin of God." Waddell, *Twenty-
nine Years*, 381 states: "A little tree of a particular kind grew in every man's yard. . . . At the foot of it
were one or two earthen pans, or basins, containing a little water. Beside it were generally seen
human skulls, and over it a land-turtle hanging to the tree. The water in the basins was never emp-
tied out, but every prayer-day a little more was added, and something like a prayer or wish expressed
for safety, success, and length of life. The basin was called God's dish. It was said that they called on
their fathers on these occasions. Sometimes prayer was made over goats and fowls killed for friends
arriving and leaving." He also reports (398) that the basins were discarded in 1849 at the behest of
King Eyo II, a son of the Eyo Willy Honesty mentioned in the diary. The custom no longer survives
among the Efik. However, an analogous custom apparently occurs among the inhabitants of Uyanga
Okposu, who call themselves the Basanga. [S, E]

65. Ambo is the name of an extended family of Creek Town. Feuds between the Ambo family
and the Eyo Honesty family frequently resulted in internecine battles. Possibly the Ambo originated
from the Ekoi. [S, E]

66. The drum referred to here is most probably a small wooden drum with a skin head, on
which are painted various *nsibidi*, or secret signs intelligible only to members of the Ekpe society. A
creditor could appeal to the Society to obtain payment from a debtor. A messenger carries the drum

May 9, 1785

At 5 a.m. at Aqua Landing, a fine morning. I went down to the landing. After that I saw Duke Ephraim "make doctor"[63] at his "god basin."[64] Soon after we had heavy rain through the day.

May 10, 1785

. . . so I went to work at my cabin. After that I saw Sam Ambo[65] carrying the Ekpe drum[66] to Dick Ephraim, because Ephraim Watt had sent [a message] to Dick Ephraim to pay what he owed, because Captain Morgan[67] had stopped trading with them.

May 26, 1785

At 5 a.m. at Aqua Landing, a fine morning. I went down to the landing. Afterwards I came up to work at my cabin. Soon after I saw Esien Duke bringing a new captain with him to my cabin. He was Captain Comberbach[68] and he said his ship was at Parrot Island.[69] Then we 3 dressed as white men [in European clothes] and went down in his boat with one big canoe to bring up his ship.[70]

to the debtor together with a message summoning him to appear at the palaver shed for adjudication of the case. The appearance of the drum with *nsibidi* signifies the importance and trustworthiness of the messenger. Cross River peoples also used large wooden drums, slit gongs, constructed from hollowed-out tree trunks—*ikorok*—to disseminate important information to villagers ([Anon], "Drum," 1). [S, E]

67. Captain William Morgan of the Bristol ship *Pearl*, who died the previous year. The *Pearl* sailed from Old Calabar in July 1784, Morgan dying on August 26. The entry refers to slaves still owed the Bristol concern William Tapscott & Co. Efik merchants presumably canceled their debt with slave shipments to Tascott's brig *Little Pearl* during fall 1785. [E]

68. Captain Peter Comberbach of the Liverpool slaver *Gascoyne* (294 tons). In 1799 Comberbach sent Duke Town merchant Ephraim Watt Ephraim Duke (or Effiwatt Efiom Edem) a large bell as a gift. The inscription on the bell reads, "Effeywatt Captain Calabar 1799." During inquiries in 1917 and 1970 this famous "Cumberbeach bell" (the name has variant spellings) proved that Ntiero House, a member of whom was Antera Duke, produced Efik civil authorities (Akak, *Efiks*, 4:423; Oku, *Kings*, 5–9; Udoh, *Report*). During Antera Duke's youth, there were four houses, or "wards," in Duke Town: Duke, Henshaw, Eyamba, and Ntiero. The term "ward" describes lineage groups to which Efik traders such as Antera Duke belonged (Jones, "Political Organization," 122). [E]

69. Wilkie's transcription inserted "(Parrot Island?)" after "porrots sand." [E]

70. Antera Duke, Esien Duke, and Peter Comberbach traveled twenty miles downriver to Parrot Island, where Comberbach had anchored the 294-ton ship *Gascoyne*. See also note 48. [S, E]

June 14 the 1785

about 6 a m in aqua Landing with fine morning so Duke send for call
wee to go for Crim house for see what his pay to Commrown Backsider
Bakassey head to be slave 560 copper for all   so the did Chop Doctor
about the will we slave for Duke   so we mak one canoq carry them hom
all obong men go to Willy Honesty town.

June 24 the 1785

about 6 a m with fine morning so I go down for Landing to go bord
Captin Combesboch   I & Esim & Egbo Young   so wee hear news about
news ship   so not Bliv.

June 25 the 1785

at 5 a m in aqua Landing with fine morning so wee see Duke send for
call wee com about Captin Osatam want to go way soon after Duke & all
wee go to Ephrim Offiong Cobin to mak Doctor for old Callabar Doctor
for 1 goat   and after 3 clock noon wee see Captin Opoter arrived and we
hear Sam Cooper in 7 father point so wee 3 go Down to canow.

---

71. The 1956 edition changed Wilkie's diary dates 14.6.1785, 24.6.1785, and 25.6.1785 to
14.5.1785, 24.5.1785, and 25.5.1785. Though Wilkie changed Antera Duke's date formatting, we assume that Wilkie transcribed the day accurately and that Antera's text proceeds chronologically, even
though his date references may err. See chapter 5. [E]

72. The Efik possess a magic liquid known as *mbiam*, which will kill anyone who swears a false
oath (see Offiong, "Social Relations," 74–75). Each individual swears an *mbiam* oath that he or she
will refrain from cheating the other on penalty of sickness or death caused by the oath medicine. The
form of the oath is usually: "If I do such-and-such, *mbiam*, you kill me." Here "chopped doctor" refers
to the *mbiam* oath potion. See also note 172. [S, E]

73. The Efik word *obong* means "king." All "obong men" may refer to the obong's retainers or
to the heads of the different Ekpe society grades. [S, E]

74. Willy Honesty's town is Ikot Etunko, called Creek Town by the English. It is known in Efik
as *obio oko*, "that town," *esik edik*, "net of creek," and *ekuritonko*. The last is probably of Efut origin. [S, E]

75. Captain Peter Potter confirms Antera Duke's diary date, writing to owners William Davenport & Co. that he arrived at Old Calabar "the 25th June after a Passage of 72 days" (Potter to Davenport, July 23, 1785, Davenport Papers, MMM). [E]

June 14, 1785[71]

About 6 a.m. at Aqua Landing, a fine morning. Duke Ephraim sent to call us to go to Crim's [Esien's] house to see what he paid to Commrown Back-sider Bakassey's headman for slaves, 560 coppers for all. So they "chopped doctor" [took an oath][72] to agree to obtain slaves for Duke. We made one canoe carry them home. All the obong[73] men went to Willy Honesty's Town.[74]

June 24, 1785

About 6 a.m., a fine morning. I went down to the landing to go aboard Captain Comberbach's ship, I and Esien and Egbo Young [Antera]. We heard news about a new ship. We did not believe it.

June 25, 1785[75]

At 5 a.m. at Aqua Landing, a fine morning. Duke Ephraim sent [a message] to call us to come because Captain Tatem[76] wanted to go away soon. After Duke and all of us went to Ephraim Ofiong's[77] cabin to "make doctor" [sacrifice], according to Old Calabar ancient ritual, with 1 goat, and after 3 o'clock in the afternoon we saw that Captain Potter[78] had arrived and we heard that some [captain] Cooper[79] was in 7 Fathoms Point.[80] Then we 3 went down to our canoes.

76. Captain John Tatem of the Liverpool slaver *Fair American* (180 tons). Wilkie's transcription inserted "(?)" after "Osatam." [E]

77. The word *ofiong* means "moon" and is used as a personal name as well as a euphemism for menstruation. Efik have an eight-day week, which consists of four day names repeated in two cycles and distinguished by the adjectives *akwa*, "big," and *ekpri*, "small." Efik personal names may be based on the day the individual was born. Thus, a man born on *Akwa ofiong* or *Ekpri ofiong* may be named *Efiong* or *Ofiong* and a woman *Afiong*. [S]

78. Captain Peter Potter of the Liverpool slaver *Essex* (150 tons). Optter antera (Potter Antera) was another Calabar merchant (see diary entry Aug.? 7, 1785). "Optter/Potter" may have been adopted from Liverpool captain John Potter, who slaved at Old Calabar from 1768 to 1772, or from Peter Potter. No Efik word commences with the letter "P" (Goldie, *Dictionary*, xx–xxi, 260). [E]

79. Captain Thomas Cooper of the Liverpool slaver *Quixote* (158 tons). Wilkie's transcription inserted "(?) (some?)" between "Sam" and "Cooper." Antera is unsure if John or Thomas Cooper arrived. He met both men, Liverpool slaving captains, on previous voyages. [E]

80. Regarding Seven Fathoms Point, see note 39. Wilkie's transcription inserted "(fathom?)" after "father." [E]

June 1 the 1785

about 5 am in aqua Landing with fine morning   so I see Duke son Run
to till he say andony poeples catch wife the Let no market go past   want to
stop men for old town plaver so I send Esin go Down for Landing and Esin
get his canow so I get Coffee Duke   so wee go Down two great canow and
Egbo Young Little canow two Cobham Little we go Down   soon after wee
see them in 7 fother point   so the run   so my canow first   wee Run at
them and the get way for Bush   so my canow get som time and poeples
Run for Bush so catch them 1 men & two slaves in the canow & I tak the
canow   so Esin Canow catch 1 men   Egbo Young canow Ephrim Coffee
Brother catch 1 men   so wee com home after wee get town have Ebrow
Optter Cosoin to go Look them 7 men in Bush.

June 2 the 1785

at 5 a m in aqua Landing with fine morning so I go for Landing after we
goin to Duke   so Duke have mak bob with Bakassey   and at 9 clock wee
have two new Captin com ashor   so wee have go on bord Optter 7 canow
for coomy   awaw com hom with Dead slave for Orroup.

June 8 the 1785

about 6 a m in aqua Landing so wee go on bord Cooper and com ashor
about at Done coomy   soon after wee 3 send for see Eyo Willy Honesty
about his no Drink Doctor wee 3 send him 3 Jar Brandy   after 9 clock night
I see Esin Duk come and till me about Arshbong Duk sister nam Ambong
his Dead his sick 8 day.

81. One of Duke Ephraim's many sons, possibly Efiom Edem, known later as Great Duke
Ephraim. He held the positions of obong and eyamba from ca. 1814 (a date based on oral testimony)
until his death in 1834 at the age of seventy-five or eighty. [E]

82. The Andoni live on the creeks on the west side of the Cross River estuary and speak a dialect of the Ibibio-Efik cluster (Westermann and Bryan, *Languages*, 133). [S, E]

83. The Andoni people were seizing women on their way to market. [E]

84. Old Town (Obutong), about three miles upriver from Duke Town. According to Liverpool
captain (later merchant) Ambrose Lace, in 1748 "there were no inhabitants in the place called Old
Town, they all lived at the place called New Town; some time after disputes arose between a party
who now called themselves Old Town people, and those who are now called New Town people"
(Lambert, *Commons Sessional Papers*, 72:345). Regarding "New Town," see note 124. [E]

July? 1, 1785

About 5 a.m. at Aqua Landing, a fine morning. I saw Duke Ephraim's son[81] run to tell us that the Andoni[82] people were "catching wives" and won't let any market canoes go past.[83] They wanted to stop [seize] men until the Old Town palaver was settled.[84] I sent Esien down to the landing and Esien got his canoe. Then I got Coffee Duke. We went down in two great canoes and Egbo Young [Antera's] little canoe and two of Cobham's little canoes. Soon afterwards we saw them at 7 Fathoms Point. They ran. My canoe being first ran at them and they got away into the bush. My canoe got there at the same time, and my people ran into the bush. They caught 1 man and two slaves in the canoe and I took the canoe. Esien's canoe caught 1 man, Egbo Young's canoe and Ephraim Coffee's brother caught 1 man. Then we came home. After we got to town Ebrow Potter had occasion[85] to go to look for those 7 men in the bush.

July? 2, 1785

At 5 a.m. at Aqua Landing, a fine morning. I went to the landing. Afterwards we went to Duke Ephraim. Duke had a discussion with [Commrown Backsider] Bakassey, and at 9 o'clock two new captains came ashore. We went on board Potter's ship with 7 canoes to collect "comey."[86] Awa Ofiong came home with a dead slave from Orroup.[87]

July? 8, 1785

About 6 a.m. at Aqua Landing. We went on board Cooper's ship and came ashore about 8 o'clock[88] having taken "comey." Soon after we 3 sent [a message] to see Eyo Willy Honesty about his not "drinking doctor."[89] We 3 sent him 3 jars of brandy. After 9 o'clock at night Esien Duke came and told me that Archibong[90] Duke's sister named Mbong was dead. She had been sick for 8 days.

85. Wilkie's transcription inserted "(?)" after "Cosoin." [E]

86. Efik merchants profited from "comey" (anchorage fees), paid to them by captains. Comey refers to a payment for "coming." The chief of each town received comey directly from individual ships' captains. See chapter 2 and also note 51. [E]

87. Perhaps Awa Ofiong brought the deceased slave to Duke Town to prove that the transaction at Ododop occurred. [E]

88. Wilkie's transcription inserted "(?)" after "at." [E]

89. Most likely the *mbiam* oath—Willy Honesty refuses to take an oath of agreement. See also note 72. [E]

90. Archibong is an anglicization of the Efik name Asibong. [S]

June 9 the 1785

at 5 a m in Arshbong Duke yard so wee have poeples mak groun for Sam
yard   after 10 clock wee putt his in grown so wee 3 firs 3 great gun and wee
see Willy Honesty com to Coomy on bord Optter & Cooper.

June 15 the 1785

about 5 I Lig in my bud so I hear Egbo Young call out for me so wee 3
go bord . . . Cooper so I get goods for 50 slaves for wee 3 soon after wee com
back

June 17 the 1785

at 5 a m in aqua Landing with fine morning so I go on bord Cooper and
com ashor so I break book for 2 slave for Captin OSatam   after 9 clock night
I have send 5 my poeples for go Yellow Bellay Daught mother Dick Ebrow
sister to stop one his house women to give ship sam as his Brother was give
one my fine girl I was give to my wife and give Captin fairwether and his
will not pay me that mak I stop.

June 18 the 1785

at 5 a m in aqua Landing with fine morning so I go down for Landing
after I have mak Doctor for one goat at my father Bason.

June 19 the 1785

at 5 a m in aqua Landing with fine morning so I go Down for Landing
with very Bad Sunday about what wee owe Captin OSatam after I go on
bord Cooper

June 20 the 1785

at 5 a m in aqua Landing with fine morning so I go on bord Cooper and
com ashor   so I stop all Day befor 3 clock noon I no eat one thing to night
I give Jug Brandy and 4 Callabash chop for Arshbong sister cry house

91. Testifying before a parliamentary select committee in 1790, Liverpool sailor Isaac Parker
stated that he went on two slave-raiding expeditions with New (Duke) Town merchant Dick Ebro
in 1766. They attacked villages twenty to forty miles upriver from Duke Town, capturing perhaps 100
men, women, and children. Ebro had a "great number" of his own slaves, whom he worked "cutting
the wood, and fishing—and going in his canoes up the country sometimes" (Lambert, *Commons Sessional Papers*, 73:126–127, 131–132, 136–137). "Dick Ebruo" also is listed in the account book of the
Liverpool slaver *Dobson* at Old Calabar in 1769–1770 (Hair, "Antera Duke," 360). For slave raiding,
see also notes 32, 134, 201. [E]
92. Antera Duke refers to Captain Patrick Fairweather's 1784 voyage to Old Calabar on board
the Liverpool ship *Tarleton* (342 tons). His term "fine girl" perhaps refers to an attractive slave given

July? 9, 1785

At 5 a.m. we were in Archibong Duke's yard and we had people make a grave in the same yard. After 10 o'clock we put her [Mbong] in the ground and fired 3 great guns, and we saw Willy Honesty come to collect "comey" on board Potter's ship and Cooper's ship.

July? 15, 1785

About 5 I was lying in my bed. Then I heard Egbo Young [Antera] call out for me. Then we 3 went aboard ... Cooper's ship. I got goods for 50 slaves for the 3 of us. Soon after we came back.

July? 17, 1785

At 5 a.m. at Aqua Landing, a fine morning. I went on board Cooper's ship and came ashore. I "broke book" for 2 slaves with Captain Tatem. After 9 o'-clock at night I sent 5 of my people to go to Yellow Belly's daughter, the mother of Dick Ebrow's[91] sister, to seize one of her house women to give to the ship, because her brother gave one of my fine girls, whom I had given to my wife, to Captain Fairweather,[92] and Yellow Belly's daughter's brother did not pay me. That's why I seized the house woman.

July? 18, 1785

At 5 a.m. at Aqua Landing, a fine morning. I went down to the landing. Afterwards I "made doctor" with one goat at my father's basin.

July? 19, 1785

At 5 a.m. at Aqua Landing, a fine morning. I went down to the landing. It was a very bad Sunday[93] because of what we owe Captain Tatem. After-wards I went on board Cooper's ship.

July? 20, 1785

At 5 a.m. at Aqua Landing, a fine morning. I went on board Cooper's ship and then came ashore. I stopped trading all day before 3 o'clock in the after-noon. I did not eat anything until night. I gave a jug of brandy and 4 cal-abashes of food to Archibong's sister's cry [mourning] house.[94]

to Fairweather for sexual purposes. Fairweather first captained a slaving vessel to Old Calabar in 1770, and he subsequently trained Liverpool-Calabar captains William Begg, William Brighouse, John Cooper, John Keatin, John Reynolds, and John Tatem, five of whom Antera Duke references. See also chapter 2. [E]

93. Antera presumably uses "bad" as a translation of *idiok*, a common Efik word with negative connotations. Here Antera's bad luck was due to the debt he owed Captain Tatem. See also Sept.? 29, 1785, a "bad Sunday" due to Egbo Young Ofiong's illness. [S, E]

94. Regarding the term "cry house," see Simmons, "Ethnographic Sketch," 22. Wilkie's tran-scription inserted "(?)" between "cry" and "house." [S, E]

at 6 a m in aqua Landing with fine morning so I go on bord Cooper and
Esin go on bord Combesboch so wee com ashor after 3 clock noon   I have
send pound with Esin to give Combesboch for get 8 slav to pay Captin
OSatam so I Done pay OSatam for all I owe and at 7 clock I Did send my
Brother Egbo Young for Boostam Trad for slaves.

about 5 am in aqua Landing with fine morning so wee Captin Osatam
Drop Down in . . Porrots iland

at 5 a m in aqua Landing with fine morning so wee have Duke go Down
for Tatam I & Abashey Offiong one canow   Esin one canow   Duke one
Canow all Captin to go Down so we get Bord in 1 clock   soon after 3 clock
wee Liv Duke on Bord and wee com Back with Tatam himself & all Captin

at 5 am in aqua Landing with fine morning so wee go on bord Combes-
boch   so wee get slave for get Duke prown and som to Ephrim Watt &
Ephrim Aqua prown   so wee go Down with Tom Cooper and Captin of
Combesboch tender and wee get on bord 2 clock and settle everry thing and
his Deash Duke and wee 143 keg powder 984 copper besides . . 3 pc pocket
Honesty for wee 4 and Duke so wee com ashor

95. In many regions of Africa, pawnship functioned as an institution of precolonial credit. After
advancing trading goods to African merchants, such as Antera Duke, captains received, in return, a
few pawns as collateral for debt. Merchants redeemed pawns—some of whom were relatives—by de-
livering slaves. Pawns were usually boys; in some African coastal markets, quantities of gold or ivory
could also be held in pawnship (Lovejoy and Richardson, "Business," 71–73). Butterworth, at Old
Calabar in 1786, recalled that when slavers prepared to depart, a "signal was hoisted, to acquaint those
who had any pawns on board, that the time of their redemption was at hand: It consisted of the fore-
topsail loosed, and waved fourteen days previous to our sailing, during which time, the fathers or
friends of the pawns redeemed them, if in their power to do so. Pawns are the sons or daughters of
inferior traders, who, from gaming or losses in trade, pledge them for what they may want in trade,
enjoying the right of redeeming them; but, if they are unable, then the pawn becomes a slave" (Butterworth, *Three Years Adventures*, 96–97). Wilkie's transcription inserted "(?)" after "prown." [E]

July? 21, 1785

At 6 a.m. at Aqua Landing, a fine morning. I went on board Cooper's ship and Esien went on board Comberbach's ship. We came ashore at 3 o'clock in the afternoon. I sent a pawn[95] with Esien to give Comberbach to get 8 slaves to pay Captain Tatem. So I have paid Tatem for all I owed, and at 7 o'clock I sent my brother Egbo Young [Antera][96] to Boostam to trade for slaves.

July? 22, 1785

About 5 a.m. at Aqua Landing, a fine morning. We saw that Captain Tatem[97] was dropping downriver to . . . Parrot Island.

July? 23, 1785

At 5 a.m. at Aqua Landing, a fine morning. We took Duke Ephraim down to Tatem's ship, I and Abashey Ofiong in one canoe, Esien in one canoe, Duke in one canoe. All the captains went down. We got on board at 1 o'clock. Soon after 3 o'clock we left Duke on board and came back with Tatem himself and all the captains.

July? 24, 1785[98]

At 5 a.m. at Aqua Landing, a fine morning. We went on board Comberbach's ship. We brought slaves to redeem Duke Ephraim's pawns and some to redeem Ephraim Watt's and Ephraim Aqua's pawns. We went down with Tom Cooper and the captain of the Comberbach tender[99] and we got on board at 2 o'clock and settled everything, and he "dashed" Duke and us 143 kegs of powder, and 984 coppers besides . . . 3 pieces of pocket Honesty [kerchiefs][100] for us 4 and Duke. Then we came ashore.

96. Regarding Antera's "brother" Egbo Young, see appendix A, diary entries July? 21, 1785, Nov.? 5, 1785, Nov.? 7, 1785, Jan. 23, 1786, Oct. 19, 1786, and note 12. [E]

97. Wilkie's transcription inserted "(Tatam?)" after "OSatam" as Antera Duke mentioned Tatam the next day. [E]

98. Wilkie replicates the date June 24, 1785; we assume Antera Duke or Wilkie incorrectly replicated the day/date. [E]

99. Captain Edward Aspinall of the Liverpool ship *William* (160 tons). [E]

100. "Pocket Honesty" denotes a kerchief or head-tie, so called because the color was unfading and thus "honest," or because the trade article was first introduced via Eyo Willy Honesty of Creek Town. The modern Efik word *bokit*, "head-tie," derives from the English "pocket," probably an abbreviation of "pocket-kerchief." [S, E]

June 27 the 1785

about 6 am in aqua Landing with fine morning so I have Abashey Commrown Back sider and one his boy to putt prown for ship so I did go on Bord Cooper to putt prown so I did give him one goods so wee Drink all Day befor night Captin Tatam go way with 395 slaves.

June 29 the 1785

at 4 wee a m with play for Arshbong Duke yard about his sister Dead so his did kill goat to us and after 10 clock Day wee have Egbo Run   sam time I see Egbo Young com and call me so I did find him   after word he say young Tom Robin his Dead be sick 7 Day   my Brother ogan & arshbong Duke son go to Orroup

July 7 the 1785

about 6 am in aqua Landing with fine morning so go Down for Landing and after 10 clock I have go on bord Captin Collins to ask him what mak his mat Drop Down   so his say Captin Combesboch Beg him to stay Little time about want get som prown out so I Did tak 2 Jar Brandy for I & Esin and I did send Optter antera for Enyong to trad of slave

July 11 the 1785

about 6 am in aqua Landing with great Rain morning wee have Captin Collins go river Barr with 230 slaves and at 1 clock noon wee go to aqua about King aqua chop new yams so wee 4 carry him 4 Jug Brandy for Deash so his killd two goat for wee 4 callabash chop   so Egbo Young and Esin com hom befor wee com for 10 clock night

101. Perhaps July? 27, 1785, was a "Calabar Sunday," when according to Nicholls, Efik leaders "drink mimbo all day long" (Hallett, *Records*, 209). See also Dec. 25, 1785 (drinking on Christmas) and Apr. 28, 1787 (another "Calabar Sunday"?). [E]

102. The *Fair American* arrived in Kingston, Jamaica, October 11, 1785, with 250 slaves, 5 of whom may have died shortly after arriving (a second source records 245 slave imports). The ship returned to Liverpool March 26, 1786, with 279 ivory tusks and West India produce (*Manchester Mercury*, Apr. 4, 1786). [E]

103. Unfortunately, the play is unspecified. Most probably it consisted of drummers and singers, but it may have been one of several costumed plays. Perhaps, from the reference to Ekpe, it was the Society's figure—though the "play" and Ekpe may not be connected. Wilkie's transcription inserted "(?)" between "wee" and "a m with play." Possibly "wee a m" means in the "wee morning"—very early. [S, E]

104. The name Hogan—one of Antera Duke's brothers—is the anglicization of the Efik name Okon. A male born at night is named Okon (a female is Akon). [S, E]

July? 27, 1785

About 6 a.m. at Aqua Landing, a fine morning. Abashey Commrown Backsider and one of his boys put pawns on board the ship, and I went on board Cooper's ship to deliver pawns and I gave him some goods. We drank all day.[101] Before night Captain Tatem went away with 395 slaves.[102]

July? 29, 1785

At 4 a.m. we carried a play[103] to Archibong Duke's yard because his sister [Mbong] had died. He killed a goat for us, and after 10 o'clock in the morning Ekpe ran. At the same time I saw Egbo Young [Antera] coming to call me and I found him. Afterwards he said that Young Tom Robin was dead after being sick for 7 days. My brother Hogan [Abashey Antera][104] and Archibong Duke's son went to Orroup.

August? 7, 1785

About 6 a.m. at Aqua Landing, a fine morning. I went down to the landing and after 10 o'clock I went on board Captain Collins's[105] ship to ask him why his mate[106] was dropping down the river. He said that Captain Comberbach begged him to stay a little longer because he wanted to get some pawns out. So I took 2 jars of brandy for myself and Esien and I sent Potter Antera to Enyong[107] to trade for slaves.

August 11, 1785[108]

About 6 a.m. at Aqua Landing, a very rainy morning. Captain Collins went over the river bar with 230 slaves,[109] and at 1 o'clock in the afternoon we went to Aqua as King Aqua was eating new yams.[110] We 4 carried him 4 jugs of brandy as a dash. He killed two goats for us and dashed 4 calabashes of chop. Egbo Young [Antera] and Esien went home before we came home at 10 o'clock at night.

105. Captain Thomas Collins of the Bristol slaving ship *Martha* (90 tons). [E]

106. One of the mates on the *Martha*. [E]

107. Enyong is the name for a cluster of villages situated in the Enyong Creek, a tributary entering the Cross River from the west above Itu. [S, E]

108. See note 109. [E]

109. Captain Peter Potter wrote to Liverpool merchant William Davenport on August 8, 1785, and gave the letter to Captain Collins as he departed Calabar. The evidence thus verifies August as the diary month. The *Martha* arrived at Dominica October 3, 1785, with 150 slaves. [E]

110. The Qua, of Big Qua Town, three miles northeast of Duke Town, speak an Ekoi dialect and held a feast to celebrate the arrival of the new yams, harvested in July and August. During annual yam celebrations in Ibibio country, "offerings are made of the new crop to *Abasi* and to the *Idem*. Till then gentleman never eat them, though their slaves were not bound to observe the rule" (Waddell, *Twenty-nine Years*, 640). [S, E]

July 19 the 1785

at 5 am in aqua Landing with small Rain morning   so wee hear Tom
Robin family cutt men head of for young Tom after 10 clock wee Duke and
all Captin go Down for Captin Brivon plaver after 4 clock time wee see one
new ship com up so wee go bord him   his be Captin Hughes com up in 7
an 7 fother pointt

July 23 the 1785

about 5 am in aqua Landing with small Rain morning I have Cooper
Capniner work for me soon after I see al Captin com ashor for tak on bord
so all wee go with King on bord Captin fairwether for coomy.

August 3 the 1785

at 5 am in aqua Landing with fine morning so wee goin in Duke yard
for mak bob to Coffee Sam Ephrim & his wife so Coffee Sam Ephrim sister
com & fight with Brother wife so Duke & all wee be Dam angiry about that
fight

August 4 the 1785

at 5 am in aqua Landing with fine morning so I go Down for Landing
so wee have Jock Bakassey com to Landing with ground Egbo in canow
about Little time wee go Down with two Egbo young Drum to fetch up and
carry Egbo to Cush and at 7 clock night I have all Captin super for my
house.

111. Tom Robin, chief of Obutong or Old Town, decapitated several slaves to honor his dead
son. The Efik sacrificed slaves at the death of an important freeman and believed that they accompanied him into the next world. [S]

112. Wilkie's transcription inserted "(?)" after "Brivon." Antera Duke refers to Captain John
Burrows, a name he had difficulty spelling (see notes 30, 40, 58). The palaver might concern sailors
who absconded from the Bristol slaver *Alexander* at Bonny and took refuge with Burrows. The
Alexander's surgeon, Alexander Falconbridge, testified that Captain James McTaggart beat regularly
almost all the sailors, and that eleven men ran away [on July 18, 1785] in a longboat belonging to another Bristol captain. From Bonny, they "intended to go to Old Calabar; but getting up the wrong
river, they were seized by the natives and stripped, and marched through the country to Old Calabar. Two or three, I am informed, died in the march. Those that remained went on board a ship called
the Lyon, Captain Burrows" (Lambert, *Commons Sessional Papers*, 72:310–311; *Alexander* muster, Sept.
29, 1785–Sept. 29, 1786, 78, BRO). On August 17, Burrows, in preparation to steer the *Lion* out of
the Cross River, transferred unsold trading goods totaling £190 to Captain Peter Potter. The *Lion* arrived at Grenada October 26, 1785, with 315 slaves, and on April 11, 1786, it arrived in Liverpool
with 427 ivory tusks and two chests Guinea pepper. [E]

113. Captain Joseph Hughes of the Liverpool slaving ship *President* (263 tons), which departed
Liverpool June 28, 1785. [E]

August? 19, 1785

At 5 a.m. at Aqua Landing, a little morning rain. We heard that Tom Robin's family[111] have cut men's heads off for Young Tom [Robin]. After 10 o'clock we, Duke Ephraim and all the captains went down [river] about Captain Burrows's[112] dispute. After 4 o'clock we saw one new ship coming up. We went aboard it. It is Captain Hughes,[113] who came up at 7 o'clock at 7 Fathoms Point.[114]

August 23, 1785[115]

About 5 a.m. at Aqua Landing, a little morning rain. I had Captain Cooper's carpenter[116] work for me. Soon after I saw all the captains coming ashore to take us on board. All of us went with King [Calabar][117] on board Captain Fairweather's ship[118] to collect "comey."

September? 3, 1785

At 5 a.m. at Aqua Landing, a fine morning. We went to Duke Ephraim's yard to discuss the dispute between Coffee Sam Ephraim and his wife. Coffee Sam Ephraim's sister came and fought with her brother's wife. Duke and all of us were damn angry about that fight.

September? 4, 1785

At 5 a.m. at Aqua Landing, a fine morning. I went down to the landing. We saw Jock Bakassey come to the landing with the Grand Ekpe[119] in a canoe. After a little time we went down with two of Egbo Young [Ofiong's] drums to fetch up and carry Ekpe to the bush, and at 7 o'clock at night I had all the captains to supper at my house.[120]

---

114. Wilkie's transcription inserted "(?)" between "7" and "an 7 fother point." [E]

115. See note 118. [E]

116. The carpenter (name unknown) of the Liverpool ship *Highfield*, Captain Thomas Cooper. European ships transported frames, windows, and other building supplies. In 1785 Captain Patrick Fairweather transported one of Duke Ephraim's houses, "about twenty yards long, and thirty feet high, with a ground floor, a first floor, and a kind of cock-loft" (Hallett, *Records*, 208). Ship carpenters and joiners frequently built and repaired Efik merchants' furniture and helped African workers build houses such as Egbo Young Ofiong's "Liverpool Hall" (see note 35) and Antera Duke's "big house" (see Sept.? 29, 1785). See also entries Sept.? 30, 1785, Dec. 30, 1785, Sept. 20, 1787, Jan. 27, 1788. [S, E]

117. King Calabar, the Ndem priest. See chapter 1. [E]

118. Captain Fairweather of the *Tarleton*, which arrived from Liverpool on August 14, 1785 (Potter to Davenport, Aug. 17, 1785, Davenport Papers, MMM), thus confirming August as the diary month. [E]

119. Grand Ekpe is Idem Nyamkpe, or the costumed figure of the Nyamkpe grade of the Ekpe society. [S]

120. See Simmons, "Ethnographic Sketch," 10–11, for a description of such a meal. [S, E]

August 14 the 1785

at 5 am in aqua Landing with fine morning so I have mak 6 Callabash of Egbo chop soon after 4 clock time we begoin carry Egbo moony for Duk plaver house for share for all old Egbo   I putt for 3 men Esin Duke putt for 3 men   Egbo Young for 2 men   Ephrim Aqua for 1 men   Ogun Antera for 1 men   so wee have great rain for all night

August 29 the 1785

at 6 am in aqua Landing with small rain morning so I go on bord fairwether to fetch his joiner for mak window for big house   so wee Bad Sunday beCause wee have Egbo Young Offiong no well.

August 30 the 1785

at 5 am in aqua Landing with fine morning so I go to see Egbo Young about his sick   so I have Joiner work for me all Day so wee super with all Captin to Esin house.

September 8 the 1785

about 6 am in aqua Landing with fine morning so I go on bord ship and com Back   so I have give King up Tabow Besides Chap so I killd goat and Deash him & poeples about 30 copper besides mimbo and Brandy   so the play all Day befor night so I mak Robirst Enyang father house to Drink Doctor with Robirst and send to trad heer for Enyang. All Cobham town give Egbo moony 12 new town Egbo 4 for guin company & old town Egbo

September 18 the 1785

about 6 am in aqua Landing with fine morning so I go Down for Landing so I have go on bord Cooper so I find Egbo Young so his tell me he say not one Captin be bord   all go down for catch fish with Willy Tom Robin so wee com ashor soon and I have Esin chop for me & Drink mimbo

121. The food usually served for initiations and so on is *ukang*, a dish prepared with large quantities of dried fish, yam, palm oil, salt, and pepper. [S]

122. Traditional Efik houses lacked windows. Slaves were never permitted to have a window if they owned a house for fear that they might observe some Ekpe society secret. [S, E]

123. This is the only instance when Antera Duke writes "Tabow." Goldie's dictionary of the Efik language defines the verb *täb-ä* or *töbö*: "To be low; to stand or lie low, or inferior in height to some other thing"; "To be short in stature, but thick in body; to be squab or squat"; "To be or become low, inconsiderable in wealth or rank" (Goldie, *Dictionary*, 283). If instead Antera refers to giving tobacco to King Calabar, the priest of the tutelary deity, Ndem Efik, the leaf may be a hallucinogen. Alternately, Antera may be referring to a "king" of the "Tabac" people (a people referenced by

September? 14, 1785

At 5 a.m. at Aqua Landing, a fine morning. I had 6 calabashes of Ekpe chop[121] made. Soon after 4 o'clock we began carrying the Ekpe money to Duke Ephraim's palaver house to share among all the old Ekpe men. I put in money for 3 men, Esien Duke put in money for 3 men, Egbo Young [Antera] for 2 men, Ephraim Aqua for 1 man, Hogan [Abasi] Antera for 1 man. We had heavy rain all night.

September? 29, 1785

At 6 a.m. at Aqua Landing, a little morning rain. I went on board Fairweather's ship to fetch his joiner to make windows[122] for the big house. We had a bad Sunday because Egbo Young Ofiong is not well.

September? 30, 1785

At 5 a.m. at Aqua Landing, a fine morning. I went to see Egbo Young Ofiong because of his sickness. I had the joiner working for me all day. We had supper with all the captains at Esien [Duke's] house.

October? 8, 1785

About 6 a.m. at Aqua Landing, a fine morning. I went on board ship and came back. I bowed before King Calabar and the shrine.[123] In addition to chop, I killed a goat and "dashed" him and his people about 30 coppers besides mimbo and brandy. They "played" all day until night. I made Robert Enyong's father's house "drink doctor" with Robert and sent him to trade at Enyong. All Cobham town gave Ekpe money for 12 New Town[124] Ekpe, 4 for Guinea Company and Old Town Ekpe.

October? 18, 1785

About 6 a.m. at Aqua Landing, a fine morning. I went down to the landing. I went on board Cooper's ship. I found Egbo Young [Antera]. He told me that not one captain is aboard because all had gone down to catch fish with Willy Tom Robin.[125] We came ashore soon afterwards and Esien came to eat with me and drink mimbo.

explorer Henry Nicholls in 1805), likely those living on the west bank of the Cross River at Ekritobako towns, twenty miles southwest of Duke Town (Hallett, *Records*, 204; Waddell, *Twenty-nine Years*, map facing 242; Latham, *Old Calabar*, frontispiece). Wilkie's transcription inserted "(?)" after "Tabow". [E]

124. In Antera Duke's time Efik referred to Duke Town as "New Town." Nicholls estimated its population at 2,000 when he visited in February 1805 (Hallett, *Records*, 206). [E]

125. Willy Tom Robin (Eso Asibong) was the fifth king of Old Town (Latham, *Old Calabar*, 11). *Willy Tom Robin* was also the name of a Liverpool schooner, captured from the Spanish in 1797, that made slaving voyages to Angola and the Windward Coast in 1799–1801. [E]

September 26 the 1785

about 6 am in aqua Landing with fine morning so I go Down for
Landing and after 5 clock I have go on bord Optter I & Esin so Esin go way
befor me   sam time I & Captin Optter see one ship come up in 7 fother
pointt   soon wee com ashor & I run to till Captin fairwether   so wee go
down for Landing and get canow to go down with Captin fairwether &
Captin Hughes & Captin Combesboch & Captin Optter & Captin William
all 5 Captin after 7 clock night wee get on bord   his be Captin Overton &
Senders for Captin fairwether soon after wee com to River & com ashor to
super for my house with them Captin and the go on bord in 10 clock with
great rain.

September 27 the 1785

about 6 am in aqua Landing with fine morning so wee hear Tom Salt or
Captin and new poeples fight with Combesboch Long Boat Captin Optter
Captin of Tender & Combesboch Captin of Tender in the Long Boat them
was go down for Look the Boat Combesboch poeples was tak for his mat
and get way with 15 good for slave so Tom Salt or Captin Androw fight with
them Captin so the poeples get Captin out in Boat so Boat one Captin stop
32 men & 1 women from them and Bring him soon after all wee go to meet
for Duk to know Duk think for Doe

October 3 the 1785

. . so I mak goods for Callabar antera to go in Commrown soon after that
wee 3 putt head togeter and settle what wee think to Doe and at 7 clock
night I have putt thing in Egbo Young Big Canow & at 12 clock night I sail
to go to Curcock.

126. See note 128. [E]

127. Captain Joseph Williams of the Bristol slaving brig *Little Pearl* (72 tons). See also note 67. [E]

128. Captain Barton Overton of the Liverpool slaving ship *Fanny* (100 tons), which arrived at Old Calabar October 26, 1785 (Potter to Davenport, Nov. 3, 1785, Davenport Papers, MMM), thus confirming October as the diary month. [E]

129. The name of a fishing village, as well as Tom Shott's point on the west bank of the Cross River estuary, probably derived from the name Tom Salt. All Efik-Ibibio dialects except Oron lack the *l* sound. [S]

October 26, 1785[126]

About 6 a.m. at Aqua Landing, a fine morning. I went down to the landing, and after 5 o'clock Esien and I went on board Potter's ship but Esien
went away before me. At the same time I and Captain Potter saw one ship
coming up from 7 Fathoms Point. Soon we came ashore and I ran to tell
Captain Fairweather. We went down to the landing and got a canoe to go
down with Captains Fairweather, Hughes, Comberbach, Potter, and Williams,[127] all 5 captains. After 7 o'clock at night we got on board Captain Overton's ship[128] and tender for Captain Fairweather. Soon after we came up the
river and came ashore to supper at my house with those captains. They went
back on board at 10 o'clock in a great rain.

October? 27, 1785

About 6 a.m. at Aqua Landing, a fine morning. We heard that Tom Salt[129]
or Captain [Andrew] and new people are fighting Comberbach's long boat.
Captain Potter's captain of the tender[130] and Comberbach's captain of the
tender went down the river in the long boat to look for Comberbach's boat,
which the people had taken from his mate, and they had got away with goods
for 15 slaves. Tom Salt or Captain Andrew fought with the captains, and the
people got the captains out in the boats. One captain's [boat] took 32 men[131]
and 1 woman from them [their canoe] and brought them back. Soon afterwards all of us went to meet Duke Ephraim to know what he was thinking
to do about it.[132]

November? 3, 1785

. . . so I got together goods for Calabar Antera to go to Cameroon. Soon
after that we three put our heads together and settled what we are thinking
to do, and at 7 o'clock at night I put the things in Egbo Young [Antera's] big
canoe, and at 12 o'clock at night I sailed to go to Curcock.

130. Captain John Howard of the Liverpool slaving ship *Christopher*, which arrived at Old Calabar August 21, after purchasing sixty-nine slaves and 5,712 pounds of ivory at Cameroon (Potter to
Davenport, Nov. 3, 1785, Davenport Papers, MMM). [E]
  131. Wilkie's transcription inserted "(2?)" between "32" and "men." [E]
  132. Duke Ephraim, as obong, brokered "diplomatic" disputes between Efik, non-Efik, and
overseas visitors. [E]

October 4 the 1785

about 4 clock I am in Egbo Young canow in 7 fother Point so I see one
Egbo Sherry fish small canow so giv the Drink Brandy and Did giv som fish
after 2 clock time I have great rain all Day befor 9 clock.

October 5 the 1785

about 5 am in Duke Canow in Tom Curcock house so I com up get ashor
from Willy Curcock old market plase so I mak poeples get chop heer soon
after com up and after 1 clock noon get from old Curcock Landing   sam
time I see my Brother Egbo Young & see bob & Apandam the com Down all
one Canow so I walk up with 4 Rods 1 Case Bottle Brandy to Deash andam
Curcock so I see Eshin

October 7 the 1785

at 5 a m in old Curcock Town with fine morning so I go Down for
Landing so I hav apandam & my Brother & see bob go Back for Boostam
soon after I did go to Enyong Creek for see potter mother house so I no find
him in heer and I get for Enyong town & I see one slave soon after I have
see potter nice father house killd goat for me & Deash 4 Rods & 2 yds
Romall so the & Callabar poeples give me about 12 callabash chop and get
time to com Back in night because be so Bad Crik

October 10 the 1785

about 5 am in Curcock town with fine morning so I go Down for Landing
so I hav give andam Curcock 1 slave goods to Live for his after 3 clock noon I
have see us Boostam canow com Down with 5 slave and yams in sam time I
sail way to com hom with slav in my canow and 3 small canow besides my

133. The etymology of "Egbosherry" is obscure; the first two syllables may represent the Efik-
Ibibio word *ekpo* (ghost). James Barbot (Hair, Jones, and Law, *Barbot on Guinea*, 2:680–681), referring
to his voyage to Old Calabar in 1698, mentions a payment of seventeen copper bars for yams to
"William king Agbisherea" and to "Robin king Agbisherea." [S, E]
134. While canoeing on the Old Calabar River near Seven Fathoms Point, five miles south of
Duke Town, Antera Duke met an Ibibio fisherman and gave him some brandy, in return receiving some
fish. Antera Duke does not seize the man; on only one occasion does the diary refer to the Efik "catching" men (see entry Jan. 30, 1785, and Northrup, *Trade without Rulers*, 67). See also notes 91, 201. [E]
135. Wilkie's transcription inserted "(Ditto canow?)" after "Duke Canow," and we accept that
Antera refers to Egbo Young Antera's canoe, as in the previous entries. [E]
136. Old Curcock or Old Ekrikok is the Ibibio town of Itu on the left bank of the Cross River,
several miles below the embouchement of the Enyong Creek. [S, E]

November? 4, 1785

About 4 o'clock I was in Egbo Young [Antera's] canoe at 7 Fathoms Point. Then I saw one Egbo Sherry[133] fishing in a small canoe. So I gave him a drink of brandy and he gave me some fish.[134] After 2 o'clock there was great rain, [which continued] all day until 9 o'clock.

November? 5, 1785

About 5 a.m. in Ditto [Egbo Young Antera's] canoe.[135] [I went] to Tom Curcock's house. I came up and got ashore at Willy Curcock's old market place. I made my people get chop here soon after we came up, and after 1 o'clock in the afternoon I went from old Curcock landing. At the same time I saw my brother Egbo Young [Antera] and I had a discussion with Apandam. They came down all in one canoe. Then I walked up with 4 rods and 1 case of bottled brandy to "dash" to Andam Curcock. Then I saw Esien.

November? 7, 1785

At 5 a.m. in old Curcock Town,[136] a fine morning. I went down to the landing. I met Apandam and my brother [Egbo Young Antera] and had a discussion about going back to Boostam. Soon afterwards I went to Enyong Creek to visit Potter [Antera's] mother's house. I did not find her there, and I went to Enyong town and saw one slave. Soon after I saw that Potter [Antera's] father's house had killed a nice goat for me; and they dashed me 4 rods and 2 yards of romal.[137] Then they and the Calabar people gave me about 12 calabashes of chop in time to return that night because the creek is so bad [difficult to navigate].[138]

November? 10, 1785

At about 5 a.m. in Curcock town, a fine morning. I went down to the landing. I gave Andam Curcock goods for 1 slave to leave at his place. After 3 o'clock in the afternoon I saw our Boostam canoe come down with 5 slaves and yams. At the same time I sailed away to come home with the slaves in my canoe, and there were 3 small canoes besides mine.

137. The *OED* defines "romal" as a silk or cotton square or handkerchief often used as a head-tie, or thin silk or cotton fabric with a handkerchief pattern, and derives the word from an Urdu compound. In 1720 romal was valued at 11s per piece; red-and-blue cotton romals cost 15s in 1725, and in silk were valued at 25s 6d in 1730 (see Donnan, *Documents,* 2:245, 324, 384). John Adams, a late eighteenth-century slaving captain, noted that romals were in great demand in Old Calabar (Adams, *Remarks,* 254–256). [S, E]

138. After the June–September rainy season, high water and strong currents hindered navigation in the Cross River system, including tributaries such as the narrow Enyong Creek. Waddell commented on the difficulty of navigating upriver to Uwet: "but the river being then in flood (October), and very strong, we had great difficulty in forcing our way up." "So strong was the current that day, that with six rowers, we could hardly make way" (Waddell, *Twenty-nine Years,* 457–458). [E]

October 11 the 1785

about 9 am in aqua Landing without sleep and wee go Down for Landing and I see Duke Sam Jack Esin about Combesboch Tender so he say his go way with 325 slave and wee have Ogon Antera and all wowo Egbo men the go with two Egbo in canow to Ebrow Ebgo Sherry fish men.

October 23 the 1785

about 6 am in Aqua Landing with fine morning so wee have go on bord Captin Fairwether Tender to get Tea to Drink after 11 clock Day wee have one foshin Ebgo for brow all men and wee Butt Egbo Young to not comig and go to not way all Day befor 5 clock time and I have be angary with my Dear Awa Ofion about water so my mother com and putt word   so his Did bring angary to my mother so I Dam more angary join about that

October 24 the 1785

about 6 am in aqua Landing with fine morning so I go Down for Landing   so I see my canow from Landing   so I see Duke send old Tom House to big me for send men to go catch cow for him so I Did go myself and I Catch for my hand soon after Duke hear that and his Did send me 1 Larg fish about that so I see tak Duke sister Daught for his house to mak were new cloth so all wee & Duke Did give abou 20 cloth and wee Did play all Day befor night & wee see Willy Tom Robin com to play with us & I Deash him some cloth.

139. The *William*, Captain Edward Aspinall, arrived at Dominica December 19, 1785, with 295 slaves, and returned to Liverpool March 19, 1786, with 293 ivory tusks (*Liverpool General Advertiser*, Mar. 23, 1786). [E]

140. Antera's "wowo" may refer to the Efik verbs *wärä* or *wara*. One definition of *wärä*, according to Goldie, is "To come forth; to come out; to proceed from; to issue." A second definition is "To come up, grow up," and he cites the phrase *Öwärä akamba owo*—"He becomes a big man." He defines *wara* as "To make haste; to be speedy, quick" (Goldie, *Dictionary*, 338). Each of these meanings sug-

November? 11, 1785

About 9 a.m. at Aqua Landing, having had no sleep. We went down to the landing and I saw Duke Ephraim, Sam, Jack and Esien about Comberbach's tender. He said it had gone away with 325 slaves,[139] and Hogan [Abashey] Antera and all the wowo [new][140] Ekpe men they went with two Ekpe in a canoe to Ebrow Egbosherry's fishermen.

November? 23, 1785

About 6 a.m. at Aqua Landing, a fine morning. We went on board Captain Fairweather's tender to get tea to drink. After 11 o'clock in the morning we had one fashion[141] [kind of] Egbo to brow [summon] all men and us, but Egbo Young [Ofiong] did not come and we did not go away all day before 5 o'clock. I was angry with my dear wife Awa Ofiong about water.[142] Then my mother came and "put in her word." She was rude to my mother, so I was damn more angry about that.

November? 24, 1785

About 6 a.m. at Aqua Landing, a fine morning. I went down to the landing. I saw my canoe go away from the landing. I found that Duke Ephraim had sent Old Tom House to beg me to send men to catch a cow for him. I went myself and caught it with my own hand. Soon afterwards Duke heard about that and he sent me a large fish. Then I saw them taking Duke's sister's daughter to his house to make her wear her new cloth.[143] All of us and Duke gave about 20 cloths and we "played" all day till night. Willy Tom Robin came to "play" with us [arrived to join the festivities] and I "dashed" him some cloth.

gests recently qualified Ekpe men and speed, those men who did the "leg work" (working as runners, for example), for Ekpe society. See also "wawa" in Antera's entry from Jan. 17, 1788. [E]

141. Our interpretation of "foshin" as "fashion" rests on Efik use of the term noted by Holman, *Travels*, 401 and Waddell, *Twenty-nine Years*, 276, 278. [E]

142. Women, children, or female slaves obtained water from springs. Probably the diarist's chief wife neglected to have the water pot filled. Water is stored in a large earthen pot called *abang ukpong*. [S]

143. The ceremony of dressing an adolescent girl in a cloth signified the attainment of womanhood (see Simmons, "Ethnographic Sketch," 15). See also notes 27, 254, 260. [S, E]

December 14 the 1785

about 5 am in aqua Landing with great fog morning so I go Down for Landing for putt yams for canow after 8 clock wee go Down 3 Big Canow I & Esin & Egbo Young with 32 slaves so his keep 25 slaves and abou 6000 yams so his Deash was wee 3 great guns and com up sam time after 8 clock night go on bord Captin Fairwether to his Tender go way with 250 slave & 2 Town.

December 22 the 1785

about 6 am in aqua Landing with fine morning so wee have Esin go down for hughes so I Did send 2 canow for 1500 yams for 150 copper to pay Captin hughes his so Captin William go Down Captin William carry 169 slave Captin Hughes carry 480 slave

December 23 the 1785

. . Captin Hughes his go way with 484 slave   Captin William go his way with 160 slave so I & Esin go on bord Cooper for brek Book for 4 slave arshbong Duk son com hom for Orroup with slave

December 25 the 1785

about 6 am in aqua Landing with fog morning so I go Down with Drehst man and Captin Fairwether Drehst & Bring his Dinner from Esin   so all wee to Esin new house Captin Fairwether & Tom Cooper Captin Potter Duke Ephrim & Coffee Duk & Egbo Young & Esim & I & Eshen Ambo Eyo Willy Honesty & Ebitim to Dinner for new year and Drink all Day befor night

144. The largest number of yams mentioned in the diary—but a fraction of the total number captains would purchase. From mid-July 1769 to January 1770, for example, Captain John Potter of the *Dobson* purchased 82,935 yams at Old Calabar. [E]

145. The *Fanny*, Captain Barton Overton, arrived at Dominica on February 18, 1786, with 234 slaves. The *Fanny* returned to Liverpool May 14, 1786, with fifty-five ivory tusks and West India produce (*Liverpool General Advertiser*, May 18, 1786). "2 Town" is Antera Duke's first diary reference to tons of produce. We assume that he refers to two tons of ivory and palm oil, since fifty-five tusks shipped to Liverpool probably weighed 750 to 1,000 pounds. Africans would have consumed palm oil on the Middle Passage, thus explaining why Captain Overton did not carry any to Liverpool. Alternatively, Overton may have offloaded some ivory on the African coast or in the West Indies. See also chapter 3. [E]

146. The *Little Pearl*, Captain Joseph Williams, arrived at Grenada February 17, 1786, with 102

December 14, 1785

About 5 a.m. at Aqua Landing, a very foggy morning. I went down to the landing to put yams in the canoe. After 8 o'clock we went down in 3 big canoes, I, Esien, and Egbo Young [Antera] with 32 slaves. He kept 25 slaves and about 6,000 yams.[144] He dashed us 3 great guns, and we came back up river. Some time after 8 o'clock at night we went on board Captain Fairweather's ship, whose tender went away with 250 slaves and 2 tons [of ivory and palm oil].[145]

December 22, 1785

About 6 a.m. at Aqua Landing, a fine morning. Esien went down to Hughes's ship. I sent 2 canoes with 1,500 yams for 150 coppers to pay Captain Hughes. Captain Williams went down the river. Captain Williams carried 169 slaves.[146] Captain Hughes carried 480 slaves.[147]

December 23, 1785

. . . Captain Hughes went away with 484 slaves. Captain Williams went away with 160 slaves. I and Esien went on board Cooper's ship to "break book" for 4 slaves. Archibong Duke's son came home from Orroup with slaves.

December 25, 1785

About 6 a.m. at Aqua Landing, a foggy morning. I went down after dressing and Captain Fairweather dressed and brought his dinner from Esien. We all went to Esien [Duke's] new house—Captain Fairweather, Tom Cooper, Captain Potter, Duke Ephraim, Coffee Duke, Egbo Young [Ofiong], Esien and I, Esien Ambo, Eyo Willy Honesty, and Ebitim—for New Year's dinner,[148] and we drank all day until night.

---

slaves, all of whom were sold. The Naval Office list reports no African produce (CO106/2, f. 21, NA). The sales record indicates that Campbell, Baillie & Co. sold 20 African men, 26 African women, 32 African boys, and 24 Africans girls for £2,585 (LivRO, 942 HOL 10). [E]

147. The *President*, Captain Joseph Hughes, arrived at Kingston, Jamaica, February 21, 1786, with 370 slaves, after having been sighted at Dominica with 390 slaves. Perhaps 62 African captives died in Kingston harbor, as agent Alexander Lindo sold 175 African male slaves and 153 African female slaves (328 total) from the *President*. The same sales record lists 230 adult and 92 child slaves sold (322 total) (*Report of the Lords*, III, Appendix, Jamaica). The *President* then returned to Liverpool on May 23, 1786, with 399 ivory tusks, 2 casks long pepper, and West India produce (*Liverpool General Advertiser*, May 25, 1786). [E]

148. Antera Duke, in referring mistakenly to Christmas as New Year's Day, indicates that Efik and Britons celebrated the two days equally. [E]

December 30 the 1785

about 6 a m in aqua Landing with fog morning and I go Down for
Landing so I find Duke in Landing & Egbo Young go on bord Captin
fairwether and I have 5 my poeples to cutt Big tree at my Big Cobin after 1
clock noon I have Tom Cooper mat Mr. Charls com to me for nail my Bud
Bottom on

December 31 the 1785

about 6 a m in aqua Landing with little fog morning so I go Down for
Landing and I have see market canow go way and at 1 clock noon wee go
bord Cooper for dinner after 4 clock time wee com back

January 1 the 1786

. . . I have see Duke send canow for Mimbo after 2 clock time wee
Captin Potter Bring his Dinner so wee have all Captin com to chop to Esim
new house about new year   wee see Eyo & Ebitim go to aqua Bakassey

January 2 the 1786

about 6 am in aqua Landing with fine morning so I go Down for Landing
and wee go bord Cooper for tea and com ashor sam time I see all Bush Ebgo
Ebrow to no man com up for house all Day after 5 clock time wee have see
one King Tom Sott com from Duke 2 canow to stay heer for settle Egbo bob.

January 3 the 1786

about 6 am in aqua Landing with fine morning . . so wee have Duke take
goat & mak Doctor with King Tom Sott so fairwether send for men to Com
on bord for tea so wee have chop for my house and wee play for Esim house
& carry to arshbong yard & play at night

149. Mate Thomas Charles of the *Quixote* (BT98/46,309, NA). See note 79. [E]

December 30, 1785

About 6 a.m. at Aqua Landing, a foggy morning, and I went down to the landing. I found Duke Ephraim there, and Egbo Young [Ofiong] went on board Captain Fairweather's ship. I had 5 of my people cut a big tree at my big cabin. After 1 o'clock in the afternoon Tom Cooper's mate Mr. Charles[149] came to me to nail my bed's bottom on.

December 31, 1785

About 6 a.m. at Aqua Landing, a little morning fog. I went down to the landing and saw the market canoe go away, and at 1 o'clock in the afternoon we went on board Cooper's ship for dinner. After 4 o'clock we came back.

January 1, 1786

... I saw Duke Ephraim send a canoe for mimbo. After 2 o'clock Captain Potter brought his dinner. All the captains came to chop at Esien [Duke's] new house for the New Year. We saw Eyo and Ebitim go to Akwa Bakasi.

January 2, 1786

About 6 a.m. at Aqua Landing, a fine morning. I went down to the landing and we went on board Cooper's ship for tea and came ashore. At the same time I saw that Bush Ekpe was being blown to keep anyone from coming to the house all day. After 5 o'clock we saw one King Tom Salt coming from Duke Ephraim with 2 canoes to stay here to settle an Ekpe dispute.

January 3, 1786

About 6 a.m. at Aqua Landing, a fine morning .... Duke Ephraim took a goat and "made doctor" with King Tom Salt. Then Fairweather sent for men to come on board to get tea. Then we had chop at my house and we "played" at Esien [Duke's] house, and carried the play to Archibong's yard and "played" at night.

January 22 the 1786

at 5 am in aqua Landing with Little fog morning so I go Down for Landing I have send 4 hand   for Little canow to mak my father Boostam misimbo to guin Company for com to mak with Ephrim Offiong about warr Copper and at 1 clock time wee Tom Cooper Tender go way with 383 slave & 4 Town

January 23 the 1786

about 6 am in aqua Landing so I go Down for Landing after 8 clock I have my Brother Egbo Young & Apandam com hom from Boostam with slave Toother and wee see Tom Cooper & Captin fairwether the com up them was carry Tender Down in aqua River

January 29 the 1786

at 5 am in aqua Landing with fine morning so all walk up to King Egbo for work to plaver house   soon after wee hear King Egbo Sam Ambo stop 3 Egbo Sherry men to the River about the was killd one his men and after 1 clock time wee hear Egbo Young Dear Brun young girl at Aqua Town

February 8 the 1786

at 5 am in aqua Bakassey Crik and with fine morning and I git for aqua Bakassey Cril in 1 clock time so I find Arshbong Duke and I go Longsider his Canow so I tak Bottle Beer to Drink with him and wee have call first for new Town and stay for Landing com way so wee go town in 3 clock time so we walk up to plaver house sam time to putt grandy Egbo in plaver house and play all night   Combesboch go way with 639 slave & Toother

150. Perhaps Guinea Company paid a fee ("war coppers") to Duke Town as tribute to avoid attack. [E]

151. The Liverpool slaving ship *Quixote* (158 tons), Captain James McGauley, arrived at Trinidad February 16, 1786, with 54 slaves and at Havana April 25, 1786, with 236 slaves. It returned to Liverpool August 20, 1786, with 3.5 tons ivory, two casks palm oil, and four casks pepper. In addition the ship carried 130 tons logwood, likely harvested in the Bay of Honduras (*Liverpool General Advertiser*, Aug. 24, 1786). Efik transported palm oil in tubs and jars. European importers then transferred the oil into wooden casks. Two tons equaled three casks. Captain John Adams, a British slave trader in 1786–1800, noted that the height of the palm-oil season in Bonny and Calabar was April–July (Adams, *Remarks*, 233). Captain McGauley thus shipped palm oil that had been stored for several months at Duke Town. [E]

January 22, 1786

At 5 a.m. at Aqua Landing, a little morning fog. I went down to the landing. I sent 4 hands in a little canoe to take my father [brother?] to Boostam.
Misimbo goes to Guinea Company to ask them to come make [an agree-
ment] with Ephraim Ofiong about war coppers,[150] and at 1 o'clock Tom
Cooper's tender went away with 383 slaves and 4 tons [of produce].[151]

January 23, 1786

About 6 a.m. at Aqua Landing. I went down to the landing. After 8
o'clock my brother Egbo Young [Antera] and Apandam came home from
Boostam with slaves and ivory,[152] and we saw Tom Cooper and Captain Fairweather come up. They had taken the tender[153] down to Aqua [Kwa] river.

January 29, 1786

At 5 a.m. at Aqua Landing, a fine morning. We all walked up to King
Ekpe to work at the palaver house. Soon afterwards we heard that King Egbo
Sam Ambo had stopped [seized] 3 Egbosherry men at the river because they
had killed one of his men, and after 1 o'clock we heard that Egbo Young
[Ofiong's] dear wife had given birth to a young girl at Aqua Town.

February 8, 1786

At 5 a.m. in Akwa Bakasi Creek, a fine morning, and I got from [out of]
Akwa Bakasi Creek at 1 o'clock. I found Archibong Duke and went alongside his canoe. I took a bottle of beer to drink with him and we called first
at New Town and stayed at the landing. We came away, then went to town at
3 o'clock. We walked up to the palaver house at the same time to put Grand
Ekpe in the house and "played" all night. Comberbach went away with 639
slaves and ivory tusks.[154]

---

152. Simmons ("Ethnographic Sketch," 75) noted that "Toother was the slave brought from
Boostam. Presumably he had done something wrong, so his master sold him to the Europeans." It is
more likely, however, that "Toother" means ivory, as in the contemporary term "elephants' teeth." [S, E]

153. Probably the *Quixote* (see note 151). [E]

154. The *Gascoyne*, Captain Peter Comberbach, arrived at Dominica Apr. 15, 1786, with 516
slaves. It returned to Liverpool July 8, 1786, with 70 puncheons palm oil, 23 puncheons pepper, and
2.5 tons ivory (*Liverpool General Advertiser*, July 13, 1786). Efik traders likely imported ivory from
Cameroon, according to Adams the biggest ivory exporter in Africa (Adams, *Remarks*, 144). See also
chapter 3. [E]

February 11 the 1786

about 5 am in Coqua Town so have Arshbong Desire me to walk up for Commrown with him so I Did and wee pas 3 Little Commrown town for way wee tak walk for 1 clock .. to get Big town so the killd goat and Deash 1 iron 2 Rod for me so wee mak long time bob for th to Arshbong good so Did pay Boy slav and the Beg wee to Drink Doctor with them so arshbong mak one his father son nam Ebetim to Drink Doctor with him to the Deash one men cow to be killd & 8 Rod about that th Chap wee us so com Down in 6 clock night

March 2 the 1786

. . . . Captin Potter go way with 284 slaves.

March 17 the 1786

. . . . We com ashor and I Did tak one goat for mak Doctor at my godBason . . . .

March 20 the 1786

. . . . Soon I see Tom Cooper com up and say Captin Fairwether go way for Barr with 440 slaves . . . .

March 21 the 1786

. . . . Duk call all wee to com for his plaver house to hear Ephrim Egbo Daught with his .. and Dick Ephrim and he say wil not marry Long Duk so wee find Everry bob be trws for him and wee hav Ephrim Duk women com and Break Duke god Bason about he Will not marry Ephrim after 7 clock night I have my wif offiong Brother Dead by his father yard and putt his 8 yds fine clothe Did putt his in grown in 6 clock time

155. Antera Duke met Archibong Duke at Akwa Bakasi Creek, and together they traveled during the night by canoe to Aqua ("Big") Town in Little Cameroon. After resting, they walked inland about forty minutes, passing through three small Cameroon villages, arriving at Big Town (Odobo). See also chapter 4 and appendix B. [E]

156. The *Essex*, Captain Peter Potter, arrived at Dominica April 15, 1786, with 235 slaves. It arrived in Liverpool August 12, 1786, with 1,000 pounds ivory and West India produce (*Liverpool General Advertiser*, Aug. 17, 1786). [E]

February 11, 1786

About 5 a.m. in Aqua Town. Archibong desired me to walk up to Cameroon with him. I did and we passed 3 little Cameroon towns on the way. We walked [about forty minutes] up to 1 o'clock . . . to arrive at Big Town [Odobo].[155] There they killed a goat and "dashed" me 1 iron and 2 rods. We had a long discussion with them about Archibong's trading goods. They paid a boy slave and begged us to "drink doctor" with them. Archibong made one of his father's sons named Ebetim "drink doctor" with him too. They dashed us one male cow to be killed and 8 rods for that chop for us, so we came down at 6 o'clock at night.

March 2, 1786

. . . Captain Potter went away with 284 slaves.[156]

March 17, 1786

. . . We came ashore and I took one goat to "make doctor" at my "god basin" . . . .

March 20, 1786

. . . Soon I saw Tom Cooper come up river and he said that Captain Fairweather was going away to the bar with 440 slaves . . . .[157]

March 21, 1786

. . . Duke Ephraim called all of us to come to his palaver house to hear Ephraim Egbo's daughter with him . . . and Dick Ephraim, and she says she will not marry Long Duke [Ephraim]. We found that every bob [troubling thing] said about him [Long Duke] was true,[158] and Ephraim Duke's women came and "broke" [made a libation in] Duke Ephraim's "god basin" because she will not marry Long Duke Ephraim. After 7 o'clock at night my wife Awa Ofiong's brother died in his father's yard and was put in the ground with 8 yards of fine cloth at 6 o'clock [the next morning].

157. The *Tarleton*, Captain Patrick Fairweather, arrived at Dominica May 9, 1786, with 360 slaves. It arrived in Liverpool September 5, 1786, with 57 puncheons and 1 butt palm oil, 50 barrels pepper, 105 ivory tusks, 8 tons redwood, and West India produce (*Liverpool General Advertiser*, Sept. 7, 1786). [E]

158. Wilkie's transcription inserted "(?)" after "trws." [E]

April 20 the 1786

. . . . I hav see the poeples about 200 hand com for mee the want me to
giv 2 my father son for pown Roonsom the men Eyo Duk was stop for what
the owe him and the say one the men Dead for Arshbong Duk hand sam
time I see the first the head men com & call me out to go up in the King
Plaver house to hear what they say soon after I see one my men was Liv him
to canow com up and tell me he say Enyong poeples tak my canow way for
Landing so I Run & go Down for Landing   I find no canow and the stop
two my Boy out in canow and putt for Iron so the com Back and stop awaw
son for my face and carry way to putt for Iron so the com Down one time
about 30 guns for the hand the Look for shoot me and after 2 clock the
Bring canow for Landing no be Little time the tak canow Back and the keep
me all Day without eat any thing and after 9 clock night the Let me hav
canow & all my men Back

May 1 the 1786

. . . . so I sail way to aqua Bakasy and I get the 1 clock noon and I call for
new Town first and I go to old Town so I firs one great gun for Crek   sam
time I find Coffe Duk heer and I hear Egbo Cry out in plaver house so I did
carry 1 Larg Cas Bottle Brandy & 4 Rods to Deash Egbo men and I Did call
the town genllmen & women and poeples to com & hear what I hav to say
so I Did settle everry bob and I give Coffee 1 Larg Cast Bottle Brandy & 10
yams   so Coffee sail away in 8 clock night

May 4 the 1786

. . . . about 4 am in aqua Bakasy Landing in Abashey offiong canow and
I com way from in 10 clock time and get Jocket Bakassey town in 7 clock
night   so wee carry grandy in th plase owe me goods   so the Did pay me
1 men slave for my goods   so Esim tell he say the was kill cow for him &
Deash 80 Rods besides 16 Rods for me

May 18 the 1786

. . . . we hear John Cobham family mak play for the father so the Did cutt
7 men head of

159. Half brothers (*eyen ete*). [S]
160. Regarding Ekpe "crying out," see Simmons, "Ethnographic Sketch," 17. [S, E]

April 20, 1786

. . . I saw the people, about 200 hands, coming to me. They wanted me to give 2 of my father's sons[159] as pawns to ransom the men Eyo Duke had stopped [seized] for what they owed him; and they said one of the men was dead by Archibong Duke's hand. At the same time I saw the first [number one] headman coming to call me out to go up into the King's palaver house to hear what they [had to] say. Soon after I saw one of my men who was left at the canoe come up and tell me that Enyong people had taken my canoe away from the landing. Then I ran down to the landing. I found no canoe; and they stopped two of my canoe boys from the canoe and put them in irons. Then they came back and stopped Awa Ofiong's son before my face and carried him away to put in irons. They came down [at] once with about 30 hand guns [musquetoons], looking to shoot me; and after 2 o'clock they brought the canoe to the landing. After a long time they took the canoe back and they kept me all day without my eating anything, and after 9 o'clock at night they let me have the canoe and all my men back.

May 1, 1786

. . . I sailed away to Akwa Bakasi and I got there at 1 o'clock in the af-ternoon, and I called at New Town first and then went to Old Town. I fired one great gun in the creek. At the same time I found Coffee Duke here and I heard the Ekpe cry out[160] in the palaver house. Then I carried 1 large case of bottled brandy and 4 rods to "dash" the Ekpe men, and I called the town gentlemen and women and people to come and hear what I had to say. I set-tled every bob [dispute] and I gave Coffee 1 large case of bottled brandy and 10 yams. Coffee sailed away at 8 o'clock at night.

May 4, 1786

. . . about 4 a.m. I was at Akwa Bakasi landing in Abashey Ofiong's canoe, and I came away from there at 10 o'clock and reached Jock Bakasi's town by 7 o'clock at night. We carried Grand Ekpe[161] to the place because they owed me goods. They paid me 1 male slave for my goods. Esien told me that they killed [sacrificed] a cow for him and "dashed" him 80 rods besides 16 rods for me.

May 18, 1786

. . . We heard that John Cobham's family were making a "play" for their father [King Calabar].[162] They cut 7 men's heads off.

161. "Grand Ekpe," the Nyamkpe (eyamba) figure. [S, E]
162. See chapter 1. [E]

May 21 the 1786

I have send 10 hand for work in Bush   after 10 clock time wee hav Bush
Egbo stop all men to no com up and I have Esim & John Cooper chop for
my house   Tom Cooper go way with 381 slaves

June 10 the 1786

we have Duk send all Egbo men go to King Egbo for shar soon Copper
Tom Sott Bring for Little Egbo plaver   so Egbo tak men tak 40 Copper for
send Egbo sherry way & one goat be killd for them at 3 clock time soon see
them two newsship com up Captin ford & one funchmen ship so wee go on
bord them two and them ashor to Duk

June 23 the 1786

I see Duk send one Boy to com & call wee 3 so wee go & find Eyo Willy
Honesty heer with Funch Coomy Book   so Duk tell wee 3 to go on bord
with Eyo so wee get Bord ship   wee go Down to Look Book   so wee find
all Henshaw town tak coomy mor what the get for Everry ship   we com
ashor & chop for abashey

July 2 the 1786

about 5 am in aqua Landing with fine morning and I go down for see
Duke with Little sick 8 clock night wee all tak 2 goat for go mak Doctor
with Duke

July 3 the 1786

about 5 am in aqua Landing with fine morning I goin to see Duke with
sick   after 1 clock time all wee going to Duke yard for chop them goat wee
was mak Doctor   and 7 clock night Duk ferry Bad

---

163. That is, stopped them coming up to work. [E]

164. The *Highfield*, Captain Thomas Cooper, arrived at Trinidad July 15, 1786, with 290 slaves,
287 of whom were sold subsequently. Cooper abandoned the ship at Trinidad (where it was condemned) and transshipped 420 ivory tusks and eight puncheons palm oil to the ship *Union*, which
arrived in Liverpool in October 1786 (*Liverpool General Advertiser*, Oct. 19, 1786). [E]

165. Captain John Ford of the Liverpool slaving ship *Ellis* (280 tons). [E]

166. Captain Moël de Kerfraval of the La Rochelle slaver *Aurore*. Significantly, Antera Duke
does not know the captain's surname (see chapter 2). [E]

167. Eyo Willy Honesty had the "comey" (port dues) book for the *Aurore*. In contrast to

May 21, 1786

I sent 10 hands to work in the bush. After 10 o'clock the Bush Ekpe stopped all men from coming up,[163] and I had Esien and John Cooper chop at my house. Tom Cooper went away with 381 slaves.[164]

June 10, 1786

Duke Ephraim sent all the Ekpe men to go to King Ekpe to share some copper rods that Tom Salt brought for the little Ekpe palaver. King Ekpe picked men to take 40 coppers to send Egbosherry way [to the Egbosherry district], and one goat was killed for them at 3 o'clock. Soon we saw two new ships coming up, Captain Ford[165] and one French ship.[166] We went on board the two and [brought] them ashore to Duke.

June 23, 1786

Duke Ephraim sent one boy to come and call us 3. We went and found Eyo Willy Honesty here with the French "comey" book.[167] Duke told us 3 to go on board with Eyo, so we got on board the ship. We went down to look at the book. We found that all the Henshaw Town people had taken more "comey" than what they [should] get for every ship.[168] We came ashore and had chop at Abashey's.

July 2, 1786

About 5 a.m. at Aqua Landing, a fine morning. I went to see Duke Ephraim who was a little sick. At 8 o'clock at night we all took 2 goats to go and "make doctor" with Duke.

July 3, 1786

About 5 a.m. at Aqua Landing, a fine morning. I went to see Duke Ephraim, who is sick. After 1 o'clock we all went to Duke's yard to eat the goats, that we had "made doctor" with, and at 7 o'clock at night Duke was very bad.

Britons, French captains traded for slaves and provisions mostly from Creek Town and Old Town merchants. See chapter 2. [E]

168. The Henshaws continued to receive comey until the 1820s. Bold (*African Guide*, 77), for example, lists Duke Ephraim, King Cobham, Young King, George Cobham, Eyo Honesty, Organ Henshaw, King Egbo, Archoban Duke, Cobbing Offiung, King Aqua, Egbo Honesty, and Jemmy Henshaw as those to whom comey is to be paid. A few years later, the Duke and Eyamba wards increased their strength sufficiently to deny the Henshaws a share of the comey. By approximately 1870 the Henshaws, the senior family of the Efiom Ekpo lineage, attempted to separate themselves from Duke Town by rebuilding and enlarging their nearby village (Latham, *Old Calabar*, 124). [S, E]

July 4 the 1786

about 4 clock morning Duk Ephrim Dead   soon after wee com up to Look way putt to grown

July 5 the 1786

about 5 clock wee Done putt Duk for grown 9 men & women go with him and all wee Look ferry poor   Captin Savage arrived

July 6 the 1786

. . . wee go on bord Everry ship 5 canow to Let all Captin know

July 9 the 1786

. . . after 10 clock night I have Esim & Egbo Young & Coffee Duke to com to my house to Look Duke Coomy Book and think what to Don

July 10 the 1786

. . . all Cobham town genllmen meet to Gorg Gobham yard with us family for chop Doctor with wee and com Back so at 9 clock time wee walk up to Long Dick Cobin with us genllmen for Drink our family Docter

July 11 the 1786

. . . at 9 clock night wee have chop Docter with henshaw family by Long Dick Cobin

July 18 the 1786

. . . after 3 clock noon wee have King Aqua Com Down with 157 hands and 16 women & girls and wee tell him for walk up to Gorg Cobham so wee and all Callabar genllmen go to meet heer for Drink Docter with aqua

July 19 the 1786

. . . wee family meet with Long Tom his be King aqua to Drink Docter with him and at 7 clock night wee family meet willy Tom Robin for Drink Docter with him

169. The death of Obong Duke Ephraim (Edem Ekpo) of Duke Town, who had been sick for two to three days. The obong always was buried secretly (see Simmons, "Ethnographic Sketch," 25). [S, E]

170. Captain John Savage of the Liverpool slaving ship *Rodney* (200 tons). [E]

171. Duke Ephraim's "comey" book itemized his debts owed to European ship captains. As obong, Duke Ephraim may have detailed other Efik traders' debts and amounts of comey. [E]

July 4, 1786

About 4 o'clock in the morning Duke Ephraim died. Soon after we came up to look where to put him in the ground.[169]

July 5, 1786

About 5 o'clock we put Duke Ephraim in the ground. 9 men and women went with him, and we all looked very poor [sad]. Captain Savage arrived.[170]

July 6, 1786

. . . we went on board every ship in 5 canoes to let all the captains know.

July 9, 1786

. . . after 10 o'clock at night Esien [Duke], Egbo Young [Ofiong], and Coffee Duke came to my house to look at Duke Ephraim's "comey" book and think what should be done.[171]

July 10, 1786

. . . All the Cobham Town gentlemen met at George Cobham's yard with our family to "chop doctor" with us,[172] and we returned. At 9 o'clock we walked up to Long Dick's cabin with our gentlemen to "drink our family doctor."

July 11, 1786

. . . at 9 o'clock at night we "chopped doctor" with the Henshaw family at Long Dick's cabin.

July 18, 1786

. . . after 3 o'clock in the afternoon King Aqua came down with 157 men and 16 women and girls, and we told him to walk up to George Cobham's. Then we and all the Calabar gentlemen went to meet there to "drink doctor" with Aqua.

July 19, 1786

. . . our family met with Long Tom who is King Aqua, to "drink doctor" with him, and at 7 o'clock at night our family met Willy Tom Robin to "drink doctor" with him.

---

172. During these ten days (July 10–19), various Efik families "chopped doctor," swearing oaths that they did not kill Duke Ephraim by witchcraft or magic and that they would not attack each other during the upcoming internecine fighting. See also note 72 and chapter 1. [S, E]

August 9 the 1786

. . . Esim till me he say one Bakassey genllmen was fear for com heer when Duke be Life now see him com and wee putt head together to carry his on bord ship for putt his for Iron and two his slav I was carry his on bord my self

September 4 the 1786

. . . about 6 am in aqua Landing with fine morning   wee have funchmen Drop Down so Esim and I go Down with 2 cow and wee com up after 3 clock wee see 6 Captin putt head together and say funchmen tak one mat beLong to Brighouse Tender and one John Cooper whitman and 3 men beLong to Savage on bord funchmen the say all be 8 hand be on bord funchmen   so all the Captin go on bord Savage and get all Ready   so wee see Eyo & Ebetim com to till see about that and wee Did go Down all wee 8 canows to Big Captin funch for Let wee have then whit maen Back he will not let wee have them men sam tim wee see them tak Savage ship and com Down so the say the mush be fight to get them whit men   so wee com up and Live them two ship heer   so at 11 clock night Eyo & Ebetim he Did Drink tea in young Duke new house   wee stay heer Little Long and Eyo & Ebetim go hom for the Town for let Willy Honesty hear that new

October 5 the 1786

. . . I see Coffee Duke send his son to till mee news about new ship after Little time I hear 5 great guns firs in 7 fatherpoint so wee see ship come up his be John Cooper Tender arrive so wee firs 3 great guns for him

173. The *Aurore* (see notes 166, 167). [E]

174. Captain William Brighouse of the Liverpool slaving ship *Preston* arrived at Old Calabar in either April or May 1786 (an event either not recorded by Antera Duke or not transcribed by Reverend Wilkie). He worked as first mate for Patrick Fairweather's 1775 voyage to Old Calabar on the *Dalrymple* (BT98/36,250, NA), and Brighouse then commanded the Liverpool slaver *Swift* to Old Calabar and Dominica in 1776, and five subsequent slaving voyages to Old Calabar and the Cameroon in 1777–1784. By 1786, he was the second-ranking British ship captain at Old Calabar, after Fairweather. Butterworth (see note 9) worked on Brighouse's tender, the Liverpool slaver *Hudibras* (150 tons), commanded by Jenkin Evans. Brighouse was taken by canoe downriver to the *Hudibras*, and then he piloted the ship to Old Calabar "as is customary for the oldest captain to do" (Butterworth, *Three Years Adventures*, 26). [E]

175. Captain John Cooper of the Liverpool slaving ship *Liverpool Hero* (211 tons). [E]

176. The muster rolls of the *Liverpool Hero* and *Rodney* (that of the *Hudibras* is not extant) give no indication that some crewmen absconded to the La Rochelle slaver *Aurore*. Butterworth, how-

August 9, 1786

. . . Esien told me that a Bakasi gentleman who feared to come here when Duke Ephraim was alive has now come, and we put our heads together to carry him on board ship to put him in irons, and also two of his slaves. I carried him on board myself.

September 4, 1786

. . . about 6 a.m. at Aqua Landing, a fine morning. We saw the Frenchman[173] drop down. Esien and I went down with 2 cows [canoes?] and came back. After 3 o'clock we saw 6 captains putting their heads together; they said that the Frenchman had taken a mate belonging to Brighouse's[174] tender and one of John Cooper's[175] white men, and 3 men belonging to Savage's ship, on board the Frenchman's ship. They said that 8 men in all were aboard the Frenchman. All the captains went on board Savage's ship and got everything ready. Then we saw Eyo and Ebetim come to tell us to see about that [incident], and we all went down in our 8 canoes, to beg the French captain to let us have the white men back.[176] He would not let us have the men. At the same time we saw them take Savage's ship and come down. They said there must be a fight to get those white men. Then we came up and left those two ships there. At 11 o'clock at night Eyo and Ebetim drank tea in Young Duke Ephraim's[177] new house. We stayed there a little time and then Eyo and Ebetim went to their town to let Willy Honesty hear that news.

October 5, 1786

. . . Coffee Duke sent his son to tell me news about a new ship. After a little time I heard 5 great guns fired at 7 Fathoms Point. We saw the ship come up. It was John Cooper's tender[178] arriving, so we fired 3 great guns for him.

ever, later recalls the incident, stating that because the French captain (Moël de Kerfraval) had behaved well to all sailors, many Englishmen "formed the resolution of seeking his protection whenever he should set sail." Looking for their missing men, the British captains "conferred together, and their conclusion was, that the scoundrels must have taken refuge in the French dog's ship, on board which they resolved to go, and inquire for the deserters." The *Rodney* unmoored and "dropt down on the French ship" near Parrot Island. Then "every man was discovered . . . and each conveyed to his respective ship almost naked." On the *Hudibras*, four of the escaped sailors "were immediately put in irons, and exposed in them for several weeks, on the forecastle" (Butterworth, *Three Years Adventures,* 85–88). [E]

177. Presumably Efiom Edem, about thirty years of age. Nicholls met Duke Ephraim in January 1805, describing him as "a very elegant formed young man, six feet high, with a very expressive countenance, and his skin rather blacker than the Calabar people in general" (Hallett, *Records,* 199). [E]

178. Captain Bryan Smith of the Liverpool slaving ship *Hannah* (192 tons). [E]

October 9 the 1786

. . . so wee hear great firs in aqua River and after 4 clock time we see one
Tender com up his be Captin Johnston ship will Tender of Captin Aspinall
so wee 3 firs great guns

October 10 the 1786

I go to my Back Cobin for plants som mimbo tree and all us family walk
up to new plaver house and tak one young Boy slave to mak Doctor and tak
2 guns for be firs for the Doctor so one guns firs and Break for Long Dick
Ephrim hand Dick mush Loos one his hand by that guns

October 14 the 1786

. . . after 10 clock I walk up to new plaver house for work and at 7 clock
night wee have see Egbo Sherry send word to know them Egbo Sherry Sam
Ambo was catch 7 men the come up for water abou 20 canow   so wee send
Egbo Drum in to brow for all abou town to no com go to market in soon
morning I send and am nothing to one good canow go up in Curock River
to tak car my Cobin Boy

October 15 the 1786

. . . I think all Day about my Cobin Boy was go in Curock for fear be
catch and I can chop all Day be 7 clock sam time I find his com hom

October 19 the 1786

. . . I have play aqua Doctor with one aqua men so I did killd one goat
for my god and Dinner with Captin Aspinall & Captin of his Tender in my
house Eyo Willy Honesty send my Brother Egbo Young to Esim Duke about
som Curock bob

179. Captain Thomas Johnston of the Liverpool slaving ship *Will* (128 tons). This is the only
instance when Antera Duke identifies the name of a European sailing vessel. [E]
180. Captain Edward Aspinall of the *William* (200 tons), which departed Liverpool May 8, 1786,
had arrived earlier (probably July) at Old Calabar, an event either unrecorded by Antera Duke or not
transcribed by Reverend Wilkie. [E]
181. The Efik planted mimbo tree groves in their household farms. [E]
182. The Ntiero family sacrificed the child. Snelgrave (*New Account*, 8) refers to his rescue of a

October 9, 1786

. . . we heard great firing in Aqua River, and after 4 o'clock we saw one tender come up. It was Captain Johnston's ship *Will*,[179] the tender of Captain Aspinall,[180] so we 3 fired great guns.

October 10, 1786

I went to my back cabin to plant some mimbo trees,[181] and all our family walked up to the new palaver house and took one young boy slave to "make doctor"[182] and took 2 guns [muskets] to be fired for the doctor. One gun fired and broke Long Duke Ephraim's hand. Long Duke must lose one of his hands by that gun.

October 14, 1786

. . . after 10 o'clock I walked up to the new palaver house to work, and at 7 o'clock at night Egbosherry people sent word to let us know that Egbosherry Sam Ambo had caught 7 men. They were coming by water in about 20 canoes. Then we sent the Ekpe drum to blow all about the town for no one to come or go to market. At sun up next morning, I sent Andam Nothing[183] in one good canoe to go up Curcock River to take care of my cabin boy.[184]

October 15, 1786

. . . I was thinking all day about my cabin boy who had gone to Curcock for fear he should be caught, and I couldn't eat all day until [at?] 7 o'clock at night when I found that he had come home.

October 19, 1786

. . . I played Aqua "doctor" with one Aqua man. I killed one goat for my god, and had dinner with Captain Aspinall and the captain of his tender in my house. Eyo Willy Honesty sent my brother Egbo Young [Antera] to Esien Duke about some Curcock dispute.

boy in Old Calabar (ca. 1713) who "was to be sacrificed that night to his god Egbo, for his prosperity" by a king called "Acqua." [S, E]. This "god Egbo" may or may not be the Ekpe figure (see Chapter 1).

183. Slaves were frequently given absurd names as a joke. [S, E]

184. Efik merchants writing in trade English adopted the maritime terminology of English ship captains. Among other tasks, Antera's "cabin boy" sent messages between merchants and ship captains. The renowned Efik leader Eyo Honesty II (d. 1858) "had been cabin boy to English captains" (Waddell, *Twenty-nine Years*, 311). [E]

October 26 the 1786

. . . I have putt water in my Bellay so I hear Egbo Run and I com to know I walk up to Egbo Young so wee see Egbo com Down & the Egbo men he say Sam Ambo and Georg Conham brow for Captain Fairwether so all us family Dam angary about brow that and wee send to call Captin Fairwether to com ashor and Break Trad first to us family abou 15 slave and firs 3 great onshor and after 3 clock noon wee see Eyo & Ebetim com Down and Eshen Ambo so the want to Sam & Georg Cobham for mak the settle with Captin Fairwether

November 2 the 1786

about 5 am in aqua Landing with fine morning wee have all us family went to Creek town for mak play first for Creek town cutt one women slave head of one cow be killd and goat and firs 7 great guns so wee com back in 5 clock time after 9 clock night I have Esim Duk com to my cobin for break one punchon Brandy for share to all Duke and sister so wee have us cason go up to guin Company with apandam for fetch wood plaver house Drun

November 4 the 1786

I go on bord Captin Fairwether and I see Effie com up 3 canow and play Egbo in after the com up for Landing with Egbo so all men & all women cry for town for Duke   I have my poeples to go wood 2 canow

November 6 the 1786

about 4 am in get up with great Rain so I walk up in town plaver house so I find all genllmen heer   so wee get Ready for cutt head of   and 5 clock morning we begain cutt slave head of   50 head of by the one Day 29 case Bottle Brandy   15 callabash chop I carry up to Everry Body and mush play for Everry yard in Town

185. The Efik administer enemas by means of a hollowed gourd having a narrow, tubular end. The patient kneels with their forehead almost touching the ground; the herbalist—wife or relative of the patient—inserts the tubular end of the gourd into the anus and pours the medicine from a clay pot into the gourd. The usual medicine used to cure constipation is *ibok ayiha*, "constipation medicine," an Efik household remedy, prepared by grinding the bark of *Cola edulis*, the bark and fruit of *Mitragyna stipulosa*, the bark of *Conlaedulis* spp., and the bark of a tree called by the Efik *enoi*. The mixture is rolled into a large ball, and a small piece is cut off, ground, and diluted with water when required. See Hallett, *Records*, 208. [S, E]

186. "Conham" in Wilkie's transcription is presumably a typographical error. [E]

187. Captain Patrick Fairweather of the slaving ship *Mary* (164 tons), which departed Liverpool

October 26, 1786

... I put water in my belly.[185] Then I heard that Ekpe was running and to find out why I walked up to Egbo Young [Ofiong]. We saw Ekpe come down and the Ekpe men said that Sam Ambo and George Cobham[186] had "blown [Ekpe]" on Captain Fairweather.[187] All our family were damn angry about that blow and we sent to call Captain Fairweather to come ashore and break trade first with our family for about 15 slaves, and we fired 3 great guns on shore. And after 3 o'clock in the afternoon we saw Eyo and Ebetim come down [from Creek Town] with Esien Ambo, and they went to Sam and George Cobham to make a settlement with Captain Fairweather.

November 2, 1786

About 5 a.m. at Aqua Landing, a fine morning. All our family went to Creek Town to make "play." First Creek Town people cut one woman slave's head off, and one cow was killed and a goat, and they fired 7 great guns. We came back at 5 o'clock. After 9 o'clock at night Esien Duke came to my cabin to break [open] one puncheon of brandy and share it with all Duke Ephraim's family and sisters. Then we had occasion to go up to Guinea Company with Apandam to fetch the wooden palaver house drum.

November 4, 1786

I went on board Captain Fairweather's ship and saw Efi[om] come up with 3 canoes and "play Ekpe" in them after they came up to the landing with Ekpe. All the men and women were crying in the town for Duke Ephraim. I sent my people for the woods in 2 canoes.[188]

November 6, 1786

About 4 a.m. I got up, a great rain. I walked up to the town palaver house and I found all the gentlemen there. We got ready to cut heads off and at 5 o'clock in the morning we began to cut slaves' heads off, 50 heads off in that one day. I carried 29 cases of bottled brandy and 15 calabashes of chop for everybody, and we must "play" in every yard in town.

Aug. 26, 1786. Sam Ambo and George Cobham had "blown Egbo" (see note 57) on Fairweather, shortly after the captain's arrival at Old Calabar. Duke Ephraim had died on July 4, 1786, but, according to the diary, final ceremonies began on November 2 when Antera Duke's family travels upriver to Creek Town to "mak play" (drumming, dancing, sacrifices). While in Old Calabar in summer 1786, Butterworth states that "[w]e were informed that, as soon as Captain Fairweather arrived, preparations would be made to commence with the grand pageant"—that is, obsequies for Duke Ephraim (Butterworth, *Three Years Adventures*, 54). See also chapter 1. [E]

188. Antera Duke sends his people out of town to protect them from the upcoming human sacrifices for Duke Ephraim. [E]

November 7 the 1786

about 4 am in aqua Landing with fine morning so I did mak all women Bring callabash for mak chop to give to Everry Body and all Country play all Day and all night all genllmen get to Dinner for Esim Duk

November 8 the 1786

. . . I see Jack Bakassey com and Bring one women slave for cutt to my father and I have send my yellow ogan abashey to market and all genllmen get Dinner for Egbo Young   wee news about new ship 3 head cutt of again

November 9 the 1786

. . . about 4 am in aqua Landing and I mak all women to Bring Callabash for mak chop soon after wee have one TaEon town cutt the Backsider town head of and Bring heer for his Duke Play and I have all genllmen Dinner for me

November 10 the 1786

. . . after 8 clock wee have Bush Egbo men brow Everry Body for stay to houses and tak . . . in 4 clock time sam time all play be again to play all night

November 11 the 1786

about 4 clock wee goin in Town plaver house and wee be again Drehst Town for Long Cloth & Egbo cloth & hatt and Jacket and Everry fine thing and obong Egbo Run for town 1 clock time wee Don for that

November 12 the 1786

. . . I Did mak all women Bring Callabash for mak chop so grandy Egbo beagain tak for women play all Day and night

---

189. Yellow was a common personal name among the Efik. It sometimes referred to skin color. See also note 54. [S, E]

190. If a ceremony is private to the Ekpe society, all nonmembers remain within the house on penalty of being whipped or decapitated. [S]

November 7, 1786

About 4 a.m. at Aqua Landing, a fine morning. I made all the women bring calabashes to make chop to give to everybody, and all the country people "played" all day and all night. All the gentlemen went to dinner at Esien Duke's house.

November 8, 1786

. . . I saw Jock Bakassey come and bring one woman slave to be beheaded in honour of my father, and I sent my [brother] Yellow[189] Hogan Abashey [Antera] to market. All the gentlemen had dinner at Egbo Young [Ofiong's house]. We heard news about a new ship. 3 more heads were cut off.

November 9, 1786

. . . about 4 a.m. at Aqua Landing, and I made all the women bring calabashes to make chop. Soon after one Taeon town man cut off the head of a Backsider town man, and brought it here for his Duke Ephraim "play." And I had all the gentlemen to dinner with me.

November 10, 1786

. . . after 8 o'clock the Bush Ekpe men "blew" everybody to stay inside their houses[190] and take . . . . At 4 o'clock all were "playing" again and "played" all night.

November 11, 1786

About 4 o'clock we went to the town palaver house, and we dressed again in town style in long cloth and Ekpe cloth[191] and hat and jacket and every fine thing. Obong Ekpe ran in town, then at 1 o'clock we were done with that.

November 12, 1786

. . . I made all the women bring calabashes of food to make dinner. Grand Ekpe was again taken to the women who played all day and night.

191. Ekpe cloth, or *ukara*, is an Ibo tie-dyed cloth in which blue triangles alternate with white; special *nsibidi*, or secret signs, usually occur in the design. [S, E]

November 13 the 1786

about 5 am in aqua Landing with fine morning so I go Down for Landing for Look plase to mak Dwelld house   soon after that wee have all Egbo men mak Duke all women for pay 5   5 copper for Egbo   after 8 clock night wee have all Egbo poeples meet for Plaver house and mak all Duke wife to com and cry Egbo   cry in town plaver house

December 8 the 1786

. . . I go Down for Landing to get all great guns Ready and wee have firs 28 great guns for ashor one one for everry ship about wee shave head first and wer fine hatt & fine clothe & Hanschiff so all Captin and wee genllmen get Dinner for Esim house

December 9 the 1786

about 6 am in aqua Landing with small fog morning and I walk up to see Egbo Sherry play wee wer new cloth and at 12 clock night Captin Fairwether Tender go way with 280 slaves

December 19 the 1786

. . . I walk up to Esim and Egbo Young and Esim play with one Country poeples Liv abou Guin Company sides the was com to see us about Duke Dead after that wee have go on bord ship and after 12 clock night Captin Brikhouse Tender go way with 420 slaves

December 24 the 1786

. . . wee have Egbo Run for abou town and after 7 clock night wee Read Letter com to Willy Honesty about what Egbo monny the putt for Willy & Tom Curcock 40 men first and 13 men mor for Cobham family in aqua Landing that

192. The diary later relates that thirty-five British sailors helped put up two sides of his new house (Aug. 18, 1787) and that a ship's carpenter laid the floor (Sept. 20, 1787). [E]

193. The Ekpe figure must whip the widows and children of a dead member. Whipping may be mitigated on payment of a small sum, but at least one stroke must be given, even if the son of the deceased is himself a member of the Ekpe society. [S]

194. We translate "one one" as two (literally one cannon fired and then another), since there were fourteen ships in the river, not twenty-eight as stated by Inikori (Inikori, "Development," 45). [E]

195. Waddell (Twenty-nine Years, 371) states that in 1848 Eyo Honesty II terminated the funeral obsequies for his uncle Eyamba, chief of Duke Town, by shaving his head. [S, E]

196. The Ibibio are noted for their masked dancers, puppet, and stilt dances. [S]

197. The Mary, Captain Robert Harrison, arrived at Dominica January 31, 1787, with 248 slaves and returned to Liverpool April 27, 1787, with 3 kegs pepper, 56 ivory tusks, 10 tons redwood, and

November 13, 1786

About 5 a.m. at Aqua Landing, a fine morning. I went down to the landing to look for a place to make a dwelling house.[192] Soon after that all the Ekpe men made all Duke women [Duke Ephraim's wives] pay ten coppers to Ekpe.[193] After 8 o'clock at night all the Ekpe people met in the palaver house and made all Duke's wives come and cry the "Ekpe cry" in the town palaver house.

December 8, 1786

. . . I went down to the landing to get all the great guns ready and we fired 28 great guns ashore, one one [two] for each ship about.[194] We shaved our heads first,[195] and wore fine hats and fine clothes and handkerchiefs. All the captains and we gentlemen had dinner at Esien [Duke's] house.

December 9, 1786

About 6 a.m. at Aqua Landing, a little morning fog, and I walked up to see an Egbosherry "play."[196] We wore new clothes, and at 12 o'clock at night Captain Fairweather's tender went away with 280 slaves.[197]

December 19, 1786

. . . I walked up to Esien's house, and Egbo Young [Antera] and Esien were "playing" with some country people living near Guinea Company side. They had come to see us about Duke Ephraim's death. After that we went on board ship, and after 12 o'clock at night Captain Brighouse's tender went away with 420 slaves.[198]

December 24, 1786

. . . Ekpe ran about town, and after 7 o'clock at night we read a letter which had come to Willy Honesty about what Ekpe money they would put in for Willy and Tom Curcock: 40 men first and 13 men more for the Cobham family. In Aqua Landing that [occurred].

West India produce (*Liverpool General Advertiser*, May 3, 1787). On December 9, 1786, Captain Fairweather discharged command of the *Mary*, transferring the captaincy to Harrison. Fairweather entered the ship *Tarleton* (342 tons) as captain on February 27, 1787 (BT98/47,137; BT98/48,221, NA). [E]

198. The *Hudibras*, Captain Jenkin Evans, arrived at Grenada February 26, 1786, with, according to one source, 350 slaves. An alternate source states 330 slave imports. Substantial harbor mortality is confirmed by the fact that agents Campbell, Baillie & Co. sold 290 slaves: 97 African men, 87 African women, 54 African boys, and 52 African girls for £8,406 (LivRO, 942 HOL 10). Antera Duke reports 420 African slaves shipped from Old Calabar; Butterworth recalls 360 slaves (Butterworth, *Three Years Adventures*, 98), though additional slaves may have been transshipped by Captain Brighouse. A few days from the Cross River estuary, the African men instigated a slave revolt, and many died in their failed attempt to gain control of the ship. [E]

December 25 the 1786

about 5 am in aqua Landing so I have Drehst & Esim & Egbo Young so
Esim & Egbo Young canow go to Boostam and after 1 clock noon wee have
all Captin Drehst and com ashor to Dinner for Esim Duke house with us
genllmen and Willy Tom Robin

December 28 the 1786

. . . so wee have meet all us family for Young Tom Curcock about his say
he say Duke was owe his father 2 Bx Rods and 3 slave so all us family find
his be Dam Lye

January 1 the 1787

about 5 am in aqua Landing with small fog morning so I have mak 8
Callabash Egbo chop and 1 clock time all Captin and us get Dinner for Egbo
Young house Liverpool Hall 3 clock time wee have putt monny for 17 men
to be Callabar Egbo

January 24 the 1787

. . . so I see Egbo Young send one his men to com and call me so all Duke
family walk up to Egbo Young house and see have mak great bob about Egbo
so I and Ephrim aqua bring Little angary word to him & I for som word his
speak about my father Willy Tom Robin pay mor Egbo moony Long Duke
mor Egbo moony belong to Imo Duk son willy Honesty and Cobham
family give old town Egbo moony for 41 men.

January 31 the 1787

. . . so I walk up Esim & Egbo Young after we hear aqua Bakassey be for
River so I & Egbo Young go Down for Landing to see and 12 clock time
wee see old town com so wee go Down to fetch them up and see Did putt
moony for 51 men Henshaw town putt for 8 men Willy Tom for one all be
60 men the Catch for wee and 7 clock night the goin hom

February 1 the 1787

. . . at 7 clock night wee have Captin Aspinall Tender go his way with 300
slaves

199. Perhaps Ekpe entry fees to the value of seventeen adult male slaves, as seventeen new Ekpe
members seems unlikely. [E]

200. Wilkie's transcription inserted "(?)" between "Imo" and "Duk." [E]

201. Thus Akwa Bakasi raiders and traders took an order for 60 men slaves: 51 for Duke Town,
8 for Henshaw Town, and 1 for Old Town. See also notes 32, 91, 134. [E]

December 25, 1786

About 5 a.m. at Aqua Landing. I dressed, as did Esien and Egbo Young [Antera]. Esien and Egbo Young's canoes went to Boostam, and after 1 o'clock in the afternoon all the captains dressed and came ashore to [Christmas] dinner at Esien Duke's house with us gentlemen and Willy Tom Robin.

December 28, 1786

. . . All our family came to meet Young Tom Curcock because he said Duke Ephraim owed his father 2 boxes of copper rods and 3 slaves. All our family found that this was a damn lie.

January 1, 1787

About 5 a.m. at Aqua Landing, a little morning fog. I had 8 calabashes of Ekpe chop made, and at one o'clock we and all the captains had [New Year's] dinner at Egbo Young [Ofiong's] house, Liverpool Hall. At 3 o'clock we put in money for 17 men to be Calabar Ekpe.[199]

January 24, 1787

. . . I saw that Egbo Young [Ofiong] had sent one of his men to come and call me. Then all Duke Ephraim's family walked up to Egbo Young's house and had a great discussion about Ekpe. I and Ephraim Aqua said some angry words to him—I because of some words he had spoken about my father. Willy Tom Robin paid more Ekpe money, Long Duke more Ekpe money belonging to Imo Duke's[200] son. Willy Honesty and the Cobham family gave Old Town Ekpe money for 41 men.

January 31, 1787

. . . I walked up to Esien and Egbo Young [Antera] after we heard that Akwa Bakasi people were in the river. I and Egbo Young went down to the landing to see, and at 12 o'clock we saw Old Town men coming. We went down to fetch them up and saw them put in money for 51 men, Henshaw Town put in for 8 men, Willy Tom Robin for one man. 60 men in all they caught for us, and at 7 o'clock at night they went home.[201]

February 1, 1787

. . . at 7 o'clock at night Captain Aspinall's tender went away with 300 slaves.[202]

202. The Liverpool slaving ship *Will* (128 tons), Captain Thomas Johnston, arrived at Dominica April 3, 1787, the number of slaves not documented. Johnston returned to Liverpool on June 18 with 15 puncheons palm oil, 5 puncheons Guinea pepper, and 1 ton ivory (*Liverpool General Advertiser*, June 21, 1787). [E]

February 2 the 1787

. . . I see Willy Honesty play Egbo and com to my yard so I Deash him
1 pc Inder Roosnall 1 g stuff 1 Rod for play poeples & 1 case funch Bottle
Brandy 1 Long whit Bottle Brandy after that all walk up to his for meet abou
first warr copper

February 16 the 1787

. . . so Egbo Young & all Willy Honesty Drehst grandy Egbo plaver house
so wee Did bought Egbo 344 men be Callabar new Egbo

February 17 the 1787

. . . at 6 clock night wee see Long Dick have som Egbo plaver with one
Boostam men so all old Egbo be Dam angary and brow all new Egbo to sleep
for Egbo plaver house

February 20 the 1787

. . . sam time wee see Willy Tom Robin send one his boy to till wee
about one my Dear father son nam Ebo Dead by sick 2 Day so I have mak
my Dear Awa ofion to go with 6 my men to went mak grandy 7 clock night
my Dear com Back

February 22 the 1787

. . . about 5 am in aqua Landing with fog morning so wee walk up to see
Willy Honesty so all old Egbo and I & Esim to meet for Egbo plaver house
to know what man be old Callabar Egbo so all Egbo men find one Ephrim
aqua son no be Town Egbo and one Robin Henshaw son and Henshaw
Robin Henshaw so all old & new Egbo brow for them to not be Egbo men
and after 8 clock night I & Esim Did carry 1 Jug 2 Long Case whit Bottle
Brandy 1 Larg Jar mimbo up to Egbo house for give all old & new Egbo to
Drink and Back 2 clock night

---

203. Wilkie's transcription inserted "(?)" between "Roosnall" and "1 g stuff." Regarding romals,
see note 137. Guinea stuffs were a popular textile manufactured in India for the African trade. An Efik
trading ledger from 1767 uses the abbreviation "G.Stuffs" (Williams, *Liverpool Privateers*, 540). [S, E]

204. Antera may refer to 344 Ekpe members or perhaps that 344 men advanced one grade in
the society. See chapter 1. [E]

February 2, 1787

. . . I saw Willy Honesty "playing Ekpe" and he came to my yard, so I "dashed" him 1 piece of Indian Romal, 1 [piece of] G[uinea] stuff,[203] 1 rod for his "play" people [performers], and one case of French bottled brandy, 1 long white bottle of brandy. After that we all walked up to his house to meet about the first war coppers.

February 16, 1787

. . . Egbo Young [Ofiong] and all Willy Honesty's people dressed Grand Ekpe in the palaver house. We paid Ekpe [money for] 344 men to be Calabar's new Ekpe.[204]

February 17, 1787

. . . at 6 o'clock at night we found that Long Dick had some Ekpe palaver with a Boostam man. All the old Ekpe were damn angry, and blew all the new Ekpe to order them to sleep at the Ekpe palaver house.

February 20, 1787

. . . At the same time we saw that Willy Tom Robin had sent one of his boys to tell us that one of my dear father's sons named Ebo was dead. He had been sick 2 days. I made my dear wife Awa Ofiong go with 6 of my men to "make Grandy."[205] At 7 o'clock at night my dear came back.

February 22, 1787

. . . about 5 a.m. at Aqua Landing, a foggy morning. We walked up to see Willy Honesty. All the old Ekpe and I and Esien [Duke] met at the Ekpe palaver house to decide who was to be in Old Calabar Ekpe. All the Ekpe men decided that Ephraim Aqua's son was not to be town Ekpe, and [neither was] Robin Henshaw's son nor Henshaw Robin Henshaw. All the old and new Ekpe "blew" for them not to be Ekpe men, and after 8 o'clock at night I and Esien carried 1 jug, 2 long cases of white bottled brandy and 1 large jar of mimbo up to the Ekpe house to give to all the old and new Ekpe to drink, and we came back at 2 o'clock at night.[206]

205. Antera's "mak grandy" may refer to digging the grave for Ebo ("making the ground"). [E]

206. Antera's distinction between old and new Ekpe may reflect the fact that new Ekpe were probationers who became old Ekpe only after they had proved their worth. Perhaps both groups of men were Ekpe runners. [E]

February 26 the 1787

. . . at 8 clock night wee have see Long King aqua send one his genllmen
to be killd by wee hand so wee send that genllmen by Long Duk for River
to be killd

March 3 the 1787

about 5 wee go on bord Captin Fairwether for tak Ephrim aqua &
Ephrim coomy and Coffee & Arshbong coomy and wee com ashor with all
captin so everry ship firs guns so one great guns com up and cutt one Captin
Tatam whit men head off

March 17 the 1787

. . . so wee have Eyo & Ebetim & Eshen com with Egbo to ogan poor
Boy Egbo plaver so all mak his pay 335 copper and one house Boy to Egbo
Cutt head of   soon after we have them again hom

March 24 the 1787

. . . at 12 clock time wee have Willy Honesty call all genllmen for meet
in Egbo Cobham Cobin for know who wee will giv King of Old Calabar
and after 7 clock night wee have all us town genllmen meet for Coffee
Cobin to settle everry Bad bob we was mak sinc wee father Dead so wee
kild 2 goat

April 13 the 1787

. . . wee have chop in Egbo Young house   wee see all Henshaw family
com to see for ask us family for now to Let the know who wee will mak be
King Egbo   so wee say   wee Don know befor wee settle about King of
Callabar first

207. The editors of Crow's *Memoirs* (280), writing in the late 1820s, mention: "At these executions the sufferers are pinioned, and tied in a sitting posture to a stake driven in the ground; and round
their heads, so as to cross their eyes, is fixed a rope, the end of which is held by some bystanders who
participate in the sacrifice. The executioner comes up with a leaden-handled sword, and generally at
one blow severs the head from the body; when it is instantaneously pulled away by the rope, and,
while yet warm, is tossed up in the air, and played with like a ball. If the executioner fails to strike
off the head at a blow, the spectators set up a laugh of scorn and disappointment." Other "sufferers"
were tied to stakes to be drowned by the tide. See also Waddell, *Twenty-nine Years*, 328. [S, E]
   208. Captain Patrick Fairweather and the *Tarleton*, which departed Liverpool December 25,
1786. [E]
   209. The only March 1787 death recorded on the muster roll of the *Langdale*, Captain Tatem,
is that of Marmaduke Aiked, who died on March 22 (BT98/48,320, NA). On Tatem's tender, the

February 26, 1787

. . . at 8 o'clock at night we saw that Long King Aqua sent one of his gentlemen to be killed by our hands. We sent that gentleman to Long Duke to the river to be killed.[207]

March 3, 1787

About 5 we went on board Captain Fairweather's ship[208] to take "comey" for Ephraim Aqua and Ephraim, and "comey" for Coffee Duke and Archibong Duke, and then we came ashore with all the captains. Then every ship fired guns. One great gun came up [recoiled] and cut one of Captain Tatem's white men's head off.[209]

March 17, 1787

. . . Eyo and Ebetim and Esien [Ambo] came with Ekpe about the Hogan poor boy[210] palaver [business]. All made him pay 335 coppers and give one house-boy to Ekpe for his head to be cut off.[211] Soon after they went home again.

March 24, 1787

. . . at 12 o'clock Willy Honesty called all the gentlemen to meet in Egbo Cobham's cabin to decide who we will make King of Old Calabar [King Calabar],[212] and after 7 o'clock at night all of us town gentlemen met at Coffee's cabin to settle every bad bob [dispute] we had had since our father died. Then we killed 2 goats.

April 13, 1787

. . . we had chop in Egbo Young [Antera's] house. We saw all the Henshaw family coming to ask our family to let them know whom we will make King Ekpe.[213] We said we didn't know as we first must settle about the King of Calabar.

Three Brothers, sailor Thomas Hartshorn was "Hurt" February 28, 1787, and was discharged in Liverpool Mar. 1, 1788, at the end of the voyage (BT98/48,89). [E]

210. Antera's "ogan poor Boy" may be a nickname for Hogan similar to Andam Nothing. [E]

211. A freeborn man who committed an action that the Ekpe society judged punishable with death could substitute a slave for decapitation. [S]

212. Efik leaders met at Egbo Cobham's cabin to select the subsequent King Calabar. Possibly they met to choose a new obong to succeed Duke Ephraim. More likely they gathered to select a new Ndem priest from the Cobham family: the Cobham family always provided the Oku Ndem; John Cobham died in May 1786 (see May 18, 1786); and Antera Duke mentions Egbo Cobham only in this March 1787 entry. See also chapter 1. [S, E]

213. King Ekpe alludes to the headship of one of the Ekpe society grades. See also the diary entry October 31, 1787. [S, E]

April 16 the 1787

. . . wee go to Creek Town 2 good canow & 1 small Dutto to mak the
guin company & old town about the 2 town want pay Egbo in one Day so
wee say never Been hear that for weer grandy grandy father so willy killd
goat for wee and I walk to Henshaw town for see my mimbo wife and com
hom in 2 clock noon

April 18 the 1787

. . . wee have Otto ephrim and willy Tom Robin com to ask wee if wee
will to the pay first or the guin company first so wee say wee will for the be
first and I have send my cobin for mimbo market

April 28 the 1787

about 5 I Lig in Bud so I have see Coffee Duke com to me and mak my
Cobin Boy call me to him so his Did tell me abou amnaty be killd in King
Aqua Landing so I did mak 7 hand go with Jimimy Antera to fetch in aqua
River so wee have been drink all Day to my girl wife in Duke sister Daught
house

April 30 the 1787

. . . I have mak my ogan abashey to go up my father men mimbo plase
for fetch mimbo so on after 10 clock Day wee brow to not men com up to
no way and wee goin chop Bush Egbo in plaver house and I walk with Egbo
Drum for Landing   sam time wee Ephrim Watt no fear and com with 7 his
men so wee walk Back in plaver house so all Bush Egbo men send word to
pay 7 goat so his Did Copper for 6 great and 1 goat for that plaver

May 21 the 1787

about 6 am in aqua Landing with fine morning wee see Captin ford send
his Tender way last night with 330 slaves so wee Done coomy on bord Potter
and wee com ashor in 4 clock time

---

214. One of his wives who lived on a small farm and looked after his palm wine (mimbo) trees. [S]
   215. The manatee is sacred to the Ekpe society. The most prized whips carried by Ekpe figures
are covered with manatee skin. Nicholls, who left a detailed description of a manatee in 1805, noted
that anyone who kills one "is obliged to take it to the king of Calabar [the Ndem priest], from whom
he receives a reward for killing it; but should he apply it to his own use, without sending it to the
king, he pays a very heavy fine to the king" (Hallett, Records, 205, 209). Wilkie's transcription inserted "(manatee)" after "amnaty." [S, E]
   216. Wilkie's transcription inserted "(goat)" after "6 great." [E]

April 16, 1787

. . . we went to Creek Town in 2 good canoes and 1 small one to meet
with the Guinea Company and Old Town men about the two towns want-
ing to pay Ekpe in one day. We said we had never heard of that since our
great-grandfather's time. Then Willy Honesty killed a goat for us, and I
walked to Henshaw Town to see my mimbo wife[214] and came home at 2
o'clock in the afternoon.

April 18, 1787

. . . Otto Ephraim and Willy Tom Robin came to ask us if we wanted
them to pay first or Guinea Company first. We said we wanted them to be
first, and I sent my cabin boy to the mimbo market.

April 28, 1787

About 5 a.m. I was lying in bed. I saw Coffee Duke come to me and
make my cabin boy call me to him. He told me about a manatee[215] being
killed at King Aqua's landing. So I made 7 hands go with Jimmy Antera to
fetch it from Aqua river. We drank all day to my girl-wife in Duke Ephraim's
sister's daughter's house.

April 30, 1787

. . . I made my [brother] Hogan Abashey [Antera] go to my father's
mimbo place to fetch mimbo. After 10 o'clock in the morning we "blew
[Ekpe]" for men not to come up no way, because we were going to eat Bush
Ekpe chop in the palaver house, and I walked with the Ekpe drum to the
landing. At the same time [nonetheless] Ephraim Watt was not afraid and
came with 7 of his men. We walked back into the palaver house, and all the
Bush Ekpe men sent word [to Ephraim Watt] to pay 7 goats. He sent coppers for 6 goats[216] and 1 goat for that palaver.

May 21, 1787

About 6 a.m. at Aqua Landing, a fine morning. We saw that Captain Ford
had sent his tender away last night with 330 slaves.[217] We settled "comey" on
board Potter's[218] ship and we came ashore at 4 o'clock.

217. The *Renown*, Captain John Holliwell, arrived at Grenada July 31, 1787, with 250 slaves, 57
hogsheads and 5 tierces palm oil, 2,800 lbs. Guinea pepper, 522 ivory tusks, 11 sea horses' teeth (hippopotamus tusks), and 540 pieces redwood. Agents Campbell, Baillie & Co. sold all 250 slaves for
£7,433: 89 African men, 82 African women, 40 African boys, and 39 Africans girls (LivRO, 942 HOL
10). The same types and quantities of African produce returned to Liverpool October 14, 1787, with
the exception that the Liverpool gazette recorded fifty-seven puncheons palm oil and six tons redwood (CO106/2, f.69, NA; *Liverpool General Advertiser*, Oct. 18, 1787). [E]
218. Captain Peter Potter of the Liverpool slaving ship *Iris* (268 tons). [E]

May 26 the 1787

. . . so I hear 18 men slave tak Boat and Run way from John Cooper Last night and 5 clock noon wee hear som them slave be to aqua town

May 27 the 1787

. . . we have see all Captin John family com to see about one the Daught marry Egbo Young was fight with another the wife and Break Toothes out   so the com to Break another wife Toothes out again   so wee Did mak Jimimy antera for tak Toothes out for the wife his Ephrim Robin Henshaw Daught

June 4 the 1787

. . . 7 clock night wee hear Captin Aspinall Dead so wee hear all pown cry out andam Ephrim mary Long duk

June 5 the 1787

. . . wee have all Captin ashor to Buary Captin Aspinall in Big plaver so wee have firs 6 great guns ashor

June 7 the 1787

. . . wee see Robin Tom King John and Otto Dutto Tom King John send them to com for mak play to Duke & my father and Egbo Young mother so the cutt one woman head of to Duke and 7 Barr Room men to be cutt for my father so the play all night

June 11 the 1787

. . . at 3 clock noon Captin Hughot & Combesboch and one Little ship belong to Hughot com from 60 slaves and one Aspinall mat Loos two his hand by firs great guns

219. Captain Edward Aspinall's death is recorded on the muster roll of the *William* (200 tons): BT98/56,139, NA. Crew members buried him on shore. Antera Duke does not comment on the deaths from disease (usually yellow fever, malaria, dysentery) of any other European crew member. At least 100 sailors, however, died at Old Calabar during the three-year period of the diary. According to Butterworth, in summer 1786 the Liverpool ship *Rodney* (see note 170) "exhibited a melancholy scene, nearly all her hands being swept away. Boats were constantly plying between the ships and the shore, with the bodies of dead sailors for interment." On his vessel, the *Hudibras*, "We lost eight in the whole. Those who had any discharge by natural issue, such as ulcerated legs, &c. escaped the fever, so fatal to many" (Butterworth, *Three Years Adventures*, 89). Only the death of senior trader Captain Aspinall warranted comment by senior Efik trader Antera Duke. [E]

220. The pawns, on deceased Captain Aspinall's ship, cried out for fear of their lives as if a big man had died in town. [E]

May 26, 1787

. . . I heard that 18 men slaves took a boat and ran away from John Cooper last night, and at 5 o'clock in the afternoon we heard that some of those slaves are at Aqua Town.

May 27, 1787

. . . All Captain John's family came to see us because one of their daughters who married Egbo Young [Antera] had fought with another wife and had had her teeth broken out. Then they came to break the other wife's teeth out. We made Jimmy Antera take out the teeth of the wife, the daughter of Ephraim Robin Henshaw.

June 4, 1787

. . . At 7 o'clock at night we heard that Captain Aspinall was dead.[219] We heard all the pawns cry out.[220] Andam Ephraim married Long Duke [Ephraim].

June 5, 1787

. . . All the captains came ashore to bury Captain Aspinall with much ceremony. We fired 6 great guns ashore.

June 7, 1787

. . . we saw Robin Tom King John and Otto [Tom King John]. Tom King John sent them to come and make a "play" in honour of Duke Ephraim, my father and Egbo Young [Ofiong's] mother. They cut one woman's head off for Duke, and 7 men prisoners[221] were to be beheaded for my father. So they "played" all night.

June 11, 1787

. . . at 3 o'clock in the afternoon Captains Hughes and Comberbach and one little ship belonging to Hughes came for 60 slaves,[222] and one of Aspinall's mates[223] lost both hands by the firing of the great guns.

221. In Efik prison is *ufok uquat* (iron-bar house). Similarly, in a letter to a Liverpool merchant, Grandy King George mentioned "the Room of irons" (Williams, *Liverpool Privateers*, 546). "Bar Room" could refer to Mbarakom people (known also as the Mbudikom) in the Cameroon grasslands (Latham, *Old Calabar*, 29). It is not likely that Antera heard "barracoon," or slave holding pen, because Britons used the word more frequently in the nineteenth century. A document from 1828 noted a barracoon on the beach by Duke Town (Latham, *Old Calabar*, 48n55). [E]

222. An auxiliary vessel of the Liverpool slaving ship *President* (254 tons), Captain Joseph Hughes. Upon reaching the African coast, carpenters sometimes built small yawls, pinnaces, or shallops to facilitate coastal trade. [E]

223. Either mates Henry Trafford or James Crozier (BT98/56,139, NA). [E]

June 15 the 1787

. . . John Cooper Deash Esim & Egbo Young 2 great guns and wee com ashor   so wee hear King aqua was mak all his wife to Drink Docter so 11 wife Dead by the Drink Docter   John Cooper Drop Down night about 8 clock time

July 15 the 1787

. . . Captin Aspinall ship go way with 328 slaves

July 18 the 1787

. . . so wee Sam Ambo beagain Cutt Cow for his god to mak play so wee see Eyo & Ebetim & Eshen send word to Let wee know the com to see Sam King ambo cutt Cow

July 25 the 1787

. . . I Did carry play to King Ambo yard about his Cutt Cow for god and I see Eyo Willy Honesty com sam time   at 11 clock night I have com Back with my play poeples

July 26 the 1787

. . . at 3 clock time wee go to Cobham town to Everry man again Deash Sam King Ambo Copper about Cutt Cow for his god so His Did get 986Copper for all Callabar so wee great Rain sam time and wee com Back with Rain all night

August 1 the 1787

. . . I com up to my work plase and goin to Egbo plaver house and I find Be som Body Tif Door out in Egbo plaver house so wee send Drum to mak all wee new Egbo to com in plaver house to fend about 3 Egbo for everry yard if will find

224. John Cooper, captain of the *Liverpool Hero*, departed Old Calabar with 560 slaves. Arriving off Barbados on August 28, 1787, after having "buried" 330 slaves (crew men threw dead Africans overboard), Cooper proceeded to Dominica, arriving at Roseau on September 3. One contemporary noted that the *Liverpool Hero* had "a great mortality." Indeed, the Middle Passage slave mortality on the *Liverpool Hero* was one of the most horrific in the history of the British slave trade. Cooper returned to Liverpool December 10, 1787, with rum, Madeira wine, 914 ivory tusks, 39 puncheons and 9 tierces palm oil, 22 barrels long pepper, 966 pounds black wood, and 1 barrel bees wax (*Liverpool General Advertiser*, Dec. 13, 1787). [E]
   225. Henry Trafford, new captain of the *William* (the name not known to Antera), disembarked

June 15, 1787

. . . John Cooper "dashed" Esien and Egbo Young [Antera] 2 great guns, and we came ashore. We heard that King Aqua has made all his wives "drink doctor." Then 11 wives died from "drinking doctor." John Cooper dropped down the river[224] about 8 o'clock at night.

July 15, 1787

. . . Captain Aspinall's ship went away with 328 slaves.[225]

July 18, 1787

. . . Sam Ambo began to cut [sacrifice] a cow for his god to make a "play." Eyo and Ebetim and Esien [Ambo] sent word to let us know that they were coming to see Sam King Ambo cut his cow.

July 25, 1787

. . . I carried a "play" to King Ambo's yard because he was cutting [sacrificing] a cow for his god and I saw Eyo Willy Honesty come at the same time. At 11 o'clock at night I came back with my "play" people.

July 26, 1787

. . . at 3 o'clock we went to Cobham Town where every man again "dashed" Sam King Ambo coppers because he cut [sacrificed] a cow for his god. He got 986 coppers from all of Calabar. At the same time it rained hard, and we came back with rain all night.

August 1, 1787

. . . I came up to my work place and went into the Ekpe palaver house and I found that somebody had thiefed [stolen] the door[226] from the Ekpe palaver house. We sent the drum to make all our new Ekpe men come to the palaver house, and we sent[227] about 3 Ekpe to every yard to see if they will find it.

130 slaves at Barbados September 15, 1787, and 170 slaves at Dominica on September 21. It is unclear whether the death of Captain Aspinall on June 4, 1787, canceled final deliveries of slaves: the *William* embarked 328 enslaved Africans but intended to purchase 350. Referring to palm oil captains, Waddell noted, "Formerly, when they died in the [Calabar] river, the payment of debts owing to them was easily evaded; indeed, they were generally held as cancelled" (Waddell, *Twenty-nine Years*, 612). [E]

226. It is not clear why someone stole the Ekpe palaver house door. [E]

227. The word "fend" in Wilkie's transcription is presumably a typographical error. [E]

August 11 the 1787

. . . after 2 clock time wee have all Captin and Callabar genllmen wee
have meet for King Ambo plaver house about one willy Curcock men was
fight with one Captin ford mat   so after Little time the mat Dead   so wee
mak that Willy Curcock men to be Cutt Ear about that fight

August 13 the 1787

. . . wee hear Captin Brighouse go way with 320 slaves

August 14 the 1787

. . . wee hear John Tom Henshaw Dead so wee Did send our poeples go
for Henshaw town with apandam

August 18 the 1787

. . . I have Captin Potter com ashor after 11 clock time Potter send on
bord his Tender & is ship to bring 35 whit men and at 12 clock the beagain
putt 2 sides house up and after 2 clock I have all Captin Dinner for me and
super

August 25 the 1787

. . . at 4 clock noon wee have Captin fairweather Tender go way with 210
slaves . .

September 5 the 1787

. . . so wee carry Egbo in King Ambo about one Tatam pown was Run
way so wee mak is give one his son for Tatam

September 16 the 1787

. . . wee tak grandy Egbo and carry to Henshaw & Willy tom for brow for
not Captin for send any Callabar poun was putt for tak my slave goods to not
send them poun way in Tender so wee have Tatam Tender go way with 330 slaves

228. According to the Liverpool muster roll of the *Ellis*, Captain John Ford, mate John Currie
died on July 22, 1787 (BT98/48,203, NA). [E]

229. On "June 24 the 1780" King Henshaw, Duke Ephraim, and Willy Honesty wrote a letter
to some Liverpool merchants in which they stated that "no whitemen shall be stop onshore any more
long as we be Callabar and we make Great Law about whitemen not hurt" (Lovejoy and Richardson,
"Letters," 109–110). Thus the murderous attack on Captain Ford's mate was a punishable offence. [E]

230. The *Preston*, Captain William Brighouse, arrived at Kingston, Jamaica November 9, 1787,
with 195 slaves. Agent Alexander Lindo sold 112 African male slaves and 74 African female slaves (186
total) from the *Preston*, of whom 131 were adults and 55 children (*Report of the Lords*, III, Appendix,
Jamaica). Brighouse returned to Liverpool March 28, 1788, with 119 ivory tusks, 10 barrels Guinea
pepper, 5 puncheons palm oil, and West India produce (*Liverpool General Advertiser*, Apr. 3, 1788). [E]

August 11, 1787

. . . after 2 o'clock we had all the captains and the Calabar gentlemen meet at King Ambo's palaver house because one of Willy Curcock's men fought with one of Captain Ford's mates. After a little time the mate died.[228] We made the decision that Willy Curcock's man should have his ear[229] cut off because of the fight.

August 13, 1787

. . . we heard that Captain Brighouse went away with 320 slaves.[230]

August 14, 1787

. . . we heard that John Tom Henshaw was dead. We sent our people to Henshaw Town with Apandam.

August 18, 1787

. . . Captain Potter came ashore. After 11 o'clock Potter sent [a message] on board his tender[231] and his ship to bring 35 white men, and at 12 o'clock they began to put up 2 sides of the house, and after 2 o'clock I had all the captains to dinner and supper with me.

August 25, 1787

. . . at 4 o'clock in the afternoon Captain Fairweather's tender went away with 210 slaves . . . .[232]

September 5, 1787

. . . We carried Ekpe into King Ambo's [place] because one of Tatem's[233] pawns had run away. We made him give one of his sons to Tatem.

September 16, 1787

. . . we carried Grand Ekpe to Henshaw and Willy Tom to "blow" forbidding any captain to send away in his tender any Calabar pawns, given for my slave goods. Tatem's tender went away with 330 slaves.[234]

231. Captain John Spencer of the Liverpool slaving ship *Ned* (193 tons). [E]

232. The *Banastre* (93 tons), Captain Thomas Smith, arrived at Grenada October 22, 1787, with 188 slaves and 21 large and 74 small ivory tusks (CO106/2, f.72, NA). Agents Harrison, Hinde & Co. sold 187 slaves for £6,131: 81 men, 55 women, 17 boys, 34 girls (LivRO, 942 HOL 10). The vessel returned to Liverpool with ninety-five ivory tusks and West India produce (*Liverpool General Advertiser*, Jan. 10, 1788). [E]

233. Captain John Tatem of the Liverpool slaving ship *Langdale* (209 tons). See also note 97. [E]

234. The *Three Brothers* (428 tons), Captain John Keatin, arrived at Dominica November 22, 1787, with 305 slaves, 143 ivory tusks, 50 puncheons palm oil, and 2 puncheons rum, and returned to Liverpool with the same quantities of African produce and additional West India produce (CO76/4, f. 53, NA; *Liverpool General Advertiser*, Mar. 6, 1788). [E]

September 19 the 1787

. . after 12 clock Day wee get Dinner in my house and Drink fine mimbo
so wee hear one guns firs so we mak 2 . . 3 Boy Run to go know who firs
guns   so them Boys com Back and till wee he say my yellow ogan abashey
shoot his wife for guns so shot not Toutch

September 20 the 1787

. . I see my yellow ogan abashey wife nam Eba com to me and he say
chop Docter and I send my Dear so my Dear send word he say his vomit so
I tell my Dear for carry him to my mother for giv mor Docter for Drink and
I go on bord after   so wee see my mother send word to me he say his be
Dead my yellow ogan wife   soon we have one Little snow Brsh ship was
in Comrown so   com to get som sail and I have Carpnter beagain Lay floor
new house first Day

. . (Here is written by another hand: Antera Duke Ejus Liber
              Archibald Forrest   Thomas Taylor)

September 26 the 1787

about 6 am in aqua Landing with fine morning his Day wee have 9 ship
in River so wee have willy Honesty and all us go on bord snow Brsh ship
for settle coomy plaver so his will pay 1000 copper for Everry Callabar Old
Otto Duk Daught Drink Docter with Husbun wife

October 1 the 1787

. . . I have see two King aqua women slave com from my yard Break one
my god Bason he say will be slave   so I Did send word to King aqua to Let
us know and after 2 clock wee all 4 Callabar new & old Egbo go to meet to
King Ambo plaver house about willy Curcock Egbo plaver

235. The Liverpool snow *Searle* (137 tons), Captain John Foulkes, which slaved at Cameroon.
Regarding snows, see note 55. [E]

236. Efik merchants purchased canvas to make sails for their canoes. In an early 1770s letter, for
example, Old Town merchant Grandy King George asked Liverpool merchant Ambrose Lace to
"Send me sum banue canvess to make sails for my canous." Williams offers "brand new" for "banue"
(Williams, *Liverpool Privateers*, 546). [E]

237. Antera Duke "his book." Asuquo and Akak translate the Latin phrase "Ejus Liber" as "free
born" (Asuquo, "Diary," 34; Akak, *Efiks*, 3:272). According to another Efik writer, "Epis Liber" is "free
born" (*Nigerian Chronicle*, Apr. 20, 1977, 13). This discrepancy is not critical: Antera Duke was a freeborn Efik trader, but the Latin phrase penned in the diary suggests that the trading ledger belonged
to Antera Duke. [E]

238. Archibald Forrest, a mate who worked on the *Gascoyne*, Captain Peter Comberbach. [E]

September 19, 1787

. . . after 12 o'clock noon we had dinner in my house and drank fine mimbo. We heard one gun [musket] fired. We made 2 or 3 boys run to find out who was firing guns. Those boys came back and told us that my [brother] Yellow Hogan Abashey [Antera] had shot at his wife with a gun but the shot did not touch [hit] her.

September 20, 1787

. . . I saw my [brother] Yellow Hogan Abashey [Antera's] wife named Eba coming to me and she said she had "eaten doctor," and I sent for my dear wife. My dear sent word that she [Eba] said that she vomited. I told my dear to carry her to my mother to give her more doctor to drink, and afterwards I went on board. Then my mother sent word to me saying the wife of my [brother] Yellow Hogan Abashey [Antera] is dead. Soon one little snow, a British ship that was in Cameroon,[235] came to get some sails,[236] and the carpenter began to lay the floor of my new house.

| *Here is written by* | Antera Duke Ejus Liber[237] | |
| *another hand* | Archibald Forrest[238] | Thomas Taylor[239] |

September 26, 1787

About 6 a.m. at Aqua Landing, a fine morning. This day we had 9 ships in the river. Willy Honesty and all of us went on board the snow, a British ship, to settle the "comey" palaver. He [the captain] will pay 1,000 coppers [among] every Calabar family.[240] Old Otto Duke's daughter "drank doctor" with her husband's wife.

October 1, 1787

. . . I saw two of King Aqua's women slaves coming to my yard and break one of my "god basins."[241] They said they would be my slaves. I sent word to King Aqua to let us know [if he agreed], and after 2 o'clock we all 4[242] and new and old Calabar Ekpe went to meet at King Ambo's palaver house about Willy Curcock's Ekpe palaver.

239. Thomas Taylor, chief mate on the *Gascoyne*. [E]

240. In the discussion about port dues, the Ekpe council ruled against Captain Foulkes, who paid a penalty of 1,000 copper rods (equal to the value of six prime slaves) to be divided among all the Calabar families. At Old Calabar in 1763, Liverpool captain James Berry's negotiations failed to reduce his port dues, and "after standing out about fifteen Day aggreed to pay 1000 Coppers among's them all" (Williams, *Liverpool Privateers*, 533). For slave prices see chapter 2. [E]

241. Apparently slaves could claim sanctuary after escaping from their masters if they broke one of the "god basins." Slaves when in trouble with their masters frequently fled to a powerful man and begged him to intercede for them. [S]

242. "We all 4" probably refers to Antera Duke, Egbo Young Antera, Esien, and Apandam. See also Oct. 22, 1787: "we 4." [E]

October 3 the 1787

. . . His Day wee 10 ship in River so I have send my cobin boy Eyo
Ebrow son in mimbo market soon after wee hear new ship in portsan

October 9 the 1787

. . . wee see Willy Honesty send to wee for com on bord Rogers to meet
so wee mak 500 coppers to give Robin John for his coomy for hav nam for
Coomy Book

October 17 the 1787

. . . I walk up to Egbo Young and Esim and after wee com Down for my
house and send my Cobin Boy for apandam Cobin to goin Bring 115
BeLong to Jimimy so wee begain shar for all 4 Callabar Egbo to mak Jimimy
Henshaw to be King Egbo

October 22 the 1787

. . . we hear all Creek town genllmen com with Willy Honesty to King
Ambo so all wee and men & women Did go to King Ambo plaver house   so
Willy send on bord Captin Fairweather to goin call Coffee Duk   so his Did
com ashor with Captin fairweather and so Callabar beagain ask him what
mak Been Run way on Bord   after word he say his hear wee 4 was Drink
Docter to killd him so wee tell Callabar wee was Drink Docter to not one
we go to his house because wee hear Duke Sister he say be his killd Duke
and to Let his Drink Docter with Duke Sister before wee settle   sam time
wee have send to call Duke Sister so his Did com to plaver house afterword
he beagain Bring all bob to all Callabar . . . and he say want to Drink Docter
with Coffee   so Everry Body ask Coffee to Drink Docter with him so
Coffee will not Drink Docter   so wee tell willy Honesty for send to 2 Egbo
Drum to carry Coffee to his house and wee say wee 4 will not settle with
Coffee if his not Drink Docter

243. Captain Richard Rogers of the Bristol slaving ship *Pearl* (375 tons). He wrote to his owners James Rogers & Co. that he arrived Oct. 4, and "found no less than eight purchasing Ships many
had been in the River sixteen months & Slaves at this instant are very scarce" (Richard Rogers to
James Rogers & Co., Old Calabar, Oct. 29, 1787, C107/12, NA). [E]

October 3, 1787

. . . this day there were 10 ships in the river. I sent my cabin boy Eyo Ebrow's son to the mimbo market. Soon after we heard of a new ship in Parrot Island.

October 9, 1787

. . . Willy Honesty sent to us to come on board Rogers's[243] ship for a meeting. We made up [collected] 500 coppers to give Robin John for his "comey" and to have it named in the "comey" book.

October 17, 1787

. . . I walked up to Egbo Young [Antera] and Esien, and afterwards we came down to my house and sent my cabin boy to Apandam's cabin to fetch 115 coppers belonging to Jimmy [Henshaw]. Then we began to share out among all 4 Calabar Ekpe to make Jimmy Henshaw King Ekpe.[244]

October 22, 1787

. . . we heard that all the Creek Town gentlemen had come with Willy Honesty to King Ambo's house. We and all the men and women went to King Ambo's palaver house. Then Willy sent [a message] on board Captain Fairweather's ship to call Coffee Duke. He came ashore with Captain Fairweather, and then the Calabar people began to ask him what made him run away on board. After these words he said he heard that we 4 had "drunk doctor" to kill him. We told the Calabar people that we had "drunk doctor" [and sworn] that not one of us would go to his house because we heard Duke Ephraim's sister say that he [Coffee Duke] had killed Duke Ephraim [with witchcraft]. We said let him "drink doctor" with Duke's sister before we settle. At the same time we sent to call Duke's sister. Then she came to the palaver house. Afterwards she began to bring the dispute to all the Calabar . . . and she said she wanted to "drink doctor" with Coffee. Everybody asked Coffee to "drink doctor" with her, but Coffee would not "drink doctor." We told Willy Honesty to send 2 Ekpe drums to carry Coffee to his house, and we said we 4 will not settle with Coffee if he does not "drink doctor."[245]

244. Antera's "4 Calabar Egbo" may refer to four branches of Ekpe. See also chapter 1 and note 250. [E]

245. Coffee Duke was to be placed under house arrest. [E]

October 25 the 1787

about 6 am in aqua Landing with small Rain morning so I walk up to see Esim and Egbo Young so I see Jimimy Henshaw com to see wee and wee tell him for go on bord Rogers for all Henshaw family coomy and wee have go on bord Rogers for mak Jimimy Henshaw name to King Egbo in Coomy Book so hear all Captin meet on bord Captin ford about ogan Captin Duk was fight with ford   soon after 2 clock time wee com ashor and I hear one my Ephrim abashey Egbo Sherry women have Brun two son one Day in plower andam Duke wife Brun young girl in aqua town

October 31 the 1787

. . . I hear one John Tom Cobham wife be Hang himself about plaver
October 17th the 1787
Jimimy Henshaw pay his for 4 Callabar Laws for be King Egbo.

Willy Honesty	20 Rods & one goat	Robin John	5 Rods
Georg old town	10 Rods	John Ambo	5 Rods
Tom Nonaw	10 Rods	Willy Tom	4 Rods
old & new Egbo	8 Rods	Tom Curcock	5 Rods
Robin Curcock	5 Rods	old & new Egbo	8 Rods
Guin Company			
King Egbo	5 Rods	Effar	5 Rods
Eyamba	10 Rods	Misimbo	4 Rods
old & new Egbo	8 Rods	King Ambo	20 Rods & goat
Tom Cobham	10 Rods	Ephrim Aqua	5 Rods
Duk Ephrim	20 Rods & goat		
Egbo Young Offion	25 Rods & goat		

---

246. The Efik regarded the birth of twins as a dire calamity. They killed the twins by putting them into pots and throwing the pots into the bush. Mothers of twins were usually expelled from the town. [S, E]

247. Wilkie transcribed Antera's date as 31.8.1787, but the entry contains the October 17 reference. Antera may have headed the diary entry "8er 31 the 1787," as ship captains occasionally abbreviated October as "8er." Placing the entry in late October fits the chronology of the diary information concerning Jimmy Henshaw (mentioned first October 17). Henshaw's payments also may have taken place October 17 (not October 31), if Wilkie disarranged the pagination.[E]

248. Hanging is the usual mode of suicide among the Efik. [S]

249. Wilkie's transcription inserted "(woman)" before "plaver," a decision with which we agree. [E]

250. Perhaps there were four branches or lodges of Ekpe (4 "Laws"). But Wilkie's transcription

October 25, 1787

About 6 a.m. at Aqua Landing, a little morning rain. I walked up to see Esien and Egbo Young [Antera]. I saw Jimmy Henshaw coming to see us, and we told him to go on board Rogers's ship to take "comey" for all the Henshaw family, and we went on board Rogers's ship to have Jimmy Henshaw's name as King Ekpe put in the "comey" book. I heard that all the captains were meeting on board Captain Ford's ship because Hogan Captain Duke had fought with Ford. Soon after 2 o'clock we came ashore and I heard in the palaver house that one of my [brother] Ephraim Abashey [Antera's] Egbosherry women had borne two sons in one day.[246] Andam Duke's wife bore a young girl in Aqua Town.

October 31, 1787[247]

. . . I heard that John Tom Cobham's wife hanged herself[248] because of the [woman] palaver[249] of October 17th, 1787.

Jimmy Henshaw paid his [dues] of 4 Calabar Laws[250] to become King Ekpe [to be distributed as follows]:

Willy Honesty	20 rods and one goat	Robin John	5 rods
George Old Town	10 rods	John Ambo	5 rods
Tom Nonaw	10 rods	Willy Tom	4 rods
Old and New Ekpe	8 rods	Tom Curcock	5 rods
Robin Curcock	5 rods	Old and New Ekpe	8 rods
Guinea Company[251]			
King Ekpe	5 rods	Effar	5 rods
Eyamba	10 rods	Misimbo	4 rods
Old and New Ekpe	8 rods	King Ambo	20 rods and goat
Tom Cobham	10 rods	Ephraim Aqua	5 rods
Duke Ephraim	20 rods and goat		
Egbo Young Ofiong	25 rods and one goat[252]		

inserted "(afaws?)" after "Laws," indicating that Antera's Efik orthography is obscure, and perhaps he meant the Efik word *ofo*, "slave." The dues total 216 copper rods and 4 goats, about the value of 2 slaves. The modest value suggests that the office of King Ekpe was not very prestigious. [S, E]

251. Though Antera Duke records no payments for Guinea Company, the fact that the community is listed indicates they were in Ekpe. [E]

252. Since Egbo Young Ofiong received the greatest share among Ekpe officers, he likely was eyamba (president of Ekpe society) in October 1787. Nicholls, on his 1805 visit, met "Egbo Young Eyambo" (Hallett, *Records*, 199). Willy Honesty, Duke Ephraim (Efiom Edem), and King Ambo, who received comparatively large payments, may have been vice presidents. See also chapter 1. [E]

November 1 the 1787

. . . at 12 clock Day wee go on bord Captin fairweather for Dinner soon
after wee have go on bord Everry ship to Let the know I will go to aqua
Bakassey to Buy Canow and after 12 clock night I sail way in Landing to
agoin in aqua Bakassey so I Did carry two Esim Duke girl with me and one
girl BeLong to my Dear that mak 3 girl wee 42 hand besides 3 girl for two
canow

December 2 the 1787

. . . wee have see Captin fairweather Docter Dead so wee have see Egbo
Run for about Town

December 4 the 1787

. . . I have my girl arshbong Duke son sister putt Larg Rods Leg mincles
in Leg so I pay the smith 1 Rods 5 Boostam yams & Jar mimbo

December 11 the 1787

. . . Tom John Cobham Dear wife Drink Docter all mush Dead so I Did
mak my Dear to go in Henshaw town to see him because be sister with him
and Esim Dear go to see him at 9 clock night my Dear com Back so I have
andam nothing com hom for orroup

December 13 the 1787

. . . wee have Esim send to go and see John Cobham in Henshaw town
and at 5 clock wee 3 Brother walk up to Henshaw town to Jimimy Henshaw
yard so Jimimy killd goat for wee and agoin for his cobin and stay heer and
call all the genllmen for mak Long time bob and com back in 9 clock time

December 22 the 1787

. . . Potter go way with Tender go way with 350 slaves

253. Surgeon Robert Fearon of Fairweather's *Tarleton* (Probate of Fearon, Dec. 13, 1788, Reel
89787, FHL; BT98/48,221, NA). [E]

254. Calabar women wore copper and brass coils or rings on their arms and legs. The armlets
(bracelets) were called *okpoho ubok* in Efik (literally "arm brass"). The Efik called the leglets *ewok*
(Goldie, *Dictionary*, 253). The English used the term "manillas" (from the Portuguese *manilhas*) to refer
to bracelets and the copper/brass currency used elsewhere on the coast. Archibong Duke's daughter
had attained womanhood. See also notes 27, 143, 260. [S, E]

November 1, 1787

. . . at 12 o'clock [mid]day we went on board Captain Fairweather's ship for dinner. Soon afterwards we went on board every ship to let them know that I will be going to Akwa Bakasi to buy canoes, and after 12 o'clock at night I sailed away from the landing to "be a going" [go] to Akwa Bakasi. I took two of Esien Duke's girls with me, and one girl belonging to my dear wife, that makes 3 girls. We were 42 hands besides the 3 girls in two canoes.

December 2, 1787

. . . Captain Fairweather's doctor[253] was dead. We saw Ekpe running about the town.

December 4, 1787

. . . I had my girl, Archibong Duke's son's sister, put large copper leg manacles [bracelets] on her leg.[254] I paid the smith[255] 1 rod, 5 Boostam yams, and a jar of mimbo.

December 11, 1787

. . . Tom John Cobham's dear wife "drank doctor," all [wives?] must die. I made my dear wife go to Henshaw Town to see her because she is her sister, and Esien's dear wife went to see her. At 9 o'clock at night my dear wife came back. Andam Nothing came home from Orroup.

December 13, 1787

. . . we sent Esien to go and see John Cobham in Henshaw Town, and at 5 o'clock we 3 brothers walked up to Henshaw Town to Jimmy Henshaw's yard. Jimmy killed a goat for us, and we went into his cabin and stayed there and called all the gentlemen for a long discussion and then came back at 9 o'clock.

December 22, 1787

. . . Potter's tender went away with 350 slaves.[256]

255. An independent craftsman, not a slave. [E]

256. The *Ned* (193 tons), Captain John Spencer, arrived at Dominica February 16, 1788, with 310 slaves, 10 of whom may have died before sale. It also carried 50 puncheons palm oil, 9 tons redwood, and 517 ivory tusks weighing 3 tons. His ivory thus averaged 13 pounds/tusk (CO76/5, f. 6, NA; *Liverpool General Advertiser*, July 17, 1788). [E]

December 25 the 1787

. . . great fog morning and at 1 clock time wee have Captin fairwer John Tatam Captin ford Captin Hughes Captin Potter Captin Rogers and Captin Combesboch and Eyo willy Honesty and willy Tom Robin so wee get Dinner in the Duke house and super so at 8 clock night the go on bord and wee Did firs 3 great guns

December 29 the 1787

. . . at 3 clock noon Captin fairweather go his way with 377 slaves

January 1 the 1788

about 5 am in aqua Landing with great fog so I go Down for Landing so I have mak my girl arshbong Duke son sister wer Cloth first Day and the women and at 1 clock wee have get Dinner with 6 Captin in Egbo Young house

January 3 the 1788

. . . I have go on bord to get som Brandy for two my Brother and at 3 clock noon I have two my Brother and my Ephrim abashey the go way from orroup   sam time wee hear Captin John King Egbo Dead in old town plaver house in all genllmen face

January 7 the 1788

. . . I see Robin John send one his old men to com and tell Everry Body is want go any Docter If be his killd Captin John King Egbo or not

January 8 the 1788

. . . I see one willy Honesty men com and tell me he say Coffee Duke he say will com heer to putt firs for all his house so I tak 2 Egbo Drum and brow to not men sleep for house sam time I hear andam Duk son Dead by Bad sick

257. This entry reveals Antera's first clear attempt to abbreviate a word ("fairwer," undoubtedly having seen "fairw^er" or "fairw^r" written). Other abbreviations occur on January 9, 1788 ("Jno") and January 27, 1788 ("Carpnt"). [E]

258. Captain Peter Comberbach of the Liverpool slaving ship *Gascoyne* (294 tons). [E]

259. The *Tarleton* (342 tons), Captain Patrick Fairweather, arrived at Dominica February 19, 1788, with 308 slaves, 45 ivory tusks, 94 puncheons, 8 butts and 15 tierces palm oil, 50 tons redwood, and 60 barrels Guinea pepper (CO76/5, f.6, NA). Shipowner Thomas Tarleton stated that Fairweather shipped 371 slaves from Old Calabar. Other sources document 305 and 302 slave imports, totals that may indicate harbor mortality. The *Tarleton* returned to Liverpool June 24, 1788; a Liver-

December 25, 1787

. . . a very foggy morning, and at 1 o'clock we [hosted] Captain Fairweather,[257] John Tatem, Captain Ford, Captain Hughes, Captain Potter, Captain Rogers and Captain Comberbach,[258] and Eyo Willy Honesty and Willy Tom Robin. We had [Christmas] dinner in Duke Ephraim's house and supper. Then at 8 o'clock at night they went on board, and we fired 3 great guns.

December 29, 1787

. . . at 3 o'clock in the afternoon Captain Fairweather went away with 377 slaves.[259]

January 1, 1788

About 5 a.m. at Aqua Landing, a great fog. I went down to the landing. I made my girl, Archibong Duke's son's sister, wear a cloth for the first time, and be a woman,[260] and at 1 o'clock we had dinner with 6 captains in Egbo Young [Ofiong's] house.

January 3, 1788

. . . I went on board to get some brandy for two of my brothers. And at 3 o'clock in the afternoon I have [hosted] my two brothers and my [brother] Ephraim Abashey [Antera]. They went away for Orroup. At the same time we heard that Captain John King Ekpe[261] had died in the Old Town palaver house in front of all the gentlemen.

January 7, 1788

. . . Robin John sent one of his old men to come and tell everyone if they want him to go and "drink doctor" to see if he had killed Captain John King Ekpe [by witchcraft] or not.

January 8, 1788

. . . One of Willy Honesty's men came and told me that Coffee Duke has said he would come here and set fire to all his houses. I took 2 Ekpe drums and "blew" to forbid any men from sleeping in the houses. At the same time I heard that Andam Duke's son had died from a bad sickness.[262]

---

pool gazette reported eighty tons of redwood (and the freighted West India produce) but did not record ivory imports (*Liverpool General Advertiser*, June 26, 1788). [E]

260. See notes 27, 143, 254. [E]

261. Captain John Ambo, King Ekpe. He also is listed in the account book of the Liverpool slaver *Dobson* at Old Calabar in 1769–1770 (Hair, "Antera Duke," 360). Little is known about this man. [E]

262. Any disease that causes the body to swell is a bad disease to the Efik, since it indicates the presence of witchcraft, the violation of an *mbiam* oath, or "bad medicine." [S]

January 9 the 1788

. . . old Robin Jno com himself and call Callabar genllmen go to King ambo plaver house and meet about the say be Robin John killd Captin John Ambo so Everry find that bob no be Tru   Duk com hom for orroup

January 17 the 1788

. . . about 6 am in aqua Landing with fine morning so I go on bord ford and com Back in 10 clock time so I have Drink in my house 6 clock I brow all wawa Egbo to again cutt firs wood in morning for putt to Town plaver house and after 9 clock night I have see firs get in to Potter antera yard so I go up in stop house myself & Everry men to Catch so firs tak 4 house soon after I see Willy Tom Robin com & Captin Tatam send one mat & 6 Boat Boy to help me

January 23 the 1788

. . . I go on bord to see Captin Potter about his cooper was Trun for water Last night about 8 clock and wee have Combesboch Tender go way with 280 slaves and 2 clock noon wee king aqua com to see Egbo Young offiong so wee Did play all noon 7 clock night his go hom soon wee carry grandy Egbo in plaver house

January 27 the 1788

about 5 am in aqua Landing with great fog morning so I walk up to see Carpnt & Joiners after that wee have Backsider Drek Comroun com to wee with the new obong men so I Did Dash them 4 Rods so wee have go Bord ford for Dinner

January 31 the 1788

about 5 am in aqua Landing with great fog morning so I goin Down for Landing and I have send my son on bord Hughes to call his ashor and give him slave and after that I & Egbo Young & Eshen Duk agoin on bord Rogers at 1 clock noon I have send two my father son for mimbo market

263. Wilkie's transcription inserted "(?)" between "wawa" and "Egbo." See also note 140. [E]
264. According to the muster roll of the *Iris*, Captain Peter Potter, Thomas Jones drowned on Jan. 24, 1788 (BT98/49,67, NA). Wilkie's transcription inserted "(drown?)" after "Trun." [E]
265. The *Will* (128 tons), Captain Thomas Johnston, arrived at Grenada May 15, 1788; the num-

January 9, 1788

. . . Old Robin John came himself and called the Calabar gentlemen to go to King Ambo's palaver house and meet, because they say that Young Robin John killed Captain John Ambo [King Ekpe]. Everyone agreed that accusation was not true. Duke Ephraim came home from Orroup.

January 17, 1788

. . . about 6 a.m. at Aqua Landing, a fine morning. I went on board Ford's ship and came back at 10 o'clock. I drank in my house. At 6 o'clock I "blew" all wawa [new][263] Ekpe men to cut firewood again in the morning to put in the town palaver house, and after 9 o'clock at night I saw fire had got into Potter Antera's yard. I went up to stop the house fire myself and everyone came. Fire took 4 houses. Soon afterwards I saw Willy Tom Robin come, and Captain Tatem sent one mate and 6 boat boys to help me.

January 23, 1788

. . . I went on board to see Captain Potter because his cooper drowned[264] in the water last night about 8 o'clock, and Comberbach's tender went away with 280 slaves.[265] At 2 o'clock in the afternoon King Aqua came to see Egbo Young Ofiong, so we "played" all afternoon. At 7 o'clock at night he went home, and soon after we carried Grand Ekpe into the palaver house.

January 27, 1788

About 5 a.m. at Aqua Landing, a great morning fog. I walked up to see the carpenters and joiners. After that Backsider Drek Comroun came to us with the new obong men. I "dashed" them 4 rods. We went on board Ford's ship for dinner.

January 31, 1788

About 5 a.m. at Aqua Landing, a very foggy morning. I went down to the landing, and I sent my son on board Hughes's ship to call ashore and give him slaves, and after that I and Egbo Young [Antera] and Esien Duke went on board Rogers's ship. At 1 o'clock in the afternoon I sent two of my father's sons to the mimbo market.

ber of slaves not documented. The ship returned to Liverpool July 6, 1788, with 27 puncheons palm oil, 3 puncheons pepper, 193 ivory tusks, 1 cask bees wax, and West India produce (*Liverpool General Advertiser*, July 10, 1788). [E]

APPENDIX A

Index of African Names

Antera Duke's diary, January 1785–January 1788, records the anglicized names of 101 men and 5 women from Old Calabar and several surrounding Cross River settlements.[1] His diary is the only source that documents most of these names, otherwise lost to history. It also preserves the greatest number of names from any single source from the beginning of European trade at Old Calabar in the mid-1600s to 1805: an Old Calabar account book from 1720 records twenty-six anglicized African names; from July 1769 to January 1770, Liverpool captain John Potter traded with fifty-four African merchants; a series of letters written by Old Calabar merchants, 1761–1773, mention names of forty-three different African businessmen; and in January–February 1805 explorer Henry Nicholls met twelve different Efik men in Old Calabar. Like the names noted in these other primary sources, most of the Efik and non-Efik men Antera Duke writes about were merchants, names he wrote in the context of Old Calabar business dealings with regional traders and those from overseas.

Antera's diary does not refer to Old Calabar residents, including important traders, documented by earlier or later sources. In some cases he simply does not have a reason to write their names in his diary. Merchant Gentleman Honesty, for example, sold thirty-nine slaves to Captain John Potter from July 20, 1769, to January 8, 1770, more than all other traders except for Willy Honesty and Antera Duke (see table 2.2). Gentleman Honesty then disappears from the historical record until Nicholls meets him on January 26,

1805. Other men had died by the time Antera began his entries in 1785. Some we assume died of old age, such as Old Cobham, Old Keneby William Henshaw, and Old Willy Ecricock, three men who sold four slaves to Captain Potter. Old Town leader Ephraim Robin John had certainly died by the mid-1780s. Cobham Tom Henshaw, Ephraim Jimmy Henshaw, Frank Jemmy Henshaw, Keneby Willy Henshaw, King Egbo Solomon Henshaw, and Tom Henshaw, names documented from 1761 to 1770, do not appear in Antera Duke's diary. Henshaw Robin Henshaw (diary entry February 22, 1787) and John Tom Henshaw (August 14, 1787), though, appear for the first time in the historical record.

This appendix contains African names recorded in Antera Duke's diary, grouped by town and family; we cross-referenced the list with sources documenting other Old Calabar names during Antera Duke's lifetime (see "Notes and Sources" at the end of this appendix). We standardized names, based on our best judgment, since Antera employs inconsistent spellings. He also sometimes penned partial trading names, such as Egbo Young rather than Egbo Young Ofiong or Eshen rather than Eshen Duke.

The name "Egbo Young" is problematic, as it is an anglicization of Efik *ekpenyong*, a common name in Old Calabar. Simmons, who conducted fieldwork at Calabar in the early 1950s, noted: "Egbo Young is an anglicization of *Ekpenyong*, the name of a supernatural power, as well as a personal name. Persons so named are believed to be self-willed and unruly, since the actions of the *Ekpenyong* supernatural power are unpredictable."[2] In the *Dobson's* accounts, 1769–1770, "Egboyoung Tom Eccricock" is one of the named Calabar merchants. There are likely two Egbo Youngs mentioned in the diary: Egbo Young Ofiong, a leading Duke Town merchant who lived at "Liverpool Hall," and Egbo Young, one of Antera Duke's brothers and close associates—hence Egbo Young Antera.[3]

There are also difficulties identifying various Esiens in the diary. Esien Duke is clearly an important trader, about whom little is known. On December 25, 1785, January 1, 1786, and again on December 25, 1786, he hosted dinners for ship captains and Efik gentlemen at his "new house." On Christmas 1785 the guests included "Esim" (Esien) and "Eshen Ambo" (Esien Ambo, from Creek Town).[4] We suggest that Esien Duke belonged to a subhouse of Duke House. Esien (spelled Crim/Eshin/Esien/Esim/Esin/Ewien) is the trader who associates frequently with Antera Duke and his brother Egbo Young. As such he may be in Ntiero ward. "Eshen Ambo" appears twice (December 25, 1785; October 26, 1786) and is referred to only as "Eshen" on March 17, 1787, and July 18, 1787—in both instances grouped with Eyo and Ebetim from Creek Town (the residence of the Ambos).

NOTE: * = uncertainty about town residence; # = uncertainty about name (spelling) or family.

Duke Town

ARCHIBONG FAMILY

Archibong Duke 1769–1770
> July? 9, 1785; July? 29, 1785; January 3, 1786; February 8, 1786; February 11, 1786; April 20, 1786; March 3, 1787

Archibong Duke's sister Mbong*
> July? 8, 1785 (dead); July? 9, 1785; July? 20, 1785; July? 29, 1785

Archibong Duke's son
> December 23, 1785

Archibong Duke's son's sister/Antera Duke's girl wife
> April 28, 1787; December 4, 1787; January 1, 1788

Ebetim (one of Archibong's father's sons) 1769–1770
> February 11, 1786

DUKE FAMILY

Coffee Duke 1769–1770
> April 22, 1785; April 30, 1785; July? 1, 1785; December 25, 1785; May 1, 1786; July 9, 1786; October 5, 1786; March 3, 1787; March 24, 1787; April 28, 1787; October 22, 1787; January 8, 1788

Coffee Duke's son
> October 5, 1786

Dick Ephraim
> May 10, 1785; March 21, 1786

Duke Ephraim 1761, 1769–1770, 1780
> January 18, 1785; February 2, 1785; March 6, 1785; March 7, 1785; March 12, 1785; March 23, 1785; April 12, 1785; May 9, 1785; June 14, 1785; June 25, 1785; July? 2, 1785; July? 23, 1785; July? 24, 1785; August? 19, 1785; September? 3, 1785; September? 14, 1785; October? 27, 1785; November? 11, 1785; November? 24, 1785; December 25, 1785; December 30, 1785; January 1, 1786; January 2, 1786; January 3, 1786; March 21, 1786; June 10, 1786; June 23, 1786; July 2, 1786; July 3, 1786, July 4, 1786 (died); July 5, 1786 (dead); July 9, 1786 (dead); August 9, 1786 (dead); November 2, 1786 (dead); November 4, 1786 (dead); November 9, 1786 (dead); December 19, 1786 (dead); December 28, 1786 (dead); January 24, 1787 (dead); June 7, 1787 (dead); October 22, 1787 (dead)

Duke Ephraim's sister
> October 22, 1787

Duke Ephraim's sister's daughter*
> November? 24, 1785; April 28, 1787

Duke Ephraim's son Egbo Abashey
  April 12, 1785
Duke Ephraim's son/Young Duke/Duke Ephraim 1769–1770, 1775, 1789, 1790a,
1792a, 1792b, 1805
  July? 1, 1785 (Duke Ephraim's son); September 4, 1786 (Young Duke
  Ephraim); October 31, 1787 (Duke Ephraim); December 25, 1787 (Duke
  Ephraim); January 9, 1788 (Duke Ephraim)
Duke Ephraim's wives
  November 13, 1786
Duke's yellow wife Pip
  March 23, 1785
Old Tom House
  November? 24, 1785

EYAMBA FAMILY

Abashey Ofiong*
  July? 23, 1785; May 4, 1786
Egbo Young Ofiong 1769–1770, 1777, 1783b, 1792a, 1805
  January 18, 1785; January 25, 1785; February 5, 1785; March 6, 1785; March 7,
  1785; September? 4, 1785; September? 29, 1785; September? 30, 1785; Novem-
  ber? 23, 1785; December 25, 1785; December 30, 1785; July 9, 1786; October
  26, 1786; November 8, 1786; January 1, 1787; January 24, 1787; February 16,
  1787; October 31, 1787; January 1, 1788; January 23, 1788
Egbo Young Ofiong's dear wife
  January 29, 1786
Egbo Young Ofiong's mother
  June 7, 1787
Eyamba
  October 31, 1787

NTIERO (ANTERA) FAMILY

Andam Nothing (slave)
  October 14, 1786; December 11, 1787
Antera Duke Ephraim 1769, 1769–1770, 1790, 1792a, 1805
  Front page of diary; September 20, 1787
Antera Duke's cabin boy (Eyo Ebrow's son)
  October 14, 1786; October 15, 1786; April 18, 1787; April 28, 1787; October 3,
  1787; October 17, 1787
Antera Duke's father
  July? 18, 1785; January 22, 1786; November 8, 1786; January 24, 1787; March
  24, 1787 (dead); April 30, 1787; June 7, 1787; January 31, 1788
Antera Duke's mimbo wife
  April 16, 1787

Antera Duke's mother
   November? 23, 1785; September 20, 1787
Antera Duke's son
   January 31, 1788
Apandam
   November? 5, 1785; November? 7, 1785; January 23, 1786; November 2, 1786;
   August 14, 1787; October 17, 1787
Awa Ofiong, Antera Duke's "dear" wife (sister of Tom John Cobham's wife)
   Front page; July? 2, 1785; November? 23, 1785; February 20, 1787; September
   20, 1787; November 1, 1787; December 11, 1787
Awa Ofiong's brother
   March 21, 1786
Awa Ofiong's son
   April 20, 1786
Calabar Antera
   November? 3, 1785
Ebo (Antera's father's son)
   February 20, 1787 (dead)
Egbo Young Antera (Antera's brother; often with Esien and Apandam)
   April 30, 1785; June 24, 1785; July? 1, 1785; July? 15, 1785; July? 21, 1785 (my
   brother Egbo Young); July? 29, 1785; August? 11, 1785; September? 14, 1785;
   October? 18, 1785; November? 3, 1785; November? 4, 1785, November? 5,
   1785 (my brother Egbo Young); November? 7, 1785 (my brother); December
   14, 1785; January 23, 1786 (my brother Egbo Young); October 19, 1786 (my
   brother Egbo Young); December 19, 1786; December 25, 1786; January 31,
   1787; April 13, 1787; May 27, 1787; June 15, 1787; October 17, 1787; October
   25, 1787; January 31, 1788
Ephraim Abashey Antera (Antera's brother)
   January 3, 1788 (my Ephraim Abashey)
Ephraim Abashey Antera's Egbosherry women
   October 25, 1787
Esien
   March 6, 1785 (Esien); March 12, 1785 (Ewien); April 22, 1785 (Crim); April 30,
   1785 (Crim); June 14, 1785 (Crim); June 24, 1785 (Esim); July? 1, 1785 (Esin);
   July? 21, 1785 (Esin); July? 23, 1785 (Esin); August? 7, 1785 (Esin); August? 11,
   1785 (Esin); October? 18, 1785 (Esin); October? 26, 1785 (Esin); November? 5,
   1785 (Eshin); November? 11, 1785 (Esin); December 14, 1785 (Esin); December
   22, 1785 (Esin); December 23, 1785 (Esin); December 25, 1785 (Esim); May 4,
   1786 (Esim); May 21, 1786 (Esim); July 9, 1786 (Esim); August 9, 1786 (Esim);
   September 4, 1786 (Esim); December 19, 1786 (Esim); December 25, 1786
   (Esim); January 31, 1787 (Esim); February 22, 1787 (Esim); June 15, 1787 (Esim);
   October 17, 1787 (Esim); October 25, 1787 (Esim); December 13, 1787 (Esim)
Esien's dear wife
   December 11, 1787

Hogan Abashey Antera (Antera Duke's brother)
> July? 29, 1785 (my brother Hogan); September? 14, 1785 (Hogan Antera); November? 11, 1785 (Hogan Antera); April 30, 1787 (my Hogan Abashey)

Jimmy Antera 1769–1770
> April 28, 1787; May 27, 1787

Long Dick[#]
> July 10, 1786; July 11, 1786; February 17, 1787

Long Duke Ephraim[#]
> March 21, 1786; October 10, 1786; January 24, 1787; February 26, 1787; June 4, 1787

Potter Antera
> August? 7, 1785; January 17, 1788

Yellow Hogan Abashey Antera (Antera's brother)
> November 8, 1786 (my [brother] Yellow Hogan Abashey); September 19, 1787 (my Yellow Hogan Abashey)

Yellow Hogan Abashey Antera's wife Eba
> September 19, 1787; September 20, 1787 (dead)

UNKNOWN FAMILIES IN DUKE TOWN

Abashey[#]
> June 23, 1786

Andam Duke's son[#]
> January 8, 1788

Andam Ephraim[#]
> June 4, 1787

Coffee Sam Ephraim[#]
> September? 3, 1785

Coffee Sam Ephraim's sister[#]
> September? 3, 1785

Coffee Sam Ephraim's wife[#]
> September? 3, 1785

Dick Ebrow's sister[#]
> July 17, 1785

Ebrow Potter[#]
> July? 1, 1785

Ephraim Coffee's brother[#]
> July? 1, 1785

Ephraim Duke's women[#]
> March 21, 1786

Ephraim Egbo's daughter[#]
> March 21, 1786

Ephraim Ofiong[#]
> June 25, 1785; January 22, 1786

Esien Duke#

> April 21, 1785 (Eshen Duke); May 26, 1785 (Esin Duke); July? 8, 1785 (Esin Duk);
> September? 14, 1785 (Esin Duke); September? 30, 1785 (Esin); December 25, 1785
> (Esin); January 1, 1786 (Esim); January 3, 1786 (Esim); October 19, 1786 (Esim
> Duke); November 2, 1786 (Esim Duk); November 7, 1786 (Esim Duk); December
> 8, 1786 (Esim); December 25, 1786 (Esim Duke); January 31, 1788 (Eshen Duke)

Esien Duke's girls#

> November 1, 1787

Hogan Captain Duke#

> October 25, 1787

King Ekpe#

> February 2, 1785; January 29, 1786; June 10, 1786

Yellow Belly's daughter, mother of Dick Ebrow's sister#

> July? 17, 1785

Henshaw Town

NSA (HENSHAW) FAMILY

Ephraim Robin Henshaw's 1769–1770 daughter

> May 27, 1787

Ephraim Watt 1770 (Effa Ewatt), 1799 (Effeywatt Captain Calabar)

> May 10, 1785; July? 24, 1785; April 30, 1787

Henshaw Robin Henshaw

> February 22, 1787

Jimmy Henshaw 1769–1770

> October 17, 1787; October 25, 1787; October 31, 1787; December 13, 1787

John Tom Henshaw

> August 14, 1787 (dead)

Robin Henshaw's 1769–1770 son

> February 22, 1787

Creek Town

AMBO FAMILY

Captain John's family

> May 27, 1787

Captain John Ambo, King Ekpe 1769–1770

> October 31, 1787 (John Ambo); January 3, 1788 (Captain John King Egbo
> dead); January 7, 1788 (Captain John King Egbo); January 9, 1788 (Captain
> John Ambo)

Ebitim (or Ebetim)# (close associate of Esien of Creek Town and Eyo)

> December 25, 1785; January 1, 1786; September 4, 1786; October 26, 1786;
> March 17, 1787; July 18, 1787

Egbosherry Sam Ambo
    October 14, 1786
Esien Ambo
    December 25, 1785; October 26, 1786; March 17, 1787; July 18, 1787
Sam Ambo, King Ekpe, King Ambo 1769–1770
    May 10, 1785 (Sam Ambo); January 29, 1786 (King Egbo Sam Ambo); October 26, 1786 (Sam Ambo); July 18, 1787 (Sam King Ambo); July 25, 1787 (King Ambo); July 26, 1787 (Sam King Ambo); August 11, 1787 (King Ambo); September 5, 1787 (King Ambo); October 1, 1787 (King Ambo); October 22, 1787 (King Ambo); October 31, 1787 (King Ambo); January 9, 1788 (King Ambo)
Sam[#]
    November? 11, 1785

COBHAM FAMILY

Cobham
    July? 1, 1785
Cobham family
    December 24, 1786; January 24, 1787
Egbo Cobham
    March 24, 1787
George Cobham 1769–1770
    July 10, 1786; July 18, 1786; October 26, 1786
John Tom Cobham's wife
    October 31, 1787 (dead)
John Cobham 1769–1770
    May 18, 1786; December 13, 1787
King Calabar (Ndem priest)
    August? 23, 1785; October? 8, 1785; March 24, 1787; April 13, 1787
Tom Cobham
    October 31, 1787
Tom John Cobham's wife
    December 11, 1787 (dead)

EYO FAMILY

Eyo Willy Honesty 1767c, 1769–1770, 1771, 1772, 1776, 1780, 1792c, 1805
    January 25, 1785 (Eyo Willy Honesty); March 12, 1785 (Willy Honesty); June 14, 1785 (Willy Honesty); July? 8, 1785 (Eyo Willy Honesty); July? 9, 1785 (Willy Honesty); December 25, 1785 (Eyo Willy Honesty); September 4, 1786 (Willy Honesty); December 24, 1786 (Willy Honesty); January 24, 1787 (Willy Honesty); February 2, 1787 (Willy Honesty); February 16, 1787 (Willy Honesty); February 22, 1787 (Willy Honesty); March 24, 1787 (Willy Honesty); April 16, 1787 (Willy); July 25, 1787 (Eyo Willy Honesty); September 26, 1787

(Willy Honesty); October 9, 1787 (Willy Honesty); October 22, 1787 (Willy
Honesty); October 31, 1787 (Willy Honesty); December 25, 1787 (Eyo Willy
Honesty); January 8, 1788 (Willy Honesty)
Eyo Willy Honesty's daughter
    January 25, 1785

UNKNOWN FAMILY

Etutim*# (perhaps Ebitim/Ebetim)
    January 18, 1785
Eyo# (Creek Town but not Eyo Willy Honesty; close associate of Ebitim/Ebetim
and Esien)
    January 1, 1786; June 23, 1786; September 4, 1786; October 26, 1786; March 17,
    1787; July 18, 1787

Old Town

ROBIN FAMILY

Robin*#
    April 21, 1785
Tom Robin 1767a
    August? 19, 1785
Willy Tom Robin
    October? 18, 1785; November? 24, 1785; July 19, 1786; December 25, 1786;
    January 24, 1787; January 31, 1787; February 20, 1787; April 18, 1787; October
    31, 1787; September 16, 1787; December 25, 1787; January 17, 1788
Young Tom Robin
    July? 29, 1785 (dead); August? 19, 1785 (dead)

ROBIN JOHN FAMILY

Little Otto 1769–1770
    January 18, 1785
Old Robin John
    January 9, 1788
Otto Ephraim [Robin John] 1767b, 1773a, 1776, 1783a, 1805
    April 18, 1787
Robin John 1761, 1767a, 1773b
    October 9, 1787; October 31, 1787; January 7, 1788;
    January 9, 1788 (Young Robin John)

UNKNOWN FAMILY

George Old Town#
    October 31, 1787
Otto Tom King John#
    June 7, 1787

Robin Tom King John[#]
    June 7, 1787
Tom King John[#]
    June 7, 1787

Little Cameroon (Efut)

Abashey Commrown Backsider★[#]
    July? 27, 1785
Backsider Drek Comrown★[#]
    January 27, 1788
Commrown Backsider Bakassey★[#]
    June 14, 1785; July? 2, 1785

Tom Shott's Point

Captain Andrew[#]
    October? 27, 1785
King Tom Salt[#]
    October? 27, 1785; January 2, 1786; January 3, 1786; June 10, 1786

Egbosherry (Ibibio)

Ebrow Egbosherry's fishermen★[#]
    November? 11, 1785
Egbo Sherry★[#]
    November? 4, 1785
Robert Enyong★[#]
    October? 8, 1785
Robert Enyong's father★[#]
    October? 8, 1785

Guinea Company

Misimbo[#]
    January 22, 1786; October 31, 1787

Bakassey (Bakasi)

Ephraim Aqua Bakassey*[#]
    April 11, 1785 (Ephraim Aqua Bakassy); July? 24, 1785 (Ephraim Aqua); Sep-
    tember? 14, 1785 (Ephraim Aqua); January 24, 1787 (Ephraim Aqua); March 3,
    1787 (Ephraim Aqua); October 31, 1787 (Ephraim Aqua)
Ephraim Aqua's son*[#]
    February 22, 1787

Jock Bakassey[#]

    September? 4, 1785 (Jock Bakassey); November 8, 1786 (Jack Bakassey)

Jack*[#]

    November? 11, 1785

Qua

Andam Duke's wife*

    October 25, 1787

Egbo Young Ofiong's dear wife

    January 29, 1786 (gives birth at Aqua Town)

John Aqua[#]

    January 30, 1785

King Aqua[#]

    August? 11, 1785 (King Aqua); July 18, 1786 (King Aqua); July 19, 1786 (Long Tom who is King Aqua); February 26, 1787 (Long King Aqua); June 15, 1787 (King Aqua); October 1, 1787 (King Aqua); January 23, 1788 (King Aqua)

Tom Aqua[#]

    January 30, 1785

Itu (Mbiabo Efik)

Andam Curcock[#]

    November? 5, 1785; November? 10, 1785

Potter Antera's mother[#]

    November? 7, 1785

Potter Antera's father[#]

    November? 7, 1785

Robin Curcock[#]

    October 31, 1787

Tom Curcock[#]

    November? 5, 1785; December 24, 1786; October 31, 1787

Willy Curcock[#]

    November? 5, 1785; December 24, 1786; August 11, 1787; October 1, 1787

Young Tom Curcock[#]

    December 28, 1786

Young Tom Curcock's father[#]

    December 28, 1786

Unknown Towns

Effar*[#]

    October 31, 1787

Efiom*[#]

    November 4, 1786

Eyo Duke*#
    April 20, 1786
Hogan poor boy*#
    March 17, 1787
Imo Duke's son*#
    January 24, 1787
Old Otto Duke's daughter*#
    September 26, 1787
Old Otto Duke's daughter's husband's wife★#
    September 26, 1787
Tom Nonaw*#
    October 31, 1787

Notes and Sources

1761. William Earle to Duke Abashy, Liverpool, Feb. 10, 1761, in Lovejoy and Richardson, "Letters," 99.

1767a. Account of goods and slaves owed the ship *Edgar* from Old Town traders, Aug. 12, 1767, in Lovejoy and Richardson, "Letters," 102.

1767b. Affidavit from Old Calabar, Aug. 22, [1767], in Lovejoy and Richardson, "Letters," 100.

1767c. Testimony from George Millar, June 9, 1790, concerning his 1767 voyage to Old Calabar, in Lambert, *Commons Sessional Papers*, 73:392.

1769. Liverpool slaver *Dobson*'s accounts, Davenport Papers, MMM, twelve brass basins engraved "Antera Duke."

1769–1770. Liverpool slaver *Dobson*'s accounts, slaves delivered on trust, July 31, 1769–January 10, 1770, Hasell MS, Dalemain House, Cumbria.

1771. Liverpool slaver *May*'s accounts, Davenport Papers, MMM, two coils of cordage addressed to "Willy Honesty."

1772. Liverpool slaver *Dalrymple*'s accounts, Davenport Papers, MMM, thirty basins inscribed "WH" (Willy Honesty).

1773a. Otto Ephraim to Ambrose Lace, Parrot Island, July 19, 1773, republished in Lovejoy and Richardson, "Letters," 105.

1773b. Ambrose Lace to Thomas Jones, Liverpool, Nov. 11, 1773, in Lovejoy and Richardson, "Letters," 107–108.

1775. Affidavit dated Old Calabar, Sept. 1775, in Herve, "Quelques aspects," 49.

1776. Otto Ephraim to Ambrose Lace, Old Town, Old Calabar, Aug. 23, 1776, in Lovejoy and Richardson, "Letters," 109.

1777. Egoboyoung Coffiong [Egbo Young Ofiong] to William Brighouse, Dec. 30, 1777, in Williams, *Liverpool Privateers*, 553.

1780. King Henshaw, Duke Ephraim, and Willy Honesty to Liverpool Gentlemen, June 24, 1780, in Lovejoy and Richardson, "Letters," 109–110.

1783a. Otto Ephraim to Ambrose Lace, Old Town Old Calabar, Mar. 20, 1783, in
Lovejoy and Richardson, "Letters," 110.

1783b. Egboyoung Offiong to Gentleman, Old Calabar, July 23, 1783, DX/1304,
MMM.

1789. Duke Ephraim to Rogers and Laroche, Old Calabar, Oct. 16, 1789, in Lovejoy
and Richardson, "Letters," 111.

1790. William Blake to James Rogers, Old Calabar, Dec. 10, 1790, C107/12, NA.

1792a. Thomas Codd to James Rogers, Old Calabar, Mar. 11, 1792, C107/6, NA.

1792b. Hamnet Forsyth to James Rogers, Old Calabar, June 11, 1792, C107/13, NA.

1792c. Halgan, "A bord," 58.

1799. Bell inscribed "Effeywatt Captain Calabar 1799," Akak, *Efiks of Old Calabar*,
4:423; Oku, *Kings*, 5–9.

1803. Jemmy Henshaw to Captain Phillips, Henshaw Town, Old Calabar, July 25,
1803, in Arthy, *Introductory Observations*, 75.

1805. Henry Nicholls testimony, 1805, in Hallett, *Records*, 195–210.

Antera Duke's Trading Expedition from Old Calabar to Little Cameroon

In chapter 4 we discussed how Efik merchants worked within a 30,000-square-mile commercial zone, traveling frequently beyond Old Calabar to trade with neighboring communities. Antera Duke made one such multiday trip in February 1786, during the dry season. At early morning on February 8 he was in "aqua Bakassey Crik," and that afternoon he found Archibong Duke. The two canoed to "new Town" and back. Three days later, at "Coqua Town," Archibong Duke asked Antera "to walk up for Commrown with him so I Did." During this trip the two Efik passed "3 Little Commrown town" and arrived at "Big town." There follows a three-week gap in Antera's diary (probably because Antera was busy or possibly omissions by diary transcriber Arthur Wilkie), a gap similar to those following two other trips Antera made to "aqua Bakassey": in May 1786 (a two-week gap) and November 1787 (a monthlong gap). Since Antera's diary presents the first evidence about Efik trading links, it is important to identify "aqua Bakassey Crik," "new Town," and the other locations and determine the route that he and Archibong Duke took to "Big town" in "Commrown." To help us reconstruct Antera's February 1786 trading expedition, we examine other evidence from his diary and draw upon the journal written by missionary Alexander Ross in 1877, the first European who ventured southeast from Old Calabar to Efut country.

Antera's February 1786 journey began in Akwa Bakasi Creek, twenty miles south of Duke Town, and continued eastward through mangrove swamps and numerous creeks fed by the Rio Del Rey. Antera's "Coqua Town," we believe, is "Aqua Town," as there is no "C" in the Efik alphabet. Perhaps the

"Co" of Coqua misreads an "A" handwritten with a loop by Antera. This "Aqua Town" was located within a one-half-day walk from three Little Cameroon towns and "Big town." Thus it is not the "Aqua Town" in the diary that references Qua Town or Big Qua Town, east of the Old Calabar villages, on the Qua River.[1] Similarly, when Antera and Archibong Duke canoe from Akwa Bakasi Creek to "new Town," they are paddling east, not north to New (Duke) Town on the Calabar River. In a May 1786 excursion to Akwa Bakasi, Antera calls at "new Town" and then reaches "old Town"— again, not a reference to Old Town on the Calabar River.

Antera's diary indicates that in the 1780s the region from Akwa Bakasi Creek east to Little Cameroon was part of the Efik trading empire, linked by a network of Ekpe lodges. On February 8, 1786, Antera and Archibong Duke walked up to the palaver house in New Town and installed "Grandy Egbo" (Grand Ekpe, Idem Nyamkpe, see chapter 1) there, followed by drums and dancing all night. In Antera's trip to Akwa Bakasi on May 1, 1786, he called at New Town, as in February, then paddled to Old Town, where he found Coffee Duke. Hearing Ekpe cry out in the palaver house, Antera carried a large case of bottled brandy and four rods to give the Ekpe men. Antera called all the town's folk to come and hear what he had to say, settled outstanding matters of business, and gave Coffee Duke a large case of brandy and ten yams. Antera stayed at Akwa Bakasi for a couple of days; on May 4 he departed the landing place in Abashey Ofiong's canoe at 10:00 A.M. and reached Jock Bakasi's town, presumably farther to the east or southeast, at 7:00 P.M. Antera and Esien Duke carried Grand Ekpe to the palaver house to settle a debt. Merchants there "Did pay me 1 men slave for my goods," and Esien and Antera received copper rods as a dash.[2]

Efik influence in Akwa Bakasi and farther into Little Cameroon had expanded when the Reverend Alexander Ross traveled there in early 1877. On January 30, 1877, Ross and his party canoed from Duke Town to King Archibong II's Farm, an all-day journey. Yellow Duke had connections with the Archibong family and guided their boat trip. The party traveled south from Duke Town, passed Seven Fathoms Point, James Island, and Fish Point on the east bank of the Cross River, steered into the Qua River estuary, and paddled ten miles east up Idibe Creek, over Bakasi River, and along two other creeks to land at King Archibong II's Farm. When Antera made his expedition, whom did he meet in Akwa Bakasi on February 8, 1786? Archibong Duke! The Archibong farms are located thirty-five miles southeast of Duke Town, off the east bank of the Akwa Bakasi Creek, close to the British-German colonial border determined at the 1884 Berlin Conference (see map 4.2).[3] Ross's expedition arrived at King Archibong's II's Farm at 5:00 P.M., and after resting three hours they resumed their voyage southeastward.

After crossing the Rio del Rey at midnight, they paddled all night and the following day, for eighteen to twenty hours, arriving at their destination in the early evening of January 31. After a forty-minute walk they arrived at the town of Odobo. From Odobo, they traveled a few miles north to Ekpri Okunde, and then twenty miles southeast beyond the falls of Kome, returning to Odobo on February 3. They departed the region on February 6 at 4:00 A.M. and reached Duke Town at 9:00 A.M. on Thursday, February 8. In recounting his weeklong trip, Ross wrote: "We visited in all thirteen towns,—three in Nsaheret, and ten in Cameroons. Seven of these speak the Efik language, and the six in Bakish speak a different language. From trustworthy sources, I ascertained that there are thirteen towns in Cameroons that speak Efik, with an aggregate population of about 22,000."[4] He added: "This country is known to us here by the name of Little Cameroons, and is entirely subject to Duke Town, with which there is continual communication. A number of Calabar people stay in Cameroons the most of their lives for trading purposes. Yellow Duke stays nine months in the year at Odobo. The Calabar people receive all their palm oil, for which they give goods in exchange."[5] Further, Ross noted, "Provisions are much cheaper here than in Calabar," and "They are governed by Egbo laws."[6]

From Ross's account it would seem that he followed the same route as Antera Duke ninety-one years earlier. Antera, too, passed through Bakasi Creek, which is where he met Archibong Duke. Three days later he arrived with Archibong at Aqua Town in the Cameroon—nearly the time it took Ross to travel from Bakasi Creek to Odobo. From Aqua Town Antera had to walk inland with Archibong Duke to "Big town." Ross, too, had to walk inland, to reach Odobo. So Obodo seems the most likely identification of "Big town" in the February 11, 1786, diary entry, both towns being inland, and both being clearly under the influence of the Archibongs. Reverend Ross's expedition in February 1877, as well as his second journey to Efut country a year later,[7] shows that there was considerable Efik influence in Little Cameroon, and that Efik traders from Old Calabar were active there. Antera Duke's business trips to the region, governed by Ekpe laws, were merely part of normal Efik activity.

Abbreviations

Add MS	Additional manuscript
BL	British Library
BRO	Bristol Record Office
BT	Board of Trade
C	Chancery Masters' Exhibits
CO	Colonial Office
FHL	Family History Library, Salt Lake City, Utah
HOL	Holt and Gregson Papers, Liverpool Record Office
IAI	International African Institute, University of London
LivRO	Liverpool Record Office
MMM	Merseyside Maritime Museum, Liverpool
MS	Manuscript
NA	National Archives, London, Kew
NAS	National Archives of Scotland
NLS	National Library of Scotland
PP	Parliamentary Papers
PROB	Probate
RAC	Royal African Company, England
RGSL	Royal Geographic Society Library, London
UPCMR	United Presbyterian Church Missionary Record
WIC	Dutch West India Company

Notes

Introduction

1. In 1908 the Foreign Mission Committee of the United Free Church of Scotland requested that the following materials be transferred from New College library: "The Museum, including all the Wall Cases, open and closed, presented to the Foreign Mission Committee by the late James Stevenson . . . with the contents, such as curios, Pictures, and Books, partly belonging to the late United Presbyterian Church." In one oak case there were two drawers "filled with Missionary Curios." Some library material transferred as early as 1905 (MS Box 40, The Library, New College, University of Edinburgh). Stevenson was secretary to the Missionary Society.

2. Arthur W. Wilkie, "The Diary of Antera Duke. 18th January, 1785 to 31st January, 1788" (typescript, Edinburgh, June 26, 1951), letter from Wilkie to Forde, Edinburgh, Sept. 9, 1951, letter from Marian B. Wilkie to Mrs. Wyatt, North Berwick, Aug. 25, [1955], *Efik Traders* book file, IAI. We examined the select correspondence (1903–1934) from Valentine, held in the National Library of Scotland, but found no testimony about the diary or its history.

3. Wilkie (1878–1958) worked in Calabar as secretary to the Church of Scotland Mission and missionary in charge of Duke Town (McFarlan, *Calabar*, 168; Cameron, *Dictionary*, 871).

4. Mrs. Wilkie to Wyatt, Aug. 25, 1955; Rev. Wilkie to Forde, Sept. 9, 1951, *Efik Traders* book file, IAI. Reverend Wilkie had six furloughs from Calabar: 1903, 1905, 1907, 1910, Mar. 2–Nov. 27, 1913, and Feb. 3–Oct. 31, 1916 (Wilkie file, Foreign Mission Office, Church of Scotland, Edinburgh; MS Box 52.5, University of Edinburgh, The Library, New College).

5. Wilkie also believed that "Duke" anglicizes "Odök"; later scholars believe that

the word might anglicize "Orök" (or "Orrock") or be a phonetic spelling for "Ekpo." The name "Duke" could derive from English captain Abraham Duke, who traded at Old Calabar in 1663 (Hair, Jones, and Law, *Barbot on Guinea*, 2:705n27).

6. Wilkie to Forde, Edinburgh, Oct. 20, 1951, *Efik Traders* book file, IAI. As Wilkie remarked, during his tenure in Calabar he "made a special study of the Efik language—particularly with the guidance and help of my great friend Chief Eyo Efiom."

7. Asuquo, "Diary," 36–39.

8. *Dobson* accounts, 1769, f. 6, Davenport Papers, MMM.

9. As Hair notes, the term "king" refers to a notable in Efik society, though it is unclear whether "King Warr" indicates that Antera Duke was a warrior who organized slave raids on other Efik/Ibibio-speaking communities (Hair, "Antera Duke," 360–361).

10. By contrast, Nicholls writes that "Egbo Young Eyamba is between sixty and seventy," the Ndem priest (King Calabar), residing at Creek Town, "is a very old man, at least eighty years of age," and King Aqua "from my own observation . . . must be about thirty-five years of age" (Hallett, *Records*, 199–200).

11. On Dec. 14, 1813, "Duke Antera, King of Eyampia," wrote a letter complaining that Portuguese captain Francisco Xavier Alves de Melo had not returned a wall clock taken from him in October 1809 (Cx. 49, D. 33, Archivo Historico Ultramarino, Lisbon, information courtesy of David Eltis, to whom we are indebted). Hair notes that "the normal Efik practice was for a son to have as the final term of his vernacular name the forename of [his] father . . . and it is likely that this practice carried over, at least to some extent, to trading names" (Hair, "Antera Duke," 360). In about 1820 Bold (*African Guide*) does not include Duke Antera in a list of Efik merchants to whom captains paid port fees (comey). In 1830 "Duke Antara" was one of the lesser twenty-eight Efik traders who transacted business with the Liverpool barque *Hamilton* (MS 24.37, University of Liverpool, Sidney Jones Library).

12. Behrendt and Graham, "African Merchants," 37–61.

13. Lovejoy and Richardson, "Letters," 103–111.

14. In 1863 Scottish missionary Hope Waddell published extracts from diary or journal entries kept by Mr. Young dated October 14, 16, and 17, 1834, documenting the death of Duke Ephraim and the subsequent poison witchcraft oaths (Waddell, *Twenty-nine Years*, 279). See also chapter 1. Waddell described several writing ledgers shortly after arriving in Calabar. In May 1846, for example, he found "Young Eyo [Honesty] writing + copying into an account book the memoranda of business transactions which his father had made on Slates. They were neatly entered and all in English" (Hope Waddell diary, May 11, 1846, MS 7739, f. 48, NLS).

15. Lovejoy and Richardson reproduce twelve of thirteen (one is a close duplicate) Efik letters or business notes and two letters written by Liverpool merchants to Efik traders ("Letters," 100–111). In addition, there is a brief note penned by Egbo Young Ofiong, dated Dec. 30, 1777, republished by Williams (*Liverpool Privateers*, 553); a letter from Egbo Young Ofiong to Captain John Burrows dated July 23, 1783 (DX/1304, MMM); and a letter from Jemmy Henshaw to Captain Phillips dated July 25, 1803, republished by Elliot Arthy (Arthy, *Introductory Observations*, 75).

16. Twenty-two of Afonso's letters, some many pages long, can be found, in Portuguese, in Brásio, *Monumenta Missionaria*, vol. 1. For a rich collection of early African writings translated from Arabic and in European languages, see Hodgkin, *Nigerian Perspectives*; for an Anglophone Atlantic perspective, see Richardson and Lee, *Early Black British Writing*. See also Jones, *Zur Quellenproblematik*, 26. Few new sources of precolonial African writing, concerning Nigeria, have been discovered. See the second edition to Hodgkin, *Nigerian Perspectives*. The most important new written African source (mostly 1860s, with some material from the 1830s) from Old Calabar discovered is the Black Davis House Book (Latham, *Old Calabar*, 88, 100).

17. See note 11 above.

18. Latham, *Old Calabar*, 98, 154.

19. Wilkie to Wyatt, North Berwick, Aug. 25, [1955], *Efik Traders* book file, IAI.

20. Hope Waddell diary, Sept. 1855–Sept. 1856, MS 7743, f. 1, NLS. Another destructive conflagration occurred at Duke Town on Dec. 22, 1882 (MS Box 52.5.6, The Library, New College, University of Edinburgh).

21. Marwick diary entry, Oct. 11, 1892, Gen 768/3, f. 88, University of Edinburgh, Special Collections.

22. Early in 1892 Elizabeth Marwick sent home to Edinburgh "a box containing some curios." On holiday in St. Andrews in 1894, Mrs. Marwick and friends examined "several Calabar curiosities" (diary entry Mar. 9, 1892, Gen 768/6, f. 40; diary entry Feb. 22, 1894, Gen 768/8, f. 16, University of Edinburgh, Special Collections).

23. The Missionary Lending Library was originally in room 31 of the George Street offices (*The Record* 210 [June 1918]: 109). A 1944 source mentions the "Church's Lending Library" in room 74 (*Life and Work. The Record of the Church of Scotland* 15 [1944]: 31).

24. Wilkie, introductory notes to "The Diary of Antera Duke," June 26, 1951 (typescript), 3, MS Box 27.5, The Library, New College, University of Edinburgh. In his correspondence to Daryll Forde in September 1951, Wilkie stated, with more certainty, that "enemy action and bombing" destroyed the diary, and Forde reaffirmed this claim in his introduction to the 1956 edition of *Efik Traders*: "During the war the offices of the United Church of Scotland suffered bombing and, though measures had been taken to store books and records in safety, some of these—including, it is feared, Antera Duke's diary—were unfortunately destroyed" (Forde, *Efik Traders*, ix).

25. Correspondence with Walter Dunlop, Foreign Mission, Church of Scotland, Dec. 10, 1998; Pamela Gilchrist, New College librarian, Edinburgh, Jan. 6, 1999; Professor Donald Macleod, Hon. Librarian, Free Church College, Edinburgh, Jan. 20, 1999; and David Kerry, acting librarian, World Mission Library, St. Colm's Education Centre and College, Edinburgh, Jan. 20, 1999.

26. Perhaps Wilkie's informants confused the George Street church building with the Presbyterian Church House in London, which indeed was destroyed by a rocket bomb in 1945 (*Life and Work* 135 [March 1957]: 66).

27. MS Box 27.5, The Library, New College, University of Edinburgh. Wilkie's handwritten diary transcription and other Calabar materials may have been destroyed when the "accumulated contents" of the attic at Cheylesmore Lodge (the

retirement home where Wilkie died) were "consigned to the bonfire" in late 1982 or early 1983 (Reverend Walter M. Ferrier to the Secretary of the Overseas Council, North Berwick, Jan. 11, 1983, Wilkie file, Foreign Mission Office, Church of Scotland, Edinburgh). Ferrier wrote to the Church of Scotland because Wilkie's "Royal Warrant for the award of the C.B.E." was retrieved from the pile of burned documents.

28. In the 1930s Forde had conducted extensive fieldwork on the Yakö people of southeast Nigeria, and a study of Old Calabar was therefore close to his own professional interests and expertise (Forde, *Yakö Studies*).

29. The most important, Waddell's *Twenty-nine Years*, included detailed information on Old Calabar from Waddell's arrival in 1847 to his 1863 departure.

30. Lambert, *Commons Sessional Papers*, vols. 72, 73, 82, evidence of John Ashley Hall, Ambrose Lace, James Morley, Richard Story; Williams, *Liverpool Privateers*, 533–553.

31. See chapter 1.

32. Eltis, Behrendt, Richardson, and Klein, eds., *Trans-Atlantic Slave Trade*; www .slavevoyages.org.

33. Hodgkin, *Nigerian Perspectives*, 181–185.

34. Fayer, "Pidgins," 313–319; Fayer, "Nigerian Pidgin English," 185–202; Görach, "Texts," 249–252; Huber and Görach, "Texts," 239–258; Noah, *Old Calabar*; Oku, *Kings*; Sparks, *Two Princes*; Lovejoy and Richardson, "Trust," 333–355; Lovejoy and Richardson, "Business," 67–89; Latham, *Old Calabar*; Northrup, *Trade without Rulers*; Northrup, *Africa's Discovery of Europe*, 61–62.

35. Wilkie to Forde, Edinburgh, Sept. 9, 1951, *Efik Traders* book file, IAI.

Chapter 1

1. On "August 23the 1776" Old Town merchant Otto Ephraim wrote how he paid "Egbo men yesterday" and was "done now for Egbo" (Lovejoy and Richardson, "Letters," 109). An earlier letter mentions "King Egbo" (99).

2. Arthy, *Introductory Observations*, 75; Holman, *Travels*, 397–399.

3. Latham, *Old Calabar*, frontispiece, 1–2, 33–51.

4. The surviving Efik writings use the word "time" when recalling present-day events.

5. Diary entry Apr. 16, 1787: "We said we had never heard of that since our great-grandfathers' time."

6. Jones, *Trading States*, 188–196; Hart, *Report*; Nair, *Politics and Society*; Latham, *Old Calabar*.

7. Simmons, "Ethnographic Sketch," 1; Nair, *Origins and Development*, 8; Latham, *Old Calabar*, 3, 9–10; Hackett, *Religion in Calabar*, 20–21. Latham's fieldwork found that the Efik called themselves "the oppressors" and were secretly rather proud of it.

8. Jones, "Introduction," in Waddell, *Twenty-nine Years*, xii–xiii. Though Antera refers to "new town" in his diary, for convenience we refer to the village as Duke Town, as known to British captains in the 1780s.

9. We follow Jones in using the term "ward" to describe the lineage group to which Antera Duke belonged (Jones, "Political Organization," 122).

10. Eyo Nsa may have been a slave, though this tradition is rejected by the Eyos and many Efik. To this day, to be remembered as of slave origin is regarded as a slight.

11. Robin Honestie, an important trader from Creek Town who received forty copper bars' comey in 1720, likely came from non-Efik origins, as Efik authorities disagree about the genealogy of his descendant Eyo Willy Honesty, ca. 1740s–1820 (Latham, *Old Calabar*, 32, 36, 46, 47). Regarding Robin Honestie, see Behrendt and Graham, "African Merchants," 46, 57, 59.

12. Waddell, *Twenty-nine Years*, 279. Young's journal, perhaps a diary like Antera's, has not been discovered. Regarding "Mr. Young" (d. 1855), see Latham, *Old Calabar*, 117–119, 156.

13. The head of Duke ward (or house) traditionally took the title "Duke Ephraim," and the name "Great Duke Ephraim" reflected the fact that Efiom Edem was the most powerful Efik leader remembered by descendants and documented by scholars.

14. Missionary Waddell referred to a chief at Duke Town as a "very old man." Regarding other aged Efik, he also used phrases or words such as "such age and dignity as he" and "patriarch" (Waddell, *Twenty-nine Years*, 352, 353, 362).

15. Latham, *Old Calabar*, 9–11. There is much debate about Efik genealogy and the dating of settlements. See, for example, Aye, "Efik Origins," 5–10; Akak, *Efiks*, 4:436.

16. It is unlikely that Efik elders interviewed in the 1950s and 1960s omitted single generations, because they would have noticed gaps in generational naming patterns. But they may have forgotten two generations, particularly if sons died at comparatively young ages. Note that there is at least a twenty- to fifty-year margin of error dating early Efik settlements.

17. Latham, "Pre-colonial Economy," 72.

18. Hair, Jones, and Law, *Barbot on Guinea*, 2:680–681. We capitalized "duke," "king," and "old." Possibly King Oyo, if at an advanced age, was Eyo Ema, one of the oldest of five founding fathers who settled Creek Town in the early 1600s (Latham, *Old Calabar*, 10).

19. Later sources provide a link between Guinea Company and the King John family. In 1847 missionary Waddell traveled up the Calabar River to the Guinea Company villages—one of which was "King John's Town." He learned that it "was once a more considerable place and maintained two kings; now it could hardly keep one" (Waddell, *Twenty-nine Years*, 361–362).

20. In 1704 Captain William Snelgrave met King Jabrue—probably King Ebrero/Ebrew/Ebro (Hair, Jones, and Law, *Barbot on Guinea*, 2:705n27).

21. In the following paragraphs all information on Horsburgh and the Efik merchants with whom he traded may be found in Behrendt and Graham, "African Merchants," 37–61.

22. Copper rods, "coppers," the unit of exchange at Old Calabar.

23. "Grande Robin" may be the traditional name for the man who headed the

Robin ward in Old Town. An early "Grande Robin" was killed on board the London slaving ship *Hunter Gally* in 1702 (T70/175, f. 23, NA). We owe this reference to David Eltis.

24. Richardson, *Bristol, Africa and the Slave Trade*, 1:121. Later in the 1700s a small British schooner was named the *Willy Tom Robin*, after an Old Town leader (www .slavevoyages.org).

25. Regarding the death of Grande Robin on board the *Hunter Gally*, see note 23 above. "We are just now firing half Minute Guns for the Death of Amboe King of Calabar. Our Captain is gone ashore to the Funeral, with our Piper, Fidler and Drummer" ("Extract of a Letter on board the Ship Castle of Bristol, Capt. Montgomery, dated at Old [C]alabar, March 10, 1729," republished in the *Whitehall Evening Post*, Aug. 12–14, 1729). We owe this reference to David Eltis.

26. Succession passed to brothers, so if in 1729 King Ambo (perhaps Esien Ekpe Oku) was succeeded by brother Ekpenyong Ekpe Oku, then witchcraft accusations would not have occurred.

27. It is difficult to know when Antera Duke's father died. He might have been alive on January 22, 1786, as on that day Antera writes "for Little canow to mak my father Boostam," which we think means "take my father [brother?] to Boostam," Boostam (Umon) being an island settlement on the Cross River northwest of Duke Town. Perhaps transcriber Wilkie misread "brother" as "father." Later that year, on November 8, a woman was killed for his father, and the diary entry on Mar. 24, 1787, states "since our father died." So we assume that Antera Duke's father died between January and November 1786.

28. Hallett, *Records*, 206.

29. "When I first went [to Old Calabar] in 1748, there were no inhabitants in the place called Old Town, they all lived at the place called New [Duke] Town; some time after disputes arose between a party who now call themselves Old Town people, and those who are now called New Town people" (Testimony of Captain Ambrose Lace, Mar. 12, 1790, in Lambert, *Commons Sessional Papers*, 72:345).

30. Liverpool merchant William Earle wrote to Duke Abashy (Abasi): "I am glad to hear Tom Henshaw first man" (Lovejoy and Richardson, "Letters," 99).

31. Butterworth, *Three Years Adventures*, 35.

32. Williams, *Liverpool Privateers*.

33. This massacre occurred in the period August 13–16, 1767, after an August 12 letter written by Captain Ambrose Lace of the Liverpool ship *Edgar* and before the *Concord*, one of the six slavers implicated in the massacre, sailed from Old Calabar on August 17. Lace wrote, "There are now seven large vessels in the river, each of which expects to purchase 500 slaves; and I imagine there was seldom ever known a greater scarcity of slaves than at present, and these few chiefly from the low country. The natives are at variance with each other; and, in my opinion, it will never be ended before the destruction of all the people at Old Town, who have taken the lives of many a fine fellow (*Liverpool Chronicle*, Feb. 11, 1768, republished in Troughton, *History*, 143). Williams also republished this letter (Williams, *Liverpool Privateers*, 535) but does not give authorship. See also Sparks, *Two Princes*, 18–19.

34. Williams, *Liverpool Privateers*, 536; Sparks, *Two Princes*, 18–25.

35. Creek Town trader Willy Honesty killed Ephraim Robin John's younger brother Amboe Robin John (Sparks, *Two Princes*, 22).

36. Captain Lace protected Ephraim's teenage son Otto Ephraim Robin John and took him to Liverpool. He arrived in April 1768 and, under Lace's care, studied at school for two years. Otto Ephraim thus would have returned to Old Calabar in 1770 or 1771 (and was still alive in 1805). See Sparks, *Two Princes*, 24.

37. Historians have not explained "King Warr," an honorific also documented in the nineteenth century. In 1846 missionary Hope Waddell met "Adam Duke, King War," but did not learn how he attained his title (Waddell, *Twenty-nine Years*, 288). For a list of Efik names, see appendix A.

38. *Liverpool General Advertiser*, Nov. 11, 1768, 3; *Voyages Database*, ID 91293. In late 1767 a slave ship from Jamaica, the *Royal African*, Captain Burney, "slaving at Old Calabar, had by some accident taken fire, and was totally destroyed, but the crew and about 70 negroes were saved" (*Liverpool General Advertiser*, Apr. 15, 1768, 2). The explosion may not have been an "accident," as this event occurred during the Old Town/Duke Town war.

39. *Dobson* Calabar account, Hasell MS, Dalemain House, Cumbria. Maurice and Eunice Schofield discovered this important document, analyzed first by Hair (Hair, "Antera Duke," 359–365). We thank David Richardson for providing us with a copy.

40. Hair, "Antera Duke," 359–365. Since the Honesty family resided historically at Creek Town, we place Gentleman Honesty in that village. In January 1805, though, explorer Henry Nicholls visited Henshaw Town, two miles south of Duke Town, and met the two "principal traders" there, Jemmy Henshaw and Gentleman Honesty (Hallett, *Records*, 200).

41. Reprinted in Williams, *Liverpool Privateers*, 543–547.

42. We discuss pawnship in chapters 2 and 3.

43. *Liverpool General Advertiser*, Feb. 21, 1788, reprinted in Lovejoy and Richardson, "Letters," 109–110.

44. The Henshaws are an interesting group, as they provided the second and third obongs, Nsa Efiom (Henshaw I) and Ekpo Nsa (Henshaw II). But at some time, presumably in the last half of the seventeenth century, the obong-ship passed to the Duke and Eyamba families. Other Efik continued to recognize Henshaw seniority, though. On Christmas Day 1872 Henshaw leaders attempted to reassert their dominance by declaring their own obong, Henshaw III—but Efik from other wards forced them to renounce their declaration (Latham, *Old Calabar*, 44–45, 124–127). Henshaws continued to be important traders, though. In 1878 Joseph Henshaw accompanied Reverend Ross in his exploration of Little Cameroon, as he had been born there and knew the district well (*United Presbyterian Church Missionary Record*, Nov. 1, 1879, 690–693, Dec. 1, 1879, 711–714. See also appendix B).

45. Hallett, *Records*, 198–205, quote on 204. Missionary Hope Waddell remarked that after the massacre (in 1767, a date Waddell does not mention), "Old Town, compelled to leave the foreign trade wholly to their rivals, fell into decay" (Waddell, *Twenty-nine Years*, 310). In 1828 Holman referred to Old Town as "Robin's Town"

(Holman, *Travels*, 361, 405). In 1803 Jemmy Henshaw admitted, "[N]ow I be trade for red-wood," a remark perhaps signaling that Duke ward had squeezed Henshaws from the export slave trade (Jemmy Henshaw to Captain [Thomas] Phillips, Henshaw Town, Old Calabar, July 25, 1803, reprinted in Arthy, *Introductory Observations*, 75). Nicholls also does not mention any Cobham "trader," though in approximately 1820 King Cobham and George Cobham received comey (Bold, *African Guide*, 77).

46. Most historians use the term "secret society" when referring to Ekpe. Offiong, though, prefers the term "traditional association," since the "existence and the declared purpose of these societies is known to every adult and quite often their many activities contribute to make them a dominant social force" (Offiong, "Functions," 78).

47. Since the first Efik at Old Calabar were fishermen, cults worshiping water spirits date from the turn of the seventeenth century. Another water spirit, a supernatural female power called Udominyang, is said to capsize canoes and seize goods that fall into her water. Today there is a Mami Wata (perhaps from "mermaid water") cult in Nigeria. See Bastian, "Married," 116–134.

48. Latham, *Old Calabar*, 9, 10, 33, 35, 43–44.

49. Waddell, *Twenty-nine Years*, 314–315, 328. See also *United Presbyterian Church Missionary Record*, Dec. 1848, 200. As Goldie puts it: "Oku Ndem Efik, A title of King Calabar" (Goldie, *Dictionary*, 254).

50. Marwick, *William and Louisa Anderson*, 361, 399.

51. Ibid., 282, 398.

52. Waddell, *Twenty-nine Years*, 315. King Calabar continued to be a key ritual figure well into the nineteenth century, despite the poverty of his office. As late as 1869 Efik worshiped Ndem Efik. In May of that year James Egbo Bassey, a rising trader, lost his big canoe when it swamped and sank in the river, loaded with his goods and people, eleven of whom drowned. When missionary William Anderson visited him the next day, James told him that "[h]is people, when sinking, cried out to Ndem Efik to save them, but there was no response" (Marwick, *William and Louisa Anderson*, 443).

53. Regarding Captain Patrick Fairweather's importance, see chapter 2. Two months earlier, on June 25, 1785, Duke Ephraim, Antera Duke, and several other Efik walked to Ephraim Ofiong's house to sacrifice a goat "for old Callabar Doctor"—according to Old Calabar ancient ritual. Antera does not explain why this traditional ceremony occurred, but given a goat's value of thirty copper rods, it may have been a prayer to Ndem Efik asking for blessings, fertility, or forgiveness. In 1805 Nicholls learned that Efik sold goats for thirty copper rods; by contrast, one fowl cost two coppers, and three "Little fish" cost one copper (Hallett, *Records*, 207).

54. Goldie, *Dictionary*, 283.

55. Latham, *Old Calabar*, 37–40.

56. Ibid., 38.

57. Hallett, *Records*, 200. Though not a trader, King Calabar probably still received comey, given his important position in Efik society.

58. Today there are Ekpe masquerades in southeast Nigeria and Cuba, where en-

slaved Africans introduced the society. In December 2004 Calabar hosted the third international Ekpe festival.

59. Ottenberg and Knudsen, "Leopard Society," 37; Northrup, *Trade without Rulers*, 108–109. Note, though, that there were significant differences between Ekpe and the Ibibio leopard cults in terms of grade structure, lodges, and credit power.

60. Told, *Account*, 26–27.

61. Holman, *Travels*, 394. When Scottish missionary Hope Waddell saw an Ekpe runner in 1846, he was "accoutred in very outré habiliments, from head to foot, and masked, with a long whip in his hand." Then, a week later, he saw a group of Ekpe runners who wore "black masks, and wild dresses of dry grass and sheep skins." Instead of leather whips, they carried long rods (Waddell, *Twenty-nine Years*, 258, 265).

62. Lacking direct evidence about Ekpe officers or the Ekpe masquerade, historians have suggested founding dates as early as ca. 1650–1700 (Lovejoy and Richardson, "Trust," 347) or as late as ca. 1750 (Latham, *Old Calabar*, 26). Lovejoy and Richardson associate Ekpe with the foundation of Old Town. Latham suggests that the Ambo ward of Creek Town founded Ekpe "at the earliest about 1720," but believes ca. 1750 is a more likely founding date. Payments or trade with "King Egbo" would indicate transactions with an Ekpe officer. In 1761, for example, Liverpool merchant William Earle mentions "King Egbo" (Lovejoy and Richardson, "Letters," 99). In 1769 Liverpool captain John Potter purchased slaves from "King Egbo Solomon Henshaw" (*Dobson* Calabar account, Hasell MS, Dalemain House, Cumbria).

63. Cited by Latham, *Old Calabar*, 42.

64. It may not be a coincidence that Silas Told's mid-1729 sighting of Ekpe occurred a few months after the death of King Ambo, perhaps the Calabar obong. One could argue that after his father died, eldest son Esien Ekpe Oku purchased the Ekpe secrets to strengthen his family's position in the ensuing power struggle, whether over the obong-ship or accusations of witchcraft in King Ambo's death.

65. Waddell, *Twenty-nine Years*, 246, 282, 313. In the 1870s James Walker learned there were nine Ekpe grades at Old Calabar (Walker, "Notes on the Politics," 120). Among the Ibibio those initiated into Ekpo grades are "decorated with white clay (*ndom*) and yellow powder (*nsei*), both signifying happiness and good fortune" (Offiong, "Functions," 80). While a youth, author Offiong, an Ibibio, entered the first and second ranks of Ekpo (78). See also Latham, *Old Calabar*, 37–40, 100–101.

66. Latham, *Old Calabar*, 65–67, 151.

67. In Antera's first diary entry, January 18, 1785, Ekpe rendered judgment in a dispute between Egbo Young Ofiong and Little Otto. Egbo Young paid a fine of one goat, indicating that he lost the decision, and each man paid a token fine of four copper rods—a total of four, we suggest, to represent the four Ekpe grades then at Old Calabar.

68. In 1805 goats cost thirty coppers each (see note 53 above). In 1787–1789 British captains stated that the price of slaves averaged 180 to 200 coppers (see chapter 2). Thus Henshaw paid a fee of 312 coppers, which represented the value of one slave and four goats.

69. Hallett, *Records*, 204. Each Ekpe step had its own obong, or "king."

70. Liverpool and Bristol captains complained that the average price of slaves, 1787–1790, had reached 180 to 200 coppers, with a ceiling for prime males at 240 to 250 coppers (see chapter 2). It is possible that "new Egbo" might have read "now Egbo"—344 men from Calabar are now in Ekpe.

71. Waddell, *Twenty-nine Years*, 313. In 1847 Waddell thought that Ekpe included 1,000 members in ten branches—a rounded figure about one-sixth the size of Duke Town, one-tenth the size of the combined Old Calabar villages, and one-sixtieth the population of Calabar and its farming areas (Latham, *Old Calabar*, 91). Latham notes, though, that it is difficult to gauge the population of Calabar's agricultural slaves, settled to the north and east. In 1805 Nicholls guessed Calabar's population, scattered in eight villages, at 5,220 but did not learn about numbers in any of the four Ekpe "laws" (Hallett, *Records*, 206). If Old Calabar's population in January 1785–January 1788—the diary years—was 4,000 to 5,000, then perhaps there were 400 to 500 society members. Antera's "344 men" thus could refer to all those then in the four Ekpe grades.

72. For "wowo Egbo," diary entry Nov.? 11, 1785; for "wawa Egbo," Jan. 17, 1788. There are five Efik names in the diary (Awa, Eyamba, Iwo, Offiong, and TaEon), the noun obong and the verb *täb-ä* or *töbö*. Antera also writes thirty-four anglicized Efik words, such as "Abashey" (for "Abasi") and, of course, his own name "Antera" (Ntiero).

73. Goldie, *Dictionary*, 338.

74. Holman, *Travels*, 394.

75. Europeans could be Ekpe members, in the grade Mbakara (white man). The earliest such evidence is from 1828.

76. Latham, *Old Calabar*, 37–39. In addition to enacting and enforcing laws for Old Calabar, Ekpe society functioned also as a place for men of similar ages and stature to meet, share a meal, and socialize.

77. *Lloyd's List*, Nov. 4, 1774; BT98/34, No. 378; BT98/35, No. 50, NA; Lambert, *Commons Sessional Papers*, 72:250–251, evidence of Hall, Mar. 2, 1790. Captain Doyle (*Hector*) died on March 4, and Fidler (*Sportsman*) died on March 6. They had sailed from Liverpool to Old Calabar the previous March.

78. On March 4, 1774, the day he died, Doyle wrote his will at Duke Town but did not explain his predicament or illness (will of Edmund Doyle, late master of the ship *Hector*, New Town, Old Calabar, Mar. 4, 1774, Reel 88822, FHL).

79. Waddell, *Twenty-nine Years*, 310.

80. Latham, *Old Calabar*, 36.

81. King Egbo was not the same as the eyamba, or president of Ekpe society, as no Henshaw has ever been eyamba (ibid., 37, 39). Here obong refers to a "king" heading an Ekpe grade—and not to the obong, or principal Old Calabar spokesman, the position held, for example, by Obong Duke Ephraim until his death in July 1786.

82. Ibid., 46–47. Young Duke Ephraim (Efiom Edem) was probably born ca. 1755. In 1769 "Young Duke" sold three slaves to Captain Potter of the *Dobson* (*Dobson* Calabar account, Hasell MS, Dalemain House, Cumbria). A Nantes document,

dated Old Calabar, September 1775, refers to "Prince Ephraim," whom we believe to be Efiom Edem (Herve, "Quelques aspects," 49).

83. In the mid-1800s missionary Waddell defined "aubong" as a native "gentleman," as "a great man on his own plantation, and very hospitable" (Waddell, *Twenty-nine Years*, 324–325). To Goldie the "Abon" was "a principal ruler, a king" (Goldie, *Dictionary*, 3). Later written and oral sources specify the obong's position and duties.

84. Regarding the Henshaw obong-ship, see note 44 above.

85. Waddell wrote a three-page summary of Calabar's history from Portuguese discovery until the 1840s, when he arrived. The first Efik he mentioned by name was "*Efium*, called by the ship captain's *Duke Ephraim*," who "was the ruler of Aqua-akpa or New Town in the beginning of this [nineteenth] century" (Waddell, *Twenty-nine Years*, 310).

86. Diary entries Jan. 3, June 10, 1786.

87. Law, "Human Sacrifice," 71. Antera does not indicate whether the nine were killed first or buried alive.

88. Simmons writes that when an obong died, high-ranking Ekpe "carried the corpse at night into the bush and dug a grave twenty feet deep" (Simmons, "Ethnographic Sketch," 25). During his fieldwork at Old Calabar, Efik elders told Latham that it was normal to bury dignitaries in their own compounds so that the graves could not be violated. See also Offiong, "Functions," 79.

89. Antera's reference to his father is puzzling, as there seems to be no reference to his father dying, but it may be in a missing part of the text. See also note 27 above.

90. In his study of twentieth-century Ibibio, Offiong states: "Until the parties to a dispute swear on *mbiam* never to mysteriously harm each other the matter is not settled, because a dispute implies the threat that one party may bewitch the other." Those swearing falsehoods on *mbiam* would "either swell or dry up and die" (Offiong, "Social Relations," 74–76). The form of the oath (in Efik) is usually, "If I do such-and-such, *mbiam*, you kill me" (see part II, extracts from Antera Duke's diary, note 72).

91. Butterworth, *Three Years Adventures*, 53–54. Schroeder claimed that the "pageant" awaited the arrival of "Captain Fairweather." Indeed, Patrick Fairweather was the senior and most important captain, the European equivalent of obong. We discuss Captain Patrick Fairweather in chapter 2. Schroeder's account lacks dates, which we supply from Antera Duke's diary.

92. When in October 1847 Waddell observed the "funeral ceremonies for old Tom Henshaw," he noted that the "patriarch had died four months previously" (Waddell, *Twenty-nine Years*, 352–353). The rainy season at Old Calabar generally lasts from May to November. Efik also needed time to invite foreign dignitaries and organize the obsequies.

93. Two days earlier, on November 2, 1786, Antera's family traveled to Creek Town. They witnessed drumming, dancing, a woman slave's execution, and sacrifices of a cow and goat, and they heard seven cannons. We assume this ceremony links to Duke Ephraim's obsequies that began on the fourth.

94. Butterworth, *Three Years Adventures*, 62–63. For a description of King Eyamba's interment in 1847, see Waddell, *Twenty-nine Years*, 336–337.

95. Butterworth, *Three Years Adventures*, 62–63. Schroeder claims that "the heads of the sad victims" were lowered into the grave—but Duke Ephraim had been buried four months earlier. The sailor thus confuses burial (July 5) with funeral (November 6) ceremonies, confirming that he did not witness the events. As he in fact stated: "These I did not see, and therefore I will not vouch for the truth of it" (63).

96. Ibid., 64–65.

97. *Nsibidi* signs, intelligible only to members, decorated Ekpe cloth. Regarding *ukara* cloth, the exclusive cloth of the highest Ekpe grade in the Cross River State, see Abalogu, "Ekpe Society," 83, 86–87. Duke Town's palaver house was located "on a site between the town and the river," and ritual executions occurred there (Butterworth, *Three Years Adventures*, 58).

98. For a discussion of traditional Efik mourning ceremonies, based on information from Efik historian E. O. Ndem, see Simmons, "Ethnographic Sketch," 23–24. There is a gap in Antera's diary (and/or its transcription) from November 13 to December 8, 1786. The significance of ten coppers is not known.

99. For a discussion of the popular witchcraft eradication crusade in the Cross River State, 1978–1979, see Offiong, "Social Relations," 81–95.

100. Antera Duke's diary indicates that witchcraft ordeals were common in 1780s Old Calabar. On June 15, 1787, King Aqua made all his wives drink the ordeal ("Drink Docter"), and eleven died. On September 20, 1787, one of Yellow Hogan Abasi's wives, Eba, is accused and forced to "chop Docter." She vomited and survived. Then Antera's mother administered the poison bean again ("giv mor Docter for Drink"), and this time Eba died. On December 11, 1787, Tom John Cobham's wives are forced to take the poison ("Drink Docter"), and all of them die, although Antera does not state the number of deaths. As these examples show, Antera did not use the term "chop nut," as Efik diarist Young did in 1834. A poison ordeal at Old Calabar in 1792 is documented in a Nantes slaver's accounts. "Tom Huescat, a black lord of certain importance," had died ("assassinated"), and two women and a man were accused. "The man vomited and was therefore not guilty. The two women were less fortunate and succumbed quickly" (Halgan, "A bord," 60).

101. Latham, "Witchcraft Accusations," 254. Pressure from British missionaries and administrators led to the abolition of the poison ordeal in 1878 (Law, "Human Sacrifice," 72).

102. Latham, *Old Calabar*, 37, 45–46.

103. *Dobson* Calabar account, Hasell MS, Dalemain House, Cumbria. Egbo Young's full trading name—Egbo Young Ofiong—first appears in 1777 as "Egoboyoung Coffiong" (Williams, *Liverpool Privateers*, 553).

104. In 1805 explorer Nicholls states that Egbo Young was between sixty and seventy years of age (Hallett, *Records*, 199). If sixty-five, he would have been born in 1740. Given that Coffee Duke was an important slave supplier in 1769, he must have been at least in his mid-thirties by 1785.

105. Egbo Young Ofiong's house: "Liverpool Hall." In 1785 Liverpool captain

Patrick Fairweather transported in pieces a house for Duke Ephraim (Hallett, *Records*, 199, 207–208).

106. Similarly, on Christmas Day in 1786 and on New Year's Day in 1787 and 1788, Egbo Young Ofiong hosted dinner for the ship captains and Efik gentlemen.

107. Brig *Sarah*'s (Captain John Goodrich) disbursements, C107/5, NA; Thomas Codd to James Rogers, Old Calabar, Mar. 11, 1792, C107/6, NA. Duke Ephraim, Egbo Young Ofiong, and Antera Duke headed the Duke, Eyamba, and Ntiero wards.

108. Both age at death and political context presumably explain why the timing of witchcraft allegations occurred 475 days after Edem Ekpo's death in July 1786, but only two days after Efiom Edem's death in October 1834. Regarding the timing when Efik were forced to "chop nut," the age-at-death difference between Edem Ekpo and son Efiom Edem needs to be considered. At Old Calabar in 1846 Waddell learned that "[w]hen a great man dies, unless of old age, his death is attributed to some secret enemy" (Waddell, *Twenty-nine Years*, 279). Unfortunately, we cannot confirm the two Duke Ephraims' ages at death.

109. Thus fifteen of these sixteen people, all accused of using witchcraft to kill the obong, died. The next day, October 17, Efiom Edem's wives all died from the ritual. In total, Waddell learned that fifty persons were made to "chop nut," of whom more than forty died (Latham, "Witchcraft Accusations," 254; Latham, *Old Calabar*, 113–115).

110. Hallett, *Records*, 199, 208. There is no exact date for the death of Egbo Young Ofiong; oral evidence given to Latham and Nair during their joint fieldwork in Calabar in 1965–1966 suggests, but does not document definitively, that he died in 1814, the year it is said that Efiom Edem became obong (Nair, *Politics and Society*, 26; Latham, *Old Calabar*, 47–48).

111. Jackson, *Journal*, 114. His text states 1892, clearly a typographical error for 1792.

112. In attempting to resolve this dispute, on October 19, 1792, Captain Patrick Fairweather transferred command of his ship *George* to another captain and remained at Old Calabar on the *Cyclops* (BT98/53, No. 287; BT98/54, No. 180, NA; www.slavevoyages.org).

113. William Blake to James Rogers, Old Calabar, Oct. 9, 1790, C107/12, NA.

Chapter 2

1. The French slaver *Luis d'Albuquerque* arrived at Old Calabar, and in 1843 disembarked 277 slaves. Little is known about this slaving venture, the last to Old Calabar, made illicit by French agreements in 1831 to end its slave trade. Historians have located more information about the twelve Brazil-Cuba-based slavers that traded at Old Calabar from 1832 to 1838 (www.slavevoyages.org).

2. After the diary entry on Sept. 20, 1787, someone, probably a chief mate on a British slaver, penned, "Antera Duke Ejus Liber" (Antera Duke "his book"). See part II, extracts from Antera Duke's diary, note 237.

3. *Voyages: The Trans-Atlantic Slave Trade Database* (www.slavevoyages.org).

4. Portuguese vessels arrived in the Cross River Region, perhaps in the late fifteenth or sixteenth century, but the first documented slaver in the area may have been the Portuguese ship *Candelaria*, which disembarked 114 enslaved Africans from "Calabar" (perhaps New Calabar) in Veracruz, Mexico, on June 25, 1625. In 1838 British cruisers captured two Portuguese-flagged vessels, the *Felicidade* and *Prova*, which had embarked 784 slaves. British cruisers captured the two Portuguese ships and escorted them to Sierra Leone. In 1841–1842 British diplomats negotiated slave trade abolition treaties with Calabar leaders.

5. Northrup, *Trade without Rulers*, 39.

6. Eltis, Lovejoy, and Richardson, "Slave-Trading Ports," 18–25. The longevity and scale of the trade disavow planter claims that they did not want to purchase "Calabar slaves." Annual shipments to the Americas demonstrate that planters demanded enslaved African labor, regardless of ethnicity.

7. Hair, "Note on Early References to 'Calabar,'" 127–128; Sweet, *Recreating Africa*, 23 (regarding the Bahia reference).

8. www.slavevoyages.org.

9. Simmons dates Jansson's *Nigritarum Regnum* to ca. 1650 (Simmons, "Ethnographic Sketch," 4), but ca. 1658 is a more reasonable approximation. The large-scale "Caerte van Rio Calabaria" (1665–1668) is clearly a drawing of the Rio Real and its tributaries—New Calabar. Building upon this chart, a French map from 1699 in fact depicted "Nouveau Kalabar" connected by a rivulet to "Vieux Kalabar," about ten miles to the southeast.

10. PROB 11/281, NA.

11. Europeans frequently termed the "Cross River" the Calabar or Old Calabar River. For example, in May 1720 four sailors from the Glasgow slaving ship *Hannover* "[w]ent ashoar at Tom Shott's in the mouth of Callabar River" (*Hannover* accounts, AC9/1042, NAS). Tom Shott's Point lies on the western banks of the Cross River's estuary. See also the "River Calabar" in Captain Adams's map ca. 1820 (Adams, *Remarks*, frontispiece) and the "Old Callebar River" in Edward Bold's map ca. 1820 (republished in Latham, *Old Calabar*, frontispiece).

12. On March 3, 1652, the London ship *Swan* "was cast away coming out of Rio del Rey, alias Calabar, in the Bight, having then aboard her above 200 Negroes, some elephants' teeth, wax, skins, and some gold" (John Paige to Gowen Paynter and William Clerke, Nov. 5, 1652, *Letters of John Paige*, www.british-history.ac.uk/).

13. Latham, "Pre-colonial Economy," 70–71; Latham, "Currency," 599–605; Watts, "True Relation," *Harleian Collection*, 2:515. Watts learned that his capture avenged "some unhandsome action of carrying a native away with their leave, about a year before" (513).

14. www.slavevoyages.org.

15. When the first British missionaries built houses at Duke Town in 1846, they commented on the historic significance of their residence. As missionary Hope Waddell wrote in June 1846: "To day we all take up our abode on shore + dedicate ourselves + our residence to God. It is the first house ever built or inhabited by white

men in Calabar or on hundreds of miles of this coast. The traders in the river confine themselves to their ships, and our coming to reside here is an era in the history of the country" (Hope Waddell diary, June 4, 1846, MS7739, f. 63, NLS).

16. Cited by Latham, *Old Calabar*, 18; Northrup, *Trade without Rulers*, 53.

17. T70/175, f. 23, NA. We owe this reference to David Eltis.

18. Alexander Horsburgh to "Gentlemen," Old Calabar, June 9, 1720, AC9/1042, NAS.

19. Liverpool merchants traded infrequently with Old Calabar until 1748: 1710 (1 venture), 1714 (1), 1725 (1), 1730 (1), 1732 (1), 1742 (10), 1743 (1), 1747 (1), 1748 (3).

20. Richardson, "Profits," 61.

21. Potter to William Davenport, Old Calabar, July 23, 1785, Aug. 17, 1785, Nov. 3, 1785, Davenport Papers, MMM.

22. Rogers to James Rogers, Old Calabar, Oct. 29, 1787, C107/12, NA.

23. Diary entries, March 7, 1785, March 12, 1785.

24. Latham, *Old Calabar*, 50–51.

25. We capitalized "duke," "king," "captain," and "old." Possibly King Oyo, if at an advanced age, was Eyo Ema, one of the oldest of five founding fathers who settled Creek Town in the early 1600s (Latham, *Old Calabar*, 10).

26. Jones, "Introduction," in Waddell, *Twenty-nine Years*, xviii–xix; Latham, *Old Calabar*, 50; Nair, *Origins and Development*, 6; Hair, Jones, and Law, *Barbot on Guinea*, 2:680–681, 705n27.

27. Latham, "Pre-colonial Economy," 72.

28. Voyage account of the ship *Florida*, Captain Samuel Paine, 1714–1716, Add MS 39946, BL. Possibly King Ambo, if elderly, was Oku Atai, one of the five founding fathers who settled Creek Town in the early 1600s (Latham, *Old Calabar*, 10).

29. Unless indicated otherwise, information on the important Horsburgh accounts come from Behrendt and Graham, "African Merchants," 37–61.

30. In about 1820 King Aqua is included in Bold's list of "Comey Paid to the Duke [Ephraim] and Traders on Entering Callebar River" (Bold, *African Guide*, 77).

31. Evidence of Morley in Lambert, *Commons Sessional Papers*, 73:154–155; Parker evidence, May 10, 1790, in Lambert 73:126; Hall evidence in Lambert, 72:226–232.

32. Simon Rottenberg first studied the Rogers papers (Rottenberg, "Business," 414). For Rogers, see also Richardson, *Bristol Slave Traders*; Richardson, *Bristol, Africa and the Slave Trade*, 4:xi–xxxvi. David Richardson first studied the Davenport Papers extensively (Richardson, "Profits," 60–90).

33. Richardson, "Consumption Patterns," 303–330.

34. Inikori, "Development," 64–65.

35. Add MS 39946, BL.

36. Alpern, "What Africans Got," 7.

37. Richardson, "Prices of Slaves," 33–46.

38. Richard Rogers to James Rogers, Old Calabar, Nov. 10, 1787, C107/12, NA. On December 22 Captain Rogers specified that red cotton textiles were in demand, and on the twenty-ninth he wrote how beads "of different colours (say) White, green, yellow & Red will answer & Go off very well" (C107/12, NA).

39. *Dalrymple* accounts, 1768–1777, Davenport Papers, MMM.

40. Egbo Young Ofiong to "Gentleman," Old Calabar, July 23, 1783, DX/1304, MMM.

41. Lovejoy and Richardson, "Letters," 106–107.

42. Information on European and Indian goods traded at Old Calabar may be found in Alpern, "What Africans Got," 6–12. He describes cushtaes as "striped blue and white or checked cloth, possibly of mixed cotton and silk," and photaes as popular "striped or checked cotton cloth, defined as a dyed calico, usually blue and white." Chelloes, another Indian textile popular among African consumers, were "striped or checked cotton cloth woven with colored threads rather than dyed after weaving" (7–8).

43. Lovejoy and Richardson, "Letters," 106–107; Antera Duke diary entry May 26, 1785.

44. *May* accounts, f. 45, *Dalrymple* accounts, f. 20, Davenport Papers, MMM.

45. *Hector* accounts, f. 57, Davenport Papers, MMM.

46. Davenport and partners paid an engraver for "Cutting Names on 2 Guns" (*Lord Cassiles* accounts, f. 6, Davenport Papers, MMM). For silver canes, see Lovejoy and Richardson, "Letters," 103, letter 4.

47. Simmons, "Ethnographic Sketch," in Forde, *Efik Traders*, 8–9. "I had Captain Potter come ashore; after 11 o'clock Potter sent his tender and his ship to bring 35 white men and at noon they began to put up two sides of the house" (translation) ("Diary of Antera Duke," in Forde, *Efik Traders*, 58). Some merchants shipped prefabricated structures, the most famous being Egbo Young Ofiong's Liverpool Hall. See also Waddell, *Twenty-nine Years*.

48. Hallett, *Records*, 208. One clock may have been similar to the eight-days clock shipped to Calabar on board the Liverpool slaver *May* in 1771. Stephen Tillinghurst manufactured this clock (housed in a mahogany case) and sold it for £10 to the *May*'s slaving firm Robert Kennedy and Company (*May* accounts, ff. 45, 51, Davenport Papers, MMM). Europeans sold or gifted a variety of clocks and watches to Calabar merchants. They cleaned and repaired the timepieces back in Europe, as the Davenport accounts reveal: "To Cleaning watches for the Calabarrs (ch[arge]d to them)," £1 10s (*Dalrymple* accounts, May 1777, f. 168). Names were inscribed on walking sticks to identify merchants' messengers. In 1846, for example, Waddell met a messenger "from Antica Cobham, accredited by his silver-heading walking staff, with his name thereon" (Waddell, *Twenty-nine Years*, 282).

49. *Dobson* Calabar account, Hasell MS, Dalemain House, Cumbria. Hair first examined this important document, and we build upon his work (Hair, "Antera Duke," 359–365).

50. Add MS 59777, vol. 1, f. 44v, BL. We owe this reference to Nicholas J. Radburn.

51. Hallett, *Records*, 209; Waddell, *Twenty-nine Years*, 247.

52. This slight percentage difference indicates that this group of six sold a few more high-priced adults.

53. According to traveler James Holman, at Old Calabar in 1828, if captains were short the slaves owed them toward the end of their trade, Duke Ephraim, then prin-

cipal dignitary, ordered other leading Efik to send to him "every individual from the neighbouring villages, who have committed any crime or misdemeanor; and should he still continue unable to make up the specified demand, they sell their own servants to him" (Holman, *Travels*, 396).

54. Captain Potter's accounts bundle slave sales, so one can only calculate slave prices by age/gender for single sale transactions: men ($n = 11$); boys ($n = 3$); women ($n = 7$); girls ($n = 4$).

55. The *Dobson/Fox* outlay totaled £5,642, but one £30 cask of textiles was earmarked for São Tomé.

56. "Rose and White, sail room, No. 3, N. and St. George's d[ock]" (*Gore's Liverpool Directory*, 1774, 65). In addition to their sail room, the *Directory* lists their residences: Joshua Rose, sailmaker, Old Hall street; James White, sailmaker, No. 4, Ranelagh Street (50, 59).

57. For an illustration of Creek Town King Eyo's state canoe and large flag ca. 1850, see Waddell, *Twenty-nine Years*, frontispiece. For a large flag on a king's canoe near Duke Town, Old Calabar, published in the *Illustrated London News* (June 1850), see Latham, "Trading Alliance," 862. Both of these flags had Union Jacks in the top corners. At Bonny/Opobo, later in the nineteenth century, King Jaja's war canoes impressed spectators: "With their imported multicoloured flags and buntings fluttering in the wind and both banks of the river resounding to the beating of scores of war drums, the canoes would land to the welcoming praise songs of the women and children" (Cookey, *King Jaja*, 83).

58. Since Davenport organized the *Dobson/Fox* voyages after the British gained Canada in 1763, it is likely that most or all of these castor hats were manufactured from beaver pelts.

59. Captains attempted to sell all perishable goods at Old Calabar, including cottons and weaponry. As Davenport instructed Captain William Hindle in February 1761: "[B]ring home only such goods as are not perishable by time, such as Iron barrs, Brass & Copper Rods, but bring no Guns back" (Davenport to Hindle, Liverpool, Feb. 7, 1761, *Tyrell* accounts, Davenport Papers, MMM).

60. Richard Rogers to James Rogers & Co., Old Calabar, Oct. 29, 1787, Nov. 10, 1787, C107/12, NA.

61. Northrup, *Trade without Rulers*, 166; Holman, *Travels*, 407; Jones, *Trading States*, 99.

62. See note 59 above.

63. By contrast, fees at Bonny totaled £150 (Adams, *Remarks*, 245, 248). Compared with Angola, customs throughout the Bight of Biafra were quite high, and with the removal of French competition from Angola in 1792 and 1793, British merchants redirected many of their ships to Cabinda, Loango, the Congo River, and Ambriz.

64. Historians, including two here, previously have assigned Adams's comey payments for palm oil to the 1790s slave-trading period. See Adams, *Remarks*, 143, 245, 248; Latham, *Old Calabar*, 20; Lovejoy and Richardson, "'Horrid Hole,'" 371n24; Northrup, *Africa's Discovery of Europe*, 58; Northrup, "West Africans," in Morgan and Hawkins, *Black Experience*, 44.

65. John Howard to William Davenport & Co., July 18, 1785, Potter to Davenport

& Co., Old Calabar, July 23, 1785, Davenport Papers, MMM; Rogers to James Rogers, Old Calabar, Nov. 10, 1787, C107/12, NA. For the period 1789–1792, slave prices at Old Calabar were £12 to £14 (Richardson, "Prices of Slaves," 38), and thus goods paid in comey to the value of 150 slaves would total £1,800 to 2,100. In 1792 Hugh Crow of Liverpool noted that customs fees at Bonny "were about £400 for each ship" (Crow, Memoirs, 43). Captain Adams believed that Old Calabar merchants lost trade to Bonny "by exacting from the vessels trading, exorbitant duties or customs" (Adams, Remarks, 143). Old Calabar's customs were thus far greater than £400, those fees at Bonny.

66. Rogers noted great inflation: comey payments 500 percent greater than his last trade at Old Calabar, which perhaps occurred in the mid-1770s (Rogers to Rogers, Old Calabar, Oct. 29, 1787, C107/12, NA).

67. Lovejoy and Richardson, "Letters," 110.

68. In 1772 Edward Tuohy, mustered on the Liverpool-Calabar slaver Swift, remarked to his father, "I expect to be out from Liverpool no longer than 8 or 9 month as she is going as a tender to another Ship which makes the time shorter than if we should stay to slave there" (Edward Tuohy to his father, Liverpool, May 18, 1772, 380 TUO 2/7, LivRO).

69. For example, mariner James Morley stated that he sailed in the Bristol sloop Marcus, "tender to the Cato, Captain Jones." William Bishop and Thomas Jones commanded these two Bristol vessels; both were experienced captains, departing for Old Calabar in tandem in late May 1763 (evidence of Morley, May 12, 1790, in Lambert, Commons Sessional Papers, 73:151; Richardson, Bristol, Africa and the Slave Trade, 3:157,161).

70. "From the first to the third quarter of the 18th century, the time spent acquiring slaves on the African coast almost doubled" (Eltis and Richardson, "Productivity," 478).

71. Falconer, Mariner's New and Complete Naval Dictionary, 327. This definition applies, for example, to two tenders identified in a list of Liverpool slaving voyages in 1799: the 54-ton Anna Bella and the 35-ton Ocean (Liverpool and Slavery, 120–129).

72. Richard Rogers to James Rogers, Old Calabar, Nov. 10, 1787, C107/12, NA.

73. Bristol muster rolls, 1791–1792, No. 32; 1792–1793, No. 52; 1793–1794, No. 172, BRO.

74. Antera Duke mentions the name of only one European ship: "after 4 clock time we see one Tender com up his be Captin Johnston ship will Tender of Captin Aspinall so wee 3 firs great guns" (diary entry Oct. 9, 1786), referring to the Liverpool slaving ship Will, as documented in www.slavevoyages.org, Voyage ID 84018.

75. Holman, Travels, 365–366.

76. In 1769 Orrock Robin John and Ephraim Robin John, for example, refer to the Bristol vessels Venus and Cato (Lovejoy and Richardson, "Letters," 102–103).

77. Jackson, Journal, 78. Antera Duke also writes about "Captin Androw," "ogan Captin Duke," and "Captin John King Egbo." These three men are Efik traders, "captain" referring to some important role in society that they played (Hair, "Antera Duke," 361).

78. "[I]t is not the duty of the mates to [purchase slaves] at Del Rey and Calabar, the captains managing that business themselves" (evidence of Hall, Lambert, *Commons Sessional Papers*, 72:253).

79. Behrendt, "Markets" 189–190. Though most captains who traded at Bonny, since they rose through the ranks, were in their late twenties or thirties, Captain Thomas Tobin commanded his first ship at Bonny (1796) at only twenty-three years of age (Behrendt, "Captains," 127).

80. Lovejoy and Richardson, "'Horrid Hole,'" 366.

81. Crow, *Memoirs*, 67, 225.

82. Lovejoy and Richardson, "'Horrid Hole,'" 372–373; Lovejoy and Richardson, "Trust," 333–355.

83. One suspects that Patrick Fairweather's prominence in Antera Duke's diary reflects the fact that the two men were about the same age. In 1851 missionary Hope Waddell intervened in a dispute involving King Eyo Honesty because, as Waddell stated: "knowing the authority attached to age, and being Eyo's equal in years, I hastened to interpose and appease him" (Waddell, *Twenty-nine Years*, 482). Because Fairweather was Antera's "equal in years," he played a key role in organizing the Liverpool slave trade with Duke Town merchants.

84. Butterworth, *Three Years Adventures*, 53–54. As we noted in chapter 1, it may have been customary for funeral obsequies to be delayed until drier November weather.

85. Captain Richard Rogers noted, "[T]he Ship *Tarleton* Capt Patrick Fairweather sails after with 450 Slaves which will be about two Months after laying in the River 14 Months but observe 3 Months living on Shore & not purchasing one Slave article" (Rogers to James Rogers, Old Calabar, Nov. 10, 1787, C107/12, NA).

86. The International Genealogical Index reports that a Patrick Fairweather was christened May 25, 1735, in Angus, Scotland, a year that accords with the future captain's maritime career. Fairweather died in Liverpool on November 24, 1799 (*Billinge's Liverpool Advertiser*, Dec. 2, 1799).

87. In 1787 a Bristol captain stated that Patrick Fairweather "has used this river 32 Years" (Richard Rogers to James Rogers, Old Calabar, Dec. 29, 1787, C107/12, NA).

88. As first mate of the *Dalrymple*, which cleared Liverpool in March 1765, Fairweather received monthly wages of £4 (*Dalrymple* accounts, Davenport Papers, MMM).

89. BT98/35,57, BT98/36,250, BT98/38,211, NA. William Begg worked as surgeon for Fairweather, the other men as mates.

90. Regarding the size of the 1783–1792 Liverpool-Calabar slave trade (total slaves, share of trade), compared with 1798–1807.

91. These sources include slave trade lists, muster rolls (crew pay lists), gazettes, and ship registers; the scattered information culled from these records is now consolidated in the transatlantic slave trade data archive (www.slavevoyages.org). For a listing of British shipping sources, most of which report captains' names, see Behrendt, "Annual Volume," 207–211.

92. In his "Notes on the Diary of Antera Duke," published in conjunction with

the diary, Simmons identifies four of these captains—all from Liverpool. In a manuscript list of Liverpool slaving voyages from 1783 to 1787, Latham finds the names of thirteen captains mentioned by Antera Duke (Simmons, "Notes on the Diary," in Forde, *Efik Traders*, 69–76; Latham, *Old Calabar*, 20).

93. www.slavevoyages.org.

94. "Diary of Antera Duke," in Forde, *Efik Traders*, 45–47, 75. For Eyo Willy Honesty, see Latham, *Old Calabar*, 47. The payment of French customs to Henshaw Town traders caused a dispute with Duke Town. French links appear strongest with Creek Town. In 1792, for example, a Nantes slaver called on Creek Town merchant Willy Honesty (Halgan, "A bord," 58).

95. On July 17, 1790, Liverpool merchant Robert Bostock noted, "Mr. Woodvill [William Woodville] is fitting out in a vessel belonging to Mr. Shaw and himself for France to be made a French Bottom" (Letterbook of Robert Bostock, 1789–1792, f. 97, LivRO). He might also have traded with Henshaw Town merchants: on the *Asia*'s muster roll is crewman "Mich^l Henshaw," the only Henshaw recorded on any Liverpool crew list (based on analysis of Liverpool muster rolls, 1775–1809, BT98/ 35–69, NA; the *Asia*'s muster is BT98/47,99).

96. The bell resides in Merchants' Hall, Clifton, Bristol. Three engraved letters on the bell have faded.

97. Lambert, *Commons Sessional Papers*, 73:156, 165. The other "Ephraim" (156) probably refers to Duke Ephraim of Duke Town.

98. William Brighouse [to Davenport & Co], Old Calabar, Dec. 23, 1776, Davenport Papers, MMM.

99. www.slavevoyages.org. The *Neptune* and *Venus* (voyage IDs 77127, 77231) owned by Harrison & Co. sailed in tandem from London to Old Calabar on July 1, 1776.

100. Evidence of Hall, Mar. 2, 1790, Lambert, *Commons Sessional Papers*, 72:250.

101. In 1750–1767 (to the year of the massacre), Liverpool ships carried 42 percent of the enslaved Africans shipped from Old Calabar. Bristol slavers transported 38 percent of the captives. In 1750–1774 (to the year of Doyle's and Fidler's deaths), Liverpool's share increased to 50 percent whereas Bristol's declined to 32 percent. By the mid-1780s Liverpool share increased further to more than 70 percent. Bristol's share declined to less than 10 percent.

102. Lovejoy and Richardson, "Trust," 343–344.

103. Hamnet Forsyth to James Rogers, Old Calabar, June 11, 1792, C107/13, NA; Society of Merchant Venturers, Bristol muster rolls, 1793–1794, 178, BRO.

104. The Duke Town settlement (or resettlement) may date from 1748. Liverpool captain and merchant Ambrose Lace recollected that in 1748, on his first visit to Old Calabar, "there were no inhabitants in the place called Old Town. They all lived in at the place called New [Duke] Town." Historians have puzzled over this remark, some believing that Lace simply erred (Sparks), others believing that Lace actually referred to the founding of Duke Town in 1748 (Lovejoy and Richardson, "Trust, Pawnship, and Atlantic History," 340). Certainly, Lace challenges Efik tradition that dates the settlement of Old Town in the late 1500s or early 1600s. A way to reconcile these

conflicting testimonies is to argue for occasional settlement, abandonment, and re-settlement of families in historic village sites.

105. Hallett, *Records*, 207–208; Richard Rogers to James Rogers, Old Calabar, Dec. 29, 1787, C107/12, NA.

106. In 1803 Jimmy Henshaw informed surgeon and captain Elliot Arthy that "now I be trade for red-wood, and every stock you may want I sell" (Arthy, *Introductory Observations*, 75).

107. Hallett, *Records*, 199.

108. Latham, *Old Calabar*, 48 (quotes), 50–51, 74; Latham, "Trading Alliance," 862–867.

Chapter 3

1. Letter dated June 24, 1780, reprinted in the *Liverpool General Advertiser*, Feb. 21, 1788, 3. Presumably Captain Begg, the only Liverpool mariner at Old Calabar in June 1780, delivered the letter.

2. Efik often pluralized words by writing two singular words, such as "gun gun" (for guns) or, in this instance "tooth tooth" (for teeth), usually indicating "many" or sometimes "large" or "big."

3. *Williamson's Liverpool Advertiser and Mercantile Chronicle*, Oct. 5, 1780, 5; BT98/ 40,191, NA. On his homeward voyage to Liverpool from Old Calabar, Begg anchored near Sierra Leone to purchase three tons camwood, a half of ton beeswax, and one ton of malagueta pepper. Begg may have purchased some of the pepper and beeswax at Calabar and some of the ivory near Sierra Leone.

4. Only two diary entries mention bulk cargoes of produce (two and four "Town," or tons, of unspecified goods)—Dec. 14, 1785, and Jan. 22, 1786. Arthur Wilkie, the diary transcriber, may have not copied all information on produce (see chapter 5, Comments on the Text).

5. *Liverpool General Advertiser*, July 13, 1786; *Manchester Mercury*, July 18, 1786. British sources, such as newspapers, generally record palm oil in puncheons. There are eighty-four (imperial) gallons to a puncheon.

6. Merseyside captains purchased 80 percent of all Biafran exports (www.slave voyages.org).

7. Jones, *West Africa*, 3, 203–206.

8. Inikori, *Africans*, 220. The eighty-one tusks weighed 2,019.5 pounds; Major purchased the ivory for trading goods that cost £126. At £1 11s per tusk, ivory cost about 25 percent the cost of a slave. Captain Major also shipped 33.5 ounces of gold, which he likely picked up on the Gold Coast en route to the Cross River.

9. The Company advertised twenty-three lots of ivory for sale in four pens. These lots totaled 4,449 ivory tusks weighing 42.5 tons and arrived on four ships, including the *Blackamore*. Two other ships traded at New Calabar, and the fourth loaded at Ardra in the Bight of Benin. Ivory tusks averaged 21.5 pounds, ranging from lots of smaller 5- to 6-pound pieces (lot 46 contained 800 tusks weighing 2 tons) to lots

whose tusks averaged 56 pounds ("Alotments of Goods to be sold by the Company of Royal Adventurers of England Trading into Africa, at the African House in Broadstreet: by the Candle, on Thursday the 18th of January 1665," Bute Broadside, Houghton Library, Harvard University). The four ships—the *Rupert, Swallow, Cormantine Frigate,* and *Blackamore*—are documented in www.slavevoyages.org. The sales advertisements do not list ivory cargoes per ship, but Cross River merchants clearly sold some of this ivory. Ardra likely supplied very little of the ivory shipped from Africa in 1664 (Wigboldus, "Trade," 324).

10. Donnan, *Documents,* 1:193.

11. Hair, Jones, and Law, *Barbot on Guinea,* 2:677, 704n21.

12. http://www.easy.dans.knaw.nl/dms, "Anglo-African Trade, 1699–1808" (hereafter referred to as Johnson, "Anglo-African Trade dataset"). In the 1970s Marion Johnson computerized English-African customs (import and export) data for the period 1699–1808 from the CUST3 and CUST17 series in the Public Record Office (London). Her data files are stored in a Dutch archive, available online as specified in the URL given earlier in this note. For a discussion of the customs data and the Johnson dataset, see Lindblad and Ross, *Anglo-African Trade.*

13. Assuming ivory averaged 14 to 20 pounds/tusk, the dealers sold 3,000 to 5,000 tusks.

14. Hair, Jones, and Law, *Barbot on Guinea,* 2:699.

15. Dutch West India Company (WIC) ships consigned ivory from the Gold Coast fort Elmina, and company records do not record quantities sourced from the Bight of Biafra. In 1699 the WIC shipped thirty-two tons of ivory from West Africa, but one-third that amount in 1700, 1701, and 1702 (Feinberg and Johnson, "West African Ivory," 438–441).

16. There were at least fifty-five London-based Royal African Company ships trading at Old Calabar from 1674 to 1704. We do not know whether any of these ships loaded redwood in the Cross River region.

17. In 1702 the *Anne Brigantine* shipped into Bristol "over 3 tons 12 cwt of redwood" from Guinea and Barbados—perhaps Captain Charles Norris traded at Old Calabar (Richardson, *Bristol, Africa and the Slave Trade,* 1:3, 10, 17; www.slavevoyages.org).

18. Voyage account of the ship *Florida,* Captain Samuel Paine, 1714–1716, Add MS 39946, f. 2v, BL.

19. Richardson, *Bristol, Africa and the Slave Trade,* 1:80–81, 84–85.

20. Letter from *Hannover* supercargo Alexander Horsburgh to "Gentleman," Old Calabar, June 9, 1720, AC9/1042, NAS. Boucher probably loaded quantities of redwood near Cape Lopez and Gabon before topping off his cargo at Old Calabar.

21. New Calabar's export slave trade declined after 1680 and may have dropped sharply in the 1690s. There are only two documented slaving vessels trading at New Calabar in the 1690s, though ten vessels slaved in that decade in the Bight of Biafra (at an unspecified location). The first documented cluster of slavers at Bonny appear in 1696–1700 (four London vessels), though these may have purchased commodities also at New Calabar, as longboats and other auxiliary craft plied creeks and rivers be-

tween New Calabar, Bonny, and Andoni (Hair, Jones, and Law, *Barbot on Guinea*, 2:672–677, 681–700). For the rise of Bonny, see Lovejoy and Richardson, "'Horrid Hole,'" 367–369.

22. If we add to these totals Guineamen that intended to slave at New Calabar, Old Calabar, and Bonny, the numbers increase to 16, 223, and 149 voyages, respectively.

23. den Heijer, *Goud*, 70, 95, 134–137; Austen and Jacob, "Dutch Trading Voyages," 5–8, 20. The trading post Agaton appears on the east bank of the Benin River, south of Benin city, on van Keulen, "Map of West Africa," www.nationaalarchief.nl/AML.

24. www.slavevoyages.org.

25. The British dominated trade there and throughout the Bight of Biafra; among rivals only French captains competed, but they offered sustained competition only in 1714–1716.

26. Similarly, English customs ledgers aggregate imports from "Africa" or in small samples of years from broadly defined regions such as "West Africa" or "North Africa." Officials do not record African ports or the names of ships, captains, or owners; cargoes are bundled together and enumerated entering customshouses in London and nonspecified outports.

27. Analysis based on produce shipments recorded in Richardson, *Bristol, Africa and the Slave Trade*, vols. 1 and 2, with African market information updated in www.slavevoyages.org. The other Bristol ships documented as purchasing ivory at known African locations: 11 tons on the Gold Coast (7 ships), 5 tons in the Bight of Benin (2 ships), and 1.5 tons at Angola (1 ship). Eighty-six Bristol ships purchased 157 tons of ivory at unknown African locations. Of 162 Bristol ships arriving with redwood, 119 ships traded for 1,082 tons of redwood at unspecified African locations, including the *Shepherd*, a nonslaver, that landed 163.5 tons of redwood directly from Africa in 1735. Eight Bristol ships loaded 115 tons of redwood along the Angola coast, and seven captains slaving along the Gold Coast purchased 20 tons, cargoes that most likely included camwood from the Sierra Leone region.

28. Average tusk weight based on evidence presented below. There was one comparably large ivory shipment from each port: in 1734 the *Seaflower* arrived in Bristol with 75 hundredweights of ivory (8,400 pounds or about 500 to 600 tusks); in 1742 the *Rising Sun* arrived in Bristol with 5 tons of ivory (11,200 pounds or about 700 to 800 tusks).

29. Richardson, *Bristol, Africa and the Slave Trade*, 1:xvi. From 1674 to 1713 the Royal African Company shipped 115.7 tons of redwood into London; Bristol vessels carried 103.8 tons of redwood into Bristol in 1725.

30. Beckinsale, "Factors," 349–362. About 1725, the peak year of Bristol redwood imports, "Cirencester, Painswick, Wooton, Marshfield, Minchinhampton and Fairford are all mentioned as making a fine Medley or mixed cloth, usually worn in England by the better class of people and also exported in large quantities to Europe" (352). For the great range of dyestuffs produced worldwide and shipped to England, see Fairlie, "Dyestuffs," 488–510, mentioning Sierra Leone camwood and Angolan barwood among the red dyes (499).

31. Thompson, "Forests," 128. In the nineteenth century English botanists studied the various African dyewoods, distinguishing between camwood (from the Sierra Leone region) and barwood (from northern Congo-Angola).

32. *Pterocarpus tinctorius*, a 40- to 70-foot tree, grows also in Angola. *Pterocarpus soyauxii*, by contrast, reaches 80 to 90 feet in height. Barwood is the more accurate term for Lower Guinea redwood (J. M. H., "Barwood," 373–375). The Gabon redwood grew in the Sette Cama region and was shipped south to Mayumba (La Fleur, *van den Broecke's Journal*, 73n2).

33. "Majumba is about seventy leagues S. S. E. of Cape Lopez, where a great deal of redwood is annually purchased, though but few slaves and very little ivory" (*Treatise upon the Trade*, 26). British "wood ships" fitting out for Lower Guinea to purchase dyewoods cleared customs for "Angola" (Enfield, *History*, 68, listing the *Hannah* clearing for "Angola, (wood)" in October 1771). In December 1752 the Liverpool slaver *Eaton* fit out for Angola for slaves and "Wood and Teeth" (*Liverpool Memorandum-Book*, [14]).

34. "[T]he greatest use that we make of [ivory tusks] here, is to make Combs, as we may see here at most Comb-makers doors in London" (*Full and True Relation*, Bute Broadside, Houghton Library, Harvard University).

35. Feinberg and Johnson, "West African Ivory," 450. Turners, according to a 1761 guide, made "Handles of Instruments, oval Boxes, Balls, &c. of Ivory" (*Parents and Guardians Directory*, 1761, 175).

36. A 1722 Bristol voting list records one "ivory turner," William Bond (*Exact List of the Votes*, 6), who appears also as the only ivory turner in a 1734 list of Bristol freeholders (*List of Free-Holders*, 48). In 1775 there were three ivory craftsmen listed in a Bristol directory: ivory turner Richard Sircom; "hard & soft wood & ivory turner" John Sutton; and "hard wood and ivory turner" William Williams (*Sketchley's Bristol Directory*, 1775, 88, 93, 106). John Sutton is listed again in a 1793 directory, along with James Baker, "Ivory and Oval Turner" (*Matthews' New Bristol Directory*, 1793, 11, 78).

37. Mason, "Birmingham," 3.

38. Lynn, *Commerce*, 1–2, 12–13; Amadi, "Palm Oil," 54–61.

39. While at Bonny in July 1699, Barbot saw "three great jars of palm-oil" and a "jar of palm-oil" (Hair, Jones, and Law, *Barbot on Guinea*, 2:687, 689). In 1724 a small group of sailors from a Bristol ship steered up the River Andoni to buy slaves and palm oil. They loaded a "small jar of Palm Oil" upon iron bars in the longboat (www.oldbaileyonline.org, Proceedings of the Old Bailey, Ref: t17250630–58). From July 1769 to January 1770, Captain John Potter of the *Dobson* purchased "Jarrs Oyl" at Old Calabar (*Dobson* Calabar account, Hasell MS, Dalemain House, Cumbria). Captains' letters (1780s) from Old Calabar to British merchants William Davenport and James Rogers mention crews and puncheons of palm oil.

40. For palm oil locations in Africa, see Lynn, *Commerce*, 1–2. Customs records indicate that 4,300 gallons of palm oil arrived in London, 1699–1744, and London merchants traded mostly in the Sierra Leone region and along the Gold and Slave Coasts. Only 500 gallons entered customs ledgers in outports during ten years from 1699 to 1745 (Johnson, "Anglo-African Trade dataset"). Because Richardson does not record

any palm oil imported into Bristol from 1698 to 1745 (Richardson, *Bristol, Africa and the Slave Trade*, vols. 1–2), we assume these small amounts arrived in Liverpool.

41. In the period 1699–1808 the customs ledgers itemizing African imports also identify Morocco (1731), Senegal (1736), and Sierra Leone (1798–1808). Officials also do not record African ports or the names of ships, captains, or owners; cargoes are grouped together, and the summary ledgers total quantities and values entering London and nonspecified outports.

42. These two Liverpool gazettes changed names, *Williamson's Liverpool Advertiser and Mercantile Chronicle* becoming *Billinge's Liverpool Advertiser* in 1794, and *Liverpool General Advertiser* becoming *Gore's Liverpool General Advertiser* in 1790.

43. There are also one-off copies of the *Liverpool Trade List* for December 8–14, 1802; October 1–7, 1807; October 15–21, 1807; November 5–11, 1807; December 3–9, 1807; December 17–23, 1807; December 31, 1807–January 5, 1808; and January 28, 1807–February 3, 1808.

44. Almost all the *Mercury's* issues survive, though detailed information on arriving ships' cargoes is lacking in three periods: April–October 1752; July 1756–April 1768; and September 1799–June 1804.

45. Shipping lists usually document produce imports from "Africa," and hence one must cross-reference all cargoes with the online slave trade database to determine African ports of embarkation. For example, the first issue of the *Manchester Mercury* listed the cargo of the *Nancy* that arrived in Liverpool from "Africa and Barbados." Captain John "Henryford" transported 133 elephants' teeth (ivory tusks) and 262 pieces of redwood. By examining the online slave trade database, we learn that the *Nancy*, Captain John Hunniford, traded at Bonny in 1752. In November 1752, Barbados shipping lists report that the *Judith*, Captain Southworth, arrived from Africa with 340 slaves and one ton of ivory. This vessel—voyage identification number 90410 in the slave trade database—also traded at Bonny.

46. African merchants also sold hippopotamus tusks, referred to as "sea horse teeth," seamorse teeth," or "sea cow teeth." According to French trader Durand, who frequented the Upper Guinea Coast, "sea-horses or hippopotami" teeth are seven to eight inches long and at the root five inches in circumference. They are "whiter and infinitely harder than ivory" and fetch a higher price than elephants' tusks. Dentists buy them "with avidity," and the teeth do not turn yellow like those of ivory (Durand, *Voyage to Senegal*, 4:77–80).

47. Excluding gold, not recorded in English customs ledgers, redwood, ivory, and gum were the most valuable African products imported into England from 1699 to 1808. Customs data indicate that during these years British ships returned with redwood valued £2,438,000, ivory valued £1,068,000, and gum (mostly gum arabic and gum senegal) valued £960,000. These three commodities totaled two-thirds of African imports, ranking ahead of beeswax (£285,000), almonds (£270,000), palm oil (£99,000), camwood (£72,000), and pepper (£45,000). We do not know how often customs officials recorded imports of camwood, a red dyewood, as "redwood." Thus camwood values were greater than the £72,000 recorded in the ledgers.

48. Isaac Hobhouse & Co. to William Barry, 1725, quoted by Richardson, "Costs of Survival," 180. Barry commanded the *Dispatch* to Old Calabar.

49. See, for example, William Brighouse to Davenport and Co., Dominica, Apr. 3, 1777; William Moore, jr. to William Davenport and Co., Barbados, June 3, 1777, Davenport Papers, MMM.

50. *Reed's Weekly Journal*, Jan. 13, 1759, reports the capture of the Liverpool slaver *Livesley*. The *Manchester Mercury* reports ivory imports from the other five ships.

51. There was always a great range in the size and quality of African ivory. In 1770 brokers advertised "445 Elephants Teeth, of remarkable good quality, their weight from 1 lb to 80 lb per tooth" (*Liverpool General Advertiser*, Oct. 26, 1770). This cargo came from the slaver *Patty* from Cape Mount on the Windward Coast. Advertisements usually group ivory pieces, as in the *Will* arrived from St. Vincent "with 334 elephant teeth and scriveloes for J & J Gregson & Co." (*Manchester Mercury*, June 21, 1791).

52. William Moore, jr. to William Davenport and Co., Barbados, June 3, 1777, Davenport Papers, MMM.

53. William Whaley and partners to Captain W. Earle of the *Chesterfield*, Liverpool, May 22, 1751, Earle Papers, MMM.

54. Davenport to Captain William Hindle, Liverpool, Feb. 7, 1761, Davenport Papers, MMM; Crosbies and Trafford to Capt. Ambrose Lace, Liverpool, Apr. 14, 1762, in Williams, *Liverpool Privateers*, 486.

55. In Potter's transactions for 499 slaves, approximately 300 sold for less than 129 coppers. Slaves were sold in lots, and thus we do not know the purchase price in coppers for all African individuals.

56. As Liverpool merchant Francis Ingram stated in March 1782: "we shall not fit [our slaver] out, having received the melancholy acc[oun]ts at one time of St. Kitts, Montserrat, Nevis, being taken & Antigua expected to go. From these circumstances prudence positively forbids our fitting out any vessels for Africa" (Francis Ingram to Richard Miles, Liverpool, Mar. 29, 1782, T70/1545, NA).

57. Register of the brig *William*, Nov. 8, 1779, C/EX/L/3/4, 17, MMM. These registers do not specify construction details, as they do after 1786. The length and breadth measurements are approximations, based on later ship registry information for brigs of fifty tons.

58. Davenport to Begg, Jan. 5, 1780, D/DAV/1, MMM.

59. Davenport to Comberbach, Dec. 27, 1781, D/DAV/1, MMM.

60. Adams, *Remarks*, 154, 171. The Duala continued to broker high-quality pink ivory. Liverpool brokers made sure to specify "Camerone ivory" in their auctions, confirming Captain Adams's opinion as to its "celebrated" quality (*Gore's Liverpool General Advertiser*, Apr. 29, 1790, 2). Newspaper advertisements did not identify the provenance for other ivory sales.

61. Arthy, *Introductory Observations*, 83–84.

62. Crow, *Memoirs*, 84, 227, 261.

63. Johnson, "By Ship or by Camel," 539. Bold, in his *African Guide* (1822), stated that English and Portuguese ships loaded sixty tons of ivory in one season in the Wouri estuary (84).

64. Waddell, *Twenty-nine Years*, 327.

65. Customs records indicate that 5,165 tons of African ivory entered England, 1750–1808 (Johnson, "Anglo-African Trade dataset").

66. Lambert, *Commons Sessional Papers*, 67:70–71, paraphrased evidence of Falconbridge and Liverpool merchant (and former captain) James Penny. The "Andonies" and "Creeks" appear in the map produced in Crow, *Memoirs*, inset, 134–135.

67. The deltas may have replaced coastal Senegal as the principal oil export region. In Mortimer's alphabetical, nonpaginated dictionary (1767), his entry "Palm-Oil" stated that the palm tree "grows in Africa, particularly at Senega[l]" (Mortimer, *Dictionary*, entry PAM–PAN).

68. Whereas customs officials recorded palm oil by weight (generally in 112-pound hundredweights and later in 2,240-pound tons), we prefer the more intuitive gallon measurements, to aid readers. An imperial gallon of palm oil weighs 9.24 pounds, given that the gallon is based on the volume of 10 pounds of water, and the specific gravity of palm oil is 0.924.

69. In Liverpool merchant William Davenport's February 1761 letter of instructions to Captain William Hindle, he tells the captain to "be looking out for ivory, and purchase all that you can of the very best." He does not mention palm oil (Davenport to Hindle, Feb. 7, 1761, *Tyrrell* accounts, Davenport Papers, MMM).

70. Johnson, "Anglo-African Trade dataset."

71. PP 1816 (506),VII, 12.

72. As Adams pointed out, when the slave trade at Bonny "was in its greatest activity, masters of vessels sometimes found much difficulty in obtaining two or three puncheons of palm-oil for the use of the slaves on the middle passage, and have been compelled to send for it to Old Calabar" (Adams, *Remarks*, 245).

73. "Mr Sparling had a Vessal lately arrivd here from Gaboon call'd the Mermaid. Captn Wilson who purchased about 170 Tons of Barwood at a very modrate Rate, we believe as low as 20 to 30 Shillings a Ton and we are informed there is great plenty of it to be had. We have sent you a sample of it by this conveyance for your government, and think wou'd be worth your while to purchase as much as you can conveniently stow in your Vessal; this wood now sells readily at 21 per Ton, and subject to no duty; Mr Sparling Vessal was bound to Majumba on the Coast of Angola but could not fetch it, so the Capt. bore away for Gaboon where he purchased this wood in three weeks. [I]t is used in dying Red Couler" (Davenport to Captain Peter Potter, May 17, 1780, D/DAV/1, MMM).

74. Lambert, *Commons Sessional Papers*, 67:59*, reports Bristol redwood imports, 1771–1778; Richardson, *Bristol, Africa and the Slave Trade*, 4:56–57, records the *Jason* and *King George*.

75. Jemmy Henshaw to Captain James Phillips, Liverpool ship *Ranger*, Henshaw Town, Old Calabar, July 25, 1803, republished in Arthy, *Introductory Observations*, 75.

76. Adams, *Remarks*, 172; Waddell, *Twenty-nine Years*, 327.

77. At Old Calabar in 1720, Scottish supercargo Alexander Horsburgh purchased £4 of "Red pepper." The *Dobson* accounts from 1769 record seven transactions for

"Pepper" in the ship's disbursements for provisions (Behrendt and Graham, "African Merchants," 61; *Dobson* Calabar account, Hasell MS, Dalemain House, Cumbria).

78. *Manchester Mercury*, Apr. 28, 1767.

79. According to Captain Hugh Crow, a Liverpool slaving ship captain (1790s–1807), at Bonny "Pod-pepper, or Cayenne . . . is found in great abundance; but I never saw any of the Malagetta pepper, the *Grana Paradisi*, or cardamoms" (Crow, *Memoirs*, 257). Writing in 1832, James Bell specified the "Cayenne-pepper" from Old Calabar (Bell, *System of Geography*, 3:500).

80. Davenport to Begg, Liverpool, Nov. 4, 1780, D/DAV/1, MMM.

81. See chapter 5, Comments on the Text.

82. Lynn, *Commerce*, 2; Latham, "Price Fluctuations," 217.

83. See chapter 5, Comments on the Text. In late December 1787, for example, Antera wrote that Captain (Patrick) Fairweather shipped 377 slaves—he did not report that the large ship also loaded 50 tons of redwood, 9,600 gallons of palm oil, 45 ivory tusks, and 60 barrels of pepper.

84. Captain Richard Rogers to James Rogers and Co., Ship *Pearl*, Old Calabar, Jan. 31, 1788, Apr. 1788, June 17, 1788; Captain John Kennedy to Rogers and Co., Ship *Juba*, Old Calabar, June 17, 1788, C107/12, NA. Rogers transshipped most of the African produce to the *Juba*. Kennedy thought he would depart in mid-July with twenty puncheons of palm oil, indicating that Africans confined on board the *Pearl* or *Juba* consumed about eight to ten puncheons. See also Richardson, *Bristol, Africa and the Slave Trade*, 4:126.

85. Undated, partial letter, Davenport Papers, MMM.

86. Baillie and Hamilton to Davenport, St. Vincent, June 12, 1784, Davenport Papers, MMM.

87. Lovejoy and Richardson, "'Horrid Hole,'" 380n62.

88. Crosbies and Trafford to Capt. Ambrose Lace, Liverpool, Apr. 14, 1762, in Williams, *Liverpool Privateers*, 486. See also Behrendt, "Markets," 196, 200.

89. Lovejoy and Richardson, "'Horrid Hole,'" 380n62.

90. Behrendt, "Markets," 200; Behrendt, "Ecology," 80.

91. Donnan, *Documents*, 2:590.

92. Behrendt, "Ecology," 59, 474n80.

93. See, for example, Lovejoy and Richardson, "Slaves to Palm Oil," 13–29.

94. Lynn, *Commerce*, 13, 18, 72–73, assuming that comey increases at Old Calabar followed the more than twofold increase in palm oil shipments, from 1820 (2,000 tons) to ca. 1850 (4,000–5,000 tons).

Chapter 4

1. In Antera Duke's day, speakers of Efik, Ibibio, Anang, and other mutually intelligible dialects had no name for their common language, although linguists now call it Efik (the first dialect to be recorded), Ibibio (the largest dialect), or Efik-Ibibio. Speakers of the many distinct dialects of what is now called Igbo were similarly dis-

aggregated in the eighteenth century but have embraced a common name and identity in the past century.

2. On October 14, 1786, "Egbo Sherry Sam Ambo," an Ibibio, captured seven men, and he and his people were coming toward Old Calabar in about twenty canoes.

3. *Abridgment of the Minutes*, 3:53; Lambert, *Commons Sessional Papers*, 73:126–127.

4. See, for example, diary entries July? 1, 1785; Jan. 29, 1786; Apr. 20, 1786. A Liverpool captain's account from 1769 refers to Antera Duke as "King of Warr," a moniker linked perhaps to his valor in small battles against Efik or non-Efik African rivals.

5. Waddell, *Twenty-nine Years*, 243; cf. Goldie, *Dictionary*, 359, entry for "Itu."

6. Earlier, on April 21, 1785, Antera's "first Boy" (head slave) returned to Duke Town from Ikot Offiong with a slave.

7. Goldie, *Dictionary*, 359, entry for "Inokun" (= Aro); interview with Chief Kanju Oji, Eze Aro of Arochukwu, Dec. 12, 1972; interview with Chief Ekpenyong Ibah, Ikot Nya Asaya, Enyong, Dec. 19, 1972.

8. Northrup, *Trade without Rulers*, provides a more detailed analysis of the chronological development of parts of these hinterland networks.

9. Ibid., 119–129; Latham, *Old Calabar*, 27–29.

10. Lovejoy and Richardson, "Letters," 109, though Efik likely wrote "place" as "places" (few Efik pluralized words).

11. Hallett, *Records*, 203.

12. In the first edition of the diary, Donald Simmons suggested that Antera Duke meant Mbiabo when he wrote Boostam (Simmons, "Notes," 69n26), but other sources nearer the time explicitly identify that term with Umon: Goldie, *Dictionary*, 361, entry for "Umon," and Walker, "Notes," 137. Another Scottish Presbyterian missionary, Waddell, *Twenty-nine Years*, 286, concurs with Goldie that Umon Town controlled the traffic from above and below the river.

13. Latham, "Pre-colonial Economy," 82; Northrup, *Trade without Rulers*, 216–217.

14. The palaver angered old Ekpe members, who then ordered all new Ekpe members, including Long Dick Ephraim, to sleep at the Ekpe palaver house. Apparently Long Dick violated some protocol.

15. See Harris, "History," 122–139. Koelle, *Polyglotta*, 10–11, 19, records the biographies of several informants from this region, including a man from the Boki, east of Ikom, who was captured about 1830 and sold from Old Calabar. For more detail on their origins, see Winston, "Nigerian Cross River Languages," 78 (1964) and 126 (1965). Dating these events is difficult. It may be that this route opened in the nineteenth century rather than the eighteenth: in 1805, according to Nicholls, "Howatt [Uwet] trades with Old Calabar people for nothing but yams" (Hallett, *Records*, 204).

16. Perhaps she returned with a dead slave to prove that the transaction had taken place.

17. W. D. Horsall & Co. to Captain Peter Comberbach, Liverpool, Dec. 27, 1781, Davenport Papers, MMM.

18. Koelle, *Polyglotta*, 12–13, 20. Dalby, "Provisional Identification," 87, identifies Ngoala with Bangongola and Param with Bagam, a place in Bamilele. See also McCulloch, Littlewood, and Dugast, *Peoples of the Central Cameroons*, 53, 59. The Tipala included Chamba, Bali, Fulani, and others.

19. Goldie, *Dictionary*, 353, entry for "Adadop" (= Ododop), says, "from Calabar, two days are spent travelling on the river, and one on land, when the village of Ekonganaku [Ekundukundu] is reached; and in another day's journey, Nkuru [Nguru]. A third day's journey on land brings the traveller to the Qua [Kwa] people in this direction, to the village named Esokhi, from which it is one day's journey to Mba-ofong; one day's journey to Mba-obe; and one and a half days' journey to Eyefen." A misprint in Goldie's entry for "Mbudikom" (*Dictionary*, 359–360) puts this place southeast rather than northeast of Old Calabar, but many of the place-names he lists there can be identified with Cameroon grassland communities: Ebafusep (= Bafussam, a part of the Bamilike, 30:1), Bamingkam (Bamekom, a name for Kom, 30:5), Baham (a part of Bamelike, 30:1), Bangang (a Bamelike town), Bamanshu (= Bamendjou, a Bamalike chiefdom), *Banda* (29:16), Bangwa (a part of Bamileke, 30:1), Mbe (a name for Bakongwang). Identifications containing numerals are based on Murdock, *Africa*. Bamendjou is listed in McCulloch, Littlewood, and Dugast, *Peoples of the Central Cameroons*, 88. The identification of Mbe is based on Dalby, "Provisional Identification," 87.

20. Goldie, *Dictionary*, 360, entry for "Mbudikom"; Great Britain, *Parliamentary Papers* 1859 xxxiv (2569-I), Hutchinson to Malmesbury, May 25, 1858, 17. For more information, see Chilver, "Nineteenth Century Trade," 233–258. "Esu[k] Orrorup" appears at the first falls on the Akpa Yafe River on H. H. Johnston's "Map of the Rio del Rey and the District Lying between Old Calabar and the Cameroons Mountains," 1888, FO84/1882/92, NA.

21. Forsyth to James Rogers, Old Calabar, July 9, 1792, C107/13, NA.

22. See appendix B.

23. Diary entries Apr. 11, 1785; July? 24, 1785; Sept.? 14, 1785; Jan. 24, 1787; Mar. 3, 1787.

24. One unnamed Bakasi "genllmen" ("gentleman"), who feared to come to Duke Town when Duke Ephraim was alive, visited the town on August 9, 1786, a month after Duke Ephraim's death. Antera and others placed this Bakasi gentleman and two of his slaves immediately in irons and carried him to a slaving ship. Antera "carry hi[m] on bord my self."

25. On November 9, 1786, during funeral obsequies for Duke Ephraim, one "TaEon town" man cut off the head of a "Backsider town" man.

26. In the 1880s the Germans extended coastal "Cameroon" far inland. German Kamerun was later divided into French- and British-administered territories and now mostly reunited as the Republic of Cameroon.

27. Northrup, *Trade without Rulers*, 191n41.

28. See Ross's map and journal in *United Presbyterian Church Missionary Record*, May 1, 1880, 149–152; Aug. 1, 1877, 605; Sept. 1877, 631–632. A better map of Ross's travels is in Langhans, "Vergessene Reisen," 48, 73–78, tafel 7.

29. Goldie, *Dictionary*, 357, entry for "Efut"; Koelle, *Polyglotta*, 13. Duala traders of the Cameroon estuary acquired other slaves from their own densely populated coastal hinterland. A map of the region, drawn a century after the diary, shows "many slave

markets" among the Basaa along the Dibamba River. "Sketch Map of the Cameroons Region Illustrating Its Chief Physical Features," enclosed in No. 13, Vice-Consul H. H. Johnston to Earl of Iddesleigh, June 17, 1886, FO403/73, NA. Cf. Austen and Derrick, *Middlemen*, 23–25; Lovejoy and Richardson, "Competing Markets," 261–293.

30. Goldie, *Dictionary*, 357, entry for *Efut*. The quote is from Roger Casement to Macdonald, July 18, 1894, quoted in Anene, *International Boundaries*, 62. Bira's story is in Koelle, *Polyglotta*, 19.

31. For Andam Nothing's journeys, see diary entries Oct. 14, 1786; Dec. 11, 1787.

32. Hallett, *Records*, 204.

33. Goldie, *Dictionary*, 354–361, entries for "Efik," "Ekri-tobacco," and "Idua." Goldie lists a number of villages of Adua that can be identified with existing settlements: Afakhaeduek (= Afaha Eduok, south of Esuk Oron), Asang (= Udua Asan, northwest of Oron Town, near Atabong), Ukpata (= Ukpata, south of Afaha Eduok). In Antera Duke's day Idua was clearly distinguished from Oron (Goldie's Adon) of which it was classified as part in the twentieth century. Little is known of the trading history of these peoples before their involvement in the palm oil trade of the nineteenth century; see Lieber, *Efik*, 58–64.

34. Latham, *Old Calabar*, 28, suggests that Nicholls meant Bakasi, the marshy territory east of the mouth of the Cross River mouth. For the Old Calabar slave trade from the Niger Delta area, see Talbot, *Life*, 335; E. H. F. Gorges, "Intelligence Report on the Ubium Clan of the Eket Division, Calabar Province," 1935, 5, Nigerian National Archive, Ibadan, Colonial Secretary's Office 26/4/32351.

35. Of ten "Moko" informants taken later in the decade who specified the port from which they had been sold, seven were from Old Calabar and three from Cameroon; Koelle, *Polyglotta*, 11–13. The possibility that the *Esperença Felis* had loaded its slaves at Cameroon is made still less likely by the very high proportion of Igbo slaves.

36. Koelle, *Polyglotta*, 11–12, 20.

37. Ibid., 7, 10–11, 18, reports that speakers of the Ibo [Igbo] language had no national name for themselves, and many had never even heard the name before coming to Sierra Leone; that Europeans used the name Calabar for speakers of the Efik language, all of whom called themselves by other names; and that Atam and Moko were also identity labels used by outsiders that were meaningless to these people in their homelands. Two of Koelle's informants from the Moko cluster of languages had each spent three years in captivity in Old Calabar before being sold abroad and so would have spoken Efik readily.

38. Northrup, "Igbo," 2.

39. Butterworth, *Three Years Adventure*, 85. For other citations and a discussion of some interpretative issues see Northrup, "Igbo," 1–3.

40. See Northrup, *Trade without Rulers*, 66–67; King, "Details," 266; "Hugh Goldie's Journal 27 January 1858," *Missionary Record* 13 (Sept. 1, 1858): 161; Waddell, *Twenty-nine Years*, 372–373.

41. Latham, *Old Calabar*, 38.

Chapter 5

1. We did compare, however, the surviving copy of Wilkie's typed transcription (ca. 1951) with the version printed by Oxford University Press in 1956. We corrected one printer error: the published diary entry of 1.8.1787 (Aug. 1, 1787) states "to fend about" instead of "to send about."

2. Wilkie to Forde, Oct. 20, 1951, *Efik Traders* book file, IAI.

3. Williams, *Liverpool Privateers*, 543–549, 553.

4. D/Earle/3, MMM.

5. Wilkie typescript, MS Box 27.5, The Library, New College, University of Edinburgh.

6. Peter Potter to William Davenport, July 23, 1785, Davenport Papers, MMM.

7. A seventy-two-day outward passage from Liverpool to Calabar falls within the sixty- to eighty-day average trip, a fact that also tells us that at least two "July" entries documenting ship arrivals refer to ones arriving one month later, in August. The Liverpool slavers *Tarleton* and *President* departed the Mersey on June 23 and 28, 1785, and are mentioned first by Antera Duke on July 19 (*President*) and July 23 (*Tarleton*). The *Tarleton*, though, arrived August 14, 1785 (Potter to Davenport, Aug. 17, 1785, Davenport Papers, MMM). Guineamen did not make the outward voyage from Liverpool to the Cross River in less than a month. Newspapers occasionally specify sailing dates, thus helping to verify Antera's diary information. The *Gascoyne*, Captain Comberbach, for example, arrived "off the Bar of Bonny 22d May [1785], all well" (*Liverpool General Advertiser*, Sept. 8, 1785). Antera notes that the captain arrived in the Lower Cross River four days later.

8. Antera's information concerning captains' arrivals and comey collection helps verify that diary entries proceed chronologically. Captains, such as Peter Comberbach, would have arrived first in Parrot Island (May 26, 1785), twenty miles downstream of Old Calabar, before disembarking at the Duke Town landing (June 24, 1785). Captain Potter arrived at Calabar on June 25, 1785, and then Efik merchants would have boarded the ship to take comey (later entry, though transcribed June 2). Captain Cooper had moored downstream off Seven Fathoms Point (June 25, 1785), and then Antera Duke and others would have taken comey (later entry, though transcribed June 8, 1785). Our assumption is that many of Antera's June and July 1785 dates, as transcribed by Wilkie, refer to July and August dates.

9. Wilkie, introduction to the Antera Duke Diary, dated June 26, 1951; Wilkie to Forde, Sept. 9, 1951, *Efik Traders* book file, IAI.

10. The diary and transcription are most comprehensive during the week of November 6, 1786 (daily recordings). Regarding the diary period June 15–29, 1785, Wilkie transcribed entries for eleven of fifteen days—though there are dating errors here. Gaps in the diary may refer to times when Antera journeyed from Duke Town without his ledger.

11. *Hector* accounts, 1776, f. 170, Davenport Papers, MMM. Similarly, in 1771 the owners of the *Lord Cassils* loaded two boxes containing eight reams "Pot Paper" and

"60 Books 1 Q:^{re} [quire] ea[ch] with Marble Covers," and the *May* (1771) shipped two reams writing paper, two books, four quires each, half-bound and lettered, and six books, three quires each, half-bound and lettered. Merchants thus exported ledgers of standard sizes.

12. Higman, *Plantation Jamaica*, 115.

13. One supposes that an English-language learner would not write in small characters.

14. Wilkie to Forde Sept. 9, 1951, *Efik Traders* book file, IAI.

15. Antera may have jotted "funchmen" because of their novelty—the English embarked the majority of slaves in Old Calabar and only English captains may have traded with Antera Duke.

16. Diary entries Feb. 14, 1785; Dec. 22, 1785.

17. Wilkie suffered from dementia or Alzheimer's disease late in life (letter from Marian B. Wilkie to Mrs. Wyatt, Secretary of the IAI, North Berwick, Aug. 25, 1955, *Efik Traders* book file, IAI); though his correspondence in 1951 is lucid, perhaps his forgetfulness had started.

18. CO76/5, f. 6, NA; *Liverpool General Advertiser*, June 26, 1788.

19. Wilkie to Forde, Sept. 9, 1951, *Efik Traders* book file, IAI.

20. Hair, "Antera Duke," 363n2.

21. As Wilkie remarked, during his tenure in Calabar he "made a special study of the Efik language—particularly with the guidance and help of my great friend Chief Eyo Efiom" (Wilkie to Forde, Edinburgh, Oct. 20, 1951, *Efik Traders* book file, IAI).

22. Simmons to Forde, June 28, 1954, Nov. 19, 1954, *Efik Traders* book file, IAI.

23. In *Efik Traders of Old Calabar*, editor Daryll Forde separated the "modern English version" of Antera Duke's diary (27–65), the notes to the diary (66–78), and the original diary extracts (79–115).

24. Hence we (1) removed "so" when Antera used this subordinating conjunction as an adverbial clause to indicate a sequential relationship; (2) retained "so" in the translation when Antera used this word to indicate a causal relationship. To standardize the translation of Antera Duke's sentence structure, we removed the conjunction "with" and rendered his time references consistent. For example, Wilkie and Simmons translated "7 clock night" as "7 o'clock at night," whereas "3 clock noon" translated as "at 3 o'clock noon"—we preferred "3 o'clock in the afternoon." Similarly, we added "in the morning," when applicable.

25. See diary entry July? 8, 1785.

26. Peter Potter to William Davenport & Company, Cameroon, Nov. 22, 1776, Davenport Papers, MMM.

27. Asuquo, "Diary," 41; Hallett, *Records*, 204; Waddell, *Twenty-nine Years*, map facing 242; Latham, *Old Calabar*, frontispiece.

28. See chapter 1.

29. Goldie, *Dictionary*, 283. See also chapter 1 regarding how chiefs "made lowly reverence" before King Calabar.

30. Williams, *Liverpool Privateers*, 546. Of course, the English vocabulary learned

by Efik merchants may differ—Ephraim Robin John, for example, used more sophisticated verbs and nouns, correctly spelling "acquaint" and "acquaintances," and attempting the difficult words "encouragement" (spelled "In Curigement") and "civility" ("Sivellety"). He also employed sophisticated verbs such as to vex, hoist, cast, prevent, write, ought, consult, and insist. Antera had learned a more simplified vocabulary.

Appendix A

1. The five women: Andam Ephraim, Awa Ofiong, Pip, Eba, and Mbong. Several other people are mentioned as wives, brothers, sisters, fathers, sons, or daughters.

2. Simmons, "Notes," 67n7. In 1847 missionary Hope Waddell learned that "[a]n object of universal reverence as a household idol was the *Ekpenyong*, a stick surmounted by a human skull, adorned with feathers, and daubed with yellow paint. It was an ugly thing, but supposed to possess great virtue in benefiting those who possessed it" (Waddell, *Twenty-nine Years*, 329).

3. It is curious, though, that Egbo Young Ofiong and Egbo Young Antera are never mentioned together in a diary entry, such as when Antera Duke lists those Efik dining together on Christmas or New Year's Day.

4. On January 1, 1787, and January 1, 1788, the party was at Egbo Young Ofiong's house, and on Christmas Day 1787, Duke Ephraim hosted the captains and Efik gentlemen. Thus something has clearly changed in the political balance. Esien Duke is also not listed as receiving Ekpe payments on October 31, 1787. He seems to have been in the second tier of big men at Old Calabar.

Appendix B

1. In January 1786 Antera heard that Egbo Young Ofiong's wife gave birth at "Aqua Town." Antera begins many dawns at "aqua Landing"—the big beach downhill from New Town—known to Europeans by the 1780s, as "Duke Town." The Efik adjective *akwa* means "big" or sometimes "old" (Goldie, *Dictionary*, 18).

2. Efik also traveled to Bakasi to buy canoes (see diary entry Nov. 1, 1787).

3. Langhans, "Vergessene Reisen."

4. *UPCMR*, Sept. 1, 1877, 631–32.

5. Ibid., 632.

6. *UPCMR*, Aug. 1, 1877, 605–608, Sept. 1, 1877, 629–633.

7. *UPCMR*, Nov. 1, 1879, 690–693, Dec. 1, 1879, 711–714.

Bibliography

Manuscript Sources

ARCHIVO HISTORICO ULTRAMARINO, LISBON
Cx. 49, D. 33

BRISTOL RECORD OFFICE
Bristol ships' muster rolls, 1783–1795, Society of Merchant Venturers

BRITISH LIBRARY
Add MS 39946, *Florida* account, 1714

DALEMAIN HOUSE, CUMBRIA
Hasell MS, *Dobson* Calabar account, 1769–1770

FAMILY HISTORY LIBRARY, SALT LAKE CITY, UTAH
Wills Proved at the Prerogative Court of Chester, 1774

FOREIGN MISSION OFFICE, CHURCH OF SCOTLAND, EDINBURGH
Arthur W. Wilkie file

HOUGHTON LIBRARY, HARVARD UNIVERSITY
A Full and True Relation of the Elephant That is brought over into England from the Indies, and Landed at London, August 3d. 1675, Bute Broadside

INTERNATIONAL AFRICAN INSTITUTE, UNIVERSITY OF LONDON
Efik Traders book file

THE LIBRARY, NEW COLLEGE, UNIVERSITY OF EDINBURGH
MS Box 27.5, "The Diary of Antera Duke" (typescript transcription)
MS Box 40, Missionary Curios
MS Box 52.5, Wilkie file, Foreign Mission Office, Church of Scotland, Edinburgh
MS Box 52.5.6, Missionary Curios

LIVERPOOL RECORD OFFICE
Holt and Gregson Papers, 942 HOL 10
Tuohy Papers, 380 TUO 2

MERSEYSIDE MARITIME MUSEUM
Davenport Papers, 1747–1785, D/DAV/1
Earle Papers, 1751, D/EARLE/1, 3
Letter from Egbo Young Ofiong to Captain John Burrows, July 23, 1783, DX/1304
Liverpool ship registers, C/EX/L/3/4

NATIONAL ARCHIVES OF SCOTLAND, EDINBURGH
AC9/1042, *Hannover* accounts, 1720

NATIONAL LIBRARY OF SCOTLAND, EDINBURGH
MS 7739, Hope Waddell diary, 1846

NATIONAL ARCHIVES, LONDON, KEW
BT98/35–69, Liverpool ships' muster rolls, 1775–1809
CO76/5, Dominica shipping lists, 1788
CO106/2–4, Grenada shipping lists, 1785–1787
C107/5–6, 12–13, James Rogers Papers, 1787–1792

UNIVERSITY OF EDINBURGH, SPECIAL COLLECTIONS
Elizabeth Marwick diary, 1892–1894, Gen 768/3–8

UNIVERSITY OF LIVERPOOL, SIDNEY JONES LIBRARY
MS 24.37, *Hamilton* logbook, 1830

Official Sources

NATIONAL ARCHIVES, KEW
FO84/1882, H. H. Johnston. "Report on the British Protectorate of the Oil Rivers (Niger Delta)." Johnston to Salisbury, Dec. 1, 1888.
Great Britain. *Parliamentary Papers* 1816 viii (506). Select Committee Report on African Settlements and Forts, Part II.
Great Britain. *Parliamentary Papers* 1859 xxxiv (2569-I). Hutchinson to Malmesbury, May 25, 1858, 17.

NIGERIAN NATIONAL ARCHIVE, IBADAN
Gorges, E. H. F. "Intelligence Report on the Ubium Clan of the Eket Division, Calabar Province." Colonial Secretary's Office 1935, 5, 26/4/32351.

Newspapers

Billinge's Liverpool Advertiser, 1794–1802

Gore's Liverpool General Advertiser, 1790–1798, 1800, 1805

Liverpool General Advertiser, 1765–1769, 1784–1789

Liverpool Trade List, 1798–1800, 1802, 1807, 1808

Lloyd's List, 1774

Manchester Mercury, 1752–1808

Nigerian Chronicle, April 20, 1977

Reed's Weekly Journal, 1759

Whitehall Evening Post, August 12–14, 1729

Williamson's Liverpool Advertiser and Mercantile Chronicle, 1780

Maps

Langhans, P. "Vergessene Reisen in Kamerun. 1. Reisen des Missionars Alexander Ross von Alt-Kalabar nach Efut 1877 und 1878." *Petermanns Geographische Mitteilungen* 48 (1902): 73–78, Tafel 7.

van Keulen, Joannes. "Map of West Africa from the Benin Bend to Cape Formosa," ca. 1675–1715. www.nationaalarchief.nl/AML, Atlas of Mutual Heritage.

"Sketch Map of the Cameroons Region Illustrating Its Chief Physical Features." Enclosed in No. 13, Vice-Consul H.H. Johnston to Earl of Iddesleigh, June 17, 1886. FO403/73, NA.

"The Entrance of Old Calebar by Cap. Pat. Fairweather 1790." *Marine Charts* 1 (1807), MR 14.C.77 (68), RGSL.

Directories

Gore's Liverpool Directory, 1774

Matthews' New Bristol Directory, 1793

The Parents and Guardians Directory, London, 1761

Sketchley's Bristol Directory, 1775

Web Sites

The Letters of John Paige, London Merchant, 1648–58: London Record Society 21 (1984), 57–82, http://www.british-history.ac.uk/.

Mason, Shena. "Birmingham: 'The Toyshop of Europe,'" 1–15. *Revolutionary Players*, http://www.revolutionaryplayers.org.uk.

Proceedings of the Old Bailey, http://www.oldbaileyonline.org.

Voyages: The Trans-Atlantic Slave Trade, http://www.slavevoyages.org.

"Anglo-African Trade, 1699–1808," http://easy.dans.knaw.nl/dms

Published Accounts

Abridgment of the Minutes of Evidence (Taken before a Committee of the whole House, to whom it was referred to consider of the Slave Trade). 3 vols. London, 1789–1791.

Adams, John. *Remarks on the Country Extending from Cape Palmas to the River Congo*. 1823. Reprint, London: Cass, 1966.

The African Pilot, or, Sailing Directions for the West Coast of Africa. 2 vols. London, 1856.

Arthy, Elliot. *Introductory Observations in Favor of the African Slave Trade*. Liverpool: T. Milner, 1804.

Bell, James. *A System of Geography, Popular and Scientific, or a Physical, Political, and Statistical Account of the World and Its Various Divisions*. 3 vols. Glasgow: Archibald Fullarton and Co., 1832.

Bold, Edward. *The Merchant's and Mariner's African Guide*. London: J. W. Norie and Co., 1822.

Butterworth, William [pseud. for Henry Schroeder]. *Three Years Adventures, of a Minor, in England, Africa, the West Indies, South-Carolina and Georgia*. Leeds: Edward Barnes, 1822.

Crow, Hugh. *Memoirs of the Late Captain Hugh Crow of Liverpool*. 1830. Reprint, London: Cass, 1970.

Durand, J. P. L. *Voyage to Senegal*. London: J. G. Barnard/Richard Phillips, 1806. In *A Collection of Modern and Contemporary Voyages and Travels*, 11 vols. London, 1804–1817.

Enfield, William. *An Essay towards the History of Leverpool, Drawn up from papers Left by the Late G. Perry, and from other Materials*. Warrington, 1773.

An Exact List of the Votes of the Freeholders and Freemen, of the City and County of Bristol. Bristol: Joseph Penn, 1722.

Falconer, William. *The Mariner's New and Complete Naval Dictionary*, ed. J. W. Norie. London: J. Badcock, 1804.

Goldie, Hugh. *Dictionary of the Efik Language*. Glasgow: Dunn and Wright, 1862. Reprint, Farnborough: Gregg Press, 1964.

———. *Calabar and Its Mission*. Edinburgh and London: Oliphant Anderson and Ferrier, 1890.

———. *Memoir of King Eyo VII of Old Calabar*. Old Calabar: United Presbyterian Mission Press, 1894.

Grosse, Francis. *Classical Dictionary of the Vulgar Tongue*. London: S. Hooper, 1785.

Hair, P. E. H., Adam Jones, and Robin Law, ed. *Barbot on Guinea: The Writings of Jean Barbot on West Africa, 1678–1712*, 2 vols. London: Hakluyt Society, 1992.

Hallett, Robin, ed. *Records of the African Association, 1788–1831*. London: Thomas Nelson, 1964.

Holman, James. *Travels in Madeira, Sierra Leone, Teneriffe, St. Jago, Cape Coast, Fernando Po, Princes Island, Etc., Etc.* London: George Routledge, 1840.

"Hugh Goldie's Journal 27 January 1858." *Missionary Record* 13 (September 1, 1858).

Hutchinson, Thomas Joseph. *Impressions of Western Africa. With Remarks on the Diseases of the Climate and a Report on the Peculiarities of Trade up the Rivers in the Bight of Biafra*. London: Longmans, 1858. Reprint, London: Frank Cass, 1970.

King, J. B. "Details of Explorations of the Old Calabar River, in 1841 and 1842 by Captain Beecroft . . . and Mr. J. B. King." *Journal of the Royal Geographical Society* 14 (1844): 260–283.

Koelle, S. W. *Polyglotta Africana*. London: Church Missionary House, 1854.

Lambert, Sheila, ed. *House of Commons Sessional Papers of the Eighteenth Century*. 145 vols. Wilmington, Del.: Scholarly Resources, 1975.

A List of Free-Holders and Free-Men. Bristol: Felix Farley, 1734.

Liverpool and Slavery: An Historical Account of the Liverpool-African Slave Trade . . . by a Genuine "Dicky Sam." 1884. Reprint, Liverpool: Scouse Press, 1985.

The Liverpool Memorandum-Book; or, Gentleman's, Merchant's and Tradesman's Daily Pocket-Journal for the Year MDCCLIII. Liverpool: R. Williamson, 1753.

Marees, Pieter de. *Description and Historical Account of the Gold Kingdom of Guinea (1602)*. Trans. and ed. Albert Van Dantzig and Adam Jones. London: Oxford University Press, 1987.

Marwick, William. *William and Louisa Anderson: A Record of Their Life and Work in Jamaica and Old Calabar*. Edinburgh: Andrew Elliot, 1897.

Mortimer, Thomas. *A New and Complete Dictionary of Trade and Commerce*. 2 vols. London: Printed for the author, and sold by S. Crowder, and J. Coote, and J. Fletcher, 1767.

Report of the Lords of the Committee of Council Appointed for the Consideration of all Matters Relating to Trade and Foreign Plantations. London, 1789.

Robertson, G. A. *Notes on Africa; particularly those Parts which are Situated between Cape Verd and the River Congo*. London: Sherwood, Neely, and Jones, 1819.

Snelgrave, Captain William. *A New Account of Some Ports of Guinea, and the Slave Trade*. 1734. Reprint, London: Frank Cass, 1971.

Told, Silas. *An Account of the Life, and Dealings of God with Silas Told*. London: Gilbert and Plummer, 1786.

A Treatise upon the Trade from Great Britain to Africa. London: R. Baldwin, 1772.

United Presbyterian Church Missionary Record. Edinburgh, 1848, 1877–1880

Waddell, Reverend Hope Masterton. *Twenty-nine Years in the West Indies and Central Africa: A Review of Missionary Work and Adventure, 1829–1858*. London: T. Nelson and Sons, 1863. Reprint, London: Frank Cass, 1970.

Watts, John. "A True Relation of the Inhuman and Unparalleled Actions, and Barbarous Murders, of Negroes and Moors, Committed on Three Englishmen in Old Calabar in Guiney." In *Harleian Collection of Voyages and Travels*, 2 vols. London, 1745–1747.

Secondary Sources

[Anon]. "Drum." *Ikorok*, Bulletin of the Institute of African Studies, University of Nigeria. 1 (July 1971–Mar. 1972).

[Anon]. *The Record* 210 (June 1918).

[Anon]. *Life and Work. The Record of the Church of Scotland* 15 (1944), 135 (1957).

Abalogu, U. N. "Ekpe Society in Arochukwu and Bende." *Nigeria Magazine* 126–127 (1978): 78–97.

Afigbo, A. E. "Pre-colonial Trade Links between Southeastern Nigeria and the Benue Valley." *Journal of African Studies* 4 (1977): 119–139.

Akak, Eyo Okon. *A Critique of Old Calabar History.* Calabar: Ikot Offiong Welfare Association, 1981.

———. *Efiks of Old Calabar.* 4 vols. Calabar: Akak and Sons, 1981–1983.

Alpern, Stanley B. "What Africans Got for Their Slaves: A Master List of European Trade Goods." *History in Africa* 22 (1995): 5–43.

Amadi, I. R. "Palm Oil Trade in the Bight of Biafra before the Abolition." *Nigeria Magazine* 57, nos. 1–2 (Jan.–June 1989): 54–61.

Anene, J. C. *The International Boundaries of Nigeria.* New York: Humanities Press, 1970.

Asuquo, Chief Ukorebi U. "The Diary of Antera Duke of Old Calabar (1785–1788)." *Calabar Historical Journal* 2 (June 1978): 32–54.

Austen, Ralph A., and Jonathan Derrick. *Middlemen of the Cameroon Rivers: The Duala and Their Hinterland, c. 1600–c. 1960.* Cambridge: Cambridge University Press, 1999.

Austen, Ralph, and K. Jacob. "Dutch Trading Voyages to Cameroon, 1721–1759: European Documents and African History." *Annales de la Faculté des Lettres et Sciences Humaines, Université de Yaoundé* 6 (1974): 5–44.

Aye, E. U. "Efik Origins and Migrations Revisited: The 'Oriental View.'" In *Old Calabar Revisited,* ed. S. O. Jaja, E. O. Erim, and B. W. Andah, 5–10. Enugu: Harris Publishers, 1990.

Bassey, Nnimo. "The Architecture of Old Calabar." In *Old Calabar Revisited,* ed. S. O. Jaja, E. O. Erim, and B. W. Andah, 123–36. Enugu: Harris Publishers, 1990.

Bastian, Misty L. "Married in the Water: Spirit Kin and Other Afflictions of Modernity in Southeastern Nigeria." *Journal of Religion in Africa* 27, no. 2 (1997): 116–134.

Beckinsale, R. P. "Factors in the Development of the Cotswold Woollen Industry." *Geographical Journal* 90, no. 4 (1937): 349–362.

Behrendt, Stephen D. "The Captains in the British Slave Trade from 1785 to 1807." *Transactions of the Historic Society of Lancashire and Cheshire* 140 (1991): 79–140.

———. "The Annual Volume and Regional Distribution of the British Slave Trade, 1780–1807." *Journal of African History* 38 (1997): 187–211.

———. "Markets, Transaction Cycles and Profits: Merchant Decision Making in the British Slave Trade." *William and Mary Quarterly* 63 (2001): 173–204.

———. "Ecology, Seasonality and the Transatlantic Slave Trade." In *Soundings in Atlantic History: Latent Structures and Intellectual Currents, 1500–1830,* ed. Bernard Bailyn and Patricia L. Denault, 44–85, 461–485. Cambridge: Harvard University Press, 2009.

Behrendt, Stephen D., and Eric J. Graham. "African Merchants, Notables and the Slave Trade at Old Calabar, 1720: Evidence from the National Archives of Scotland." *History in Africa* 30 (2003): 37–61.

Brásio, António, ed. *Monumenta Missionaria Africana. Africa Occidental (1471–1531).* 20 vols. Lisbon: Agência Geral do Ultramar, Divisão de Publicações e Biblioteca, 1952–1988.

Cameron, Nigel M. de S., et al., eds. *Dictionary of Scottish Church History and Theology.* Downers Grove, Ill.: InterVarsity Press, 1993.

Chilver, E. M. "Nineteenth Century Trade in the Bamenda Grassfields, Southern Cameroons." *Afrika und Übersee* 45 (1962): 233–258.

Clinton, J. V. "King Eyo Honesty II of Creek Town." *Nigeria Magazine* 69 (August 1961): 182–190.

Cookey, S. J. S. *King Jaja of the Niger Delta: His Life and Times, 1821–1891.* New York: NOK, 1974.

Dalby, David. "Provisional Identification of Languages in the *Polyglotta Africana*." *Sierra Leone Language Review* 3 (1964): 83–90.

den Heijer, Henk. *Goud, Ivoor en Slaven: Scheepvaart en Handel van de Tweede Westindische Compagnie op Afrika, 1674–1740.* Zutphen: Walburg Pers, 1997.

Donnan, Elizabeth, ed. *Documents Illustrative of the History of the Slave Trade to America.* 4 vols. Washington, D.C.: Carnegie Institution of Washington, 1930–1935.

Eltis, David, Stephen D. Behrendt, David Richardson, and Herbert S. Klein, eds. *The Trans-Atlantic Slave Trade: A Database on CD-ROM.* New York: Cambridge University Press, 1999.

Eltis, David, Paul E. Lovejoy, and David Richardson. "Slave-Trading Ports: Towards an Atlantic-Wide Perspective, 1672–1832." In *Ports of the Slave Trade (Bights of Benin and Biafra)*, ed. Robin Law and Silke Strickrodt, 18–25. University of Stirling, Occasional Paper Number 6, October 1999.

Eltis, David, and David Richardson. "Productivity in the Transatlantic Slave Trade." *Explorations in Economic History* 32 (1995): 465–484.

Fairlie, Susan. "Dyestuffs in the Eighteenth Century." *Economic History Review*, n.s., 17, no. 3 (1965): 488–510.

Fayer, Joan M. "Pidgins as Written Languages: Evidence from 18th Century Old Calabar." *Anthropological Linguistics: Exploring the Languages of the World* 28 (1986): 313–319.

———. "Nigerian Pidgin English in Old Calabar in the 18th and 19th Centuries." In *Pidgin and Creole Tense-Mood-Aspect Systems*, ed. John Victor Singler, 185–202. Amsterdam: Benjamins, 1990.

Feinberg, Harvey M., and Marion Johnson. "The West African Ivory Trade during the Eighteenth Century: The ' . . . and Ivory' Complex." *International Journal of African Historical Studies* 15 (1982): 435–453.

Forde, Daryll, ed. *Efik Traders of Old Calabar.* London: Oxford University Press, 1956.

———. *Yakö Studies.* London: Oxford University Press, 1964.

Görach, Manfred. "Texts: Broken English from Old Calabar." *English World-Wide* 15 (1994): 249–252.

[H_____], J. M. "Barwood (Pterocarpus Soyauxii, Taub.)." *Bulletin of Miscellaneous Information (Royal Gardens, Kew)* 1906, no. 9 (1906): 373–375.

Hackett, Rosalind I. J. *Religion in Calabar: The Religious Life and History of a Nigerian Town.* Berlin and New York: Mouton de Gruyter, 1989.

Hair, P. E. H. "A Note on Early References to 'Calabar.'" *Journal of Niger Delta Studies* 1 (1977): 127–128.

———. "Antera Duke of Old Calabar: A Little More about an African Entrepreneur." *History in Africa* 17 (1990): 359–365.

Halgan, Georges. "A bord du navire négriere nantias 'le Mars' vers l'Afrique et vers la Guyane, 1791–1793." *Bulletin de la Société Archéologique et Historique de Nantes et de la Loire-Inférieure* 78 (1938): 52–65.

Harris, Rosemary. "The History of Trade at Ikom, Eastern Nigeria." *Africa* 42 (1972): 122–139.

Hart, A. K. *Report of the Enquiry into the Dispute over the Obongship of Calabar, Official Document 17.* Enugu, Eastern Nigeria: Govt. Printer, 1964.

Herve, Bruno. "Quelques aspects de la traite négrière nantaise, 1772–1778." *Cahiers des Anneaux de la Mémoire* 1 (1999): 45–57.

Higman, B. W. *Plantation Jamaica, 1750–1850: Capital and Control in a Colonial Economy.* Kingston, Jamaica: University of the West Indies Press, 2005.

Hodgkin, Thomas, ed. *Nigerian Perspectives: An Historical Anthology.* London: Oxford University Press, 1960.

———, ed. *Nigerian Perspectives: An Historical Anthology.* 2nd ed. London: Oxford University Press, 1975.

Huber, Magnus, and Manfred Görach. "Texts: West African Pidgin English." *English World-Wide* 17 (1996): 239–258.

Inikori, Joseph E. *Africans and the Industrial Revolution in England: A Study in International Trade and Economic Development.* Cambridge: Cambridge University Press, 2002.

———. "The Development of Entrepreneurship in Africa: Southeastern Nigeria during the Era of the Trans-Atlantic Slave Trade." In *Black Business and Economic Power,* ed. Alusine Jalloh and Toyin Falola, 41–79. Rochester, N.Y.: University of Rochester Press, 2002.

Jackson, Roland, ed. *Journal of a Residence in Bonny River on Board the Ship Kingston During the Months of January, February and March 1826, by R. M. Jackson.* Letchworth, Hertfordshire, 1934.

Johnson, Marion. "By Ship or by Camel: The Struggle for the Cameroons Ivory Trade in the Nineteenth Century." *Journal of African History* 19 (1978): 539–549.

Johnston, Bruce F. *The Staple Food Economies of Western Tropical Africa.* Stanford, Calif.: Stanford University Press, 1958.

Jones, Adam. *Zur Quellenproblematik der Geschichte Westafrikas, 1450–1900.* Stuttgart: Steiner, 1990.

———, ed. *West Africa in the Mid-Seventeenth Century: An Anonymous Dutch Manuscript.* Madison, Wis.: African Studies Association, 1995.

Jones, G. I. "The Political Organization of Old Calabar." In *Efik Traders,* ed. D. Forde, 116–157. London: Oxford University Press, 1956.

———. *The Trading States of the Oil Rivers: A Study of Political Development in Eastern Nigeria.* London: Oxford University Press, 1963.

La Fleur, J. D., ed. *Pieter van den Broecke's Journal of Voyages to Cape Verde, Guinea and Angola (1605–1612).* London: Hakluyt Society, 2000.

Latham, A. J. H. "Currency, Credit and Capitalism on the Cross River in the Precolonial Era." *Journal of African History* 12 (1971): 599–605.

———. "Witchcraft Accusations and Economic Tension in Pre-colonial Old Calabar." *Journal of African History* 13 (1972): 249–260.

———. *Old Calabar, 1600–1891: The Impact of the International Economy upon a Traditional Society*. Oxford: Oxford University Press, 1973.

———. "A Trading Alliance: Sir John Tobin and Duke Ephraim." *History Today* 24 (Dec. 1974): 862–867.

———. "Price Fluctuations in the Early Palm Oil Trade." *Journal of African History* 19 (1978): 213–218.

———. "The Pre-colonial Economy: The Lower Cross Region." In *A History of the Cross River Region of Nigeria*, ed. M. B. Abasiattai, 70–89. Enugu, Nigeria: Harris Publishers in Association with University of Calabar Press, 1990.

Law, Robin. "Human Sacrifice in Pre-colonial West Africa." *African Affairs* 84, no. 334 (1985): 53–87.

Lieber, J. W. *Efik and Ibibio Villages*. Ibadan: Institute of Education, University of Ibadan, 1971.

Lindblad, J. T., and Robert Ross, eds. *Marion Johnson, Anglo-African Trade in the Eighteenth Century*. Leiden: Intercontinenta, 1990.

Lovejoy, Paul E., and David Richardson. "Competing Markets for Male and Female Slaves: Prices in the Interior of West Africa, 1780–1850." *International Journal of African Historical Studies* 28 (1995): 261–293.

———. "Trust, Pawnship, and Atlantic History: The Institutional Foundations of the Old Calabar Slave Trade." *American Historical Review* 104 (1999): 333–355.

———. "The Business of Slaving: Pawnship in Western Africa, c. 1600–1810." *Journal of African History* 42 (2001): 67–89.

———. "Letters of the Old Calabar Slave Trade, 1760–1789." In *Genius in Bondage: Literature of the Early Black Atlantic*, ed. Vincent Carretta and Philip Gould, 89–115. Lexington: University Press of Kentucky, 2001.

———. "From Slaves to Palm Oil: Afro-European Commercial Relations in the Bight of Biafra, 1741–1841." In *Maritime Empires: British Imperial Maritime Trade in the Nineteenth Century*, ed. David Killingray, Margarette Lincoln, and Nigel Rigby, 13–29. London: National Maritime Museum, 2004.

———. "'This Horrid Hole': Royal Authority, Commerce and Credit at Bonny, 1690–1840." *Journal of African History* 45 (2004): 363–392.

Lynn, Martin. *Commerce and Economic Change in West Africa: The Palm Oil Trade in the Nineteenth Century*. Cambridge: Cambridge University Press, 1997.

McCulloch, Merran, Margaret Littlewood, and I. Dugast. *Peoples of the Central Cameroons*. London: International African Institute, 1954.

McFarlan, Donald M. *Calabar: The Church of Scotland Mission, founded 1846*. London: T. Nelson, 1957.

Murdock, G. P. *Africa: Its Peoples and Their Cultural History*. New York: McGraw-Hill, 1959.

Nair, Kannan K. *Politics and Society in South Eastern Nigeria, 1841–1906: A Study of Power, Diplomacy and Commerce in Old Calabar*. London: Frank Cass, 1972.

———. *The Origins and Development of Efik Settlements in Southeastern Nigeria.* Ohio University, Papers in International Studies, Africa Series 26 (1975): 1–36.

Noah, Monday Efiong. *Old Calabar: The City States and the Europeans 1800–1885.* Uyo, Nigeria: Scholars Press, 1980.

———. "Pre-European Economic Organization among the Ibibio People." *Africana Research Bulletin* 12, nos. 1–2 (March 1983): 30–55.

Northrup, David. *Trade without Rulers: Pre-colonial Economic Development in Southeastern Nigeria.* Oxford: Oxford University Press, 1978.

———. "Igbo and Myth Igbo: Culture and Ethnicity in the Atlantic World, 1600–1850." *Slavery and Abolition* 21 (2000): 1–20.

———. *Africa's Discovery of Europe, 1450–1850.* New York: Oxford University Press, 2002.

———. "West Africans and the Atlantic, 1550–1800." In *Black Experience and the Empire*, ed. Philip D. Morgan and Sean Hawkins, 35–57. New York: Oxford University Press, 2004.

Offiong, Daniel A. "Social Relations and Witch Beliefs among the Ibibio." *Africa* 53, no. 3 (1983): 73–82.

———. "Social Relations and Witch Beliefs among the Ibibio of Nigeria." *Journal of Anthropological Research* 39, no. 1 (1983): 81–95.

———. "Witchcraft among the Ibibio of Nigeria." *African Studies Review* 26, no. 1 (1983): 107–124.

———. "The Functions of the Ekpo Society of the Ibibio of Nigeria." *African Studies Review* 27, no. 3 (1984): 77–92.

———. "The Status of Ibibio Chiefs." *Anthropological Quarterly* 57, no. 4 (1984): 100–113.

———. "The Status of Slaves in Igbo and Ibibio of Nigeria." *Phylon* 46, no. 1 (1985): 49–57.

———. *Witchcraft, Sorcery, Magic and Social Order Among the Ibibio of Nigeria.* Enugu: Fourth Dimension Publishing, 1991.

———. "Conflict Resolution among the Ibibio of Nigeria." *Journal of Anthropological Research* 53 (1997): 423–441.

Oku, Ekei Essien. *The Kings and Chiefs of Old Calabar (1785–1925).* Calabar: Glad Tidings Press, 1989.

Ottenberg, Simon, and Linda Knudsen. "Leopard Society Masquerades: Symbolism and Diffusion." *African Arts* 18, no. 2 (1985): 37–44, 93–95, 103–104.

Paley, Ruth. "After *Somerset*: Mansfield, Slavery and the Law in England, 1772–1830." In *Law, Crime and English Society, 1660–1830*, ed. Norman Landau, 165–184. Cambridge: Cambridge University Press, 2002.

Richardson, Alan, and Debbie Lee, eds. *Early Black British Writing.* Boston: Houghton Mifflin, 2004.

Richardson, David. "West African Consumption Patterns and Their Influence on the Eighteenth-Century English Slave Trade." In *The Uncommon Market*, ed. Henry A. Gemery and Jan S. Hogendorn, 303–330. New York: Academic Press, 1979.

————. *The Bristol Slave Traders: A Collective Portrait.* Bristol: Bristol Record Society, 1985.

————. "The Costs of Survival: The Transport of Slaves in the Middle Passage and the Profitability of the 18th-Century British Slave Trade." *Explorations in Economic History* 24 (1987): 178–196.

————. "Profits in the Liverpool Slave Trade: The Accounts of William Davenport, 1757–1784." In *Liverpool, the African Slave Trade, and Abolition: Essays to Illustrate Current Knowledge and Research,* ed. Roger Anstey and P. E. H. Hair, 60–90. 1976. Reprint, Liverpool: Historic Society of Lancashire and Cheshire, 1989.

————. "Prices of Slaves in West and West-Central Africa: Toward an Annual Series, 1698–1807." *Bulletin of Economic Research* 43 (1991): 33–46.

————, ed. *Bristol, Africa and the Eighteenth-Century Slave Trade to America.* 4 vols. Bristol: Bristol Record Society, 1986–1996.

Rottenberg, Simon. "The Business of Slave Trading." *South Atlantic Quarterly* 66 (1967): 409–423.

Simmons, D. "An Ethnographic Sketch of the Efik People." In *Efik Traders of Old Calabar,* ed. Daryll Forde, 1–26. London: Oxford University Press, 1956.

Simmons, D. "Notes on the Diary of Antera Duke." In *Efik Traders of Old Calabar,* ed. Daryll Forde, 66–78. London: Oxford University Press, 1956.

Sparks, Randy. "Two Princes of Calabar: An Atlantic Odyssey from Slavery to Freedom." *William and Mary Quarterly* 59, no. 3 (2002): 555–584

————. *The Two Princes of Calabar: An Eighteenth-Century Atlantic Odyssey.* Cambridge, Mass.: Harvard University Press, 2004.

Sweet, James. *Recreating Africa: Culture, Kinship, and Religion in the African-Portuguese World, 1441–1770.* Chapel Hill: University of North Carolina Press, 2003.

Talbot, P. A. *Life in Southern Nigeria.* London: Macmillan, 1923.

Thompson, H. N. "The Forests of Southern Nigeria." *Journal of the Royal African Society* 10, no. 38 (1911): 121–145.

Troughton, Thomas. *The History of Liverpool, from the Earliest Authenticated Period down to the Present Time.* Liverpool: William Robinson, 1810.

Udoh, E. A. *Report of Enquiry into Obong of Calabar Dispute.* Vol. 1. Calabar, 1971.

Walker, J. B. "Notes on the Old Calabar and Cross Rivers." *Proceedings of the Royal Geographical Society* 16 (1871–1872): 137.

————. "Notes on the Politics, Religion, and Commerce of Old Calabar." *Journal of the Anthropological Institute of Great Britain and Ireland* 6 (1877): 119–124.

Westermann, Diedrich, and M. A. Bryan. *The Languages of West Africa.* London: Oxford University Press, 1952.

Wigboldus, Jouke S. "Trade and Agriculture in Coastal Benin c. 1470–1660: An Examination of Manning's Early-Growth Thesis." *Afdeling Agrarische Geschiedenis Bijdragen* 28 (1986): 299–380.

Williams, Gomer. *History of the Liverpool Privateers and Letters of Marque with an Account of the Liverpool Slave Trade.* London, 1897. Reprint, Montreal: McGill Queen's University Press, 2004.

Winston, F. D. D. "Nigerian Cross River Languages in the Polyglotta Africana." *Sierra Leone Language Review* 3 (1964): 74–82.

———. "Nigerian Cross River Languages in the Polyglotta Africana." *Sierra Leone Language Review* 4 (1965): 122–127.

Zupko, Ronald Edward. *A Dictionary of English Weights and Measures from Anglo-Saxon Times to the Nineteenth Century*. Madison: University of Wisconsin Press, 1968.

Index